HOSPITALITY MARKETING MANAGEMENT

HOSPITALITY MARKETING MANAGEMENT
SECOND EDITION

Robert D. Reid

James Madison University

 VAN NOSTRAND REINHOLD
New York

Editorial Production Services: Spectrum Publisher Services, Inc.
Project Editor: Maureen P. Conway

Copyright © 1989 by Van Nostrand Reinhold

Library of Congress Catalog Card Number 88-5396

ISBN 0-442-27848-9

Printed in the United States of America

Text Design Rita Naughton

Van Nostrand Reinhold
115 Fifth Avenue
New York, New York 10003

Van Nostrand Reinhold International Company Limited
11 New Fetter Lane
London EC4P 4EE, England

Van Nostrand Reinhold
480 La Trobe Street
Melbourne, Victoria 3000, Australia

Nelson Canada
1120 Birchmount Road
Scarborough, Ontario M1K 5G4, Canada

16   15   14   13   12   11   10   9   8   7   6   5   4   3   2

Library of Congress Cataloging-in-Publication Data
Reid, Robert D.
   Hospitality marketing management / Robert D. Reid.—2nd ed.
      p.   cm.
      Rev. ed. of: Foodservice and restaurant marketing. © 1983.
      Includes bibliographies and index.
      ISBN 0-442-27848-9
      1. Food service—Marketing.   2. Restaurants, lunch rooms, etc.—
   Marketing.   I. Reid, Robert D.   Foodservice and restaurant
   marketing.   II. Title.
   TX911.3.M3R443 1989
   647'.95068—dc19

For Susan and "the Girls"

Contents

Preface

Developing the manuscript for this book has given me the opportunity to reexamine the way that I had structured the original edition. Since the first edition was published in 1983, many changes have occurred in the hospitality industry. Recent developments have been closely monitored, and necessary additions and adjustments were made. Perhaps the increasing importance of marketing as one of the management functions is the most significant change that has taken place.

In order to broaden the scope of the book and increase its usefulness for educators, students, and hospitality industry managers, several new chapters have been added to the book. The most significant change is the addition of an entirely new section, "Hospitality Group Sales." An additional chapter has been added in hospitality services marketing, broadening the scope of the coverage of this fast-developing aspect of marketing. In addition, a chapter focusing on promotions and public relations has been added.

The book is divided into six major sections:

1. *Introduction to Marketing.* The first three chapters provide a solid foundation in basic marketing principles. The first chapter, "Functions of

Marketing," introduces the reader to the marketing concept, the hospitality marketing mix, the role of management in hospitality marketing, and other principles and concepts.

The second chapter, "Introduction to Services Marketing," introduces the broad subject of services marketing by examining how services differ from products, how consumers make service purchase decisions, and how managers can successfully manage in the service economy.

The third chapter, "Overview of Marketing in the Hospitality Industry," studies the product life cycle and trends that are affecting the industry, as well as provides an overview of the major corporations in the industry.

2. *Marketing Planning, Information, and Research*. "Developing a Marketing Plan," the fourth chapter, provides a solid foundation for the chapters that follow by introducing the reader to a systems model for developing a successful marketing plan.

"Marketing Information Systems," Chapter 5, studies the crucial information needs of contemporary hospitality managers. It reviews the management of marketing information systems as well as the design of such systems.

The last chapter of this section, "Market Research Methodology," introduces the reader to research topics that include research methodology, sampling, and survey instrument design. More specific topics related to the industry include marketing audits, feasibility studies, and product development.

3. *Understanding Hospitality Consumers*. One of the keys to successful marketing is understanding the consumer. Chapters 7 and 8 are designed to provide this level of understanding. Chapter 7, "Market Segmentation and Positioning," reviews the nature of segmentation and criteria for effective market segmentation. Methods used to measure demand are reviewed, and positioning the product-service mix is discussed.

Consumer behavior is the topic of Chapter 8, reviewing such topics as models of consumer behavior and consumer satisfaction. A contemporary consumer decision-making model is introduced and serves as a foundation for a complete discussion of extrinsic and intrinsic factors that influence consumer behavior.

4. *Advertising and Promotion*. The fourth section consists of three chapters that provide a thorough review of advertising and promotion. Chapter 9 reviews subjects related to the management of the advertising function. Advertising terms, relationships with advertising agencies, and advertising budgets are thoroughly discussed and reviewed. The chapter also provides an overview of the development and management of successful advertising campaigns.

Chapter 10, "Advertising and Promotional Media," introduces the reader to each of the major media. Techniques that will lead to successful advertising in each of the media are reviewed.

Chapter 11, "Promotions and Public Relations," is a new chapter. The important area of sales promotion provides an introduction to the chapter. Types of sales promotion and techniques are discussed. Internal promotion and public relations management are also thoroughly reviewed.

5. *Hospitality Group Sales.*   This section is totally new in this edition. Chapter 12, "Marketing Organizational Structure and Management," discusses the manner in which hospitality organizations seek group business. The chapter also provides a complete outline and discussion of the manner in which forecasts and marketing plans aimed at the group market are developed, implemented, and evaluated. Finally, a review of both manual and computerized group rooms and food and beverage management systems are discussed. Chapter 13, "Group Sales," focuses on selling to group markets, including selling effectively to meeting planners and to different market segments such as the association and corporate markets. The personal selling process and key account management techniques are also highlighted.

6. *Menu Design and Pricing Strategies.*   The final section of the book consists of two chapters. Chapter 14 reviews the menu-planning principles that have been shown to lead to successful menus, as well as accuracy in menus, cycle menus, and methods to evaluate the success of menus.

The final chapter, "Pricing Theory and Practice," discusses contemporary pricing strategies, marketing factors that affect prices, and effective pricing guidelines and policies.

An instructor's manual is available from the publisher.

I believe that you will find this book useful in your pursuit of a successful career in the hospitality industry. Writing the book has helped me continue to learn. I trust that it will have the same influence on you.

Acknowledgments

Many individuals have had a positive influence on my professional development and my life and have in their own way contributed to the writing of this book. To each of them, I would like to say, "Thank you!" A few specific people who deserve special thanks are Robert E. Holmes, Harold B. Teer, Karen W. Wigginton, Edward Pease, and especially Susan J. Reid, who was always there with her quick wit or a kind word of encouragement. I would like to acknowledge the contributions of the following reviewers for the development of this book: Kenneth Crocker, Bowling Green State University; Eugene J. Spaziana, South Central Community College; and John Stefanelli, University of Las Vegas, Nevada.

PART I

INTRODUCTION
TO MARKETING

CHAPTER 1

Functions of Marketing

This chapter will introduce the subject of marketing and will define terms used by those individuals engaged in managing the marketing function. It serves as the foundation for subsequent chapters. The chapter is divided into the following major sections:

INTRODUCTION
☐ Economic
☐ Political
☐ Social
☐ Technological

MARKETING DEFINED

MARKETING VERSUS SELLING

THE MARKETING CONCEPT

MARKETING AS A COMPETITIVE FORCE

THE ROLE OF MANAGEMENT IN MARKETING

MARKETING PLANNING

MARKETING EXECUTION

MARKETING EVALUATION

MANAGING PERSONNEL FOR IMPROVED MARKETING

THE HOSPITALITY MARKETING MIX

THE TRADITIONAL MARKETING MIX

THE MARKETING MIX FOR HOSPITALITY OPERATIONS
☐ Consumer Perceptions, Attitudes, and Behavior
☐ Industry Attitudes and Trends
☐ Local Competition
☐ Trends
☐ Governmental Policy and Legislation

SUMMARY

KEY WORDS AND CONCEPTS

QUESTIONS FOR REVIEW AND DISCUSSION

INTRODUCTION

During the past decade, a great many changes have taken place within the hospitality industry in the United States. Changes in four major aspects of American life—economic, political, social, and technological—have had an impact on the hospitality industry. Several broad trends in each of the four areas mentioned above are noteworthy.

Economic

☐ The percentage of independently owned hospitality operations has declined, indicating the ever more powerful influence of large hospitality chains.

☐ The percentage of the household food budget spent outside the home has increased. The hospitality industry today receives in excess of 40 percent of all consumer expenditures for food. This has increased over 7 percentage points in the last ten years.

☐ Hotel occupancy rates have declined from over 70 percent to the mid-60-percent range. This is the result of increased competition and a tremendous growth in the number of available rooms.

☐ Market segmentation has been the dominant strategy, especially in the lodging segment of the industry. Most of the major lodging chains now have established multiple brands, each vying for a small market segment. Examples of this segmentation include all-suite, budget, luxury budget, mid-priced, upscale, and residential hotel properties.

Political

☐ During the past decade, favorable tax treatment, such as industrial revenue bonds and special tax concessions granted by localities, has resulted in the building of many new hotel properties in urban areas.

☐ Most recently, changes in the federal tax codes have made hotel developments less desirable than they were under previous tax codes. So-called passive investments, in which the investor is not an active participant in the daily management of the facility, are not treated as favorably under the new federal tax codes. Future hotel development decisions will be based more on operational feasibility and less on the real estate investment aspects of the project.

Social

☐ The advent of two-income families has had a very positive impact on the foodservice and lodging segments of the hospitality industry.

☐ The increase in the proportion of older Americans will have an increasing impact on the hospitality industry. Long ignored by most major marketers, this market segment is now coming to the forefront. It has the numbers and purchasing volume to affect both the foodservice and lodging segments.

☐ The dietary habits of the American people have also changed, as many individuals are showing increased concern about the food they eat. The trend has been toward more "natural" and "healthy" foods. In support of this, the United States Department of Agriculture has published *Dietary Guidelines for Americans,* which outlines the dietary goals for the nation. The American Heart Association provides menu review and recipes that meet their dietary guidelines for good health. Many foodservice operations now feature menu items that have been approved by this organization. The National Restaurant Association has also been active in this area, especially in the form of education for its members.

Technological

☐ Labor shortages and the high cost of labor have resulted in an increase in self-service within the hospitality industry. This is occurring within all segments, from fast-food restaurants to upscale hotels.

☐ The increasing sophistication and decrease in price of computers has had a significant impact. Further examples will be discussed within several chapters. If the technology is managed properly, detailed relational data bases and property management systems can provide managers with the potential to better serve the guests' needs.

Along with these changes, the hospitality industry has experienced dramatic growth, and the future looks very positive. All major projections point toward continued growth and development. Certainly, a few large obstacles loom on the horizon. Existing economic cycles will cause some upward and downward shifts in the hospitality industry, and further changes in the tax codes may have some negative impact on business travel and entertaining.

In recent years, most of the growth in the hospitality industry has occurred in chain operations or in the industry's corporate segment. The hospitality industry leaders, such as McDonald's, Pillsbury, Holiday, and Marriott Corporations, continue to increase their share of the market, at the expense of smaller chains and independent operators. Independent operators have continued to prosper, especially in the foodservice sector, but the marketplace is much more competitive today than it was even five short years ago. An increased level of competition has meant greater emphasis on marketing. No longer is it possible for an individual to open and operate a foodservice facility successfully on good food alone. To assure a steady flow of clientele, a hospitality manager must possess a thorough understanding of marketing. Without the marketing management skills the hospitality industry demands, a hospitality manager is less likely now to achieve total success.

With this continual change and increased competition, what are the marketing functions that a successful hospitality manager must fulfill? This chapter introduces basic marketing concepts; the following chapters will explore specific areas of professional hospitality marketing management. Throughout this text, your overriding questions should be "What are the functions of marketing, and how can I apply these concepts?"

MARKETING DEFINED

Marketing is a word used and often abused in the daily conversations of business people throughout the United States. It is used in business conversations, meetings, and professional publications. Some of those who use the word have a clear understanding of it; others do not.

Think for a moment: What does marketing mean to you? Managers use the term to discuss marketing strategies, marketing concepts, marketing tools, and marketing research. But what does the word *marketing* really mean?

The term *marketing* is indeed used to encompass many different activities. To confuse matters further, marketing has been defined in many different ways. The following paragraphs offer several of the major definitions of the term. Compare these definitions with your own.

Historically, marketing was defined as the business process by which products are matched with markets and through which transfers of ownerships are affected. Since this definition was written, there has been tremendous growth in sales of intangibles known as services. Much of the economic growth in the United States in the last fifteen years has been in the area of services. Part of this is the growth of the hospitality industry, which alone accounts for more than $200 billion in annual sales and represents a significant segment of the total value of services purchased each year.

A service is defined as an intangible product that is sold or purchased in the marketplace. A meal purchased at a fast-food restaurant or an occupied room in a hotel is considered a part of the service segment. Why? Simply stated, after the meal is consumed and paid for, or after the individual checks out of the hotel, the individual patron leaves the facility and does not have a tangible product in exchange for the money spent. This individual has consumed a service that is a part of the hospitality industry, one of the largest service industries.

Each year, millions of individuals spend billions of dollars vacationing and traveling for business and other reasons, yet when the trip is over, nothing tangible remains. On the other hand, if you purchase a new automobile or washing machine, the purchase is considered a tangible product and as such is not part of the service industry segment.

To reflect the role of service industries, such as the hospitality industry, more clearly, the definition of marketing must include references to services. Two such definitions follow.

1. Marketing is the performance of business activities that direct the flow of goods and services from product to consumer.

2. Marketing is defined as the merging, integrating, and controlled supervision of all the company's or organization's efforts that have a bearing on sales.

These definitions are certainly adequate. The vast majority of hospitality establishments, however, are being operated to generate a satisfactory return on investment in the form of profits. These profits are used to pay dividends to stockholders and are reinvested by the organization to promote expansion and further development. Even nonprofit hospitality operations, such as selected hospitals, nursing homes, college or university hospitality operations, and governmental hospitality operations, must be concerned with marketing. Managers of nonprofit operations must still understand the needs and wants of their consumers in order to succeed. A universal concern of all hospitality managers is the financial well-being of the organization. Whether a manager is trying to achieve a 20 percent annual return on investment or is instead aiming to break even on a very limited budget, the overriding concern is still financial. This overriding financial concern must be considered in the definition of the word *marketing* as it applies to the hospitality industry.

Another factor that any definition of marketing must include is the consumer, for the consumer should be the manager's first priority. Unlike factories, which sell large quantities of manufactured products to distributors and other suppliers and may never have direct contact with the final consumer, a hotel or restaurant contacts each consumer individually and must deal with each consumer on an individual basis.

Therefore, a suitable definition of the word *marketing* must account for the financial concerns of management as well as the need to satisfy consumers on an individual basis. Hospitality marketing is therefore defined as encompassing the following:

☐ Ascertaining the needs and wants of the consumer

☐ Creating the product-service mix that satisfies these needs and wants

☐ Promoting and selling the product-service mix in order to generate a level of income satisfactory to the management and stockholders of the organization

This definition satisfies the objectives of the two major groups, the consumers and the stockholders and management.

The definition of marketing can be illustrated by the marketing cycle (Figure 1.1). In the marketing cycle, a hospitality manager engages in the three components, or steps, that make up the definition of marketing, and also obtains feedback from the consumer regarding the degree of consumer satisfaction. Financial reinvestment must also occur if the organization is to remain a viable business, for without some portion of the profits being reinvested, it will slowly decay and will eventually fail to meet the ever-changing needs and wants of the consuming public.

MARKETING VERSUS SELLING

Many hospitality managers engage in a series of activities that they incorrectly refer to as marketing. These activities include promotional functions, such as advertising in newspapers and on radio; internal promotions, such as posters and table tents; direct mail efforts, such as following up with a prospective client by sending a direct mail promotion concerning a specific event; and personal selling, such as making a sales presentation for a prospective con-

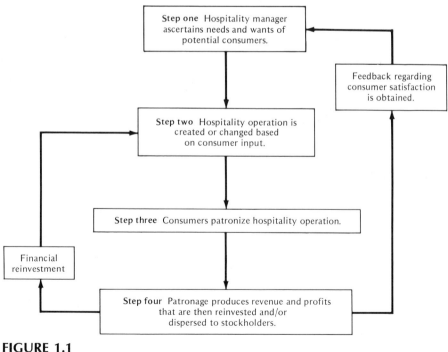

FIGURE 1.1
The Marketing Cycle

vention group. While such activities are without question a part of the marketing function, alone and unsupported they cannot be referred to as marketing.

Managers engaged in activities of this type are merely attempting to sell their product-service mix. The product-service mix is composed of all the tangible and intangible products and services that make up a hospitality operation. The product-service mix includes the food, beverages, guest rooms, meeting facilities, atmosphere, table appointments, and personal attention by service personnel, as well as a host of other tangibles and intangibles. This type of activity, when practiced exclusively, is very "self-centered" or "product-service mix oriented." The focus is only on the hospitality operation's product-service mix, and the goal is to convince the consuming public to purchase and consume a portion of the product-service mix. Little consideration is given to the needs and wants of the consuming public; instead, the hospitality manager is hoping that a sufficient number of consumers will patronize the operation to allow the operation to achieve its financial objectives.

The hospitality industry, especially the foodservice segment, is filled with examples of operations that have failed because the owners created hospitality operations they liked or "always wanted to operate," yet the owners and managers failed to consider fully the needs and wants of potential consumers. The results are predictable: low volume, poor sales revenue, and frequent bankruptcy. A simple fact is clear—restaurants have one of the highest failure rates of any type of business in the United States.

Marketing is not the same activity as selling, and the two should not be confused. Selling is an activity that pushes the existing product-service mix on the consuming public; marketing seeks to satisfy the needs and wants of the consuming public. The following mini case study will illustrate the difference between selling and marketing.

A MINI CASE STUDY:

A New Oriental Restaurant

This mini case study focuses on the foodservice market of a town with a population of 40,000. Several wealthy individuals who lived in this town frequently dined at an Oriental restaurant in a large metropolitan area located 45 miles north of the town. These individuals noted that if Oriental food and service were available in their hometown, they would not have to drive the 90 miles to and from the city each time they desired Oriental food and service.

After many hours of conversation over a two-month period, these individuals decided to combine their resources and build an Oriental restaurant in the town where they lived. They spared no expense in constructing and equipping the facility and in hiring and training a first-quality kitchen staff. In mid-October, the investors along with the management personnel welcomed the first guests.

Business was quite brisk for a period of eight weeks, averaging 275 covers per day for lunch and dinner combined. The investors and management were very proud indeed. None of the investors had ever operated a restaurant before, but all clearly thought they had built a "sure winner." In the weeks that followed, however, the number of lunch and dinner guests began to decline steadily to a point where the number of average daily covers had fallen below 100. In an attempt to discover the problem, the owners and management pursued several avenues. The quality of both food and service had slipped slightly, but were very nearly as high as during the opening weeks of operation. Those customers who were patronizing the restaurant seemed very satisfied. They conducted interviews with selected guests. What could be the problem?

After careful consideration, the investors and management launched an intensive promotional and advertising campaign using all available local media, and such internal promotional methods as tent cards and increased personal selling. After a four-week period, the results of the media blitz were disappointing. The average daily number of covers served hovered around 110 and showed no signs of increasing. Additionally, the level of banquet business activity exhibited further decline, despite the extraordinary promotional efforts.

The owners then hired a team of marketing consultants to conduct an in-depth study to determine the hospitality consumer trends in the town and surrounding areas. After several days of study, the consultants' final report concluded that the area lacked a sufficient number of people to support a restaurant with this concept. Consumers seemed willing to patronize the operation, but not with the frequency necessary to make it a financial success. Based on the marketing research, the consulting report projected that the average number of daily covers was not likely to increase beyond 100 to 110. Simply stated, the consultants concluded that the potential market was too small to support a restaurant of this type. Business had fallen off because of a lack of steadily returning clientele.

The consultants' report was carefully reviewed by both the owners and management of the restaurant. They decided, however, that the restaurant should continue to operate in the same manner, with only minor menu changes. The owners still believed very strongly in their original concept and felt that it could be successful. After an additional thirty days, the level of business remained the same, and at that time, the owners terminated the general manager and hired a new individual to fill the position.

The level of business increased slightly under the direction of the new manager, but not to the extent necessary for the restaurant to be a success. Debts continued to mount, and the restaurant was forced to settle all of its accounts on a cash-on-delivery (C.O.D) basis only. None of the local purveyors would extend credit to the restaurant for fear of not receiving payment. The situation continued to deteriorate for another four months as losses mounted each week.

After being in business for a total of ten months, the restaurant closed in mid-August and was later sold to another group of investors. This second group remodeled the restaurant and operated a successful family steak house operation.

Questions for Consideration

1. Review and analyze the actions taken by the first group of investors.
2. What might the first group of investors have done differently? What would you have recommended to them?
3. Why do you think the second group of investors was successful where the initial group had failed?
4. What conclusions can you draw from this example?

This example clearly shows a group of rational business investors who let their personal feelings interfere with their critical evaluation of a business opportunity. Instead of investing in a restaurant that would appeal to a large group of potential consumers who would patronize the facility frequently and therefore assure financial success, they chose instead to build a facility that failed to attract a large enough percentage of repeat clientele to be successful.

The difference between selling and marketing is very simple. Selling focuses on the needs of the seller. These needs include the very basic need of having a product-service mix that must be sold to generate revenue necessary to remain in business. Clearly, the needs of the seller are very strong.

Marketing, however, focuses on the needs of the consumer. When a product or service is truly marketed, the needs of the consumer are considered from the very beginning of the process of product or service development, and the product or service is designed to meet the unsatisfied needs of the consuming public. When a product is marketed in the proper manner, very little selling is necessary because the consumer need already exists and the product or service is merely being produced to satisfy the need.

Another brief example will illustrate the critical difference between selling and marketing. During the 1970s, many chain foodservice operations became very successful by catering to the under-30 single market segment. The pattern for success was to develop a "high-energy" lounge type of operation that sold a high proportion of liquor to food. These operations were often called "fern bars," due mainly to the light wood and many plants that typically made up the decor of the restaurant. For many years, these operations were very successful, generating very substantial sales and profits.

However, in the 1980s, several factors combined to cause a potential problem. First, the market segment to which this type of facility was appealing was declining in size. Those who had previously patronized the fern bars were now seeking a more relaxed atmosphere. Second, the attitude toward alcohol consumption, especially as it related to drinking and driving, had undergone significant change. Consumption of alcohol was declining. Third, nutrition was seen by consumers as being more important. The relationship between diet and overall health and well-being was becoming more pronounced. With these three factors in mind, the fern bar concept began to change. Less emphasis was placed on the consumption of alcohol in a high-energy lounge. Rather, increased emphasis was placed on food sales. Menus were researched and rewritten, and music volume levels were reduced. More emphasis was placed on service. Clearly, the fern bar has evolved to meet the needs of ever-changing consumer tastes. Even the most successful concept will not be successful for an indefinite period. If the operators of these restaurants had continued to "sell" their product-service mix, they would not have been successful. Instead, they were sensitive to the changes occurring in the market and were able to adapt their product-service mix to meet the needs of consumers. This is a key to successful marketing—recognizing trends and being ready and willing to make changes that are necessary to assure continued success.

THE MARKETING CONCEPT

If a hospitality organization is to market its product-service mix successfully, it is essential that the marketing concept be not only thoroughly understood but also fully implemented. Understanding the concept is not difficult, but implementing it may prove to be very challenging for management.

Simply stated, the marketing concept is a consumer-oriented philosophy that focuses all available organizational resources on the profitable satisfaction of the needs and wants of the consumer. As an old rhyme states,

> To sell Jane Smith
> What Jane Smith buys,
> You've got to see things
> Through Jane Smith's eyes.

Clearly, it is difficult to sell something to someone who has no need for it. If the organization adopts a consumer-oriented marketing philosophy, however, the product-service mix will be designed in direct response to unsatisfied consumer needs, and as a result, very little actual selling will be necessary. In such instances, supply and demand are in balance, and both the consumer and hospitality ownership are satisfied.

Table 1.1 illustrates the two different philosophies of the marketing concept that are often practiced in the hospitality industry. One shows the reactions of a hospitality manager using the marketing concept, while the other shows reactions that are not governed by the marketing concept.

Many hospitality organizations subscribe to the marketing concept, but many others do not. Does your organization believe in and subscribe to the marketing concept? Here is a key question to ask: "Are consumers given priority, or is the operation run to suit the needs of the employees and management?

A manager of a hospitality operation has a difficult series of challenges to face each day. First, a manager is expected to successfully satisfy the needs of the hospitality consumers. Second, the owners expect a manager to maintain the level of expenses within certain predetermined limits that are usually defined in absolute dollars or as a percentage of gross sales. Third, a manager is expected to generate a satisfactory return on investment for the owners.

TABLE 1.1
How the Marketing Concept Is Used and Abused

Decisions	When the Marketing Concept Is Applied	When the Marketing Concept Is Not Applied
Menu Design	"Let's conduct a focus group using our current guests to determine the desirability of adding new items to the menu."	"Let's add two more steak items to the menu—that's what I like."
Pricing	"What do you think is the best price to achieve the best return on investment and the highest occupancy rate?"	"Let's raise room rates by 8 percent; that's what we did last year."
Guest Requests	"We don't have any rooms with a king bed available right now, but I can have one for you in 30 minutes. Can I have the bellman check your bag for you?"	"We don't have any rooms with king beds at that price; you'll have to take one with two double beds."
Reaction to Negative Guest Comments	"That's a great idea, we'll try to use it to improve our guest service."	"Your idea isn't feasible; we don't do things that way."

This return might be the breakeven point in a nonprofit operation or it might be a very high rate of return in a commercial operation.

The point is that a manager is faced with a series of difficult objectives to achieve, and these objectives often conflict with one another. Even in the most successful of companies, there are limited resources that must be used to accomplish seemingly unlimited goals and objectives. No matter how well the company has performed in the past, it is human nature always to want a little more. Guests develop ever-increasing expectations for all aspects of the product-service mix. Owners want ever-increasing profits and the employees want a little more each year. The manager's task is to balance the three objectives mentioned in the preceding paragraph. Managers often view profitability as the single most important objective of the firm, yet for the long-term financial well-being of the firm, profits may not be the most important objective. It is quite possible, as many short-sighted owners and managers have demonstrated, to achieve high levels of short-term profitability at the expense of long-term consumer satisfaction and long-term profits. After a period of time, consumers will perceive that they are not receiving a high level of value for their money, and the operation will develop a reputation for being overpriced and providing poor price-value. As a result, the number of patrons is likely to decline, and so too will long-term profitability.

If the management establishes consumer satisfaction as the number one objective, however, the consumers are more likely to be pleased. As a result, they will return more frequently to the hospitality operation, and this will have a positive influence on sales and profits. In addition, by telling their friends and associates about their positive experiences, satisfied consumers are likely to induce others to patronize the establishment. Some managers refer to this as "word-of-mouth advertising." By strict definition, there is no such thing as word-of-mouth advertising, as you'll learn in a later chapter. However, the comments made by one individual to others can have a tremendous influence on the behavior of consumers. As volume (number of covers served) increases, profits should also increase.

When the marketing concept is established as a high priority, other objectives can also be achieved because the number of guests served and the revenues are likely to be high. Experience shows that when the marketing concept has been adopted by all members of the management and staff, substantial changes have often been made in the establishment's manner of operation, and the financial results have often been improved significantly.

It is critical to instill the marketing concept in all employees. Marketing is not something done by those who work in the sales and marketing department: It is part of every employee's job. All employees must develop a guest orientation and try to ensure that every guest is satisfied. This will not happen by accident. It takes a concerted effort on the part of all of the management staff, beginning with the general manager. It must be developed

through orientation and training of hourly employees and through the examples that managers set.

MARKETING AS A COMPETITIVE FORCE

Marketing and intensity of competition feed on each other in circular fashion.
As the level or intensity of competition increases, an individual hospitality
operation is forced to devote more time and attention to marketing in order to
maintain its share of the market. Vast amounts of human energy are often
devoted to marketing programs that allow the operation to gain a very slight
advantage over other primary competitors.

Yet as more marketing efforts are undertaken, this fuels the competitive
fires, increasing competition and thereby creating the need for still more
marketing efforts. A hospitality manager might be tempted to say, "The heck
with all of this; I'm not going to do any marketing." This is an extremely
short-sighted view that in the long run is likely to result in reduced sales
volume, greatly diminished levels of profitability, and perhaps even failure of
the business.

The competitive arena in marketing is due in large part to two factors.
These are the increased tendency of the consumer to (1) dine outside the
home and (2) travel frequently, which results in an increased level of competition within and among all segments of the hospitality industry. In recent
years, more and more families have undertaken dual careers, and the results
have been very positive for the hospitality industry. More meals are being
consumed away from home because, after long work days, the family members decide that no one wants to cook a meal and clean the kitchen. They dine
out instead, and with both husband and wife working, more and more meals
are eaten in a wide variety of hospitality operations. These two-income
dual-career families allow greater independence and increased selection
when dining away from home, and they represent a very large potential
market. Two-income families also tend to travel more frequently, resulting in
a large potential market for lodging as well.

Both independent and chain hospitality operators have seen and responded to this increased demand in a predictable manner: They simply built
more hotels and restaurants. Therefore, the intensity of competition has
increased dramatically in the last several years, and many inferior hospitality
operations have been the victims.

Some managers view competition as a productive force, one that is
dynamic and growing, and results in innovation. Competition tends to increase marketing efficiency, keep price increases more modest, and promote
innovation in new products and services. The result of all of this is a wider
selection of hospitality operations from which the consumer may choose.

Simply stated, competition forces managers to work harder to attract and satisfy consumers.

THE ROLE OF MANAGEMENT IN MARKETING

As stated earlier, marketing is the responsibility of all hospitality employees, both managers and hourly employees. It is management's role to establish a marketing orientation among all members of the staff.

Within hotel and lodging properties, the marketing and sales staff handles the more formal sales and marketing functions. These functions and how they are accomplished will be discussed in a later chapter.

In large hospitality organizations, the marketing function is performed by marketing managers whose sole responsibility is the management of marketing activities. In most hospitality units, and especially independent operations, however, the marketing function is the responsibility of a manager who must be concerned with other functions as well. Because of the nature of these positions, the marketing function may be relegated to a position of secondary importance. When this occurs, the results are usually predictable: The hospitality operation suffers declining sales and sagging profits because competitive hospitality operations are actively marketing their product-service mix and, as a result, are winning consumers away from other operations.

The successful marketing of a hospitality operation is not something that can be accomplished overnight, nor is it something that can be successful with only a few hours of attention each week. The establishment and maintenance of a successful marketing program requires the management's time and effort.

The activities of management in marketing a hospitality operation can be divided into three major areas:

☐ Marketing planning

☐ Marketing execution

☐ Marketing evaluation

A brief overview of the activities of marketing management for each of these areas follows.

MARKETING PLANNING

☐ Assess the competitive environment and evaluate the activities of the competition

☐ Develop marketing strategy

☐ Develop marketing objectives

☐ Develop short- and long-range plans

☐ Develop and continually refine the elements of the marketing mix

☐ Forecast sales

MARKETING EXECUTION

☐ Develop advertising and promotional materials

☐ Establish and maintain effective communication within the different departments of the organization

☐ Train all sales personnel

☐ Engage in personal selling and follow-up activities

MARKETING EVALUATION

☐ Develop and evaluate the data collected from a marketing information system

☐ Analyze organizational performance in comparison with forecasts

☐ Analyze the effectiveness of advertising and promotional efforts

☐ Evaluate the performance of the sales staff

☐ Review relative competitive position

These points, while no means complete, provide an overview of some of the major activities that a manager must perform to market a hospitality operation successfully. The three major functions—planning, execution, and evaluation, form a continuous marketing management cycle, as illustrated in Figure 1.2.

Marketing is not an on-off situation. It needs constant attention to be successful and it must therefore be ongoing. Management must constantly obtain feedback and use it in developing revised strategic plans. Management's role in the marketing effort is critical, for without diligent effort, the results will be less than satisfactory.

MANAGING PERSONNEL FOR IMPROVED MARKETING

Management assumes a series of important responsibilities in the marketing efforts for a hospitality organization. If an organization is to achieve its desired objectives, the manager must make serious efforts to carry out these specific responsibilities.

First, the management establishes and maintains the tone for the entire operation. Employees look to the manager to set an example for them to follow and to set performance standards. For example, everyone has been in restaurants where all the service personnel seemed happy and were smiling. The orders were taken efficiently, and perhaps the service person engaged in some suggestive selling. The food and beverage items were served in the proper manner, and maybe, just maybe, customers were persuaded by the waiter or waitress to have belt-tightening desserts. Dining out in this manner is extremely pleasant. What makes some restaurants a pleasure to go to and others an ordeal? The management sets the tone and is responsible for these activities. A manager can and must convey the marketing concept to the employees and must also teach them to engage in suggestive selling and other marketing activities. In short, the manager must convey to all employees that they are part of the marketing effort. To achieve the maximum success, all employees must become marketing oriented.

Second, a manager is responsible for his or her own personal development. Managers can easily become so wrapped up in day-to-day operational activities that they fail to engage in self-development. If managers do not undertake some type of self-directed development, however, chances are that they will stagnate and lose some of their effectiveness on the job. For this reason it is important for managers to belong to professional organizations through which they can meet and talk with other managers. In this way, they can discuss common problems and perhaps learn about possible solutions. There are numerous professional organizations that a manager might choose to join. The National Restaurant Association (NRA) and the American Hotel

FIGURE 1.2
The Marketing Management Cycle

and Motel Association (AH&MA) are the best-known associations. A manager might also consider a state or local hotel or restaurant association. Those who are pursuing a career in the hotel sales and marketing field should be active members in the Hotel Sales and Marketing Association International (HSMAI). Each of these associations provides a variety of member services, including continuing education, publications, and other services of interest and value to the members. Managers should make an honest effort toward continuing education and lifelong learning. It would be desirable for a manager to annually attend one or two seminars that were related to the specific focus of the individual's position. Such seminars are sponsored by numerous groups, including professional associations and colleges and universities.

Third, if managers are to achieve the highest possible level of marketing success, they must pay particular attention to the selection process for guest-contact employees. Employees who deal directly with guests must be able to make guests feel welcome and appreciated even under the most trying of circumstances. It takes a special type of person to do this successfully. For this reason, the screening process by which guest-contact employees are selected must be examined closely. Too often, managers simply hire the first applicant or hire an individual without checking any of the applicant's credentials or references. This practice can be termed "the warm-body approach to staffing." Often, the first individual who applies for a position is hired, and the results are regrettable. Not all individuals are suited for guest-contact positions, and therefore some effort must be made to screen out those individuals who would have a negative impact on internal marketing efforts. The labor market, particularly for entry-level positions, is often very tight, making recruiting even more difficult.

Fourth, a manager must assume responsibility for the development of the entire staff. All employees need initial training and refresher training to learn new skills and refine older skills. In addition, training serves as a motivating tool, showing that management does indeed care and wants the best possible operation. One of the most common foodservice refresher in-service training activities is in the area of wine service. Many employees do not feel totally comfortable with their knowledge of wines and wine service. As a result, they fail to promote wine as actively as they should, simply because they lack the self-confidence. It is normally quite simple for a restaurant manager to arrange an employee wine seminar with the cooperation of a local wine purveyor from whom wines are purchased on a regular basis. Purveyors are usually helpful in arranging and conducting such seminars, and the results from this type of training can be very positive. Employees are motivated, and this obviously has a direct effect on sales and profits.

Fifth, management must acknowledge that the guest-contact employees are the first-line salespeople. They deal personally with every guest, and they represent the operation's manager and owners. In the eyes of the guest, these employees *are* the hotel or restaurant. A manager must devise strategies to motivate these employees. Again, no single strategy will work for all individuals in all situations, and a manager must devise new motivational techniques and strategies. Broadly defined, motivational techniques can be divided into two categories, monetary and nonmonetary rewards. Monetary rewards involve money or something of value, which is awarded to the employee, while nonmonetary rewards are intangible. Both techniques can be used, either separately or in combination. Trade journals and in-house company literature often provide ideas for innovative incentive programs.

THE HOSPITALITY MARKETING MIX

Several years ago, Neil Borden first coined the term *marketing mix.* Since that time, the concept of the marketing mix has gained universal acceptance. It is an important concept to understand, both conceptually and strategically. This section outlines the major components of a traditional marketing mix for the hospitality industry; the next section covers the contemporary marketing mix.

A successful hospitality organization is one that focuses on the needs and wants of the consumers and markets the product-service mix of the operation. The management of this type of operation is engaged in mixing or stirring these components into a form that the potential consumer will find attractive and will patronize time and time again. The results are obvious: The consumer is satisfied, and the operation achieves financial success through repeated patronage.

THE TRADITIONAL MARKETING MIX

The marketing mix, many believe, consists of four elements, sometimes called the *four Ps:*

1. *Product.* The unique combination of products and services

2. *Place.* The manner in which the products and services are sold, including channels of distribution

3. *Promotion.* The methods used to communicate with the tangible markets

4. *Price.* A pricing policy that stimulates sales and allows the firm to achieve its financial goals

To achieve success in marketing a hospitality operation, a manager must closely examine and understand all of the components of the hospitality marketing mix. In order to be successful, these components must be combined and managed in the proper manner. There is no magical formula that, when followed, will guarantee success. If this were the case, no hospitality operation would ever fail or go out of business. Yet each year, many hospitality operations are not able to achieve the correct blend of these elements.

Even without a magical formula, however, there are guidelines and principles that, when followed and monitored closely, will greatly increase the chances for success. This book presents and discusses these guidelines and principles in the following chapters.

THE MARKETING MIX FOR HOSPITALITY OPERATIONS

Just as researchers have demonstrated distinct differences between products and services, some researchers believe that the traditional four Ps approach to the marketing mix does not apply to the hospitality industry. Rather, a more contemporary marketing mix is appropriate. This marketing mix consists of three sub-mixes:

1. *Product-Service Mix.*   This is a combination of all the products and services offered by the hospitality operation, including both tangibles and intangibles. More will be discussed in Chapter 2 concerning the unique nature of services. Keep in mind that once a hospitality consumer leaves the hotel or restaurant, there is nothing tangible to show. Because the consumer has purchased and consumed the service, the largest part of the hospitality industry product-service mix is indeed service.

2. *Presentation Mix.*   This includes those elements that the marketing manager uses to increase the tangibility of the product-service mix as perceived by the consumer. This sub-mix includes the following: physical location, atmosphere (lighting, sound, and color), price, and personnel.

3. *Communication Mix.*   This involves all communication that takes place between the hospitality operation and the consumer. It includes advertising, marketing research, and consumer perception. The communications sub-mix should be viewed as a two-way communications link, rather than a simple one-way link with the hospitality operation communicating to the consumer. This two-way link allows for the traditional advertising and promotion that flow from the seller to the buyer, but also allows for marketing research and other data collection vehicles. In these cases, the seller is seeking information and data from the consumer, thereby establishing open communication with the various market segments.

The marketing mix, whether designed in the traditional or a more contemporary format, is an important concept for managers of marketing functions. Initially, the marketing mix is used to formulate marketing strategy (see Chapter 4), but it pervades all aspects of marketing management.

As a manager attempts to professionally manage the components of the hospitality marketing mix, several external factors can reduce the effectiveness of the manager's efforts. These factors, which either directly or indirectly influence the hospitality marketing mix, are consumer perceptions, attitudes, and behavior; industry attitudes and trends; local competition; broad national and international trends; and government policy and legislation.

Consumer Perceptions, Attitudes, and Behavior

It is commonly accepted that people change their minds and that, as a result, their tastes also change. As tastes change, travel patterns and dining habits will also change, as evidenced by the increase in dining out and by the decline of several old favorites in the last ten years in different parts of the country. For example, changing consumer tastes and preferences have spurred the development of lighter and more "healthy" types of menus, in all segments of the foodservice industry. Today, salad bars and pre-packaged salads are commonplace in fast-food restaurants; five to ten years ago they were rare. In other segments of the foodservice industry, menu designers have added lighter entrees in order to satisfy the consuming public's ever-growing demand for lower calorie and more nutritious food. These innovations originated in direct response to changing consumer perceptions, attitudes, and behavior.

The point to remember is that no hospitality operation can afford to stand still and continue to offer the same product-service mix. Eventually, the consumer's perceptions of the operation will change, and the level of business will decline. The successful marketing manager must keep abreast of current trends and be willing to change and modify the operation in order to satisfy the ever-changing needs of the consumer.

Industry Attitudes and Trends

Just as a manager must be aware of and responsive to the changing needs of potential consumers, so too must a manager be aware of changing attitudes and trends within the entire hospitality industry. Consider, for example, the growth of the various segments of the lodging industry. Just a few short years ago, a lodging organization would have only one brand of lodging product. For example Holiday Corporation's sole brand was Holiday Inn, while Marriott Corporation's sole brand was Marriott Hotels. All of this has changed, and the majority of the major corporations now offer several different brands, each attempting to satisfy the needs of different market segments. This and other industry trends will be discussed in greater detail in Chapter 3.

Local Competition

In addition to national competition and ever-changing trends, the successful manager must be very much aware of the efforts the local competition is engaged in to attract new and repeat clientele. The competition must be constantly checked to determine changes in the quality of products and services, types of products and services offered, pricing strategies employed, advertising and promotional activities used, design and decor changes, and personnel changes. A change in any one of these sub-factors could dramatically affect the competitive relationship among hospitality operations in a local area.

Even traditionally noncompetitive and nonprofit hospitality operations need to be aware of such factors. For example, a hospital foodservice facility had been operated for several years as a nonprofit operation and had been subject to very little competition from local foodservice operations. As a result, the hospital achieved a very high level of employee and physician participation in the cafeteria. A new foodservice operation, however, was developed and located half a block from the hospital. After the new restaurant opened, the level of employee and physician participation in the hospital cafeteria fell sharply, and it was obvious that these individuals were patronizing the new restaurant despite the fact that prices were much higher there than at the hospital cafeteria.

The hospital foodservice director and the hospital administrator assumed that, after the novelty of the new restaurant wore off, the staff would resume eating in the hospital cafeteria. Yet after six months, participation in the cafeteria continued to be greatly reduced, and the cafeteria was operating at a loss. Clearly, something had to be done to appeal successfully to the former clientele. Eventually the management decided that revised menus and prices should be offered to the staff. These changes would reflect the changes in tastes and needs of the staff, and would compete directly with the restaurant. Once these changes were thoroughly planned and implemented, the hospital was able to increase staff participation and was again able successfully to achieve their financial goals.

All hospitality operations, both foodservice and lodging, for profit and nonprofit, need to be concerned with local competition. No hospitality establishment operates in a vacuum. All types of hospitality operations are immediately subject to competition and must engage in marketing efforts.

Trends

An old phrase says that "you can't see the forest for the trees," meaning that, one can get too focused on the small details of the near environment and can lose sight of the broader environment. The details of the immediate task overshadow the broader issues. This affliction often affects managers in the hospitality industry. They become so preoccupied with the immediate needs of operating the foodservice or lodging facility that they lose sight of broad trends that are occurring all around them. These trends are normally divided into four areas: social, political, economic, and technological.

Governmental Policy and Legislation

The government at the federal, state, and local levels exerts a major influence on the operation of all businesses, including those of the hospitality industry. New and existing legislation, policies, and regulations seem to dictate every move that a manager wishes to make. Examples include such items as wage and hour laws, tax laws, alcoholic beverage laws, local zoning ordinances, local sign ordinances, and truth-in-menu legislation. Clearly, today's hospitality manager must strive to keep abreast of proposed as well as new legislation. Professional associations, such as the NRA, AH&MA, and HSMAI can be a tremendous aid to a hospitality manager in this effort. Professional associations work very hard to inform and educate members of the various elected bodies, as well as the general public. Lobbying is a vital part of this effort, for the professional associations have as one of their goals the support of legislation that will have a favorable impact on the hospitality industry as well as the opposition to governmental actions that will adversely affect the well-being of the hospitality industry.

These five factors—the consumer, industry attitudes, local competition, trends, and government policy and legislation—all influence the formulation, adjustments, and readjustments that a hospitality manager must make in the marketing mix of a hospitality organization. A manager can exert only very limited control over these influential factors, but management must be prepared with contingency plans to deal with the changes that these factors might easily bring.

SUMMARY

This chapter serves a vital function in introducing and reviewing several key points. These will serve as the foundation for discussions in the future chapters. A major point is the definition of the word *marketing*. There are several definitions of marketing, but within the context of hospitality marketing as presented in this book, marketing is defined as ascertaining the needs and wants of the consumer, creating the product-service mix that satisfies these needs and wants, and promoting and selling the product-service mix in order to generate a level of income satisfactory to the management and stockholders of the hospitality operation.

Marketing is different from selling because marketing focuses on the needs of the consumer, while selling focuses on the needs of the seller. In addition, the marketing concept advances the philosophy that the needs of the consumer should be given priority over any financial goals that the firm may have. The concept holds that if the consumer's needs and wants are totally satisfied, then financial success will follow.

Marketing as a competitive force and the role of management in marketing suggest that the activities of the marketing manager focus on three major areas: planning, execution, and evaluation of marketing activities.

Management must assume responsibilities for the marketing efforts of the organization and its employees. The responsibilities having a direct bearing on marketing include establishing and maintaining the tone of the operation, engaging in personal development, recruiting and selecting the best possible guest-contact employees, training and development of the entire staff, and acknowledging the importance of guest-contact employees by using motivational techniques to encourage their achievements.

Finally, a marketing mix must be specifically designed for a hospitality operation. The traditional four Ps marketing mix includes product, place, promotion, and price. The contemporary hospitality marketing mix is a combination of three sub-mixes: the product-service mix, the presentation mix, and the communication mix. Environmental factors such as consumer perceptions and attitudes, hospitality industry attitudes and trends, local competition, broad trends, and governmental policy and legislation affect the marketing mix.

KEY WORDS AND CONCEPTS

☐ Trends in economic, political, social, and technological areas

☐ Market segmentation

☐ Two-income families

☐ Dietary habits and changes in dietary behavior

☐ Labor shortages

☐ Marketing

☐ Corporations versus independent operators

☐ The marketing concept

☐ Marketing planning, execution, and evaluation

☐ The traditional marketing mix, the four Ps: product, place, promotion, and price

☐ The hospitality marketing mix: the product-service mix, presentation mix, and communications mix

Questions for Review and Discussion

1. Why has marketing assumed a position of increased importance in the management of hospitality organizations?
2. Explain the difference between selling and marketing. How are the two similar? Different?
3. If a manager wanted to hire the very best possible guest-contact employees, how do you think he or she should recruit and select these individuals?
4. If you were employed as a manager in a large foodservice operation, what motivational techniques would you employ with service personnel? What techniques would you employ if you were a front office manager within a large hotel?
5. Discuss the components of the traditional and contemporary marketing mix. What role does the hospitality manager play in managing the marketing mix? How is the marketing mix used?
6. What factors can affect the marketing mix? How might these factors affect the marketing mix? How might a manager anticipate the impact that these factors might have?
7. What is the marketing concept? What role should the marketing concept play in managing a hospitality facility?
8. What is the marketing cycle? Explain and discuss the major activities with which a manager must be concerned.

CHAPTER 2

Introduction to Services Marketing

The growth in the services sector of the economy has been nothing short of phenomenal in the last ten years. Services now account for over 66 percent of the Gross National Product (GNP) and the growth rate continues to increase each year. The largest proportion of new jobs are created in the service sector, with the growth in the hospitality industry being a major contributor to this growth. This chapter will introduce the concepts of services marketing and will explore some of the critical differences between product and services marketing.

THE NATURE OF SERVICES
☐ Intangibility
☐ Simultaneous Production and Consumption
☐ Consumer Involvement in Service Production
☐ Absence of Inventories
☐ Lack of Service Consistency
☐ Distribution Channels
☐ Classification of Services

CONSUMER BEHAVIOR WITH REGARD TO SERVICES
☐ Search and Experience Qualities
☐ Relationship Marketing

MANAGING IN THE SERVICE ENVIRONMENT
☐ Conflicts Between Operations and Marketing
☐ Managing Supply and Demand
☐ Improving Guest Service and Guest Satisfaction

SUMMARY

KEY WORDS AND CONCEPTS

QUESTIONS FOR REVIEW AND DISCUSSION

INTRODUCTION

Until very recently, the emphasis within the marketing community has been on products. Now, services have surpassed products and have taken on a more important role in marketing. Services, such as those offered by providers in the hospitality industry, have developed marketing practices that are unique. It has been established that the strategies, tactics, and practices that have been used successfully for product marketers do not always work successfully for those who market services. With the very distinct differences between products and services in mind, a new field of services marketing has evolved.

What are services? Unlike products, which are tangible, services are for the most part intangible. A service is not a physical good; rather, it is the performance of an act or a deed. This performance is generally done on a personal basis, often face-to-face between individuals. What the hospitality industry is selling is an experience. This experience is created to a large extent by the providers of the services—the front desk clerks, the hostesses, the service personnel in the restaurants, the bell staff, and all the other providers of services to the guest. This chapter will explore some of the attributes that make services unique.

While the growth in services has been remarkable, several reasons underlie this growth. Lovelock[1] points out four distinct reasons. First, the decline in government regulation has spurred the growth of services. In the last ten years, there has been a very noticeable shift toward the government taking a much less active role in the regulation of business activities. The most noteworthy of these shifts have been in the airline, trucking, and telecommunication industries. Reduced government regulation results in the occurrence of several things including the following:

☐ *Easier entry into markets.* The absence of government regulation allows service providers to enter and exit from markets more quickly. This is most evident in the airline industry. Carriers no longer have to seek governmental approval for new routes and they are able to respond much more quickly to changes in consumer demand.

☐ *More freedom to compete on price.* Industries such as airlines and trucking no longer have to charge prices that are regulated by the government. Rather, the prices are determined by market supply and demand forces.

☐ *Removes geographic restrictions on service delivery.* There are virtually no restrictions imposed by the government to limit the growth and development of a service provider. Again, growth is determined by market supply and demand forces.

☐ *Incentive to differentiate services.* As will be discussed in later chapters, the providers of all services are seeking to make their services more tangible and to make their services seem different to the consumer. By doing so, their goal is to increase sales, market share, and profitability.

☐ *Ability to use mass media to promote the service.* The growth in the amount of advertising time and space purchased by service providers is quite remarkable. Until the last few years, for example, it was unusual to see hospitality industry advertisements appearing on national television. Today, advertisements of this type are very common.

A second reason for the growth of service are the changes that have taken place within professional associations or industry standards. A new element of competition has been introduced into professions such as law and medicine as more of these area's practitioners advertise their services. Within the hospitality industry, standards have changed. We see an increase in advertising in which the product-service mix of the competition is directly attacked or compared with the advertiser's product-service mix. This would not have been the case a few years ago.

A third reason for the growth of services has been the revolution in computerization and technology. This has altered the manner in which we do business with the consumer. In all types of businesses, consumers are taking a more active role in the service delivery system. For example, we see machines in hotel lobbies that allow guests to check themselves in and out, much as consumers use automated teller machines (ATM's) at banks. The ease with which a company can maintain and access a data base has permitted the development of sophisticated reservation systems and has fueled the development of frequent traveler programs. The use of more sophisticated reservations and property management systems has the potential to improve the level of service provided to guests.

A fourth reason for the growth in services has been the growth in franchising. Much of the growth of the hospitality industry has been the direct result of franchising efforts by some of the major companies. Notable lodging organizations such as Holiday, Sheraton, and Quality, as well as foodservice firms such as McDonald's, Burger King, Kentucky Fried Chicken, and Wendy's have all used franchising as a major vehicle for growth. Much of the growth of these organizations has been at the expense of independent owners and operators.

THE NATURE OF SERVICES

Services, including hospitality services, differ from products by their nature. Among the important differences are the following:

Intangibility

Marketing as practiced by product-oriented industries differs tremendously from hospitality marketing. In many other industries, marketing involves tangible manufactured products, such as automobiles, washing machines, and clothing. The product-service mix of a hospitality operation, however, combines tangibles and intangibles. Consider the following as a partial listing of the product-service mix of a hotel operation: service, convenience, hospitality, social contact, atmosphere, relaxation, entertainment, escape, guest rooms, and food and beverages.

The hospitality industry shares characteristics with other service industries, which in turn are vastly different from manufacturers. First, the product-service mix is more intangible that it is tangible. For example, in the preceding list, note that most of the items are intangible in nature. Services are "consumed," but are not "possessed" in the same manner as a tangible product, such as an automobile or a washing machine.

Simultaneous Production and Consumption

Hospitality services are generally produced and consumed simultaneously, unlike product manufacturers, who produce, distribute, and then sell their products. In a restaurant operation, customers order meals, followed by placement of the order, the meals are then produced, served, and consumed within a short time. In essence, production and consumption are simultaneous.

Consumer Involvement in Service Production

Because consumers tend to be present when the service is provided within a hotel or restaurant, they are involved in the service production. In many instances, they are directly involved through the element of self-service. Examples of this can be seen in fast-food restaurants as well as in hotels that provide automated check-in and check-out by means of either a machine or a video connection through the television. In all instances, a dialogue takes place between the service provider and the guest, as the provider determines the exact nature of the product-service mix desired by the guest.

The satisfaction of the guest will be determined by several factors—the nature of the interaction with the service provider, the nature of the physical facilities in which the service is provided, and by the nature of the other guests present in the facility at the time the service is provided.

Absence of Inventories

In some service settings, there is an absence of inventories. This is not particularly true in the hospitality industry. Some elements of the product-service mix are tangible and therefore some levels of inventory must be maintained. These inventories revolve around the food and beverage items available, as well as the guest environment items such as sheets, towels, and furniture.

Lack of Service Consistency

Service marketing differs from product marketing in that services are less uniform than products. It is easy to standardize a product-manufacturing process simply by establishing an automated assembly line, but this method has limited application to the hospitality industry. The hospitality industry is people based rather than equipment based. Within the hospitality industry, the people become a major part of the product-service mix. For example, the waitress who serves the guest becomes a major part of the product-service mix that the customer consumes.

Distribution Channels

When the services provided are highly intangible, there are not likely to be any distribution channels. However, within the hospitality industry, the distribution channels are well established and in many cases are quite lengthy. Consider the units operated by a fast-food company such as McDonald's. The individual unit must receive all of the food and beverage products that appear on the menu, as well as the packaging material in which the products are served. In addition, point-of-sale promotional material must be received from the corporate offices. While in many service instances, the distribution channels are quite short or nonexistent, within the hospitality industry the channels are well established for those elements of the product-service mix that are tangible.

Given the relative intangibility of the product-service mix of hospitality operations, how can the product and service be successfully marketed? The management can adopt several strategies, but the following should be considered. First, because people become a major part of the product-service mix, personnel should be selected with great care and trained in a professional manner. Poorly trained personnel can sabotage in a few minutes what the marketing effort has sought to establish over a period of weeks or even months. Personnel should be considered an investment in much the same manner that manufacturers view equipment as an investment.

Second, people can be used to give the product-service mix more tangibility. Personnel can be featured in advertising and promotional efforts, thereby giving the product-service mix a tangible human quality. An example of this technique within the hospitality industry is Ronald McDonald. In the battle to win the children's market, McDonald's got off to a fast start with the Ronald McDonald character. This same personalization has been used successfully by many other hospitality firms and by firms within other service industries as well.

Third, the service aspect of the product-service mix can be customized to the needs of the consumer. For many years Burger King used the slogan "Have it your way" in an effort to capitalize on custom-designed service. Wendy's has proudly promoted hamburgers with 256 possible topping combinations, thereby custom-designing the product-service mix.

Fourth, the environment in which the product-service mix is consumed is very important. Creation and maintenance of a specific type of environment is critical to the success of the operation. The environment includes many factors, including design, decor, personnel uniforms, lighting and table appointments. For example, when McDonald's began in the 1950s, special attention was given to the environment. Cleanliness was seen as critical to the success of the fledgling fast-food operation, and cleanliness was correctly perceived as a means to gain a distinct competitive advantage. Control of the environment is even more important today.

Controlling the environment affords the hospitality marketing manager the opportunity to develop a tangible representation of a predominantly intangible product-service mix. This tangible representation is more easily perceived by the consumer and can favorably affect the success of the marketing effort.

Classification of Services

Products and goods have been classified for years. Is it possible to classify services as well? Products are classified using a variety of typologies, for example:

☐ Convenience, shopping, and specialty goods

☐ Durable and nondurable goods

☐ Consumer and industrial goods

Lovelock[2] has suggested that it is also possible to classify services. He suggests posing several questions, including these:

☐ What is the nature of the service act?

☐ What type of relationship does the service organization have with its customers?

☐ How much room is there for customization and judgment on the part of the service provider?

☐ What is the nature of the demand for the service?

☐ How is the service delivered?

☐ What are the attributes of the service product?

The service act can be categorized in terms of both tangible and intangible actions or elements. Within each of these two categories, service acts can be targeted toward either people or things. In essence, who or what is the direct recipient of the service act? Within the hospitality industry, the nature of the service act is a mixture of tangible and intangible elements directed toward people. The hospitality industry involves a high-contact situation between the guest and the service provider.

The nature of the relationship between the customer and the service organization can be divided into four distinct categories by asking two questions: (1) What is the nature of the service delivery? and (2) what is the type of relationship between the customer and the service organization? The nature of the service delivery can be either continuous delivery of service or discrete transaction. The type of relationship established can be either membership or no formal relationship. Within the hospitality industry, the nature of the relationship is discrete transactions without formal membership in most cases. Within a club setting, a membership has been established. Several of the hotel chains have established frequent traveler programs in order to develop more of a membership orientation with their guests and thereby establish more brand loyalty and repeat purchase behavior.

The extent to which the service organization will customize the service or allow for judgment is a third way in which services can be classified. This element can be classified by asking two questions: (1) To what extent do customer-contact employees exercise judgment in meeting individual customer needs? and (2) to what extent are service characteristics customized? Within the hospitality industry, the service provider generally does not exercise a great deal of judgment in meeting the needs of the individual consumer. However, the services provided can be customized to meet the needs of individuals by simply changing the nature of the services provided. With increased emphasis on training of guest-contact personnel, there is a great deal of potential to allow these personnel to exercise more judgment in individual situations.

The nature of demand for hospitality services is one of the greatest challenges for service marketers and providers in the industry. Unlike product marketers, service providers are not able to build up an excess inventory level in anticipation of a peak demand period. Rather, if a hotel room is not occupied tonight, the potential revenue gained from the sale of the room is forever lost. Conversely, if demand exceeds supply, no additional revenue can be gained because the property is operating at maximum capacity. Within the hospitality industry two conditions are quite common: Demand will fluctuate over time, and supply is constrained and is not easily and quickly expanded to meet increasing and/or fluctuating demand.

The method of service delivery is another method of classifying services. Services can be available at a single site or at multiple sites. Within the hospitality industry, the greatest number of units are part of chain organizations, and therefore the majority of hospitality services are available at multiple units. Second, the nature of the service organization-customer interaction can be classified. In some instances the customer must go to the service organization, in others the service organization goes to the customer and in still others the customer and service organization transact business via electronic media or the mail. In the vast majority of hospitality businesses, the customer must come to the service organization's site. However, some of this may be changing with the advent of increasing the customer's convenience. Organizations such as Domino's Pizza saw the unmet consumer need for delivery convenience and developed the service delivery method to provide this service. The results have led to great success for Domino's Pizza.

The final manner in which services can be classified is by examining the attributes of the product-service mix. Classifying services based on attributes requires evaluating the relative contributions to the product-service mix of people-based attributes and of equipment and facility attributes. In the hospitality industry, both of these elements are high.

The study of services has evolved a great deal in the last ten years. We can establish that there are clear differences between the marketing of products and services. Classifying services is more difficult and less precise. However, services can be classified by asking six questions and determining the classification of specific types of services based on the answers to these questions.

CONSUMER BEHAVIOR WITH REGARD TO SERVICES

Search and Experience Qualities

Consumer behavior will be explored in greater depth in a later chapter, but, an brief introduction to the subject as it relates to services will be useful at this point. Several models attempt to explain consumer purchase behavior. When consumers make purchase decisions, they move through a series of steps that explain the thought process leading up to and following purchasing a product or service. Prior to making a purchase decision, consumers look for information about the product or service, referred to as *search qualities*. Search qualities are attributes that the consumer can investigate prior to making a purchase decision. When consumers attempt to check out the service attributes related to a service, they find that there are few available. The second set of qualities that the consumer can check out are the experience qualities. These attributes can be discerned only after the purchase of the service or during the consumption phase. Service purchase decisions are heavily slanted toward experience qualities. Purchase decisions related to services are more difficult, because of the lack of search qualities. Consumers tend to rely on their own past experience and the past experiences of others when making purchase decisions.

Relationship Marketing

Marketing efforts are devoted in many cases to attracting new customers. Relationship marketing is based on the proposition that it is less expensive to keep the customers that you already have than to acquire new customers. It is short-sighted to think that merely attracting new customers will keep the business headed in a successful direction. Rather, an equal amount of attention and resources should be devoted to keeping the customer base that is already in place. In times of slow market growth and increasing competition, it will be less expensive to hold onto the existing customer base than to seek new customers.

Relationship marketing as defined by Berry[3] is attracting, maintaining, and enhancing customer relationships. This long-term view toward the customer must be seen as being equal in importance to attracting new customers. Attracting new customers is merely the first step—everything else follows.

The adoption of a relationship marketing approach is most desirable when several conditions exist:

☐ There is an ongoing or periodic desire for the service on the part of the service customer.

☐ The service customer controls the selection of the service organization.

☐ There are alternative service organizations, and customer switching between service organizations is common.

All three of these conditions are met within the hospitality industry today. Examples used in this section will focus on the marketing of services within a convention- or group-oriented hotel. However, the conditions exist generally across all segments of the hospitality industry and the principles discussed will apply equally to the restaurant segment.

Several recommended strategies are discussed below:

Core Service Strategy. This is the central service provided to the consumer, around which other services can be grouped. The ideal core service is one that will (1) attract new consumers because it meets their needs and (2) build toward a long-term relationship because it provides quality service. An example of this is the core of services provided by a sales manager in a hotel. This individual should seek to develop a relationship with the group of clients that he or she services. The relationship between the client and the sales manager can make an excellent foundation and a core service for the reasons discussed above. As the client and the sales manager develop a better relationship, the sales manager can provide additional services, ones that the client values and is not likely to find available at other hotels.

Customizing the Relationship. To continue the example further, as the sales manager better understands the client's specific needs and the type of meeting, food and beverage offerings, and budgets preferred, he or she will be in a better position to customize the services provided. Specific meeting room setups, guest room arrangements, and food and beverage offerings can be tailored to better satisfy the needs of specific clients.

Service Augmentation. Another strategy is to build extras into the service repertoire. These extras serve to differentiate the service organization from competitors. By providing augmented service not readily available from others and valued by the guest, the service organization can gain a competitive advantage. Example of service augmentation within the hotel segment includes concierge service, multilingual staff, 24-hour room service, and complimentary newspapers for all guests. Hotel frequent traveler programs are another example of service augmentation, although the services provided by most of these programs are similar to those provided by other competitive programs and thus offer limited opportunity for gaining competitive advantage.

Relationship pricing.   As the relationship builds, the prices offered to the client can be reduced to provide a more favorable perceived price value relationship. Prices might be reduced slightly to recognize the contribution that the client has made to the success of the hotel by providing a significant level of volume. Another step that can be taken is upgrading a guest to more luxurious accommodations or providing additional services at no additional charge.

Internal marketing.   A final strategy that will help to foster relationship marketing is to view the staff as part of the marketing efforts as well. Efforts should be made to communicate successfully with all members of the service staff. Those individuals who come in contact with the guests are very important to the long-term success of the hotel or restaurant. The quality of the services provided is determined by those hourly employees who come in contact with the guests. For this reason, it is critical to attract, train, retain, and motivate quality personnel. The ability to deliver consistent and high-quality service depends on the organization's ability to recruit, train, retain, and motivate high-quality service personnel. It is wise to interact frequently with those responsible for providing the direct service to guests. How satisfied are they with their positions? What steps could management take to allow them to provide better service? The answers are readily available, if management will take the time to listen to those who have the most contact with guests.

MANAGING IN THE SERVICE ENVIRONMENT

Conflicts Between Operations and Marketing

Within any service organization there are bound to be differences and in some case conflicts between those responsible for sales and marketing and those with operational responsibilities. In virtually every hotel, those working in operating departments could share stories of how sales and marketing personnel have made promises to clients that were impossible to fulfill to the satisfaction of the client. Similarly, sales and marketing personnel could share stories of how the operating personnel were unwilling or unable to deliver on a simple client request for some type of product or service that was within their talents and skills to deliver.

In well-managed hospitality facilities these situations occur occasionally; in poorly managed facilities they seem habitual. One of the best ways to keep the conflicts to a minimum is to understand the perspective of the person on the other side and to make every effort to "walk a mile in their shoes." Holding a management position in either sales and marketing or operations is a challenge: It demands great skill and talent and the ability to be flexible. One way to better understand the other side's point of view is to try to see things from their perspective.

First, sales and marketing personnel tend to view the world through a revenue perspective. That is, everything that they attempt to do is targeted toward increasing revenue. Every new group that is booked into the hotel is seen as additional revenue. If a promotion is developed to increase the number of covers served in the dining room, the goal was to increase revenue.

Operations personnel, on the other hand, tend to view the world through a cost containment perspective. All efforts are focused on increasing efficiency and reducing costs to the lowest level that will still keep the operation running smoothly. Both groups, sales and marketing and operations, want to increase profits, but they simply want to take dramatically different routes to do so.

Second, with respect to time horizons, sales and marketing personnel tend to want to have everything completed tomorrow, or better yet, today. If the food production personnel are working on a new theme banquet that will be offered to special convention groups, the operations personnel will likely want to wait until "all of the bugs are worked out" before it is served to an important client group. Sales and marketing personnel on the other hand, will want to offer it to several groups, beginning right away.

Third, when it comes to offering expanded products and services as a means of gaining a competitive advantage, the sales and marketing staff will be a bountiful source of ideas. They may not stop to think how the new products and services will integrate with those that already exist. Operations personnel will tend to take a very conservative point of view, trying to keep the operation as simple and straightforward as possible.

The responsibilities of sales and marketing personnel include the booking of room nights (guest rooms) as well as managing the marketing functions of the business such as advertising and public relations. The compensation package and rewards structure for sales and marketing personnel are based on salary and bonuses. The bonuses are determined by quotas based on revenue and the amount of business that is brought to the property.

Sales personnel sometimes tend to view operations managers as being too internally focused, too negative about new ideas and new concepts to increase sales, and too focused on the process and not focused enough on guest satisfaction.

Operations managers are responsible for maintaining a smooth operation, while at the same time maintaining costs at predetermined levels. Their compensation package is based on salary and bonuses as well. The bonuses are usually based on attaining the targeted cost figures. Operations managers often have the perspective that sales personnel have too many crazy ideas that are not feasible, that they do not understand the limits of time and skill that exist within operations, and that working in sales is glamorous and is not as hard as working in operations.

This view of sales and marketing personnel conflicting with the operations personnel may be a little bit oversimplified. However, if each individual begins to better understand the other's point of view and primary motivation, the overall result will be the improved delivery of service to the consumer.

Lovelock[4] recommends three ways that operational managers can be persuaded to adopt a more marketing focus:

1. Decentralize revenue responsibility by giving operational managers responsibility for both revenue and cost goals

2. Increase internal marketing efforts, particularly those focused on providing more training to guest-contact employees

3. Develop additional company standards and standard operating procedures (SOP's) that focus directly on service standards for guests. An example might include the maximum amount of time a guest should have to wait before a service person provides service.

Managing Supply and Demand

Managing supply and demand in a service organization, such as a hotel or restaurant, is very difficult. Demand for services comes in waves and often is not as consistent as one would like. The demand may be seasonal, as with a resort hotel, or it may fluctuate by time of day, as with restaurants. It might also fluctuate by day of the week, as is the case with business-oriented hotels that are busy Monday through Thursday but quite slow on Friday through Sunday. Managing the fluctuations in demand and the corresponding supply is perhaps one of management's greatest challenges.

One method to evaluate the extent to which the supply and demand are being successfully managed is to calculate the Asset Revenue Generating Efficiency (ARGE).[5] This technique evaluates the relationship between actual revenue and maximum potential revenue. For example, within a hotel operation, the ARGE will examine the occupancy percentage and the average daily rate to determine the extent to which the revenue potential is being realized. Suppose that a hotel has 400 available rooms each day with a rack, or maximum, rate of $100. If all of the rooms were sold each day at rack rate, the maximum daily revenue would be $40,000. It is rare, however, that a hotel would be able to do this on a consistent basis. Assume that over a period of time, such as a month, the hotel achieved a 68 percent occupancy rate and had an average daily rate of $75. This means that on average, 272 rooms were sold each day at an average daily room rate of $75, resulting in total revenue of $20,400. This figure is then divided by the maximum potential daily revenue of $40,000 (20,400/40,000 = .51) and the ARGE is calculated to be 51 percent. The ARGE is useful as an evaluation tool of sales and marketing personnel because it takes into account both volume and average daily room rate. The ARGE could also be applied in other situations.

While it is difficult to "micromanage" either supply or demand, several broad strategies can be employed:

☐ *Modify price.* Changing price to meet the demand schedule can be used to encourage demand during periods of low demand to maximize revenue during periods of high demand.

☐ *Develop programs to boost nonpeak demand periods.* Several years ago, most of the fast-food companies began to develop breakfast programs, which have resulted in a very significant increase in total revenue. This represents an example of how they stimulated demand during a nonpeak period. In the case of companies that had not previously had any type of breakfast menu, it was really stimulating business during a zero volume period. Business-oriented hotels adopt the same sort of strategy when they offer special weekend rates and packages in order to boost occupancy during low-demand weekends.

☐ *Shift demand through reservations.* All of the major hotel chains maintain toll-free telephone reservation services. If demand for a particular location exceeds capacity, rather than losing the business, they will simply try to refer the potential guest to their property that is closest to the desired location. In this way, the chain will still derive the revenue and they will also provide service to the guest.

☐ *Increase personnel efficiency.* Though the use of part-time employees and cross-training employees to perform two or more jobs, management can improve employee productivity.

☐ *Increase consumer involvement in self-service aspects of the service delivery system.* For example, hotels can increase the productivity of the front desk personnel and provide improved service to the guests by enabling guests to check themselves out via video check-out on the television.

Improving Guest Service and Guest Satisfaction

Improving guest service and providing high-quality service on a consistent basis is likely a top priority of all managers working in the hospitality industry. This is much easier said than done. However, it is not impossible. As each of us travels, we encounter service personnel in hotels and restaurants who provide exceptional service. This type and consistency of service does not happen by accident; it begins with a commitment by management to make it that way. Conversely, when the opposite occurs, the finger should be pointed at management as well.

An excellent source for studying to improve service is *Quality Service: The Restaurant Manager's Bible* by William Martin.[6] Martin recommends a five-step process for improving customer service, shown in Figure 2.1 and expanded here:

1. *Define your standards of quality service with measurable indicators.* Before you can evaluate the level of service provided by personnel within your organization, it is imperative that you establish the standards by which they will be judged. These standards must be observable and measurable. For example, it might be reasonable to expect a guest seated at a table within the dining room to be approached and greeted by a service person within two minutes. Once these standards are developed, it is important that they be communicated to all personnel. It is crucial that standards be clearly defined before any plans are developed to improve the level of service. Martin uses two major dimensions to define quality service, the procedural dimension and the convivial dimension. The procedural dimension includes incremental flow of service, timeliness, accommodation to consumer needs, anticipation of consumer needs before they occur or are requested by the consumer, communication that is clear and concise, consumer feedback, and proper coordination through supervision. The convivial dimension includes

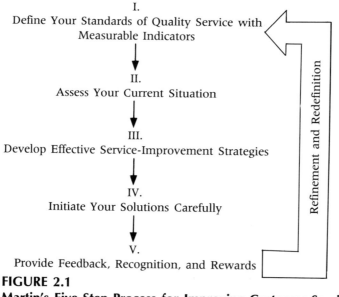

FIGURE 2.1
Martin's Five Step Process for Improving Customer Service
William B. Martin, *Quality Service: The Restaurant Manager's Bible*, © 1986 School of Hotel Administration, Cornell University, p. 162.

service personnel displaying positive attitude, positive body language, and positive and upbeat tone of voice; employing tact; using the guest's name as a means of delivering personal attention; attending to the guest on a personal basis; providing guidance to guests who are indecisive; suggestive selling; and solving problems should a problem or complaint arise.

2. *Assess your current situation.*   Just as in any development program, before you move forward you must determine your current position. This can be done by objectively assessing the level of service currently provided within the organization. It calls for an audit of the service provided by those responsible for service within the organization. Listing the strengths and weaknesses is important, for this will provide a means to build on those aspects of service that are positive and to improve those areas that are deficient.

3. *Develop effective service improvement strategies.*   This must be accomplished through well-planned and thorough training of service personnel. Attention must be paid to identifying objectives for the training and providing specific instructions and clear descriptions of the expected outcome of the training.

4. *Initiate your solutions carefully.*   As is the case with any plan, the implementation stage is the most critical. It is best to proceed with caution, taking steps incrementally rather than all at once. It is best to build on small successes, rather than trying to accomplish too much too soon.

5. *Provide feedback, recognition, and rewards.*   Positive feedback must be provided if the change in behavior is to continue. A reward structure must be provided that will maintain the level of interest and enthusiasm among the service personnel that exists when the training is completed. This represents a major challenge for management, but one that is well worth the efforts.

6. *Refinement and redefinition.*   No plan is ever fully complete or fully implemented. Rather, by using a feedback loop, management must continually evaluate the degree of success that has been achieved. Standards of service must be continually evaluated and the process begun anew.

SUMMARY

The growth in the service economy has been remarkable in the last ten years, and the contribution of the hospitality industry has been a major part of this growth. The growth in services can be attributed to several factors, including (1) reduced governmental regulation of services, as shown by easier entry into markets, more freedom to compete on price, removal of geographic restrictions on service delivery, incentive to differentiate services, and the ability to use the mass media to promote services; (2) changes in professional association and industry standards; (3) a revolution in computerization and technology; and (4) the growth in franchising.

Several key differences between products and services were discussed at length in the chapter. Including among the differences are intangibility, simultaneous production and consumption, consumer involvement in service production, absence of inventories, lack of service consistency, and short or nonexistent distribution channels.

Services can be classified just as products are classified. It is suggested that a series of questions be used to accomplish this, including the following:

☐ What is the nature of the service act?

☐ What type of relationship does the service organization have with its customers?

☐ How much room is there for customization and judgment on the part of the service provider?

☐ What is the nature of the demand for the service?

☐ How is the service delivered?

☐ What are the attributes of the service product?

When consumers make a service purchase decision, they rely more heavily on experience qualities than search qualities, due to the nature of services. The purchase decision for services offers considerable opportunity for relationship marketing, especially within hotels that have focused on group business as a major target.

It is normal for conflicts and disagreements to develop between the operations personnel and sales and marketing personnel. The underlying reasons behind this conflict were discussed, as well as methods to reduce the conflict.

The management of supply and demand within a service organization is very difficult. The nature of this challenge was explored, as well as methods to better manage supply and demand. These methods include changing prices, developing programs to boost nonpeak demand periods, shifting demand, increasing personnel efficiency, and increasing consumer involvement in self-service aspects of the service delivery system.

Finally a quality service model developed by Martin was presented and discussed. Due to the inconsistency of service delivery, the development of a means to improve and ensure quality service is imperative for service organizations such as hotels and restaurants.

KEY WORDS AND CONCEPTS

☐ Characteristics of products and services

☐ Reasons for the growth of services in the economy

☐ The nature of services

☐ Strategies for successfully marketing services

☐ Classification of services

☐ Consumer behavior with regard to the purchase of services

☐ Relationship marketing

☐ Managing in the service environment, coordinating operations and marketing, supply and demand, improving guest service and satisfaction

☐ Quality service and service standards

Questions for Review and Discussion

1. What are services? Do you believe that service marketing should be studied separately from product marketing? Why or why not?
2. List and discuss several of the reasons behind the growth in services. Which of these do you consider to be the most important? Why?
3. How do services differ from products?
4. What criteria can be used to classify services? Describe each of these criteria.
5. What are search and experience qualities? How are they used by consumers as they make purchase decisions?
6. What is relationship marketing? How can it be applied to the hospitality industry?
7. How can supply and demand be managed? To what extent to you believe it is possible to manage supply or demand within a hotel or restaurant?
8. Define and describe the steps in Martin's quality service model.

CHAPTER 3

Overview of Marketing in the Hospitality Industry

This chapter will focus on the management function of marketing as it applies to the hospitality industry. The chapter is divided into the following major sections:

INTRODUCTION
☐ Operations
☐ Finance
☐ Administration
☐ Human Resource Management
☐ Research and Development
☐ Marketing

THE PRODUCT LIFE CYCLE
☐ Pros and Cons of the Product Life Cycle
☐ Developing Strategies for the Product Life Cycle

INTRODUCTION

Marketing management as practiced today differs tremendously from the techniques used several years ago. Hospitality marketing is in a constant state of flux, as corporations plan, implement, and evaluate new marketing strategies and tactics. General marketing management practices and techniques should be analyzed and used as guidelines, but it is necessary for each hospitality organization to adjust and modify these general guidelines and techniques as dictated by the competitive environment. The one constant within the hospitality industry is change, and this serves to attract management personnel who want to be stimulated by the ever-changing competitive environment.

It is also important to remember that marketing is but one of the functions with which management must be concerned. Within large hospitality organizations, specialists are hired to staff positions within each of the functional areas. In small organizations, however, management must wear many hats and successfully perform all of the managerial functions. The following discussion places marketing in its proper place as a major part of the successful management of any hospitality organization. To fulfill an organization's potential, management must place its various functions in perspective and manage each successfully. The functions are interdependent and must support each other, thereby increasing the overall strength of the organization.

The major management functions include the following:

Operations

Management is responsible for the day-to-day operation of the hospitality facility. This includes such diverse activities as purchasing, receiving, inventory control, production, service of guest rooms, and all of the other activities that take place each day within a successful hotel or restaurant operation. Without a strong focus on operations, the quality of the product-service mix is likely to be poor and/or inconsistent. The results of this are fully predictable—declining customer counts and possible business failure.

Finance

A central and overriding goal of all businesses, including hospitality organizations, is to increase the wealth of the owners or stockholders. In periods of economic uncertainty, such as during high rates of inflation, high interest rates, or periods of recession, the management of the financial function becomes even more critical to the success of the hospitality organization. All hospitality organizations need to focus considerable attention on this function to manage the organization's assets and financial affairs successfully.

Administration

This function is very much a behind-the-scenes function and is often neglected. Administration includes such areas as accounts receivable, accounts payable, and payroll. The increasing emphasis on computer applications both in the front and back of the house is an administrative responsibility.

Human Resource Management

The hospitality industry, as a part of the service industries, is a people business. As discussed in Chapters 1 and 2, people assume a major role in the product-service mix. The success of a hospitality venture depends to a large extent on the success of the individual employees. Management is responsible for establishing the overall direction, but it is left to each employee to implement the management's wishes. The major activities of human resource management include recruitment, selection, orientation, training, professional development, and personnel relations. Historically, the turnover rate in the hospitality industry has been much higher than in other industries.

High rates of turnover for all positions, but especially among key positions, adversely affect the entire organization. The human resources of a hospitality organization are just what the name implies—valuable resources that should be developed. Some hospitality firms expend very little effort in professional development, much to the detriment of the organization.

Research and Development

In order to compete successfully in the years ahead, hospitality firms must invest time and money for research and development. These efforts typically focus on developing new market segments and new elements of the product-service mix. The growth of new concepts and new types of product-service mixes is an example of the outgrowth of research and development efforts. Lodging organizations such as Holiday, Quality, Marriott, and others developed all-suite hotels in response to research and development efforts that identified a substantial consumer market for small suites at affordable prices.

Because it is unlikely that a single hospitality concept will be successful indefinitely, management must be future oriented and must anticipate necessary changes. Research and development efforts must be attuned to what consumers will want in the future. Being ready and able to change to meet future consumer needs is the real challenge of research and development.

Marketing

The final area for which management is responsible is marketing. Successful marketing calls for the professional management of the marketing mix and the three sub-mixes discussed in Chapter 1. Management must always be ready to adapt the elements of the marketing mix in order to gain a competitive advantage in ever-changing market conditions.

THE PRODUCT LIFE CYCLE

A major goal of operating a hospitality organization or facility is to maximize the wealth of the owners. In the case of a noncommercial organization, such as a nonprofit hospital, a similar goal would be to achieve a break-even point based upon a very limited operating budget. To reach this goal, hospitality organizations have adopted numerous strategies. Historically, one of the most popular strategies has been the rapid growth strategy. It was believed by many hospitality firms that the best strategy to employ would be one that led to rapid expansion in number of units or properties. The anticipated results would, of course, be increased sales and profits. This strategy was employed very successfully by numerous corporations, including most of the giants in the fast-food segment of the industry.

Many leading management experts have studied the phenomenon and have identified what is known as the product life cycle of an organization. The product life cycle of an organization can be divided into five separate and unique stages, as illustrated in Figure 3.1.

Stage I of the life cycle is called the introduction stage. Here the organization is in its infancy, having just been created by a single entrepreneur or a group of investors. During this stage, the operation is seeking to establish itself firmly in the marketplace and is seeking to build a firm clientele base. The primary emphasis is to establish brand awareness which will then lead to trial and repeat purchase by guests. Those first guests are generally innovators, those who will take a chance on an unknown brand. If the first guests' experience is a positive one, they will help to establish brand awareness by telling their friends and colleagues. Advertising is also used to establish brand awareness. Well-known brands within the hospitality industry, such as Wendy's, Holiday Inn, Marriott Hotels, and Embassy Suites, were once unknown to potential consumers. At this stage, the business is struggling to survive. Financing is usually quite difficult and the organizational structure is very simple. The owners are usually very involved in the daily operation of the business.

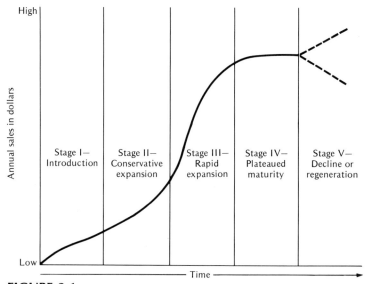

FIGURE 3.1
The Life Cycle of Hospitality Organizations

If the organization succeeds in establishing itself, business soon begins to increase, and the owners may be faced with a decision regarding expansion.

Stage II, or conservative expansion, is a period of slow and steady growth, usually in the form of an increase in the number of units. New units are constructed using the original unit as a model. Minor changes may be made in the unit design and concept, but normally the owners attempt to standardize the physical plant, thereby reducing developmental costs. The owners' rationalization is that if the original unit was successful, then additional units will also be successful.

This thinking is often the downfall of the owners, for in expanding, they fail to consider the market structure in which new units are located and therefore fail to achieve the level of profitability they desire. Standardization and consistency of the product-service mix are very desirable qualities, and these attributes were critical to the success of companies such as Holiday Inn and McDonald's. However, a blind faith in standardization can have detrimental affects on the success of the business. As hospitality companies have segmented their markets, they have found that it is critical to meet the needs of the smaller segments, not always targeting for the larger mass market. With this in mind, the needs and wants of the specific market segment must be paramount in the minds of hospitality marketing managers. The hospitality market in the United States is not made up of one large mass market; rather, there are many smaller market segments.

Franchising is also a potential method to foster more rapid growth. By engaging in franchising, the owners are able to expand the concept more rapidly than they could using their own resources. The decision to begin franchising is a serious one, for with it comes a more complex organizational structure. Support services must be provided to the franchisee group in areas such as operations, finance, administration, marketing, human resource management, and research and development. These extra services and the interactions between the corporate office and the franchisees result in a more complex organizational structure.

Many companies, however, do achieve success when expanding from a single unit to perhaps as many as ten. At this stage, economies of scale may begin to play a more important role in the management of the organization. These economies of scale apply to the marketing function as well, particularly in the areas of advertising and promotion.

Assuming that the organization is able to overcome the problems that may arise during the conservative expansion stage, the firm then advances to Stage III, the rapid expansion phase. It is during this stage that the organization commits itself to expand as rapidly as possible, either through franchising or through financing obtained through other sources and managed directly by the organization. During the rapid expansion stage, the organization typically expands with many new units in a process known as cookie cutting. Cookie cutting involves the establishment of new units that are modeled on existing ones and are merely placed in new locations. These units are often located in clusters within geographic regions. The development of the Courtyard by Marriott concept is an illustration of this approach. Following a period of test marketing and research and development in the Atlanta area, the Courtyards were developed in clusters around major cities. This clustering allows the consolidation of staff support services in a central location where it can be provided to several hotel properties, thereby reducing the operating cost of each hotel.

During Stage III, the product-service mix is standardized, and the role of marketing is heavily oriented toward site selection. This is an area in which many regional chains make fatal errors. Instead of concentrating their efforts on both expansion and product-service mix research and development, they place too much emphasis on expansion, and research and development of new products and services suffer.

Assuming that the organization is able to achieve the desired success in the rapid expansion stage, it will then enter Stage IV, the plateaued maturity stage. At this point, the organization has expanded as much as the market will allow, and volume, as measured in annual gross sales, will level off. Companies in this stage of the product life cycle find that the market is often saturated and competition is increasing from alternative options. There may also be changes in consumer preference, as the consumer turns toward newer and more innovative concepts for food and lodging. It is imperative that management take decisive steps to hold onto the current market, thereby protecting market share. Steps must also be taken to tighten up operations to preserve and enhance the quality of the product-service mix. The stage typically finds an increase in marketing efforts in an attempt to boost stagnant sales. This mature life cycle may remain stable for some time, perhaps many years, but eventually this stage too will end.

The organization then enters into Stage V, which is a real turning point. Rarely will the plateaued maturity stage continue indefinitely. Instead, the organization will slowly decline, or sales will again increase and the process may begin again. Stage V is called decline or regeneration.

The McDonald's Corporation serves as an excellent illustration of the way a corporation progresses through the organizational life cycle. McDonald's Corporation, under the direction of Ray Kroc, began with a few units in the middle 1950s. The corporation quickly achieved a sound financial base and rapidly moved into Stages II and III of the life cycle. New units were continually under construction, and soon the familiar red and white buildings with the golden arches could be found throughout the country. As McDonald's reached Stage IV of the life cycle, however, an important decision was made.

The upper-level management felt that the red and white buildings with the golden arches had lived their useful life and that a new image was needed. With this in mind, the entire corporation began to rethink the design and decor of all new units as well as the vast majority of existing units. They determined that a more subdued appeal was needed in order to attract different target markets. The term *fast-food* was not used in any promotional or corporate literature. Instead, emphasis was placed on the image of McDonald's as a restaurant. Instead of leveling off sales, McDonald's was able to inject new life into their concept and therefore continued to expand and increase the number of units, total sales, and bottom line profits. This type of thinking has continued today, as McDonald's remains the dominant foodservice company, with a substantial gap in number of units, gross sales, and profitability between them and the number two and three contenders.

While this section has focused upon the product life cycle as it pertains to hospitality organizations, the product life cycle is also frequently applied to such elements of the product-service mix as individual menu items and design and decor treatments.

Pros and Cons of the Product Life Cycle

As you might expect with most concepts or theories, the product life cycle concept has its supporters and its opponents. Supporters argue that firms that use the concept successfully are able to identify the stage in which the organization or an individual product finds itself and then use this knowledge in formulating better marketing plans. Experts believe that these firms are able to find out where each of their products and services are positioned within the life cycle, determine the correct mix of products and services to improve the performance of the entire organization, and analyze trends in the product-service mix as well as the impact this mix will have on short- and long-term financial performance.

Those supporting the product life cycle concept indicate that specific strategies can be adopted for each stage in the life cycle. When implemented properly, these strategies can have a positive impact on the financial performance of the organization. In effect, proponents claim that the product life cycle is not merely charted; instead, the organization's marketing managers seek to shape the life cycle by prolonging its positive aspects and improving profitability.

The opponents of the product life cycle concept state their case with equal vigor. They contend that few products or services actually conform to the life cycle curve illustrated in Figure 3.1. Rather, the curve may rise and fall in any number of patterns, each unique to the product or service itself. If managers believe that a product follows the normal life cycle curve when a decline (Stage V) begins, they may choose to discontinue the product. Those who do not support the product life cycle concept contend that this "death" may be inappropriate and that the product may instead be experiencing a temporary plateau or slight decline prior to a growth period. This premature death could result in reduced profitability. Furthermore, some products may remain in the plateaued maturity stage (Stage IV) indefinitely.

Opponents of the concept also claim that it is often difficult to determine the exact stage in which a product lies. There are clearly no indicators to mark the transition from one stage to another. Similarly, if a product experiences a slowdown in growth following a period of rapid growth does this mean that Stage IV, plateaued maturity, has begun? Or is this simply a slight slowdown in growth prior to continued expansion?

Finally, opponents of the product life cycle concept indicate that some marketing managers place too much faith in it. It is as if they were wearing blinders like those used on race horses. These individuals focus too much attention on the product life cycle and forget about all the other environmental factors that can influence the success of a product or service.

Developing Strategies for the Product Life Cycle

A wide variety of strategies have been used for the various stages in the product life cycle. To develop strategies, however, management must first analyze the life cycle. This can be done in a seven-step process, as follows:

1. *Compiling historical data.* It is imperative that a hospitality firm compile as much historical sales data as possible. Ideally, these data should be available for the entire history of the organization. The specific type of data needed include number of units sold and total sales revenue, profit margins, total profit contributions, return on investment, and prices.

2. *Identifying competitive trends.* Recent activities of major competitors should be monitored closely to determine changes in market share and position, as well as changes in quality of the product-service mix. Additionally, the other elements of the marketing mix, presentation mix, and the communication mix (as discussed in Chapter 1) should be monitored for significant changes.

3. *Determining changes in product-service mix.* The marketplace must be monitored in order to learn about new products and services that other hospitality operations are introducing. What are the potential effects of their changes on your operation?

4. *Studying the product life cycles.* It is helpful to study the product life cycle of similar products or services to determine whether a pattern exists. Rarely is a product or service so new and unusual that it is not possible to compare it with a previous one.

5. *Projecting sales.* Based on the data collected, sales for a three- to five-year period should be projected. Statistical applications using a computer

are particularly useful at this stage, as recently developed forecasting models can improve the accuracy of these forecasts. In addition to projecting sales, management should also measure other indicators of financial success, including profits, return on investment, and debt-to-equity ratios. Use of ratio analysis using both the organization's balance sheet and income statement will be particularly useful.

6. *Locating current position on the life cycle.* Based on the historical data, as well as the projections, it should now be possible to locate the position on the product life cycle.

7. *Developing strategies.* Once the position is located on the product life cycle, strategy formulation begins. Table 3.1 illustrates the characteristics and strategies that apply to different stages in the product life cycle. These strategies should not be viewed as absolute, but they do represent the most widely accepted ideas in the marketing community.

McDonald's Through the Life Cycle

Every organization must continue to innovate and to develop new products and services if it is to continue to be successful. McDonald's serves as an excellent example of an organization that has done just this. As the industry's well-established leader, McDonald's might find it easy to sit back, not introduce new items, and become complacent. This is not the case. A brief review of annual reports and trade journals reveals that McDonald's has a long history of introducing new products and services. Each of these has been introduced with the goal of boosting sales and customer counts. Some have been more successful than others. However, the important point to remember is that the organization took chances—calculated risks—and continues to be the industry leader.

A brief review of some of the product service mix changes that McDonald's has made include the following:

1963   The Filet-o-Fish™ sandwich is introduced. This was done in partial response from franchisees located in Catholic neighborhoods in which no beef was consumed on Fridays. Hence, sales on Fridays were very low.

1967   The building is redesigned to include indoor seating, representing a move toward more of a restaurant look.

1968   Newer, more contemporary building design replaces the red and white building with the golden arches.

1972   Quarterpounder™ is introduced, increasing per unit sales.

1973   A limited breakfast program is introduced, featuring the Egg McMuffin™.

1974   McDonaldland cookies™ are introduced.

1975   Drive-through windows are introduced. In some cases, drive-through windows account for 50 percent of total unit sales.

1976   New uniforms are rolled out.

1977   A complete breakfast menu and sundaes are introduced.

1981   Chicken items are added to the menu.

1982   McRib sandwich™ is added to the menu. It proves to be unsuccessful and is later removed.

1983   Chicken McNuggets™ are added to the menu, boosting sales by 10 percent. Biscuits are also added to the breakfast menu.

1987   A variety of individual salads are added to the menu.

1990   Further innovations and changes in the product service mix???

The Concept of the Wheel of Retailing

The concept of the wheel of retailing is one that can apply to the hospitality industry. The wheel of retailing advances the notion that as companies continue to develop products and services, they will add new features to existing products and services. This continual upward movement of products and services provides an opportunity for new competitors to enter the market at the lower end of the market.

The retailing world and the hospitality industry are filled with examples of the application of the wheel of retailing. For example, the original strength of the Japanese automobile industry movement into the United States was based on the fact that Japan produced a series of small automobiles that were superior to and cheaper than the small cars produced by American manufacturers. American manufacturers had largely ignored the lower end of the automobile market, thereby permitting the Japanese to gain a competitive advantage at the lower end.

Within the foodservice segment of the hospitality industry, McDonald's and Wendy's serve as excellent examples of the application of the wheel of retailing. Presented above was a listing of the new products and services that McDonald's has introduced since the early 1960s. If one considers the origins of the chain, it was based on a very simple menu consisting of hamburgers, french fries, soft drinks, and milk shakes. That was it—nothing else. As McDonald's added new items to their menu, they allowed room for others to enter the market with simpler, less complex menus and service delivery systems. Wendy's is the best example. When Wendy's began, they too had a simple menu with far fewer items than McDonald's. Over the years Wendy's menu and range of products and services has also grown.

TABLE 3.1
Characteristics and Strategies for the Stages of the Product Life Cycle

	Stage I- Introduction	Stage II to Stage III— Conservative Expansion and Rapid Expansion	Stage IV— Plateaued Maturity	Stage V—Decline or Regeneration
CHARACTERISTICS				
Sales	Low	Fast increases	Little or no growth	Declining
Profits	Negligible	Peak levels	Declining	Very low or zero
Cash flow	Negligible	Moderate	High	Low
Customers	Risk takers/innovators	Target markets	Target markets	Small segment of late adaptors
Competitors	Few	Increasing in number and strength	Highly competitive	Declining in number and strength
STRATEGIES				
Strategic focus	Expanded market	Market penetration to capture target markets	Maintaining competitive position and market share	Prepare to remove from market; milk of all possible benefits
Marketing expenditures	High	Continued high but declining as percentage of total sales	Declining	Very low
Marketing emphasis	Awareness of products and services	Building repeat patronage and word-of-mouth promotion	Maintaining repeat patronage	Selective patronage
Price	High to cover initial costs	High due to high demand	Declining to retain competitive advantage	Declining to increase volume
Advertising strategy	Aimed at needs and wants of innovators	Make mass market aware of products and services	Used to differentiate among major competitors	Emphasize low price to increase volume

TRENDS AFFECTING THE HOSPITALITY INDUSTRY

Identifying trends within any business is one of the keys to success. Being in a position to identify what is occurring and what is likely to occur in the future is very important. As discussed in Chapter 1, when studying trends, one should examine four major areas: economic, sociocultural, technological, and political issues.

Research conducted at Virginia Tech has identified several broad trends that are having an impact on the hospitality industry. These serve as examples of the type of issues and trends that hospitality managers should be identifying and acting upon to stay ahead of the competition. The broad trends identified include the following:

1. *Changing consumer attitudes and tastes.*   Consumers have developed an increased interest in and knowledge about nutrition. They are more interested in the types of foods that they consume and are more conscious about the relationship between diet and general health.

Consumers have also changed their life styles. Single-parent families have become quite common, as have two-career families. Both men and women are marrying at an older age. These changes have resulted in changing patterns for foodservice and lodging consumption. No longer do the majority of families take a two-week vacation in the summer; rather, the mini vacation and long weekends have become more the norm. Consumers have also become more demanding, seeking novel concepts. They will not tolerate sameness; they want something new and unique.

2. *Increasingly active political environment.*   All of the professional associations that represent segments of the hospitality industry have launched more active lobbying campaigns, in response to a more active political climate. Examples of political activity include changes in the federal tax codes that are having an impact on the industry, franchisee groups that are gaining strength, and an increase in consumer protection legislation.

3. *Defensive strategies.*   The hospitality marketplace is more competitive than ever, and it will become even more so. This has resulted in a number of activities, including these:

   (a) Chain organizations have become more dominant by capturing a larger market share. There has also been some consolidation among the largest corporations through mergers and acquisitions.

   (b) Most of the primary markets in the United States are fully developed, so expansion in foreign markets has increased, especially in the foodservice segment.

   (c) The availability of alternative products has increased. An example of this is the expansion by convenience stores, such as the Southland Corporation (the 7-11 chain), into the foodservice business.

(d) There has been an increasing emphasis on quality assurance and quality control. Leading hospitality firms have successfully implemented programs to assure that specific quality standards of products and services are provided for guests, thereby pleasing guests.

(e) Corporations have attempted to define and defend market niches. This has increased the development of regional or "second-tier" chains.

(f) Expenditures for marketing activities have increased.

Specific Trends Affecting Hospitality Marketing

Several issues and trends are critical to understanding hospitality marketing. They help to put into proper perspective what is occurring in the competitive marketplace. Three trends that are having and will continue to have an impact on the hospitality industry are discussed in the following section.

1. *Shrinking guest loyalty.* Advertising and promotions for the hospitality industry's product-service mix have traditionally focused on the product, the services provided, and the physical plant or atmosphere in which the guest enjoys the product-service mix. Often a focus of the promotion was on price; that is, the price offered to the consumer was reduced. It was believed that a price reduction would accomplish two goals: first, increased patronage, and second, repeat patronage and brand loyalty. We find, however, that there is less brand loyalty today than at any time in the past. Consumers often shop around for the best "deal" and are loyal only to those organizations that give them a consistently good deal.

Recognizing this, companies have sought ways to increase brand loyalty, especially among heavy users of the product-service mix. The best examples of this approach are the frequent flyer programs promoted by the airlines, and the frequent traveler programs promoted by the lodging companies. The basic concept common to all of these programs is to (a) identify those individuals who use your product-service mix frequently, (b) recognize the contribution these individuals make to the success of your company, and (c) reward these individuals with awards and incentives that will increase their loyalty to your company's brand. Tie-ins with other companies providing travel-related services are also frequently used. For examples it is common for airlines, hotels, and rental car companies to offer bonus points within their programs if the traveler uses the services offered by one of the companies participating in the tie-in. Both the airlines and hotel companies are constantly making minor alterations to their programs. In addition, the Internal Revenue Service (IRS) is considering ways to tax these awards and incentives as individual income.

2. *Increasing consumer sophistication concerning the price-value relationships.* The budget segment of the lodging industry has undergone significant

growth in the last several years. This growth has been fueled by the consumer demand for affordable accommodations that provide a high value. Companies have responded with brands such as Hampton Inns, Comfort Inns, and Marriott Courtyards. Each of these brands feature very nicely appointed guest rooms, limited or no public meeting space, and limited or no foodservice provided on the hotel site. Each of the brands has been able to reduce the development and operating expenses, and thereby provide guests with a lower price and a high price-value relationship, something that all consumers are seeking.

Other types of hotels in the upscale segment also try to increase the consumer's perception of price-value. They continually provide a broad assortment of amenities, such as health clubs on property, telephones and televisions in the bathrooms, and personalized concierge service. These properties are striving to become terminal destinations, providing a complete product-service mix that includes a variety of food and beverage outlets, in-house office services, a wide variety of meeting room configurations, and other services, such as recreation, that will appeal to potential guests.

Within the fast-food service segment, companies often "bundle" their products in an attempt to increase sales and provide a better price-value for their customers. For example, they might bundle a large hamburger, large french fries, and a large soft drink at a price lower than the normal price if the same items were purchased separately.

3. *Market segmentation.* The markets within both foodservice and lodging have been segmented to some extent for a long time. During the 1980s, however, this trend has become even more pronounced. No longer were the services offered fairly uniform; they were being tailored to meet the specific needs of a small sub-set of travelers and diners. Examples exist to illustrate this point in foodservice as well as lodging, but the example within the lodging segment is perhaps the best. During the last several years, most of the major lodging chains began to develop and operate several new brands or types of lodging properties, each tailored to meet the needs of a market segment. Market segmentation will be discussed further in Chapter 7.

The major hospitality marketing trends for the years ahead will be the ones you read about in the trade journals, but each manager needs to identify a target market and develop a plan for appealing to that particular market.

Marketing plays an important role in the profit planning of any hospitality operation. Managers must undertake efforts to generate a continuous flow of new consumers and stimulate as large a percentage of repeat patronage as possible. Even nonprofit operations need to allocate resources for marketing efforts when planning for budget expenditures. These operations normally expend money for special events to stimulate consumer interest, and they conduct surveys of patrons and other marketing activities.

The old phase, "In order to make money, you have to spend money," rings true for marketing. Every day, a typical American consumer is exposed to hundreds of advertisements and personal marketing efforts for a wide range of products and services. Given this deluge of information and organized persuasion, it is difficult for the average consumer to develop a strong brand loyalty to any one foodservice or lodging organization. It is therefore important for all hospitality managers to engage in organized and well-planned marketing campaigns. The simple fact remains that those managers who fail to implement some type of marketing program are likely to fail to achieve the highest possible level of success.

The amount of money allocated for marketing activities varies greatly in the hospitality industry. Typically, marketing efforts account for 1 to 8 percent of gross sales. This figure represents the total cost of marketing, not just the cost of advertising and promotional efforts. The total expenses for marketing include such expenses as salaries, office expenses, travel for sales personnel and all other costs associated with marketing efforts. The lower figures may apply to noncommercial operations or those that are so well established that they find themselves operating in a relatively noncompetitive environment. Operations that are newly established or that function in highly competitive markets may spend more than 8 percent of total sales for marketing efforts. No formal guidelines can be used to determine an ideal amount to allocate for marketing. Instead, each manager must carefully plan a marketing program that will achieve the desired results while being cost effective.

It is highly desirable for a manager or group of managers to establish a firmly defined marketing budget that allocates specific dollar figures to specific activities (e.g., radio advertising and consumer surveys) for well-defined periods, such as monthly intervals. In this manner, a plan or frame of reference is created, and managers are able to gauge the extent to which they are following the predetermined plan. Marketing budgets can be either fixed or flexible. Fixed budgets use dollar figures, which are precise and not subject to change even though sales volumes may vary. Flexible budgets, on the other hand, are normally based on two or more projected levels of sales and would allow more flexibility, as may be necessary in certain competitive situations. The development of marketing plans and budgets will be discussed further in Chapters 4 and 12.

SIZE, SCOPE, AND MAJOR CORPORATIONS IN THE HOSPITALITY INDUSTRY

The hospitality industry has clearly established itself as one of the leading service industries in the United States today. One cannot pick up a trade journal or a publication of one of the professional associations such as the National Restaurant Association or the American Hotel and Motel Association without seeing a new all-time high figure for industry sales. Figures published by the NRA and AH&MA indicate that the hospitality industry currently employs more than 10 million people. Total industry sales will exceed $400 billion by the early 1990s.

The hospitality industry is made up of a wide variety of segments, including restaurants and foodservice operations, hotel and motels, private clubs, food brokers and distributors, manufacturers, professional associations, and hospitality education.

Just as it is important to be a student of industry trends, so too is it important to keep up with the developments of the major corporations within each of the major industry segments. These are the organizations that will continue to set the pace for the industry. While it is true that some of the most creative and innovative ideas are those started by smaller independent operators, it is the major corporations that will set the pace.

Foodservice Corporations

The NRA claims that the foodservice segment is the number one retail employer in the United States, employing more than 8 million individuals in nearly 600,000 units. Growth in employment in foodservice operations accounted for 50 percent of the growth in the retail sector during the period 1975–1985. The foodservice segment represents nearly 5 percent of the nation's gross national product (GNP). Employment growth looks very positive. It is projected that by 1995, the foodservice segment will hire 25 percent more managers and supervisors.

Of the nearly 600,000 foodservice units operating in the United States, most are single-unit operations, and about half are sole proprietorships or partnerships. Yet at the same time, the chain organizations are becoming more dominant. In 1972, chains accounted for 33 percent of the foodservice segment's sales, while today their market share of total sales is nearly 50 percent.

McDonald's Corporation has long been the industry leader, enjoying a greater than two-to-one lead over the number two corporation in annual sales. Operating in excess of 8500 stores and showing annual sales in excess of $10 billion, they are the major force. The ten largest corporations, based on annual sales, are shown in Table 3.2. Within some of the largest corporations, several brands exist. Table 3.3 provides a listing of the top fifteen brands, based on annual sales volume.

Lodging Corporations

According to the AH&MA, the lodging segment employees nearly 1.5 million individuals and creates over 100,000 new positions each year. Total lodging

TABLE 3.2
Leading Foodservice Corporations and Operators

Rank	Corporation	Headquarters	Number of Units
1	U.S. Dept. of Agriculture Food and Nutrition Service	Alexandria, VA	90,000
2	R. J. Reynolds Industries, Inc.	Winston-Salem, NC	9,500
3	McDonald's Corp.	Oak Brook, IL	8,500
4	PepsiCo Food Service Division	Purchase, NY	6,900
5	Pillsbury Co. Restaurant Group	Minneapolis, MN	4,900
6	Holiday Corp.	Memphis, TN	3,800
7	Wendy's International Inc.	Dublin, OH	3,200
8	ARA Services, Inc.	Philadelphia, PA	2,700
9	Imasco, Inc.	Rocky Mount, NC	2,600
10	Marriott Corp.	Washington, DC	2,000

TABLE 3.3
Top Fifteen Brands within the Foodservice Industry Based on Annual Sales

Rank	Brand/Corporation	Headquarters
1	McDonald's	Oak Brook, IL
2	Burger King	Miami, FL
3	Kentucky Fried Chicken	Louisville, KY
4	Wendy's	Dublin, OH
5	Hardee's	Rocky Mount, NC
6	Pizza Hut	Wichita, KA
7	Dairy Queen	Minneapolis, MN
8	Denny's	LaMirada, CA
9	Taco Bell	Irvine, CA
10	Red Lobster	Orlando, FL
11	Big Boy	Washington, DC
12	Arby's	Atlanta, GA
13	Ponderosa	Dayton, OH
14	Jack in the Box	San Diego, CA
15	Domino's Pizza	Ann Arbor, MI

segment sales exceed $50 billion per year, representing approximately 1 percent of the GNP.

The leaders in the lodging segment of the industry are equally dominant. Each year, fewer and fewer independent properties continue to operate successfully. Most of the new development is done by the corporations themselves or through other methods of expansion such as franchising, management contracts, and joint ventures. According to *Hotel and Motel Management*, fully 75 percent of the hotels and motels operated in the United States are franchised. Growth projections for the next five years are greater than 40 percent.

Table 3.4 provides a listing of the ten largest lodging corporations, based on the number of rooms.

SUMMARY

This chapter provides an overview of marketing in the hospitality industry. In addition to the marketing function, managers are also held responsible for operations, finance, administration, and research and development.

Historically, hospitality organizations have adopted a growth strategy founded on rapid growth and expansion in the number of units. This rapid expansion has been studied and is incorporated in the model illustrating the product life cycle. This cycle has five stages—introduction, conservative ex-

TABLE 3.4
The Top Ten Lodging Corporations

Rank	Corporation	Number of Rooms
1	Holiday	295,000
2	Best Western	180,000
3	Hilton	95,000
4	Sheraton	94,000
5	Ramada	89,000
6	Quality International	75,000
7	Marriott	70,000
8	Howard Johnson	65,000
9	Days Inn	60,000
10	Motel 6	58,000

pansion, rapid expansion, plateaued maturity, and decline or regeneration. Marketing experts do not all agree about the relative merits and weaknesses of the product life cycle, but managers may find it a useful tool. Specific characteristics and strategies are suggested for each stage in the product life cycle.

Being a student of trends is an important skill to develop. Several broad and specific trends were presented in the chapter. Broad trends affecting the hospitality industry include changing consumer attitudes and tastes, an increasingly active political environment, and the adoption of defensive strategies by companies. Specific marketing trends discussed were shrinking guest loyalty, increasing consumer sophistication concerning price-value relationships, and market segmentation.

Marketing must assume a role in the profit planning for all hospitality operations. Hospitality managers must engage in marketing activities if they are to prosper and achieve desired financial goals. In some instances, firms may allocate more than 8 percent of total sales to the marketing effort. It is important that this money be budgeted in an organized manner if its maximum use is to be assured.

KEY WORDS AND CONCEPTS

- ☐ Management functions
- ☐ Stages of the product life cycle
- ☐ Pros and cons of the product life cycle
- ☐ The wheel of retailing
- ☐ Trends affecting the hospitality industry
- ☐ Guest loyalty
- ☐ Price-value relationship
- ☐ Market segmentation

Questions for Review and Discussion

1. What are the major functions for which a hospitality manager must assume responsibility? Briefly define and discuss each function.
2. Cite and discuss each of the five stages of the product life cycle.
3. What are the pros and cons of using the product life cycle as a marketing tool? Do you believe that it should be used in developing marketing plans and strategies? Why or why not?
4. Do you think that the rapid growth strategy was a wise strategy for

corporations to have followed? What type of growth strategy do you think will be most favored in the next five to ten years? Why?

5. Cite and discuss the major trends affecting the hospitality industry in general and marketing specifically. Based on your reading of current trade journals and literature, what do you believe are the emerging trends? What impact do you think they will have on the hospitality industry? Why?

PART II

MARKETING PLANNING, INFORMATION, AND RESEARCH

CHAPTER 4

Developing a Marketing Plan

This chapter will introduce the concept of strategic planning as it pertains to the marketing function. A model for strategic planning will be presented and discussed at some length, and aspects of this model will be discussed in further depth in the chapters that follow. The model is designed to provide an overall framework into which material in later chapters can be placed. The chapter is divided into the following major sections:

INTRODUCTION

Planning for Effective Marketing
☐ Types of Plans
☐ Definition of Planning Terms
☐ Advantages to Planning
☐ Disadvantages to Planning

A SYSTEMS MODEL FOR DEVELOPING A MARKETING PLAN
☐ The Strategic Marketing Planning Model
☐ Why Some Plans Fail

SUMMARY

KEY WORDS AND CONCEPTS

QUESTIONS FOR REVIEW AND DISCUSSION

INTRODUCTION

Each year the process of successfully marketing a hospitality operation becomes more difficult. New types of lodging facilities come into the marketplace and new types of foodservice concepts and menus enter the marketplace as well. The level of competitive activity continues to increase, as other hospitality operations loom on the competitive horizon as either direct or indirect competitors. Consider, for example, the tremendous growth throughout the lodging segment of the hospitality industry in the late 1970s and 1980s. Most of the major chains experienced rapid growth and the total number of available rooms grew significantly. Growth rates of 15 to 20 percent per year were not uncommon. Similar growth has occurred in the foodservice segment as well.

As these chains rapidly expanded, hundreds of independent operations and small chains were forced to appraise the competitive environment and develop strategies to allow them to counteract this new competition successfully. Many of these independent and small chains, however, were unsuccessful in their efforts. What caused these operations to fail?

Numerous factors contribute to the failure of a hospitality operation; a list of such factors would be very long. Factors that consistently play a part in the failure of a hotel or restaurant include poor financial planning, poor overall operational management and control, inconsistent quality of the product-service mix, employee theft, and poor location. In addition, poor marketing planning and execution often contribute to operational failures. This means that management has simply neglected to anticipate the impact that increased competition would have upon the organization. This neglect results in a lack of contingency planning, and the result is the failure of many hospitality organizations.

An old saying that still holds true today indicates that there are three types of companies: those that make things happen, those that watch things happen, and those that wonder what happened.

Those companies that make things happen are generally engaged in planning. They have established corporate objectives, which in turn lead to the formation of overall strategies that serve as the basis for the day-to-day action plans that guide operations. The truly successful companies are those that never lose sight of the organization's broadly defined mission, the strategies that the organization will follow, and the objectives. Becoming overly concerned with day-to-day operations is a major pitfall that causes the downfall of many hospitality organizations. The result is that managers become so engrossed in the various aspects of operations management that they fail to see the overall picture; they "can't see the forest for the trees." They are not aware of trends, and when the competitive environment does change, they are not prepared for it.

Successful planning is a key element in the financial success of all hospitality organizations. Those organizations that allocate human and monetary resources for planning are much more likely to reach their financial goals than those that do not.

PLANNING FOR EFFECTIVE MARKETING

Types of Plans

Within most corporations, there are two levels of management: operational and strategic. The planning that takes place at each of these levels pertains to a variety of managerial functions, including marketing. Specific marketing planning efforts are related to each of these levels.

Operational marketing planning is planning undertaken by management at the individual unit or individual property level. The unit management must formulate a market plan to serve as a guide for the marketing activities for a period normally not to exceed one year. This plan will direct the efforts at the unit or property level, but must also be consistent with the corporate-level planning. Plans prepared at the unit level might focus on some of the following issues and questions:

- ☐ What is our market share? Is it increasing or decreasing?

- ☐ What are the strengths and weaknesses of our unit?

- ☐ How has our mix of guests changed in the last year?

- ☐ What advertising and promotions were the most and least successful during the last year?

- ☐ What types of promotions and sales efforts should be undertaken to build business during our slow periods?

- ☐ What types of advertising media schedules should be planned?

- ☐ What in-house promotions should we schedule?

Within small chains and independent operations, the unit management is often granted great autonomy. Within larger chain organizations, most aspects of the marketing function are tightly controlled, and the management of an individual unit assumes the role of implementor rather than planner. This is done to assure coordination of marketing efforts and consistency throughout the chain. Marketing managers representing the corporate office will normally work with the management at the unit level to help them formulate and implement plans that will allow the unit to be successful, while at the same time supporting the overall corporate marketing efforts.

Strategic marketing planning is undertaken by multiunit organizations or chains. Within organizations of this type, all aspects of the marketing function are the responsibility of the corporate vice-president of marketing. This individual, working in conjunction with other staff members, is responsible for planning and implementing the marketing program for several units. In addition, the unit management must be supplied with input for planning the local marketing program. Inherent in the responsibilities at the corporate level is the coordination of marketing activities within the entire organization. Larger corporations have the advantage of economies of scale, particularly in the area of advertising.

Definition of Planning Terms

It is useful at the outset of the chapter to set the record straight by defining several planning words and phrases.

Mission.   A corporation's mission statement is the guiding framework within which all decisions should be made. Typically, mission statements are brief, usually less than two paragraphs, and define the scope of business for the corporation. A corporate mission statement should answer the question "what business are we in?" For example, if a corporation defined its mission as providing hospitality services in the budget-priced segment of the market, this would be the primary focus for the corporation. It would not fit with the broadly defined mission for this corporation to seek business in nonbudget segments.

Strategy.   A strategy is the manner by which an organization attempts to link with, respond to, integrate with, and exploit its environment. Strategy is a pattern or plan that integrates an organization's major goals, policies, and action plans. Strategies that are well formulated will help the organization maximize its resources and will guide it to a unique and viable position within its competitive environment. Strategy gives an organization its identity, based on its pattern of making decisions.

Goals.   Goals are broad statements of what the corporation seeks to accomplish. For example, a corporation may develop a goal which states, "we are seeking to achieve the number one market share in the mid-Atlantic region." The goal does not tell how the results are to be achieved; rather it states in broad terms the desired end result.

Objectives. An objective is a refinement of the broad goal statement. Following the goal, an objective or series of objectives will further refine the goal statement, by stating (1) what will be accomplished in measurable terms, (2) within what specific time frame it will be accomplished, (3) which individual or group will be responsible for achieving the objective, and (4) how the results will be evaluated.

Policies. Policies are the formal rules and guidelines that direct all of the actions an organization takes. The relative structure of different organizations will determine the extent to which a formal policy structure exists. Some organizations are established with a minimum of formal policy structure and managers are relatively free to make decisions, while others are highly structured and the corporate policies dictate the framework within which decisions can be made.

Action Plans and Marketing Programs. Action plans and marketing programs describe in detail the specific steps that are necessary to achieve the stated goals and objectives, within the limits set by the corporate policies. Action plans should also assure that adequate resources are committed to achieve the goals, and that a specific individual is held accountable for attaining the stated goal or objective.

Strategic marketing planning involves establishing of goals and objectives and a long-range marketing plan. The top management of the organization, working in conjunction with the owners or board of directors, must establish broad goals and specific objectives. Questions concerning the strategic future of the organization must be addressed. These might include the following: To what new target market(s) should we appeal? At what rate should we develop new units? By what methods should we strive to raise the volume of sales within our existing units?

The plans formulated by this group should serve as the basis for all other marketing decisions, as well as management decisions made within the operating departments. The strategic options from which the organization may choose are shown in Figure 4.1 The four options are the following:

1. Market penetration, in which the existing product-service mix is sold within existing market segments

2. Product-service mix development, in which new or modified product and services are offered for sale within existing market segments

3. Market development, in which the existing products and services are sold in new or revised market segments

4. Diversification in which new or modified products and services are offered for sale in new or revised market segments

A market penetration strategy is selected when the existing product-service mix is sold to the existing market segments. In an effort to increase sales, management attempts to increase the rate of repeat patronage, building on a solid base of clientele. Another part of this strategy is to increase initial patronage among those members of existing markets who have not previously patronized the hospitality operation. This is done by drawing patrons away from competing operations, thereby increasing the market share. The overall goal is twofold: to increase sales, and to increase market share. This strategy is commonly used during periods of economic uncertainty, such as rapid inflation. As it becomes more expensive to borrow capital for physical expansion, one of the best ways to grow is to increase sales within existing units. In this manner, a larger percentage of the increased sales will eventually become profits.

Product-service mix development involves using marketing information concerning the unmet needs and wants of existing market segments. New products and services are introduced in an attempt to increase sales. No hospitality operation can remain unchanged for too long and expect to continue to prosper. Markets change, consumer needs and wants change, and so too must the product-service mix of any hospitality organization. Consider, for example, the product-service mix development of any of the fast-food chains. New menu items have been added continually over the years to increase unit sales and expand the total market. Meal period or day parts such as breakfast, were successfully introduced, adding significantly to total sales of the individual units and the total corporation. In some cases, the addition of breakfast increased total unit sales volume by more than 25 percent. The addition of drive-through service also increased total sales significantly. Product-service mix development should be an ongoing aspect of any marketing program.

Market development as a strategy has proven to be very successful

	Existing Product-Service Mix	New or Modified Product-Service Mix
Existing Market Segments	Market penetration	Product-service mix development
New and Revised Market Segments	Market development	Diversification

FIGURE 4.1
Marketing Strategy Options

during the last thirty years. It involves expansion into new market segments using the existing product-service mix. As hotel and restaurant concepts are developed successfully, management usually begins to look for new markets. New units are constructed, and soon a regional and, perhaps eventually, a national chain has emerged. The undisputed leader in this area is, of course, McDonald's, with well over 8500 units worldwide.

Finally, a diversification strategy can be employed, but normally only by the largest of hospitality organizations. Diversification occurs when the organization purchases or takes control of other firms. These firms may or may not be in the hospitality industry. The most common form of diversification within the hospitality industry occurs when a hospitality firm seeks to control its suppliers and distributors. In this manner, the firm can lower its operating costs and increase profits. If a hospitality firm is sufficiently large and financially stable, this can be a very successful strategy.

Many hospitality organizations, particularly small organizations, often do not devote the human and monetary resources necessary to develop adequate strategic marketing plans. Without such plans, the marketing strategy can easily become reactionary; the organization merely reacts to each new competitive force and lacks an overall sense of direction and purpose. Conversely, an organization that develops well-defined strategic marketing plans has laid the groundwork necessary for a proactive marketing effort, one that sets the pace rather than merely react to what competitors do.

Advantages to Planning

Formulating an organized and well-conceived marketing plan can have a tremendously positive impact on a hospitality organization. First, it helps the organization cope with change more effectively. If the competitive environment changes rapidly, an organization that has developed strategic plans with several contingency options is in a better position to effectively deal with the change.

Second, planning related to the marketing function helps assure that the objectives the organization establishes are either achieved or modified. The plans formulated serve as guides used to achieve the objectives. If, in some unforeseen circumstances, the objectives cannot be achieved, revised objectives and plans can be formulated. This is done after a very careful analysis of the situation investigating why the original objectives could not be achieved.

Third, establishing a marketing plan aids management in decision making. The established plans can easily serve as a point of reference for management to consult when confronted with a difficult decision. Given the alternative choices, managers can ask which one will contribute the most to the achievement of their objectives.

Fourth, planning can serve to lessen misunderstanding and can provide a vehicle for clear and organized thought. By providing an opportunity for managers to present ideas, the development of a strategic plan can be a very positive force.

Fifth, the development of both short- and long-range marketing plans aids management in the eventual evaluation of the marketing efforts. Results of marketing efforts can be compared with projected results, thereby giving management a control process for the marketing function. Just as management is concerned with the financial progress of an organization and compares the actual performance with what was budgeted, so too management assesses the degree to which the marketing objectives have been achieved.

Disadvantages to Planning

Establishing a marketing plan is not without its drawbacks. First, establishing objectives and formulating a marketing plan is very time-consuming. The time that management invests in planning can be expensive, and the results of planning must be cost-effective. The overall benefits of these efforts, however, normally far exceed the cost to the organization.

Second, if planning is to be successful and have the desired impact on an organization, it must have the support and commitment of the top management. If those involved in the planning process perceive that they are merely "going through the motions" and that their activities will not have any impact, they will view the planning process with disdain.

Third, if plans are poorly conceived or are based on false assumptions, they can be inaccurate or ineffective. For this reason, some managers feel that planning is of little value. Additionally, unplanned scenarios can develop rapidly, rendering marketing plans much less effective.

Fourth, plans often need to be prepared with very short lead time. If this is the case, the resulting plan may not be fully refined. The development of a plan should be viewed as a means to an end, such as increased performance, not as an end unto itself.

A MINI CASE STUDY:

Poor Marketing Planning at XYZ Fast-Food Company

Several years ago, a fast-food company located in the western part of the United States specialized in hamburgers and fried chicken. Business was brisk, and the small company began to expand, first to ten units, then fifteen and eventually thirty-five units. With the opening of each new unit, the owners proudly felt that with the additional profits from each unit, rapid expansion was just around the corner. When there were a total of thirty-five units in the chain, the owners seemed ready to embark on a major expansion program. They had gained recognition in one of the national trade journals as one of the growth chains, and the future looked bright.

Beneath the veneer of rapid expansion, however, lay many problems at the core of the organization. First, the owners of the firm were proud entrepreneurs, individuals who spent most of their time dealing with the operating problems of each of the thirty-five individual units. Little time had been devoted to strategic planning, and as a result, the company lacked a unified, well-defined plan for the future. Second, sites for all the units had been selected without considering future shifts in population. Failure to consider these population trends had resulted in several units' falling well below sales projections. Third, no overall advertising and promotional strategy had been formulated. Instead, each individual unit manager was instructed to "run a few newspaper advertisements featuring coupons when business was slow."

Despite the existing and potential problems, which may appear obvious, the owners did not perceive any major problems. Decreasing sales at one or more units were discounted with such rationales as "the economy is hurting everyone," or "the weather's been bad," although at the same time, other national and regional fast-food chains prospered and were rapidly expanding in the same geographic area. Their target market was not narrowly focused. The owners were attempting to be "all things to all people," offering a very broad menu by fast-food standards.

Unfortunately, a declining spiral had been set in motion, and despite top management's efforts, the organization eventually filed for bankruptcy. With some careful thought and diligent planning, the situation might have been avoided.

Questions for Consideration

1. What marketing errors did management make?
2. What course of action would you have proposed they take?
3. What were the critical decisions that they should have made? How should each of these decisions have been approached?
4. What type of planning efforts should have been undertaken? How might these have been done?

A SYSTEMS MODEL FOR DEVELOPING A MARKETING PLAN

Establishing and implementing a marketing plan is not a difficult task. It is, however, time-consuming and requires a considerable amount of in-depth thought if it is to be of any significant value.

One of the major problems for many hospitality managers is that an overall comprehensive marketing plan is never fully developed and implemented. To accomplish this task, managers must draw information from several sources and combine it into a unified and logical plan. Many hospitality managers are unable to do this, and therefore the marketing efforts of the organization never fully realize their potential.

For this reason, this chapter approaches the task of developing a marketing plan from a systems perspective. Using a systems approach provides both a visual and a descriptive step-by-step planning and implementation process that a manager can use to a develop a marketing plan for an organization. This planning system moves the initial planning through final evaluation of the results. The systems model is illustrated in Figure 4.2.

Two major aspects must be considered when formulating strategic marketing plans: (1) the current situation in which the organization finds itself, and (2) the organization's desired market position. An analysis of the

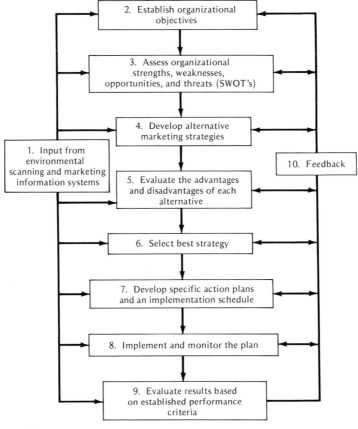

FIGURE 4.2
A Strategic Marketing Planning Model

current situation involves careful consideration of several questions, including the following: Where are we now? Where will we be if we continue on our present course and our environment either remains unchanged or changes in the manner we predict? What are the most significant activities of our competitors? Considering the second aspect requires asking where the firm desires to be two, five, or even ten years from now. This look into the future must expand beyond one year and should yield long-term plans. Those companies that do not look carefully into the future are often those that become overly involved in the day-to-day operational concerns and the activities of the current marketing program.

Examining the current situation and the desired future marketing position should reveal a gap between the two. This gap is called the *strategic gap*. The goal of strategic planning is to conceive and implement a plan that will allow the organization to reduce or eliminate the strategic gap by moving from the current position toward the desired market position.

The Strategic Marketing Planning Model

The strategic marketing planning model consists of ten steps that are discussed in the following paragraphs. Several of these steps will be discussed in greater depth in the next chapter. The development of a marketing plan specifically for hotel marketing departments will be discussed in Chapter 12.

1. *Input from environmental scanning and marketing information systems.* Figure 4.2 shows that input from environmental scanning and a marketing information system influence each step of the model. Managers who formulate marketing plans for the future do not plan in a vacuum. All hospitality operations—large or small, publicly or privately owned, gourmet or fast-food, nonprofit or for profit—are subject to influences from the environment. Failure to account for these influences can be disastrous. Determining the impact that these environmental factors will have on the strategic plans of a hospitality organization is indeed difficult and will require considerable time and study. The term *environmental scanning* is used to describe the process whereby the environment is examined and the most significant events are noted. The environmental variables are categorized as economic, social, political, and technological components of the system.

First, management must take into account the relative state of the economy within the geographic area in which the organization operates. What are the trends for future business growth, consumer spending, population changes, and other economic indicators? On a broader scale, what are the national economic indicators projecting? What effect will changes in these indicators have on the hospitality organization? Trade journals and other business and economic publications can serve as invaluable resources for hospitality managers to review.

Second, management must consider the effects of the social environment on the marketing plan. The rate of social change continues to increase.
Two major social changes that have occurred in the last ten years are
important for hospitality, yet many hospitality managers have failed to adapt.
The first social change is the tremendous growth in the number of individuals
in the United States over the age of 55; this is a growing market that many
hospitality organizations continue to ignore. The second change is in the
traditional role of women; this has changed dramatically, yet many managers
planning their marketing programs are ignoring the large market segment
made up of working women.

The third variable that management must take into account is the
political environment. All levels of government have a tremendous impact on
the operation of every hospitality operation in the country. For example,
changes the federal government makes in the minimum wage laws have an
immediate impact on hospitality operations. Government at the state and
local level controls sales taxes, and additional taxes are often imposed on the
hospitality industry. For example, suppose that the state sales tax is 5 percent
and the local government is considering an additional 4 percent sales tax on
restaurant meals. The result would be a 9 percent sales tax on restaurant
meals. When this additional tax is imposed, what is the likely effect on the
sales volume of an individual foodservice operation? As prices increase
because of the additional sales tax, to what extent will this negatively affect
sales volume? Based on the analysis of the environment, how can
management develop a marketing program to maintain or increase sales
volume in light of the additional 4 percent restaurant meals sales tax?

The fourth area that managers must take into consideration is
technological change. Even though the hospitality industry remains a service-
and people-oriented business, the role of technology continues to grow. The
impact of computer applications has just begun to manifest itself.

Other aspects of environmental scanning and the role that it should play
in the management of a hospitality organization are discussed in greater detail
in Chapter 5.

Input must also be generated from a marketing information system.
Marketing information systems will be discussed in Chapter 5. In general, a
marketing information system should generate information concerning
consumer behavior patterns, demographic patterns of consumers, sales
trends, and activities of major competitors. It is important, when developing a
marketing plan, to have available current information that can serve as the
basis for sound marketing plans.

2. *Establish organizational objectives.* Based on the environmental
scanning and the marketing information system, management is now ready
to take the next step—establishing marketing objectives. These objectives
should be based on the organization's overall mission, and the mission should

reflect the nature of the business and describe what it is all about. It is the mission that should guide future decisions. It should also define the fundamental and unique purpose that differentiates the corporation from others, and should identify the scope of the corporation's activities.

Based on the corporation's foundation—the mission—the organization's objectives are then developed. The objectives serve several functions. First, they enable management to come to some consensus concerning the goals of the organization. Second, responsibility for specific objectives can be assigned to various managers, thereby establishing accountability. If a specific manager is assigned the responsibility for following through and seeing that an objective is completed, the results are likely to be more positive than if no one individual is assigned responsibility. Third, establishing objectives with the input of all management personnel serves as a brainstorming and motivational device. When each individual has input into formulating the organizational marketing objectives, individuals develop both a sense of ownership and allegiance for the objectives, because they have played important roles in establishing them. As a result, managers are likely to work more diligently in attempting to achieve stated objectives.

The formulation of well-written and measurable objectives will take time, and care should be taken to assure that the objectives are feasible. Several characteristics of good objectives follow:

- [ ] Operational objectives should be specific and well understood. They should not be broad and difficult to define. Everyone involved in formulating the objectives should clearly understand the precise objectives toward which the organization seeks to move. For example, the objective "to increase sales within the next six months" is so unspecific as to be meaningless.

- [ ] Objectives should identify expected results. If at all possible, they should be quantitative so that no "gray" area will exist for purposes of evaluation. When the objective is stated in quantitative terms, the expected results are more readily understood. For example, the objective "to increase the number of dinner patrons by 15 percent on Monday, Tuesday, and Wednesday evenings" is a well-stated quantitative objective.

- [ ] Objectives must be within the power of the organization to achieve. When establishing objectives, management must keep in mind the relative abilities of the organization. For example, the objective "to successfully open ten new units within the next eighteen months" will make little sense if the organization currently has only six units and lacks the necessary capital to undertake such a large expansion program.

- [ ] Objectives must be acceptable to the individuals within the organization. The management must come to a consensus concerning the objectives. It is extremely difficult for an organization successfully to achieve the stated objectives if the managers with input into the formation of the objectives do not agree. The extra time spent at this stage in achieving a consensus will make the remaining planning and implementation steps proceed more smoothly.

3. *Assess the organization's strengths, weaknesses, opportunities and threats (SWOT's).* Once the organizational objectives are formulated, management should critically assess the organization's strengths, weaknesses, opportunities, and threats. The assessment of the strengths and weaknesses focuses on the internal operation of the business, while the assessment of the opportunities and threats are externally focused. The internal strengths and weaknesses should focus on those internal aspects of the operation over which management has control. The opportunities and threats are external to the operation. Opportunities are areas that could be exploited. For example, if a foodservice operation found that there would be minimal competition for an off-premise catering business in addition to their existing restaurant operation, this would represent an opportunity or an area for potential growth. Using the same example, if they decided to enter the off-premise catering business, then competition might follow. This potential action by the competition represents an external threat.

Inherent in this analysis is the need to examine very critically what the business does well and what it could improve on. At the same time, a very critical assessment of the market is needed to determine as specifically as possible the threats and potential opportunities that exist external to the business.

Management must critically ask, "What do we have or offer that is different, unique, or excellent in comparison with the competition?" Management must also examine the organization's shortcomings by asking, "What do we have or offer or do that is below average?"

The process of identifying the internal strengths and weaknesses, or the external threats and opportunities is similar to examining a balance sheet with assets and liabilities. The strengths and opportunities should be used to promote the business and to make decisions about new directions that should be taken. At the same time, management must make every effort to correct or neutralize the weaknesses and threats. Many managers find it difficult to identify an organization's weaknesses or threats clearly, tending to overlook or downplay negative factors.

As a minimum, the evaluation of the strengths, weaknesses, opportunities, and threats should consider the following areas:

☐ The product-service mix of your organization and each of the major competitors based on these areas:
  - Quality of the products, guest rooms, food, and beverage
  - Quality of service
  - Location
  - Parking

- Exterior and interior structure and decor
- Meeting facilities
- Price
- Personnel
- Image in the consumer's mind
- The financial status of the organization
- Success of current marketing programs and activities

☐ The market for your property and the competition
- Profile of current guests based on segmentation criteria (to be discussed in depth in Chapter 7)
- Profile of potential guests

☐ The broad environmental trends
- Economic
- Political
- Social
- Technological

4. *Develop alternative marketing strategies.*   Based on the assessment of the environment, the competitive situation, and the strategic gap, the next step is to develop alternative marketing strategies. This involves discussions of "what if" situations. For example, what if the major competitor launches an advertising blitz that reduces sales volume by 15 percent? What if the inflation rate doubles in the next three years? What if the tax code further reduces business deductions for travel and entertainment? What if unemployment in the area increases by 2 percent during the next six months because a major manufacturing plant is closed?

All management personnel with marketing responsibilities should be involved in a series of brainstorming sessions designed to get as many alternatives strategies recorded as possible, for only when all potential ideas are explored will the very best strategy or strategies emerge.

A common method of contingency planning involves the use of sales forecasts. In order to develop an effective marketing plan, an accurate projection of sales is necessary. Data supplied by a marketing information system are used to project revenue and expenses for each revenue center. These projections are usually based upon historical sales data. The use of a computer in simulating sales projections is of tremendous potential value.

Tables 4.1 and 4.2 illustrate sales projections for a restaurant operation. This operation is open from 11:30 AM until 10:00 PM and uses the menu during the entire time. In Table 4.1 the expected number of covers served has been projected for optimistic, moderate, and pessimistic levels of sales. The expected number of covers served is determined using the sales histories supplied by a well-organized marketing information system and the input from environmental factors.

The expected number of covers served is then multiplied by the expected check average. The check average figure is based on historical data and the

TABLE 4.1
Sales Projections for a Restaurant

	Expected Number of Covers Served		Expected Average Check		Weeks Open per Year		Projected Total Revenue
Optimistic Projection							
Sunday	400	×	$14.95	×	52	=	$310,900
Monday	245	×	12.85	×	52	=	163,709
Tuesday	245	×	12.85	×	52	=	163,709
Wednesday	250	×	12.85	×	52	=	167,050
Thursday	290	×	12.85	×	52	=	193,778
Friday	440	×	12.85	×	52	=	294,008
Saturday	475	×	12.85	×	52	=	317,395
Total	2175			Projected annual revenue			$1,610,609
Moderate Projection							
Sunday	350	×	$13.45	×	52	=	$244,790
Monday	210	×	11.45	×	52	=	125,034
Tuesday	210	×	11.45	×	52	=	125,034
Wednesday	215	×	11.45	×	52	=	128,011
Thursday	250	×	11.45	×	52	=	148,850
Friday	395	×	11.45	×	52	=	235,183
Saturday	400	×	11.45	×	52	=	238,160
Total	1825			Projected annual revenue			$1,245,062
Pessimistic Projection							
Sunday	300	×	$13.45	×	52	=	$209,820
Monday	175	×	10.95	×	52	=	99,645
Tuesday	175	×	10.95	×	52	=	99,645
Wednesday	180	×	10.95	×	52	=	102,492
Thursday	210	×	10.95	×	52	=	119,574
Friday	350	×	10.95	×	52	=	199,290
Saturday	360	×	10.95	×	52	=	238,160
Total	1565			Projected annual revenue			$1,035,450

expected menu price increase for the coming period (in this case, one year). These figures are then multiplied by the number of days that the operation is open per year, and the result is the projected total revenue figure. By projecting sales revenue for three separate volumes, management is able easily to determine a projected range of sales. In Table 4.1, the projections of annual revenue range from a low of $1,035,450 to a high of $1,610,609.

Table 4.2 illustrates how management can carry these projections one step further in more finely tuning the operation. Each projected annual

TABLE 4.2
Projected Annual Revenue with Assigned Probabilities

	Projected Annual Revenue		Probability Assigned		Weighted Projected Annual Revenue
Optimistic Projection	$1,610,609	×	0.30	=	$ 483,182.70
Moderate Projection	1,245,062	×	0.60	=	747,037.20
Pessimistic Projection	1,035,450	×	0.10	=	103,545,00
			1.00		$1,333,764.90

revenue figure is assigned a probability that indicates the relative likelihood of the pessimistic, moderate, and optimistic projections. In the example, the pessimistic figure is assigned a probability of 0.10, or 10 percent; the moderate figure is assigned a probability of 0.60 or 60 percent; the optimistic figure is given 0.30, or 30 percent. These assigned probabilities must add up to 1.00, or 100 percent. How are these probabilities assigned? Each represents management's best estimate of the likelihood of a given sales projection being correct. The probabilities are assigned based on historical data, marketing research, and judgment.

The projected revenues are then multiplied by the assigned probabilities, and these answers are added together to provide a weighted annual revenue figure. This figure ($1,333,764.90 in the example) represents management's best projection of revenue for the period. The projected annual revenue range ($1,035,450–1,610,609) and weighted projected annual revenue figure ($1,333,764.90) can then be used to prepare budgets and other financial forecasts.

5. *Evaluate the advantages and disadvantages of each alternative.* It is important, however, that suggested strategies be evaluated for the contribution they will make to the achievement of the organization's mission, as well as the objectives. Any strategy that is selected will potentially affect the organization's objectives, and only those strategies that contribute positively to these objectives should be considered.

A useful way to evaluate the alternatives is to examine the advantages and disadvantages of each one. In this way, management can more clearly see both sides of each alternative, as well as assess the risks associated with each one.

6. *Select the best alternative strategy.* Based on the brainstorming sessions and discussions to date, the management group should work toward a consensus regarding the most desirable strategy or combination of strategies. Some give-and-take among individuals is desirable, as the goal of this discussion is group consensus. The group consensus process of evaluating the alternative strategies to produce the most viable strategy is more desirable than having one individual make all the marketing decisions. The process allows the thoughts and opinions of many individuals to be incorporated into the final decision.

It is also a sound management practice to involve managers from the operational departments, those outside the marketing function, because their input can prove to be invaluable. For example, if a change in menu content is deemed desirable from a marketing point of view, what effect will this have on the operational aspects of the organization? Operations managers would be able to discuss the implications of such a change.

7. *Develop specific action plans and an implementation schedule.* Unless the marketing strategies are refined into action plans that are then properly implemented, the results are often less than fully successful. Once the best strategic alternative is selected, management must develop specific action plans and a timetable for implementation. The action plan should focus on the following:

☐ Who will assume primary responsibility for each part of the action plan
☐ How they will proceed to implement the action plan
☐ When they are to have it completed by
☐ Where they will need to go to implement the action plans
☐ What resources will be needed to fully implement the action plan
☐ What method or measures will be used to evaluate implementation of the action plan

Following the development of the action plans and before implementing the plans, two activities should be completed. First, an implementation schedule should be developed. Not all the action plans can be implemented at the same moment. Instead, an orderly timetable or schedule should be established to show, in detail, when the specific parts of the action plans will be implemented. Second, a series of performance criteria for evaluating the relative success of the action plans should be established. Performance criteria should be precise, so that the marketing plan can be carefully evaluated. For example, performance criteria should be established for degree of consumer satisfaction, market share, product-service mix, quality assurance, sales volumes, and advertising effectiveness. Specific sales objectives should be established based on breakeven analysis and other measures of financial performance. The performance criteria should be established in relation to current and future environmental trends. Will the desired performance criteria be satisfactory in times of economic instability, inflation, recession, or growth? It is extremely important that the performance criteria be clearly defined prior to implementation of the plan, for without clearly defined criteria, evaluation becomes subjective and not nearly as meaningful as it should be.

8. *Implement and monitor the plan.*   This step is the moment of truth. The old phrase "plan the work and work the plan" could not be more appropriate. The preceding steps have carefully spelled out the goals, objectives, SWOT's, marketing strategies, and specific action plans. Now it is time to see if the plans will work in the way that management thought would lead to success. After all, the plan was undertaken in order to be implemented. Planning is done to increase the probability of success. Once the plan is implemented, it is important for management to monitor the results. Any variance from the predicted results should be noted and evaluated.

9. *Evaluate results based on established performance criteria.*   After the plan has been implemented and has been in place for a significant period of time, an evaluation should be conducted. The results of the plan should be evaluated in light of the established performance criteria. These results should also be evaluated for the degree to which they contribute to the achievement of the organizational objectives.

10. *Feedback.*   It is important that this model not be viewed as a purely linear process. It is possible, and in many cases desirable, to recycle through various steps of the process. As the environment changes or the results vary, management should return to the appropriate step to reformulate marketing strategy. This strategic marketing model is best viewed as a dynamic model, with sufficient flexibility to allow for changes in strategies or implementation schedules due to ever-changing environmental and competitive conditions.

Why Some Plans Fail

Despite the best efforts of management planners and all those involved in the planning process, some plans fail to fully achieve the desired results. Why do some plans fall short of the desired objectives? The following are the most common reasons that some plans fail, based on the findings of several research studies:

☐ *Strategic planning is not integrated into the day-to-day activities of the marketing function.* In these cases, the plan is seen as an end in itself, and is not made operational. Plans that are carefully developed but sit on a shelf and are not used are almost worse than no plans at all. The planning process is a dynamic, ongoing process, as Figure 4.2 illustrates. Plans should be implemented, evaluated, revised, and implemented again. Only when this cycle is continual can planning truly succeed.

☐ *The planning process is not understood by the planners.* It is important that the planning group carefully work through all of the steps of the entire model. Sometimes, managers want to jump ahead and draw conclusions before all environmental variables are considered and before a clear consensus has been formed. This tendency should be avoided at all costs, for the results are usually less than desirable. Every member of the planning team must fully understand the steps involved in the planning process and should actively contribute during each step.

☐ *There is a lack of input from nonmarketing managers.* For a marketing plan to succeed, it must be implemented in part by managers who have major responsibilities in areas removed from the marketing function. The plan's failure is more likely without the input of these managers, who will in part implement it.

☐ *Financial projections are not plans.* Some hospitality organizations make projections or forecasts for sales and label this activity planning. Projections by themselves should not be equated with plans. Only when clearly defined strategies are identified for achieving the desired sales projections does planning take place.

☐ *There is inadequate input and insufficient consideration of all environmental variables.* Although it is impossible to consider all the variables, the real danger is not too much information, but too little. Managers often want to rush to a conclusion rather than consider information that is readily available. Again, this information comes from environmental scanning and marketing information systems.

☐ *Planning focus is placed too heavily on short-term results.* The emphasis should be placed in formulating plans that will allow the organization to move toward the successful achievement of long-term objectives. Too frequently, the emphasis is placed on short-term profits at the expense of long-term objectives and profits.

Of course, hundreds of other reasons might also explain why plans sometimes fail to achieve the desired results. If, however, the members of the planning group focus their attention clearly on the initial stages of the planning model, the later stages will become much easier to complete, and the chances for success will also increase. It is important to avoid the tendency to rush through the initial steps in order to produce results.

SUMMARY

This chapter focused on the necessary steps for formulating a strategic marketing plan. An example of a fast-food chain illustrated the disastrous financial results that can occur when an organization does not engage in strategic marketing planning. Planning for effective marketing includes operational and corporate levels of marketing planning. Although there are several advantages and disadvantages to planning, several research studies have clearly demonstrated that those organizations engaging in marketing planning hold a decisive advantage over the competition and exhibit improved financial performance.

The last section of the chapter introduced the concept of strategic planning. Strategic planning includes three important concepts: (1) analysis of the current situation, (2) the desired market position, and (3) the strategic gap. A 10-step strategic marketing model provides managers with a procedure to follow in formulating marketing plans. Common reasons for the failure of marketing plans can be identified, but by referring to the model outlined here, managers can avoid common mistakes.

KEY WORDS AND CONCEPTS

- ☐ Contingency planning
- ☐ Operational marketing planning
- ☐ Strategic marketing planning
- ☐ Mission
- ☐ Strategy
- ☐ Goals
- ☐ Objectives
- ☐ Policies
- ☐ Action plans and marketing programs
- ☐ Market penetration
- ☐ Product-service mix development
- ☐ Market development
- ☐ Diversification
- ☐ Environmental scanning and marketing information systems
- ☐ Strengths, weaknesses, opportunities, and threats (SWOT's)

Questions for Review and Discussion

1. What types of planning are done within hospitality firms?
2. What are the common advantages and disadvantages associated with planning? What others would you add to the list in the chapter? Do you agree or disagree with those in the chapter?
3. Illustrate and discuss the steps in the strategic planning model. Which steps do you feel are the most critical? Why?
4. If you were involved in developing a strategic marketing plan, how would you seek input from operational managers?
5. Why do some plans fail? How can the probability of success be increased?

CHAPTER 5

Marketing Information Systems

This chapter focuses on the marketing informational needs of hospitality managers. It introduces the concepts and principles pertaining to the design and management of a marketing information system. It highlights the areas of use for marketing information, as well as the sources of both internally and externally generated marketing information.

INTRODUCTION
☐ The Critical Need for Information
☐ Definition of a Marketing Information System
☐ The Components of a Marketing Information System

USE OF A MARKETING INFORMATION SYSTEM
☐ Timely Uses for a Marketing Information System
☐ Requirements for a Successful Marketing Information System

INTERNALLY GENERATED MARKETING INFORMATION
☐ Sources of Information

EXTERNALLY GENERATED MARKETING INFORMATION
☐ Sources of Information
☐ Primary Data
☐ Secondary Data

SUMMARY

KEY WORDS AND CONCEPTS

QUESTIONS FOR REVIEW AND DISCUSSION

INTRODUCTION

The Critical Need for Information

Since the advent of personal computers, the United States has experienced an information explosion, and all industries have made substantial advances in information collection, analysis, storage, and retrieval. The hospitality industry was very much a part of this trend. As the environment in which organizations operate becomes more complex and more competitive, the informational needs become more complex. Those organizations that are able to collect, analyze, store, retrieve, and utilize information most effectively and efficiently are likely to be the most successful organizations in the future.

In making effective marketing decisions, management needs information about the marketing environment in which the organization functions. Without the proper types of information available on a timely basis, management is more likely to make decisions that will adversely affect the performance of the organization.

A simple example will illustrate this point. Suppose that the management of a small restaurant chain must make a decision concerning the allocation of the advertising budget among the available media for the upcoming quarter. Two of the advertising objectives of this restaurant are (1) to reinforce the chain's high level of perceived value among current customers, increasing the rate of repeat patronage by 10 percent; and (2) to increase by 10 percent the number of customers who are patronizing one of the chain's restaurants for the first time. To make an effective decision about media allocation, the management of this chain has specific informational needs. Here, management needs access to the following types of information:

(1) characteristics of the current clientele, (2) characteristics of the target market segments most likely to patronize the chain's restaurants for the first time, (3) media habits of both of these groups, and (4) characteristics of the consumers of all available media (e.g., television, radio, print) and the individual media vehicles (for example, individual radio stations).

Without this specific information available on a timely basis, the management of this restaurant chain will be forced to make a less than fully informed decision. The results of a less-informed decision could directly and adversely affect the advertising effectiveness of the organization and directly affect the financial performance of the organization. All too often, management is forced to make critical decisions without the necessary marketing information.

Most managers are not satisfied with the quality and quantity of information available to them. They must frequently work with too much of some types of information and too little of others. What type of information is needed if management is to make informed decisions? A broad overview of the informational needs of management is shown in Table 5.1. This list is by no means all-inclusive, but it is shown here to provide a starting point for the

TABLE 5.1
An Overview of the Informational Needs of Hospitality Managers

Type of Information	Example
Demographic variables	Age, sex, income, occupation
Geographic variables	Location of home or office. Zip code analysis is used by hotels to determine the geographic origin of guests.
Psychographic variables	Indicators of lifestyle and personality, such as the terms *Yuppie* and *Dink* (Dual income, no kids)
Behavioral variables	Travel patterns and dining-out patterns while on business or pleasure. Also includes expenditure patterns and frequency.
Perceptions of quality of the product-service mix	Includes such things as the price-value relationship, assessment of the service, quality of the guest rooms, food and beverage, other services provided.
Competitive situation	Analysis of actions taken by the direct and indirect competitors
Macroenvironment	Scanning of the economic, political, social, and technological environments.
Guest histories	Analysis of trends in business patterns.

development of a list of informational needs specific to an individual hospitality organization. Some types of information may be critical to one organization, yet of little value to another. Each hospitality organization should compile a list of informational needs, and then design and implement a method of collecting this information.

Initially, management needs information that will provide insight into the needs and wants of both current and potential customers. These insights allow management to understand the customer better, and they aid in developing a product-service mix with a higher probability of satisfying the customers. Generally, management focuses on demographic, geographic, psychographic, and behavioral variables, as shown in Table 5.1. Information related to these four variables will allow management to have a sufficient understanding of the target market segments. Other informational concerns include marketing activities of direct and indirect competitors, influences of the product-service mix, macroenvironment, and guest histories and trends for each hospitality facility within the organization.

Definition of a Marketing Information System

A hospitality marketing information system is a structured organization of people and procedures designed to generate a flow of information from inside and outside the organization. These are the data to be used as a basis for marketing decisions. *Marketing information system* is a broader and more encompassing term than *market research*. Marketing research indicates that information is collected for a specific reason or project; the major objective is one-time use. For example, a potential restaurant owner may undertake a feasibility study and use market research to determine whether to build a new restaurant. Such an information-gathering study is designed to answer a very specific question and is not intended to be used for other purposes.

A marketing information system, on the other hand, is an ongoing data-gathering process involving initial data collection as well as routine and systematic data-collection procedures. For example, a manager may choose to collect data by means of a zip code analysis of guest registration information to determine the profile of the guests of a hotel. This systematic and routine information gathering is not intended to address one specific question but is instead part of an overall system designed to monitor the degree of marketing success that the operation is able to achieve.

A well-designed marketing information system satisfies four basic criteria:

1. It must include a structured organization or established system of people and information-gathering procedures.

2. The system should be designed to generate a continuous flow of

information to provide accurate and current marketing information for management.

3. Information should be gathered from inside and outside the organization, involving external information-gathering methods, such as consumer surveys, and internal information-gathering methods, such as employee meetings, guest comment cards, analysis of point of sale and registration information, and in-house guest surveys.

4. Information should be compiled so that management can use it as a basis for marketing decisions.

It would be extremely difficult and quite hazardous for the management of a hospitality organization to make decisions without accurate and up-to-date marketing information. Professional management demands that decisions be based on sound information. Managers who are able to use information as the basis for marketing decisions are likely to make better and more consistent decisions. The Marriott Corporation serves as a good example. For many years, this corporation has relied upon a widely based decision-making process. The resulting decisions have consistently been very good and have thereby allowed Marriott to establish and maintain a leadership position in the hospitality industry. This is not to say that a very good marketing information system alone will allow an organization to achieve financial success, but it will be of tremendous benefit to management.

The Components of a Marketing Information System

If a marketing information system is to be fully effective, information relative to the environment in which the hospitality organization operates must be available on a timely basis. The foundation for this data collection is environmental scanning. *Environmental scanning* is a term used to describe a process whereby variables that could affect a hospitality organization are given a quick evaluation. Based on this initial evaluation, those with the greatest potential impact, either positive or negative, are examined in greater detail. From a theoretical standpoint, if management is to make a rational decision, all information that could affect the hospitality organization should be examined and evaluated. Realistically, however, this is not possible because of the finite limits on the valuable resources of time, money, and personnel. Instead, only those environmental variables that appear to be the most important or most critical are examined in greater detail.

In short, a marketing information system that uses environmental scanning provides an overview of the entire environment as well as further detail concerning those variables within the environment that are most critical to the successful operation of the hospitality organization.

Within the environment in which a hospitality organization functions are three sub-environments. These sub-environments are (1) the macroenvironment, (2) the competitive environment, and (3) the organizational environment. A conceptual model of the components of a marketing information system is shown in Figure 5.1. Data are generated for each of the three sub-environments through an environmental-scanning process. The data are then compiled, summarized, and stored until needed by management. At the appropriate time, management can readily retrieve data summaries, evaluate marketing trends, and formulate marketing plans and strategies. The overriding objectives of a marketing information system are (1) to collect relevant data concerning each of these sub-environments; (2) to compile, summarize, and store the data; and (3) to have data readily available for management on a timely basis.

The macroenvironment concerns the broadest possible effects. Macroenvironmental effects are those that the individual hospitality organization is almost powerless to control, including economic, social, political, and technological aspects of the environment. As conditions change within the macroenvironment, the management of hospitality organizations should collect data concerning these changes. Knowledge of existing conditions will

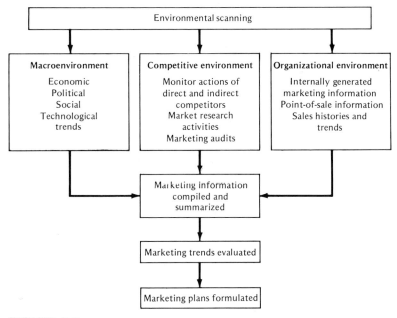

FIGURE 5.1
Components of a Marketing Information System

provide a basis for calculating the impact that these variables will have on the operation of a hospitality organization. For example, if the tax deductibility of business travel and entertainment is further reduced, or if the inflation rate rises to exceed 10 percent annually, what impact is this likely to have on sales volume? Nearly 20 percent of the population moves each year, how will these demographic changes affect a hospitality organization? These are the influences that the management of a hospitality organization is virtually powerless to control. At best, management can monitor the variables of the macroenvironment and can gauge the effects that they might have on business.

The competitive environment immediately surrounds the hospitality organization. The organization exerts some degree of control over this environment but can never control it totally. The major concern for management is to monitor closely the marketing and operational actions taken by direct and indirect competitors. Attention should be focused initially on changes made in the marketing mix, guest profile, room and menu prices, and sales volume as measured in both dollars and in guest counts. Management should also be concerned with the degree of concentration of competition, entries and exits among competitors, and changes in market share among competitors. Exact figures are not likely to be available, but all competitors should be monitored closely so that management can be prepared for changes before or at the time they occur, rather than weeks or months later. By monitoring competition in this way, management can ready an appropriate competitive response, thereby gaining a differential competitive advantage.

The two other aspects of the competitive environment for a marketing information system are market research activities and marketing audits. Market research encompasses a wide range of activities undertaken to generate information about a specifically defined problem. Marketing audits are evaluations of the effectiveness of current marketing practices. Both of these topics will be addressed in greater detail later in this text.

The third sub-environment that is a part of a marketing information system is the organizational environment. Data collection in this sub-environment involves examining all relevant information sources within the hospitality organization. The basis for data collection in this sub-environment is guest histories, although information can be generated from other sources as well. Guest histories are records that a hotel maintains for all types of guests, both individual and groups. In addition, histories should be maintained within all retail outlets, especially food and beverage. Within the food and beverage area, all sales should be recorded, broken down by menu group and menu item. Only when managers have access to records of previous sales are they able to make informed decisions concerning the product-service mix for the organization.

USE OF A MARKETING INFORMATION SYSTEM

Timely Uses for a Marketing Information System

The overall purpose of a marketing information system is to provide accurate and timely information to which management can refer in the decision-making process. This information can be used in many situations, including the following:

- ☐ Decisions concerning market segmentation
- ☐ Decisions involving advertising and promotional efforts
- ☐ Decisions involving capital investment and expansion of existing units or construction of new units
- ☐ Decisions concerning changes in the product-service mix offerings
- ☐ Identifying new or different sales opportunities
- ☐ Decisions concerning hours of operation
- ☐ Decisions involving changes in design, decor, and atmosphere
- ☐ Decisions concerning the market position of an organization

The use of a marketing information system should allow a hospitality manager to speed up the reaction time to changing market conditions, thereby allowing the organization to gain a competitive advantage.

Requirements for a Successful Marketing Information System

To generate data that is useful to hospitality management, it should fulfill three requirements.

1. *It should be objective.*   Management should be able to quantify and analyze the information gathered. Management needs as much purely objective data as possible in order to make sound decisions. For example, which of these two statements seems to provide better information for decision-making purposes?

- ☐ *Statement A:* "As the owner of this restaurant, I think we should modify our menu so that we can appeal to more family business."
- ☐ *Statement B:* "A recent study has indicated a 10 percent increase in the number of families with children under the age of 10 in our area."

Statement B would appear to be more objective and offer quantitative data on which to base a decision. Statement A is, on the other hand, merely an opinion and is not supported by any quantitative data.

Too many hospitality managers rely heavily on subjective opinions for decision-making purposes. As a result, their decisions are often incorrect. Decisions based on purely personal opinion are often less than successful when implemented. Decisions based on a combination of data and managerial thought generally yield higher-quality decisions.

2. *It should be systematic.* The marketing information system is not an on-off process; it is a system that should be designed to provide a continuing information source for management. When information is collected in a systematic and continuous manner, more and better information is available.

3. *It should be useful.* Many studies produce information that is of little value. This is obviously not the purpose of a marketing information system. One rule of thumb to follow is this: Collect, compile, and store information only if it is used actively; do not collect information and then file it away without using it. This is a needless and expensive waste of time and effort, yet many hospitality operators, in attempts to gather any quantitative information, maintain data that are never used and are truly useless. The advent of low cost and increased capacity hard disk storage within personal computers has partially encouraged this storage of little-used data. Hard disks with 40 to 300 megabytes of capacity are common. Every effort should be made to collect and store only information that is useful.

INTERNALLY GENERATED MARKETING INFORMATION

The component of a marketing information system that is the simplest to design and implement is an internal system, or the component designed to collect data from within the organizational environment. When considering the organizational environment, management need only be concerned with information available from within the physical confines of the organization's units, be they hotels or restaurants. This component of a marketing information system requires less time and money than does the competitive environment, or externally generated marketing information. The internal component of a marketing information system is very valuable to management because it provides a wealth of information.

Sources of Information

Management has three main sources of internal marketing information: (1) guest histories and sales data, (2) hourly employees and management staff, and (3) guests who patronize the facility.

1. *Guest histories and sales data.* No rules can tell a manager exactly what records should or should not be maintained. The management of every hospitality organization must make this decision based on individual needs. Within a hotel operation, the minimum records that should be maintained are both individual and group guest histories. These will permit management to have knowledge and monitor changes in: zip code origin of guests, length of stay, guest expenditure per day, and other pertinent data concerning guests. Within a restaurant operation, the records maintained should include customer counts for all meal periods, and sales for each menu item over a specified period of time.

The cost of storing data by computer has been reduced significantly, making this a very feasible alternative for a great many hospitality managers. All larger organizations have a sophisticated management information system in place. However, for the smaller organization, the design of a management information system is much easier than it has been in the past. Many point-of-sale terminals will interface with personal computers, making the transfer of data to "off the shelf" data base management and accounting software relatively easy. By using a personal computer, a manager is better able to manage the data. It is obvious that, with accurate information readily available, a manager is more likely to consult such marketing information prior to making a marketing decision.

2. *Employees and management staff.*   All too often hospitality management ignores the wealth of information that is informally gathered by hourly employees, such as front desk personnel, telephone operators, restaurant service people, hosts, and hostesses. These individuals are in constant contact with guests, yet they are rarely asked to relay customer comments and reactions to operational changes, such as new menu items or guest room decor changes. These employees represent an excellent source of information, although the information they provide may not be totally objective. It is a good idea for management to meet with employees on a regular basis to discuss problems and opportunities. Employees like to feel recognized by their supervisors; this recognition by a superior can be a motivator. All employees need to be exposed to some motivation techniques, although many managers ignore the simple and basic needs of employees as individuals.

The subject of employee meetings is, of course, the responsibility of each individual manager, but the following list of questions provides several possibilities:
- ☐ Who are our present customers? Where do they come from? How have they changed in the last year?
- ☐ Do they come for business or pleasure?
- ☐ Into what age groups do they fall? Has this changed in the last few months?
- ☐ What is their approximate socioeconomic level?
- ☐ Where else do they go to eat and drink? What other hotels do they stay in when they travel?

☐ What new features and changes in our product-service mix would guests prefer?

☐ To what new or different market segments might our hotel or restaurant appeal?

☐ What are the wants and needs of these new segments? How do these needs differ from the needs of our current guests?

☐ Will these new potential market segments mix with our current clientele?

☐ How does our hotel or restaurant compare with others in the area?

☐ What do our competitors offer that we do not and that guests find attractive?

☐ Based on feedback that you hear, how do guests rate our quality of products and services?

☐ Is our service as friendly and prompt as possible?

☐ How do the building appearance and decor compare with those of the competition?

This is just the beginning for a hospitality manager. A creative manager could easily add dozens more questions that might serve as starting points for an informal discussion.

3. *Guests who patronize the facility.*   The focus of the marketing concept is the hospitality operation's clientele. All aspects of the entire operation should be aimed at satisfying these individuals. The purpose of using an internal marketing information system is to solicit opinions and comments from the current clientele. This can be done in a number of ways, such as having the manager talk with a few of the customers or having service personnel check with the customers. One method used frequently is the comment card. These cards are placed in guest rooms, or are provided to the guest upon check-out or when they have finished a meal in a restaurant. The purpose is to solicit their opinions and comments concerning the operation's quality. Figures 5.2, 5.3, and 5.4 (pages 102–107) illustrate the comment cards used by three hospitality chains—Marriott, Embassy Suites, and Stouffers. Each of these comment cards is designed as a folding postage paid mailer and, solicits feedback concerning all aspects of the guest stay, including quality of service, quality of the guest room, and quality of food and beverages received. Similar comment cards are used by companies involved in just the foodservice segment of the industry.

All three internal sources of marketing information are very valuable. Together they can provide a great deal of useful information with which to make decisions. Historically, hospitality managers have failed to use these sources to maximum advantage, but the current competitive situation in the hospitality industry dictates that all sources of information be used to gain a competitive advantage and to earn maximum financial rewards.

EXTERNALLY GENERATED MARKETING INFORMATION

While externally generated marketing information is extremely valuable, it is normally not collected on a daily basis, as is the case with internally generated marketing information. This is due to a much larger investment of time, money, and other scarce resources that externally generated information requires.

Sources of Information

Management should consider using a wide variety of sources of external marketing information. Literally thousands of sources are available, and these sources are limited only by management's own efforts to locate them. The following are a few typical sources of external marketing information:

☐ Trade associations, such as the National Restaurant Association, the American Hotel and Motel Association, or the Hotel Sales and Marketing Association International

☐ City Visitor or Convention Bureau, city Chambers of Commerce, or local planning boards

☐ Trade journals and periodicals, such as *Restaurants & Institutions, Restaurant Hospitality, Nation's Restaurant News, Restaurant Business, Lodging Hospitality, Lodging Magazine,* and *Hotel and Motel Management*

☐ Broader-based business periodicals such as *Business Week, The Wall Street Journal, Fortune, Barron's,* and *Forbes*

☐ University bureaus, foundations, and the Cooperative Extension Service

☐ Government publications concerning population and retail business census data

☐ Syndicated services, such as Harris or Gallup Polls, Target Group Index, or W. R. Simmons

☐ Public or university libraries

A number of guidelines should be followed when collecting external information. If they are not followed, much time, effort, and money are likely to be wasted. They are outlined below.

1. *State known facts.*   Before undertaking an external study, make an accounting of all data currently available. It makes little sense to conduct an

"Will you let me know?"

Welcome to our hotel. We are pleased to have you stay with us.

It's very important to us that we do things right for you. That means . . .

- Reservations should be easy to make
- Quick, hassle-free check-ins
- Rooms that are pleasant, immaculate
- Restaurants so good that many times they're local favorites
- A staff brimming with vitality—and smiles
- Expertise in handling meetings
- Fast, painless check-outs

You're the one who can tell us whether we have been successful or not. We value your comments and want to hear about the things we do right and the things we need to improve.

Will you let me know?

I have to make sure we do things right. After all, it's my name over the door.

Bill Marriott

President, Marriott Corp.

We need your assistance to help us provide the service you expect.

Will You Let Me Know?

Berkeley Marina Marriott

Berkeley Marina Marriott
OCA 237

1. How would you rate our hotel on an overall basis?
   ☐ Excellent ☐ Good ☐ Average ☐ Fair ☐ Poor

2. Was your room reservation in order at check in?
   ☐ Yes ☐ No

3. How would you rate the following?

	Excellent	Good	Average	Fair	Poor
Check in, speed/efficiency	☐	☐	☐	☐	☐
Cleanliness of room on first entering	☐	☐	☐	☐	☐
Cleanliness and servicing of your room during stay	☐	☐	☐	☐	☐
Decor of your room	☐	☐	☐	☐	☐
Check out: speed/efficiency	☐	☐	☐	☐	☐
Value of room for price paid	☐	☐	☐	☐	☐

4. Was everything in working order in your room?
   ☐ Yes ☐ No
   If you checked NO, would you please tell us what was not in working order?
   ☐ Room air conditioning
   ☐ Room heating
   ☐ Bathroom plumbing
   ☐ Television
   ☐ Light bulbs
   ☐ Other _____

5. How would you rate the following in terms of their friendly and efficient services?

	Excellent	Good	Average	Fair	Poor
Reservation staff	☐	☐	☐	☐	☐
Front desk clerk	☐	☐	☐	☐	☐
Bellstaff	☐	☐	☐	☐	☐
Housekeeping staff	☐	☐	☐	☐	☐
Telephone operators	☐	☐	☐	☐	☐
Gift shop staff	☐	☐	☐	☐	☐
Engineering staff	☐	☐	☐	☐	☐
Front desk cashier	☐	☐	☐	☐	☐

If any members of our staff were especially helpful, please let us know who they are and how they were helpful so that we can show them our appreciation.
Name _____
Position/Comments _____

6. Please rate the following which you have used on this visit:

A. Restaurant
Please indicate name of restaurant. _____
☐ Breakfast ☐ Lunch ☐ Dinner

	Yes	No
Were you seated promptly?	☐	☐
Was your order taken promptly?	☐	☐
Was your food served promptly?	☐	☐

	Excellent	Good	Average	Fair	Poor
Friendly service	☐	☐	☐	☐	☐
Quality of food	☐	☐	☐	☐	☐
Menu variety	☐	☐	☐	☐	☐
Value for price paid	☐	☐	☐	☐	☐

B. Room Service

	Excellent	Good	Average	Fair	Poor
Prompt service	☐	☐	☐	☐	☐
Friendly service	☐	☐	☐	☐	☐
Quality of food	☐	☐	☐	☐	☐
Menu variety	☐	☐	☐	☐	☐
Value for price paid	☐	☐	☐	☐	☐

C. Cocktail Lounge

	Excellent	Good	Average	Fair	Poor
Prompt service	☐	☐	☐	☐	☐
Friendly service	☐	☐	☐	☐	☐
Quality of drinks	☐	☐	☐	☐	☐
Value for price paid	☐	☐	☐	☐	☐

D. Banquet/Convention Event

	Excellent	Good	Average	Fair	Poor
Prompt service	☐	☐	☐	☐	☐
Friendly service	☐	☐	☐	☐	☐
Quality of food	☐	☐	☐	☐	☐

7. Did you use "The Marriott Hot Line" to register any dissatisfaction with our hotel?
   ☐ No
   ☐ Yes .... problem was resolved.
   ☐ Yes .... but problem was not resolved.

Please explain any problem which remains unresolved.
_____
_____
_____

8. What was the primary purpose of your visit?
   ☐ Pleasure
   ☐ Convention/group meeting/banquet
   ☐ Business (other than above)

9. Have you stayed at this hotel previously?
   ☐ Yes ☐ No

10. If in the area again, would you return to this Marriott?
    ☐ Yes ☐ No

PLEASE PRINT THE FOLLOWING INFORMATION
Departure date: _____
Length of stay: _____ days. Room number _____
☐ Mr. ☐ Mrs. ☐ Miss ☐ Ms.
Name _____
Home address _____
_____ Zip _____
Company or organization _____
Business address _____
_____ Zip _____

THANK YOU VERY MUCH FOR YOUR RESPONSE.
YOUR EVALUATION WILL MAKE A DIFFERENCE.

FIGURE 5.2
Marriott Hotels Guest Comment Card
Courtesy: Marriott Corporation, Washington, DC

103

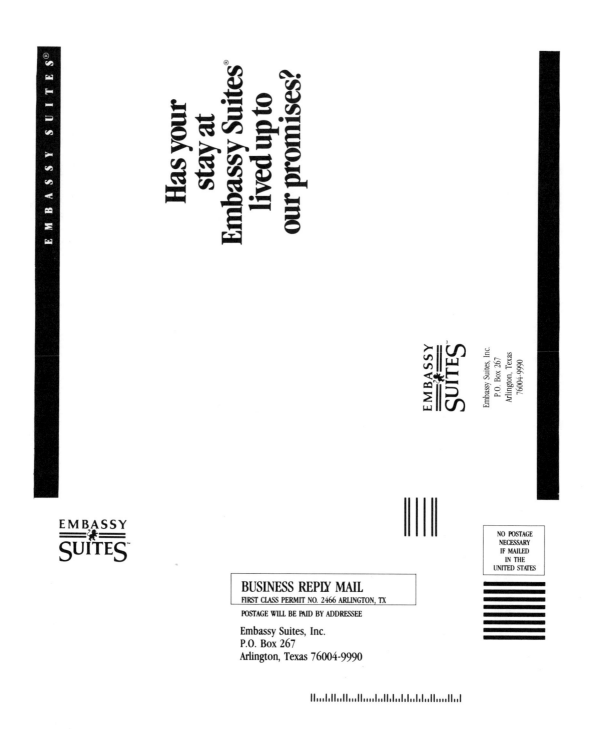

EMBASSY SUITES®

Has your stay at Embassy Suites® lived up to our promises?

EMBASSY
SUITES™

Embassy Suites, Inc.
P.O. Box 267
Arlington, Texas
76004-9990

BUSINESS REPLY MAIL
FIRST CLASS PERMIT NO. 2466 ARLINGTON, TX

POSTAGE WILL BE PAID BY ADDRESSEE

Embassy Suites, Inc.
P.O. Box 267
Arlington, Texas 76004-9990

NO POSTAGE
NECESSARY
IF MAILED
IN THE
UNITED STATES

There's only one person we want to impress. You.

ow we need to know if we succeeded. We promised you The Suite Life®. And all of us at Embassy Suites® hope your visit was everything we said it would be. In fact, we hope you were so impressed with our suites, our services, our staff—with our whole approach to serving you—that you'll become a regular guest each time you return to our area.

Now we need to know how well we kept our promise.

So won't you please take a minute to tell us how you rate our Embassy Suites hotel . . . and how we can make your stay even better in the future.

Thank you so much for your comments and for choosing Embassy Suites.

Hervey A. Feldman

Hervey A. Feldman,
President and
Chief Executive Officer
Embassy Suites, Inc.

We welcome your comments about Embassy Suites® accommodations and service.

How Would You Rate:

	Excellent	Good	Average	Fair	Poor
1. Our Hotel on an Overall Basis?	☐	☐	☐	☐	☐
2. Our Suite on an Overall Basis?	☐	☐	☐	☐	☐
3. The overall value you received for the price paid?	☐	☐	☐	☐	☐
4. Our Services?					
Reservations Handling	☐	☐	☐	☐	☐
Check-in-Speed	☐	☐	☐	☐	☐
Check-out-Speed	☐	☐	☐	☐	☐
Cleanliness of Public Areas	☐	☐	☐	☐	☐
Free Breakfast Service	☐	☐	☐	☐	☐
Free Breakfast Quality	☐	☐	☐	☐	☐
Free Bar Quality	☐	☐	☐	☐	☐
Free Bar Service	☐	☐	☐	☐	☐
Limousine (if available)	☐	☐	☐	☐	☐
Recreational Facilities	☐	☐	☐	☐	☐

If you met an outstanding employee(s), please let us know his/her name(s)

_____

	Excellent	Good	Average	Fair	Poor
5. Our Public Restaurant/Lounge?					
(If available)					
Appearance	☐	☐	☐	☐	☐
Restaurant Food Quality	☐	☐	☐	☐	☐
Restaurant Service	☐	☐	☐	☐	☐
Lounge Drink Quality	☐	☐	☐	☐	☐
Lounge Service	☐	☐	☐	☐	☐
Room Service (Speed and Quality)	☐	☐	☐	☐	☐
Entertainment	☐	☐	☐	☐	☐
6. Your Suite					
Appearance	☐	☐	☐	☐	☐
Cleanliness	☐	☐	☐	☐	☐
Comfort	☐	☐	☐	☐	☐
Furnishings	☐	☐	☐	☐	☐
Bathroom	☐	☐	☐	☐	☐
Supplies/toiletries	☐	☐	☐	☐	☐
Security	☐	☐	☐	☐	☐

Was everything in working order? Yes ☐ No ☐
If not, please comment _____

---

7. What was the purpose of your stay?
Pleasure ☐   Relocation ☐   Other _____
Group Meeting ☐   Business Trip ☐
How many people stayed in your room? 1 2 3 4 More ☐
Any Children? Yes ☐ No ☐

8. Did you stay during week ☐ During weekend ☐ Both ☐
Length of stay? _____ days.

9. Have you stayed at an Embassy Suites or Granada Royale® hotel before this trip?
Yes ☐ No ☐

10. Would you stay again at this Embassy Suites hotel when you return to the area?
Yes ☐ No ☐

11. What did you like most about this Embassy Suites hotel?
_____
_____

12. Is there anything we can do to make your next visit with us more enjoyable?
Yes ☐ No ☐
If so, please indicate:
_____

Comments: _____

Optional:
Name: _____
Company: _____ Suite #: _____
Address: _____ Date: _____
City: _____
State: _____ Zip: _____
Telephone: _____

LOS ANGELES - AIRPORT

When you've completed this questionnaire, please drop it off at the front desk or mail it to us.

The management of Embassy Suites appreciates your response and will carefully consider each of your comments. We look forward to having you as our guest the next time you visit our area.

FIGURE 5.3
Embassy Suites Guest Comment Card
Courtesy: Embassy Suites, Irving, TX

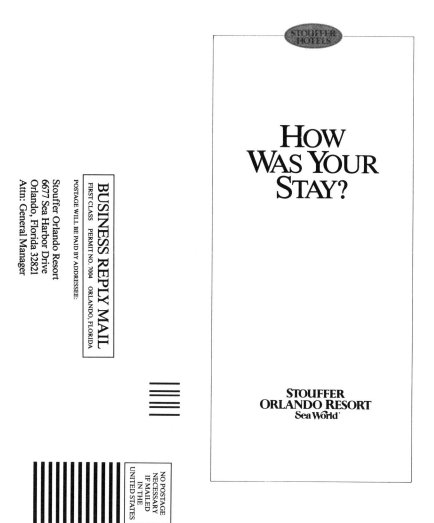

HOW
WAS YOUR
STAY?

STOUFFER
ORLANDO RESORT
Sea World

Thank you for staying with us.
At Stouffer Hotels we proudly maintain a long established tradition of superb service and luxurious accommodations, and we sincerely hope your stay is comfortable and trouble-free.

If for any reason you're not satisfied, or there is some way we can make your stay more pleasant, we'd like to know. Our goal is to continue to provide the kind of service that discriminating travelers from all over the world have come to expect from Stouffer Hotels.

The following questionnaire will help us evaluate our services. Please take a minute at your leisure to give us your impressions, then leave the questionnaire at the front desk or drop it in the mail.

Again, thank you for giving us the opportunity to serve you.

Sincerely,

William N. Hulett
President, Stouffer Hotels

	Highest				Lowest
1. Overall, how would you rate our hotel?	A	B	C	D	F
2. Your Room:					
Appearance	A	B	C	D	F
Cleanliness	A	B	C	D	F
Comfort	A	B	C	D	F
Furnishings	A	B	C	D	F
Bathroom	A	B	C	D	F
3. Restaurant/Lounge Name _____					
Food Quality	A	B	C	D	F
Service Quality	A	B	C	D	F
Price	A	B	C	D	F
4. Room Service					
Food Quality	A	B	C	D	F
Service Quality	A	B	C	D	F
Price	A	B	C	D	F
5. Staff Personnel: (Friendliness & Efficiency)					
Desk Clerk/Concierge	A	B	C	D	F
Food & Beverage Server	A	B	C	D	F
Telephone Operator	A	B	C	D	F
Housekeeper	A	B	C	D	F
Bell Staff	A	B	C	D	F
6. Complimentary coffee/ newspaper with wake-up call	A	B	C	D	F

7. When you return to this area, would you stay at our Stouffer Hotel or look elsewhere?
Stay Here ☐
Look Elsewhere ☐

8. Have you stayed at our Stouffer Hotel before?
Yes ☐   No ☐

Comments: _____
_____

Date of stay: _____ Room # _____
Name _____
Home address _____
_____ Zip _____
Company or organization _____
Business address _____
_____ Zip _____

FIGURE 5.4
Stouffer Hotels Guest Comment Card
Courtesy: Stouffer Hotels Corporation, Solon, OH

107

extensive study or pay to have one conducted only to produce information that is available from existing sources. By stating all known facts, management establishes a base from which to work. This base may easily be established by looking at all internal sources previously discussed and collecting all data available internally before proceeding with more expensive, external information-gathering techniques.

2. *List specific goals and objectives.*   Once a base of information has been established, a plan must be formulated. Goals and objectives are the basis for this plan. Without goals and objectives, an external study could easily go astray and would not yield the information needed by a hospitality manager. The manager needs to ask, "What do I want to learn? What types of information about my clientele, my competition, or my own operation would be most useful?" Having answered such questions, an operator can begin to formulate potential questions for a survey to provide the desired information.

3. *Collect all relevant data.*   At this point the actual legwork must be done to ensure an adequate sample. The information gathered must be both valid and reliable. Validity is the degree to which the data gathered measure what they are supposed to measure. Reliability is the degree with which data consistently measure whatever they measure. Data collection is extremely important and is not a process to be treated lightly. The information generated will only be as accurate and valid as the procedures used to generate the information. For this reason, great care must be taken to assure that the information is gathered correctly.

4. *Summarize the data and analyze the situation.*   No matter what data collection methods are used, some type of summary and analysis must be done to reduce the data into a manageable package. This may then be used by management to make a wide variety of decisions.

Primary Data

Primary data consist of original research done to answer current questions regarding a specific operation. An example is a foodservice manager who attempts to ascertain consumer attitudes toward new menu offerings or to solicit consumer perceptions of increased menu prices or different portion sizes. This type of data is very pertinent to an individual operation but may not be applicable to other situations.

The advantages to primary data include the following:

☐ *Specificity.* These data are tailored to one operation only and can provide excellent information for decision-making purposes.

☐ *Practicality.* Just as the data are geared toward one operation, they can provide solid "real-life" information and a practical foundation to be used in the decision-making process.

Drawbacks to using primary data include the following:

☐ *Cost.* For an individual manager, gathering primary data is extremely expensive. To gather primary data even from a city of 100,000 people may prove to be a monumental task for an operator and may cost too much in time and money.

☐ *Time lag.* Marketing decisions often must be made quickly, yet it requires a good deal of time to conduct a thorough information-gathering study. While a manager is collecting the data, the competition may be driving the hospitality operation into bankruptcy.

☐ *Duplication.* While primary data are geared toward a specific operation, other sources of existing data may closely duplicate the information collected and would therefore be appropriate for decision-making purposes. This duplication of effort is very expensive, and primary data collection should therefore be undertaken only after all secondary data sources have been exhausted.

Secondary Data

This type of data is information already available from other sources. All of the trade associations and trade journals listed earlier publish a wealth of secondary data each year. These data summarize a wide variety of information about operations, marketing, human resource management, financial performance, and other topics of interest to management.

A shrewd manager will make a thorough check of all available secondary data sources before undertaking primary data collection. Secondary data can save many personnel hours and a great deal of money. The major advantages of using secondary data follow.

☐ *Cost.* It is much less expensive to obtain information from existing sources than to develop entirely new data. These existing sources may require a nominal charge for the information, but it will be much less than the cost of undertaking primary data collection.

☐ *Timeliness.* Secondary data are available almost instantaneously. A manager can have access to data very quickly and therefore does not have to wait weeks or perhaps months for primary data to be collected, analyzed, and summarized.

By using secondary data whenever possible, a manager saves the frustration of developing the research methodology design, designing the data collection instrument, pretesting the instrument, devising a sampling plan, gathering the data, checking the data for accuracy and omissions, analyzing the data, and summarizing and reporting the results. Instead, a manager can merely locate the appropriate source and extract and record the information desired. This process can be completed in a few hours or days, while primary data collection can take weeks or months to complete.

Secondary data collection is not, however, without drawbacks, some of which follow:

☐ *Limited applicability.* A manager has no assurance that information gathered by others will be applicable to a particular hospitality operation. For example, information gathered in New York about the popularity of a specific menu item may not be useful to a manager located in the Midwest. Information that pertains to one operation may apply only to that operation and be of limited value to anyone else.

☐ *Information frequently out of date.* Managers need current and accurate information on which to base decisions. All too often, secondary data are not as useful as they might be merely because they are not current. For example, a consumer attitude survey concerning restaurant price and value perceptions conducted four years ago would be of little use to a hospitality manager making plans today. During the four years, a great many changes in consumer attitudes are likely to have taken place. These changes in attitudes will make the original data outdated and useful only in a historical sense. If a hospitality manager were to make use of less than timely data, the results are likely to be less than satisfactory.

☐ *Reliability.* Whenever a hospitality operator uses secondary data as the basis for a decision, the manager runs the risk that the information may not be reliable and accurate. A manager would do well to ask, "Who collected the data and what method of data collection was used?" Information is only as good as the individuals who collect it and the methods they use. If a study is administered in a haphazard manner, the results and conclusions should be viewed with caution.

SUMMARY

Marketing information systems should be designed for the purpose of producing data that are useful to a hospitality manager. This information can be used as a basis for decisions. This information should not, however, be used as the sole determining factor when making any decision. Two other factors also come into play when making a decision—experience and intuition. If all decisions could be based solely on information produced by marketing information systems, there would be no need for managers. Instead, machines could be used to tabulate the information and predict the correct answer. Managers, however, have far too many uncontrollable variables to contend with in gathering marketing information. For this reason a hospitality manager must view the situation by considering (1) marketing information, (2) previous experience in similar situations, and (3) intuition as to what the future holds. Based on these three factors, a decision must be made, and the hospitality manager must accept the final responsibility for the decision.

A hospitality marketing information system is a structured organization of people and procedures designed to generate a flow of data from inside and outside the operation. It is used as a basis for marketing decisions. A marketing information system can be used in many ways by a resourceful hospitality manager. It can, for example, be an information source for decisions related to market segmentation, advertising, and menu item changes. A marketing information system makes use of environmental scanning of three subenvironments: (1) the macroenvironment, (2) the competitive environment, and (3) the organizational environment.

Marketing information systems involve both internally and externally generated marketing information, each with its own set of sources for information and its own methodology for obtaining necessary information. Data collected may be classified as either primary or secondary. Primary data result from original research, while secondary data are information taken from sources that already exist in printed form.

KEY WORDS AND CONCEPTS

- ☐ Demographic variables
- ☐ Geographic variables
- ☐ Psychographic variables
- ☐ Behavioral variables
- ☐ Macroenvironment
- ☐ Competitive environment
- ☐ Organizational environment
- ☐ Guest histories
- ☐ Marketing research and marketing audits
- ☐ Guidelines for external data collection
- ☐ Primary and secondary data

Questions for Review and Discussion

1. Why would it be useful for a hospitality organization to implement a marketing information system?

2. Cite those sources for internal and external marketing information that you consider to be the best. Discuss the advantages and disadvantages of each.
3. Differentiate between primary and secondary data, including their advantages and disadvantages.
4. What role should a marketing information system play in the management of a hospitality establishment?

CHAPTER 6

Market Research Methodology

This chapter serves as a continuation of Chapter 5 by examining the important aspects of marketing research. All successful companies rely to some extent on developing new and innovative ideas through marketing research. This chapter focuses on the area of marketing research projects, exploring research methodology and specific research applications typical of the hospitality industry.

INTRODUCTION

MARKETING RESEARCH METHODOLOGY
☐ The Experimental Method
☐ The Observational Method
☐ The Survey Method
☐ Sampling Methodology
☐ Survey Instrument Design

SPECIFIC MARKETING RESEARCH APPLICATIONS
☐ The Marketing Audit
☐ Feasibility Studies
☐ Product Development

SUMMARY

KEY WORDS AND CONCEPTS

QUESTIONS FOR REVIEW AND DISCUSSION

INTRODUCTION

Market research efforts are undertaken to answer a wide variety of questions, which might include, "Where do our guests come from? How frequently do people dine out in this area? In what types of restaurants do they most frequently dine? If the seating capacity of restaurant X is expanded by 20 percent, what impact will this have on sales and profits? If the city builds a new convention center, how many additional room nights is that likely to bring to the city?"

Conducting a market research effort is not an inexpensive proposition, and when research is undertaken, care must be taken to assure that the proper methods are used. This remains true whether the hospitality organization conducts its own market research or relies on external consultants. Market research data are only as good as the methodology used. If poor methodology is used, the results are not likely to describe the situation accurately, and marketing decisions based on this information are not likely to be very appropriate.

MARKETING RESEARCH METHODOLOGY

Following are six steps that will generally ensure that the outcome of the research project will accurately reflect the true situation:

1. *Define the problem.* Before initiating any marketing research effort, the problem should be clearly defined. What does the research effort propose to do? What types of questions need to be asked? What solutions are sought? A strong tendency among all researchers, especially novice researchers, is to rush into data collection without giving adequate thought to defining the problem. This tendency should be vigorously avoided. A small amount of time spent in defining and refining the problem will save many hours later on.

2. *Conduct a preliminary investigation.* The purpose of this step is to save both time and money. Little can be gained by researching an area or problem that has been researched before. Therefore, all internally generated marketing information should first be examined to collect data that may be relevant to the stated problem. Second, all available secondary data should also be reviewed for the same reason. These two generic types of information

should save a great deal of time and are likely to produce a few tentative answers to the research problem. These tentative answers can then be tested in later steps.

3. *Plan the research.* Based on the defined problem and the data collected from secondary sources, plans should be formulated concerning the method by which further data should be collected. Numerous methodologies are commonly used; they include telephone and direct mail surveys, personal interviews, consumer focus group interviews, and consumer motivation research.

4. *Collect the data.* Once the research methodology has been planned, the data should be collected in the manner prescribed. No shortcuts should be taken; a slow, systematic approach is best. Every effort should be taken to avoid contamination of the data by extraneous variables which would bias the results.

5. *Analyze the data.* As statistical procedures have become more sophisticated, so too have the approaches to data analysis. Procedures that used to take hours of calculation by researchers can now be done by computers in a matter of seconds or minutes. The general rule in analyzing data is to complete the relatively simple analysis before advancing to the more sophisticated.

6. *Summarize the data and reach conclusions.* Based on the five previous steps, management should now have a clear picture of the problem, the key variables, the relationships among these variables, and the courses of action available. In many cases, the decision will be clear-cut; in other cases, managerial judgment will be the deciding factor. The important point to remember is that when a methodical approach is taken to the research effort, better decisions are likely to result.

Step 3 involves a research plan. Following are three common approaches to a research plan: (1) the experimental method, (2) the observational method, and (3) the survey method.

The Experimental Method

The experimental method is the most formal of the three and finds only limited use in the hospitality industry. When using this method, a researcher divides the sample of people into groups and exposes each group to a different treatment. For example, all of the national fast-food companies use cities across the country as test-market centers. In each of these centers, the companies will introduce or "test-market" new products to obtain customer reaction to new items and to project future sales of these items. Sales may then be compared with those at other test-market centers to determine popularity of new and old items and to decide which products will be introduced systemwide. It is quite expensive to conduct this type of study, and it is also quite difficult to control all external variables that may affect the outcome of the experiment. For example, such external variables as the weather or the advertising efforts of competitive hospitality operations could easily have an effect on the sales volume of new products. Because of the expense, only the large chains are able to conduct such studies on a regular basis.

Many large chains, such as McDonald's, Burger King, and Wendy's, are continuously conducting experimental test-market studies. Such studies allow these hospitality giants accurately to predict the future sales of a new product. A corporation that has the financial size and stability needed to engage in test-marketing is able to gain additional competitive advantage.

The Observational Method

The observational method involves observing consumer behavior and making organized notes to document or record the observed behavior. When doing this type of research, it is important that all individuals acting as observers record their observations in the same manner. Therefore, if more than one individual is recording observations, it is imperative that a common method of observing behavior and recording information be established. This is done to ensure consistency among the different observers. The observational method will not be effective unless it is carried out in this way.

The observational method might be used to record observed reactions of consumers to various personal selling approaches. Suppose a manager instructed the service personnel to use three different sales approaches for the promotion of wine. Each service person would then be instructed to record both the approach used and the customer's reaction. After a period of time, perhaps two weeks, the manager could then compare the recorded information of all service personnel and might better determine which promotional technique would likely be most effective for future use.

Such information is easily used in the hospitality industry, but the observational method is not without its drawbacks. The major drawback is that it is difficult to observe and document all relevant customer behavior. It is also difficult to instruct and train all the observers so that they all observe and record information in exactly the same manner.

The Survey Method

When used properly, the survey method can gather a great deal of useful information for a hospitality manager. The survey method is adaptable to a variety of situations and is relatively inexpensive. Surveys may be accomplished using a number of different methods, including telephone surveys, direct mail surveys, or personal interviews.

Telephone surveys are the easiest to implement and produce very quick results. One major advantage to this type of survey is the cost. No travel is involved, and a single individual may contact and solicit answers from a large number of people in a fairly short period of time. On the other hand, there is no face-to-face contact, and people are often not inclined to answer questions over the phone. The reliability of the answers received over the telephone is also in question.

Direct mail surveys are used a great deal too. They offer ease of completion and moderate cost, but they present two major drawbacks. First, the rate of return is normally quite low. Often, less than 25 percent of the surveys are properly completed and returned, and it is extremely hazardous to base business decisions on such a small return. The risk always exists that those individuals who returned the surveys are atypical and may not provide answers and opinions that truly represent the majority of the targeted market segment. Second, direct mail surveys do not allow any in-depth questioning, and they do not allow for follow-up questions. The respondent merely sees the written questions and has no opportunity for clarification. This may make it more difficult to generate answers that reflect the complexity of opinion within the targeted market segments.

Personal interviews allow more in-depth questioning. An interviewer normally uses a guide sheet to direct the interview and may adjust the questioning to focus on a point of special interest or to follow-up an answer given by the respondent. There are two drawbacks to personal interviews as a surveying technique. The major drawback is cost. It is extremely expensive to have an interviewer spend a long period of time with one individual in order to gather information. An in-depth interview can last as long as two hours; hence the number of individuals that can be interviewed is limited, and the cost per interview is quite high. The cost of travel also makes this type of survey expensive. Second, a good deal of interviewer training must be done for interviewers to be effective. In addition, supervision is required in order to have control over the interviewers.

Step 5 of the six-step research methodology is data analysis. The most basic approach to data analysis is to calculate the relevant measures of central tendency such as the mean (arithmetic average), the median (midpoint), and the mode (the most frequently selected response). Additionally, the measures of variability should include the range (difference between the highest and lowest score, such as a 1–10 rating) and the standard deviation (the distribution of scores on both sides of the mean).

Once these calculations are completed, cross tabulations are often performed to determine whether a relationship exists. Correlation coefficients can be calculated to describe not only the relative strength of the relationship but also whether it is positive or negative. For example, suppose a hospitality market researcher wanted to determine whether there was a relationship between annual income in dollars and the number of times per week that adults dine outside the home. The results of the research study might indicate a high positive correlation (+0.90) between annual income and the number of times per week adults dined outside the home. This means that as annual income rises, so too does the number of times that an adult dines outside the home. A negative correlation is just the opposite; if the relationship in the example were a high negative (−0.90) correlation, the number of times per week that adults dine outside the home would decrease as annual income increases. Correlation coefficients can range from −1.00 to +1.00. The larger (closer to 1.00) the correlation coefficient (positive or negative), the stronger the relationship.

Multivariate statistical techniques are also commonly used in marketing research. These techniques include multiple regression analysis, discriminant analysis, and factor analysis. Multiple regression analysis seeks to analyze the influence that one or more variables (independent variables) have on another variable (the dependent variable). For example, what influence does radio advertising have on sales volume? Discriminant analysis seeks to classify variables rather than assign a numerical value. For example, what are the traits or characteristics of those individuals who dine outside the home more than ten times per week on average? Factor analysis is a statistical technique used to discover a few basic factors that may explain intercorrelations among a large number of variables.

Statistical procedures are very useful in analyzing data, but managers must also rely on critical thinking and the role of intangibles in reaching their conclusions.

Sampling Methodology

Market research data are often based on probability sampling; a relatively small sample of people is randomly selected, and the results from this sample are generalized to the larger population. It is imperative that the market researcher select the random sample with care, for errors in sample selection can affect the results and hence the generalizations. Three sampling methods pertinent to the hospitality industry are (1) simple random sampling, (2) cluster sampling, and (3) systematic sampling.

For any of these methods, the first requirement is to define the population from which to gather information. (The population is simply a definition of the group of individuals from which to gather information.) For example, two specific populations might be (1) all males and females between the ages of 20 to 26 who are not married, and (2) all males and females who earn more than $25,000 per year and work within 1 mile of our restaurant.

The next step or requirement is to determine the number of individuals to survey. This is known as the *sample size*. The size of the sample really depends on the risk a hospitality manager is willing to assume. As more individuals are surveyed, the degree of risk is reduced because the information gathered is more likely to represent the entire population, or universe. The risk is reduced because the information gathered tends to be more valid and reliable as more individuals are surveyed. But the question arises: How many people should be surveyed? This is not an easy question, and there is no set answer. Precise sample sizes can be calculated based on the degree of accuracy that is desired in the results . In order to obtain results that are accurate within plus or minus 10 percent is relatively easy and the sample size required is not that large. However, to obtain results that are accurate within plus or minus 1 percent, a much larger sample size would be necessary. Sampling is a very complex science.

The sample size necessary is directly related to the size of the population. As the number of individuals in the population increases, the percentage of the population that must be included in the sample decreases, as illustrated in Table 6.1.

Having identified and defined the population and determined the number of individuals to be surveyed, the next steps are to select the individuals and implement the survey. If a survey is to have any usefulness, it must be implemented with great care. A poorly chosen sample is not likely to produce information that represents the opinions of the entire population. Without information that is truly representative of the entire population, it is extremely difficult to make a sound decision. Any decisions based on insufficient or inaccurate data are tenuous at best.

One of the most popular methods of sample selection is random sampling. This method allows each and every member of a population an equal chance of being selected. Random sampling is probably the best method for a hospitality marketing researcher to use when undertaking a survey. It does not guarantee a representative sample, but it comes as close as any available method. Here are the steps for selecting a random sample:

TABLE 6.1
Sample Size as a Function of Population Size

Population Size	Necessary Sample Size
500	217
5,000	357
50,000	381
100,000	384

1. Identify and define the population.

2. Determine the desired sample size.

3. List all members of the population.

4. Assign each member of the population a consecutive number starting with 1.

5. Select an arbitrary number from a table of random numbers. Random numbers tables are easily generated by computer program, and can also be found in research methodology textbooks. The number will correspond with the numbers assigned in Step 4.

6. Repeat Step 5 until enough individuals are selected to complete the desired sample size.

Another sampling method that a hospitality marketing researcher should consider is cluster sampling. Cluster sampling involves the use of previously formed groups rather than separately chosen individuals. If a manager surveyed all the consumers who patronized a particular hospitality operation on a given day or during a specific meal period, this would be a cluster sample, and the patrons would be the cluster. The manager has no control over the selection of the individuals that make up the cluster but uses the entire cluster as a sample. Similar clusters might be all the guests checking out of a hotel on a particular day, or the individuals who live in one apartment building or in a series of buildings.

Systematic sampling is also of potential interest to a hospitality marketing researcher. Systematic sampling involves using an existing listing of names (often in alphabetical order) and selecting a representative sample from these names. The steps are shown in Table 6.2.

Survey Instrument Design

Survey questionnaires are commonly used by market researchers within the hospitality industry because they are relatively inexpensive, and with them, a broad range of information can be collected. Figure 6.1 is an example of a survey instrument. This instrument was developed by the National Restaurant Association and is reprinted from *Market Research for the Restaurateur*.

Surveys can be used in direct mail, personal interviews, and telephone interviews. The design of surveys, however, is by no means a simple task. It may appear to be fairly easy to jot down a few questions and develop a survey instrument, but this is far from the truth. Designing a successful questionnaire is a difficult task, and a great deal of time and thought needs to go into development. Following is a series of questions to help a survey instrument designer begin.

TABLE 6.2
Systematic Sampling

	Step		Example
1.	Identify and define the population.	1.	The entire population of city XYZ, population 100,000
2.	Determine the desired sample size.	2.	The approximate sample size for a population of 100,000 is 384 individuals.
3.	Obtain a list of the population.	3.	Source: Telephone directory
4.	Determine k by dividing the size of the population by the sample size.	4.	$k = 100,000 \div 384$ $k = 260$
5.	Start at a random point near the top of the list.	5.	Randomly selected name near the top of the list
6.	Take every kth name on the list until the desired size is reached.	6.	Every 260th name until the desired size sample is reached

☐ Who does what, when, where, and how?

☐ What do the respondents know about the subject?

☐ How do the respondents feel about the subject?

☐ Why do the respondents act or feel the way they do?

When developing a survey questionnaire, the designer should make it clear to follow and as interesting as possible. By starting the survey with easy yet interesting questions, the designer allows the respondent to become involved and respond to all of the questions on the survey instrument. Two types of questions may be included in a survey: open-ended and closed-ended questions. An open-ended question might read like this: "Please offer any comments and suggestions as to how we might improve our restaurant." (This is followed by a few blank lines on which the respondent may write a response.) On the other hand, a closed-ended question might look like the following example:

Please check the response that most closely represents your feelings.

	Excellent	Very Good	Average	Fair	Poor
Quality of food	_____	_____	_____	_____	_____
Quality of beverage	_____	_____	_____	_____	_____
Quality of service	_____	_____	_____	_____	_____

National Restaurant Association
Customer Attitude Questionnaire

We would appreciate it if you would take a few minutes to complete the following questionnaire so that we can find out more about our customers.

1. Which of the following best describes where you were just prior to coming to this restaurant? (Check one)
    _____ 1 At work
    _____ 2 At home
    _____ 3 Shopping
    _____ 4 Social or recreational activity
    _____ 5 Travel or vacation
    _____ 6 Other, please specify _____

2. Which of the following best describes where you will go immediately after you leave this restaurant? (Check one)
    _____ 1 Work
    _____ 2 Home
    _____ 3 Shopping
    _____ 4 Social or recreational activity
    _____ 5 Travel or vacation
    _____ 6 Other, please specify _____

3. Excluding this restaurant, what is your favorite restaurant for dinner? (Please give full name of restaurant.)
    _____

4. Please compare this restaurant with the favorite dinner restaurant you have mentioned for each of the categories listed below. (Check under the appropriate word how you feel this restaurant compares with your favorite one.)

Characteristics	Much Better	Better	Same	Worse	Much Worse
Service	( )	( )	( )	( )	( )
Cleanliness	( )	( )	( )	( )	( )
Quality of food	( )	( )	( )	( )	( )
Menu variety offered	( )	( )	( )	( )	( )
Employee friendliness	( )	( )	( )	( )	( )
Atmosphere	( )	( )	( )	( )	( )
Convenience of location	( )	( )	( )	( )	( )
Value for the price	( )	( )	( )	( )	( )

5. How many people are in your party today?
    _____ 1 One   _____ 4 Four
    _____ 2 Two   _____ 5 Five
    _____ 3 Three   _____ 6 Six or more

FIGURE 6.1
Example of a Consumer Attitude Survey
Source: National Restaurant Association, *Market Research for the Restaurateur*

6. How often do you eat at this restaurant?
    _____ 1 More than once a week
    _____ 2 About once a week
    _____ 3 About every 2–3 weeks
    _____ 4 About once a month
    _____ 5 About once every 2–3 months
    _____ 6 Less than once every 3 months
    _____ 7 First visit

7. Who chose this restaurant for today's meal?
    _____ 1 Myself
    _____ 2 Another family member
    _____ 3 Co-worker
    _____ 4 Friend
    _____ 5 Other, please specify _____

The last few questions are just for classification purposes. All answers will be confidential.

8. How old are you?
    _____ (1) 18 to 24   _____ (4) 45 to 54
    _____ (2) 25 to 34   _____ (5) 55 to 64
    _____ (3) 35 to 44   _____ (6) 65 or older

9. Are you a male or a female?
    _____ 1 Male   _____ 2 Female

10. How many members are there in your household?
    _____ 1 One person   _____ 4 Four persons
    _____ 2 Two persons   _____ 5 Five or more persons
    _____ 3 Three persons

11. How many wage earners are there in your household?
    _____ 1 One   _____ 2 Two   _____ 3 Three or more

12. What is the best description of your occupation?
    _____ 1 Sales   _____ 7   Management/Administration
    _____ 2 Clerical   _____ 8   Service Worker
    _____ 3 Farmer/Rancher   _____ 9   Housewife
    _____ 4 Self-Employed   _____ 10 Retired
    _____ 5 Professional/Technical _____ 11 Student
    _____ 6 Government   _____ 12 Other, please specify _____

13. What is your approximate household income?
    _____ 1 Under $10,000   _____ 4 $20,000 to $24,999
    _____ 2 $10,000 to $14,999 _____ 5 $25,000 to $29,999
    _____ 3 $15,000 to $19,999 _____ 6 $30,000 and over

FIGURE 6.1 *(continued)*

Both types of questions are widely used and offer certain advantages. An open-ended question allows the respondent to reply more personally, but this type of survey does make analysis and summary of the results more difficult. On the other hand, a closed-ended question is easy to analyze, but the respondent has very little choice of response and merely decides the most appropriate preworded answer. Open-ended questions are most effective if used to determine subjective opinions, while closed-ended questions are best for gathering objective information and facts.

Surveys are used for a multitude of reasons, and it is difficult to establish rules that will apply in all situations. The following general guidelines, however, apply to the construction of all survey instruments:

- ☐ Avoid talking down to the respondent or using technical language. Ask the questions using language the respondent understands and is familiar with.

- ☐ Avoid long and wordy questions. These will tend to discourage the respondent and may reduce the number of respondents to a written survey.

- ☐ Avoid questions that are vague and general in nature.

- ☐ Avoid including more than one idea per question.

- ☐ Avoid personal questions that might embarrass the respondent. Make certain that there is a legitimate reason for asking each question.

- ☐ Avoid putting any personal bias into the questions.

- ☐ Make sure that you fully understand the purpose of the question, for if you do not, the respondent is not likely to understand the question.

- ☐ In closed-ended questions, provide a "don't know" or "no opinion" response where appropriate.

- ☐ All responses in a closed-ended question should be mutually exclusive.

- ☐ The number of choices in a closed-ended question need not be limited to five or six responses; a larger number of responses can be used where appropriate.

- ☐ Indicate very clearly in the directions the number of choices a respondent should check for a closed-ended question.

- ☐ Watch for words and phrases that have more than one meaning, as this can confuse the respondent.

☐ Questions of a personal nature, such as income, are generally less threatening if they are placed toward the end of the survey.

Surveys are extremely useful to the management of a hospitality organization. They can help gather a great deal of valuable information about present and potential patrons.

The design of marketing research surveys is much more difficult than one might first imagine. Should the reader desire to learn more about survey design, one of the best sources for further information is *Mail and Telephone Surveys: The Total Design Method,* by Don A. Dillman.

SPECIFIC MARKETING RESEARCH APPLICATIONS

The Marketing Audit

In recent years, the term *marketing audit* has been used more frequently by owners and managers of hospitality organizations. What does the term mean? How can a marketing audit be used? Should all types of hospitality operations engage in marketing audits? A marketing audit is simply a tool used to examine and evaluate the effectiveness of an organization's marketing strategies and practices. In an audit, management takes a broad view and seeks to analyze the organization's performance against prestated objectives as well as environmental conditions.

To achieve maximum use, it is recommended that hospitality operations undertake a marketing audit in a systematic way and on a regular basis. The vast majority of hospitality firms should plan to conduct an audit on at least an annual basis. Many will use marketing audits monthly. Each manager must determine precisely the marketing elements that are to be subject to an audit. The following is a suggested list of components for a thorough marketing audit:

☐ *Marketing environment audit.* It is advisable to begin with a brief study of the macroenvironment surrounding the hospitality operation; this means looking at the large-scale economic, social, political, and technological factors that play on the industry. In addition, the microenvironment should also be reviewed; this means examining the competitive environment that immediately surrounds the hospitality operation. This study should consist of markets, consumers, and competitors.

☐ *Marketing strategy audit.* In light of environmental conditions, the firm's marketing strategies must be carefully reviewed. Goals and objectives related to marketing must be reviewed carefully to determine (1) whether the goals are still appropriate and (2) the best strategies for successfully achieving goals if the goals are still appropriate.

☐ *Marketing sales effectiveness audit*. Consumer reaction to the sales and marketing efforts must be studied carefully. How effective are the service and sales personnel? Do they really serve the needs of the hospitality operation's consumers? Do they adequately engage in personal selling of the products and services offered?

☐ *External and internal marketing productivity audit*. Efforts that have been undertaken to increase sales must be examined. All advertising and promotional efforts must be examined carefully to determine which efforts yield the best results per dollar spent. Zero-based budgeting is a technique that might prove to be very useful in this effort.

Marketing audits can prove to be extremely useful, for the following purposes:

☐ To search for new opportunities to pursue

☐ To search for weaknesses within the organization that should be eliminated

☐ To provide current information about the micro- and macroenvironments

Feasibility Studies

When a new hotel or restaurant is being considered, a special type of research project is undertaken, called a *feasibility study*. The overriding concern of a developer, or someone who is going to invest money in a hospitality facility, is whether the venture will be a success. The investor is concerned about the return that the investment will pay, relative to the amount of money invested and the degree of risk involved. Typically, investors are concerned primarily with the return on investment (R.O.I.).

Feasibility studies generally contain two major sections. The first focuses on the market feasibility of the project. The project is evaluated based on supply and demand of the local area, to include demand generators within the local area. Even though guests will travel long distances to reach a hotel property, the supply-demand analysis focuses on local demand attractions and reasons why potential guests visit the area. The majority of hotels are transient in nature; only resorts and conference centers attract guests as a terminal destination. Along with the supply-demand analysis, a projection of operating statistics is also typically included in this section of a feasibility study.

The second section of the study covers the financial feasibility of the hospitality development. This economic aspect of the project typically examines the discounted cash flow of the investment, giving the potential investor a better idea of the true economic viability of the project. The acceptable rate of return on investment will differ with each project. Generally speaking, however, the more risk involved in the project, the higher the return on investment should be to compensate for the element of risk.

Feasibility studies are very critical to managers and investors in the hospitality industry. Development costs of urban hotel properties typically exceed $100,000 per guest room, so the stakes are very high. It is critical that the potential investors have sound and accurate feasibility studies on which to base their decisions.

A well-researched and well-written feasibility study will assist the developer in obtaining financing and securing potential investors, and obtaining and negotiating a lease or franchise agreement, and will also serve as the basis for the development of initial pre-opening marketing plans, guide the planning and development of the project by the architects and project managers, and serve as a target when preparing the annual and five-year capital and operating budgets.

According to the American Hotel and Motel Association, in *A Practical Guide to Understanding Feasibility Studies*, these projects normally contain the following sections:

☐ *Introduction.*

☐ *Summary and Conclusions.* The section is written as an "Executive Summary" so that a potential investor or other interested individual can get an overview of the project and the recommendations without reading the entire report.

☐ *Market Area Characteristics.* This section provides a geographic definition of the area, along with a summary of the area's demographics and economic forecasts. The focus is on the area's future economic potential, typically covering population, income, retail sales, employment, commercial development, transportation, and tourism growth potential.

☐ *Project Site and Area Evaluation.* This section focuses on the micro aspects of the area, to include accessibility to the local attraction, visibility, adaptability of the site for the type of project planned, and local zoning, licensing, and building codes.

☐ *Competitive Analysis.* This section provides a complete inventory of current and planned competition, divided into the respective market segments. A complete analysis of the proposed property's strengths, weaknesses, opportunities, and threats should be presented.

☐ *Future Demand Analysis.* Each of the major market segments is examined to determine the current and future trends. For each of the consumer markets, demand is calculated for room nights, public meeting space needs, and restaurant needs.

☐ *Recommended Facilities and Services.* Based on the current market conditions, the competitive situation, and the economic feasibility of the proposed facility, this section makes recommendations concerning the type of facility that offers the best chance of success. The targeted market segment is identified, the facilities concept is identified, and a recommended product-service mix is proposed.

☐ *Economic Projections.* The final section gets to the heart of the issue— what will be the expected return on the initial investment? What will the operating projections for revenue and expenses be for one, two, and five years? These figures are usually broken down by major department. What are the projected cash flows?

Product Development

No matter how successful a foodservice or lodging concept is, if the company behind the concept doesn't innovate and change, it will be left behind. Looking over the list of the top 100 companies in the lodging and foodservice segments each year shows that some older companies fade away and new ones emerge. Corporations such as McDonald's continue to lead the industry, because they have been very successful in developing products and services that will enhance their market position. It has been said that the days when a foodservice company could expand sales and market share simply by build- ing new stores is over; today it must be done within existing stores by product-service mix development.

This development takes two forms: innovation, and "follow the leader." Innovators are the risk-takers, always seeking to be the first into the market with a new product. However, given the ease with which hospitality products and services can be duplicated, those who subscribe to the "follow the leader" approach can introduce their competing products and services soon after the market leader introduces its own products and services.

New products and services don't just happen. They rarely occur by accident. Most companies have a fairly regimented process for guiding the development of new products and services. The following section examines this process as it is typically implemented by a foodservice company develop- ing new menu items.

1. *Assemble a new product group.*   Some new ideas are generated from the units within the chain or from those working in the field. However, it usually is the charge of one group at the corporate office to manage new product development. This group should have representation and input from a variety of departments, including marketing, operations, accounting, and finance. Each of the members of the new product group should serve as a liaison between the new product group and his or her respective department. The goal is to keep the lines of communication and ideas open.

2. *Establish new product priorities.*   It is all too easy to race off in a hundred directions seeking to develop new products that are hoped to be market winners. All new product candidates should fit with the company's overall mission and future direction. Current products should be evaluated to determine which are candidates for increased emphasis, or perhaps deletion. New products in various stages of test marketing should be evaluated as well, to determine potential winners and losers. If a product in test market appears to be a winner, perhaps it should be introduced systemwide more rapidly. On the other hand, if a product appears to be unsuccessful, it should be reformatted or dropped.

3. *Potential new products.*   Ideas should be sought from all potential sources. Menu items usually are thought to expand, extend, or enhance the current foodservice menu. Current new menu item development appears to be most active in breakfast foods, light and healthy menu items, new tastes in foods such as regional cuisine, foods that cannot be prepared easily at home, foods that lend themselves to take-out, and finally food that is delivered.

4. *Screening potential new products.*   Once ideas have been generated by brainstorming and other techniques, it is now a major task to screen the list of potential products to select the ones with the greatest potential. This is normally done by examining the product by both qualitative and quantitative analysis.

The qualitative standards involve questions such as these: To what extent will the product increase sales and check averages? Will the product attract new customers, and to what extent will it cannibalize from the sale of current products? What price would consumers pay for the product? Do we have the talent and capacity to produce this product within our units? Does the competition offer a similar product? If so, how can we differentiate our product?

The quantitative analysis involves a weighted scoring of each new product to determine potential based on criteria such as the following: image of the product and the company; overall company goals; strengths,, weaknesses, opportunities, and threats; current and potential customers; voids in the current product-service mix; equipment necessary to produce the new item; and sources of supply for the new product or the necessary ingredients.

Once the two types of analyses are completed, the most product ideas with the most potential are selected for further development.

5. *Further product development.* At this stage, the products are typically tested further in test kitchens. The emphasis is on recipe development to refine the product so that it can be produced consistently. Standards are established for portions, preparation, and holding times, as well as presentation. If the development plan proceeds according to schedule, the product is then tested in a few select units. At this stage of the development, the product will likely be evaluated by focus groups made up of representatives of the target markets. The focus groups, led by a skilled facilitator, will assess the product's potential impact by conducting taste tests and soliciting consumer feedback about the product, price, and other attributes. If this process continues to be successful, the product is then ready to undergo limited test-marketing in more units. Market testing should last approximately three to twelve months. During the test-market period, the product is evaluated based on (1) consumer feedback concerning quality, price, and response to various forms of advertising and promotion; (2) sales figures during various days of the week and times during the day; and (3) the financial contribution that the menu item has made.

6. *Final decision concerning a total new product rollout.* At this point a decision must be made concerning the future of the product. The choices are simple, yet the decision is difficult. The options are to introduce the new product in all the company's stores, to reformulate the product or the rollout plans, or to abandon the product and let it die a natural death.

SUMMARY

Marketing research as it is practiced in the hospitality industry is quite similar to such research in other fields. There is a constant need to know more about current and potential guests, actions and future plans of competitors, current trends in the marketplace, and other issues of concerns to management. Marketing research projects are designed to seek the answers to real questions that are raised every day by management.

The basics of conducting marketing research are not difficult, but the specifics of designing, implementing, analyzing, and interpreting the results of a marketing research project are very demanding. It requires great skill to successfully manage a marketing research project. This chapter provided an overview of the research method, which involves six steps: (1) define the problem, (2) conduct a preliminary investigation, (3) plan the research, (4) collect the data, (5) analyze the data, and (6) summarize the data and reach conclusions.

Within the broad context of marketing research methodology, three methods are most commonly used—the experimental method, the observational method, and the survey method. The chapter provides a brief overview of each of these methods, in which the advantages and disadvantages of each are presented.

Other critical areas of interest include sampling and research questionnaire design. The most commonly used methods to select samples for research studies are simple random sampling, cluster sampling, and systematic sampling. The design of research questionnaires is also critical to the success of a research project. The chapter provided guidelines and examples that will be useful in the design or evaluation of questionnaires.

Specific marketing research applications include marketing audits, feasibility studies, and new product development methods. These applications do not just happen by chance. Rather, each one has a specific format and process that is typically used to ensure that the research is conducted and presented in as unbiased a manner as possible.

The marketing audit can be a very useful tool for a hospitality manager. An audit can identify potential strengths and pinpoint existing weaknesses that a manager can work toward improving. Just as other types of audits, such as financial audits, have tremendous value to a manager, so too does a marketing audit, which critically examines the marketing function of a hospitality organization.

Feasibility studies are usually divided into the following sections: Introduction, Summary and Conclusions, Market Area Characteristics, Project Site and Area Evaluation, Competitive Analysis, Future Demand Analysis, Recommended Facilities and Services, and Economic Projections.

The steps in new product development include assembling a new product group, establishing new product priorities, determining the new products with potential for development, screening the potential new products, further developing the new products, and making final decisions concerning whether to roll out the new product in all units within the company.

KEY WORDS AND CONCEPTS

- ☐ Market research methodology
- ☐ Preliminary research
- ☐ Data collection
- ☐ Experimental method
- ☐ Observational method
- ☐ Survey method
- ☐ Mean, median, mode, correlation, multivariate statistics
- ☐ Simple random sampling, cluster sampling, systematic sampling
- ☐ Survey instrument
- ☐ Marketing environment audit
- ☐ Marketing strategy audit
- ☐ Marketing productivity audit

☐ Feasibility study, marketing feasibility, financial feasibility

☐ Product development process

☐ Qualitative standards

☐ Quantitative standards

Questions for Review and Discussion

1. Discuss the three methods for collecting marketing data. Which method would work best in a specific situation with which you are familiar?
2. How is random sampling done?
3. If you were hired by a hospitality firm and were asked to design and implement a marketing information system, how would you approach the task?
4. What role does a feasibility study play in development?
5. What are the major sections of a feasibility study? What are the contents of each major section?
6. If you had to evaluate the thoroughness of a feasibility study, how would you complete this task?
7. What is the process by which companies typically develop new products?

PART III

UNDERSTANDING HOSPITALITY CONSUMERS

CHAPTER 7

Market Segmentation and Positioning

For any hospitality organization to achieve the highest possible level of success, management must have a clear understanding of the market segments that it serves. This chapter focuses on two elements that are critical to the success of a hospitality marketing program—market segmentation and product-service mix positioning. Both of these concepts can be applied so that the organization is able to gain the maximum competitive advantage. The chapter also deals with measuring demand, and on two growing segments— women travelers and those individuals over the age of 55.

The chapter is divided into the following sections:

INTRODUCTION
☐ The Nature of Segmentation
☐ Segmentation Variables
☐ Criteria for Effective Segmentation

MEASURING DEMAND
☐ Evaluating Market Segments
☐ Forecasting Methods

TWO CONSUMER MARKETS WITH EXCELLENT GROWTH POTENTIAL
☐ Working Women and Women Business Travelers
☐ Individuals over 55

POSITIONING THE PRODUCT-SERVICE MIX
☐ Positioning Defined
☐ Constructing the Space of the Product-Service Mix
☐ Developing the Positioning Statement

SUMMARY

KEY WORDS AND CONCEPTS

QUESTIONS FOR REVIEW AND DISCUSSION

INTRODUCTION

The Nature of Segmentation

Until recently, most hospitality organizations have attempted to serve the needs of a fairly wide variety of target markets. These groups include the young and old, the wealthy and not so wealthy, men and women, and people from all ethnic backgrounds. National hospitality chains serve the needs of target markets living in all fifty states, and most take into consideration the sometimes not-so-subtle differences among those living in the East, South, Midwest, and West. Difference in geographic location, demographic variables, life style, and consumer behavior add special challenges to the marketing of the product-service mix of a hospitality organization.

More recently, nearly all of the successful organizations in the hospitality industry have begun to use market segmentation more actively. The successful ones use market segmentation to help them plan strategies, develop advertising and promotional plans, and evaluate the success of those plans. Market segmentation has been more widely used within the lodging segment of the industry, but it is employed just as effectively within the foodservice segment.

Gaining and maintaining a competitive advantage in the broad consumer market for foodservice or lodging is a very difficult task. It is much easier to be successful if one tries to carve out a smaller niche or segment of the market, in which one can establish a competitive uniqueness—hence, the development of market segmentation. Marketing managers have long used market segmentation to separate the market into smaller homogeneous groups. Therefore, a simple definition for *market segmentation* is pursuing a marketing strategy whereby the total potential market is divided into homogeneous subsets of customers, each of which responds differently to the marketing mix of the organization.

Figures 7.1, 7.2, 7.3, and 7.4 illustrate the concept of market segmentation. Figure 7.1 illustrates a market that is not segmented, one in which no attempt has been made to divide the entire market into homogeneous subsets. Figures 7.2 and 7.3 illustrate markets that have been segmented by age and annual income, respectively. Figure 7.4 illustrates a market that has been segmented using both age and income as criteria. It is, as this chapter

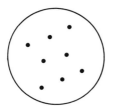

FIGURE 7.1
A Nonsegmented Market

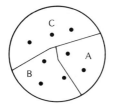

FIGURE 7.2
A Market Segmented with Age as the Criterion (A = 18–34, B = 35–49, C = above 49)

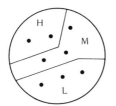

FIGURE 7.3
A Market Segmented by Annual Income (H = high, M = moderate, and L = low)

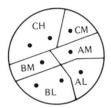

FIGURE 7.4
A Market Segmented by Annual Income and Age

will show, a common marketing practice to segment markets based on a variety of criteria.

Why segment the market? Many owners and managers of hospitality organizations, especially those that are independently owned, ask this question. Often, they believe that they are trying to appeal to all potential consumers and that by segmenting the market they will weaken their competitive position. They believe that if they segment the market and aim their marketing and promotional efforts squarely at a few segments, their sales volume will fall.

This approach really misses the reasons for segmentation. Segmentation, when done properly and when based on solid data, can actually improve sales and profits because it allows the organization to target specific market segments that are much more likely to patronize the organization's facilities. Segmentation is used to identify those market segments that are likely to be heavy users of the products and services. At the same time, segments that hold little potential receive little or no attention, and scarce marketing resources are not used chasing after market segments with little sales potential. The basic approach to segmentation is to put the resources where the markets are. Advertising dollars should not be allocated for attracting market segments that do not hold the potential for a substantial volume of business.

Marketing managers hold that no single homogeneous market exists for any product or service. This is also true of the hospitality industry. Think for a moment of McDonald's, Burger King, Steak and Ale, Red Lobster, T.G.I. Friday's, and Chi-Chi's. Initially, each may seem to be appealing to a mass market that includes nearly all consumers in the United States, but this is simply not the case. Each of these hospitality organizations has clearly defined several market segments as either primary or secondary. All of their marketing efforts evolve from their segmentation of the total market into clearly defined segments. For example, the television commercials run by the large hospitality chains are clearly aimed at specific target market segments, and the programs on which they appear are carefully chosen to deliver the largest number of individuals from the specific target markets and at the highest cost-efficiency. The fact that the programming aimed at children aired on Saturday morning is saturated with advertising by the fast-food companies is certainly no accident. These companies know that one of the best vehicles for reaching this potential market segment is to advertise on the Saturday morning children's programming. Advertising for fast-food restaurants is not different from that for any other product or service sold, in that the best method of advertising is via the medium that will provide the best access to those who are heavy users or purchasers of the product or service.

When the market is segmented, different product-service mixes can be promoted to meet the needs of the different segments. For example, a cocktail lounge manager may appeal to a variety of market segments by varying the type of entertainment offered. One manager in particular was able to increase sales volume by more than 40 percent simply by establishing specific nights of the week as "jazz night," "fifties night," "disco night," and "blues night." Each of these "nights" offered a specific type of entertainment that appealed to specific clientele. The approach proved to be very successful because the operator was able to attract many more customers. Within the lodging segment of the industry, hotels that cater to the business traveler are usually busy on Monday through Thursday night and are often quite slow on the weekends. Therefore, one of the advertising thrusts is toward those segments with the most potential for boosting weekend occupancy. Each hotel chain attempts to represent the total package of amenities, room, and food and beverage in an appealing manner. By attempting to appeal to those target segments seeking a get-away weekend or a mini vacation at a reduced price, the hotel is able to boost occupancy and total revenue during a time when the hotel would normally not be running at 100-percent occupancy.

Segmentation Variables

Five basic variables used by marketing managers typically segment consumer markets. These variables can be categorized as geographic, demographic, psychographic, behavioral, and benefit segmentation.

Geographic Variables.   A geographic variable, as the name implies, relates to the consumer's geographic area of residence. Markets are often segmented by region of the country, such as the New England, Mid-Atlantic, North Central, and Pacific regions. Segmentation is also often accomplished by examining the population of a given area. Several different terms are used to describe cities and metropolitan areas. The term *metropolitan statistical area* (MSA) describes small-to-medium-sized cities. The largest cities such as New York, Chicago, or Los Angeles are known as *consolidated metropolitan statistical areas* (CMSA's), while those cities inside the CMSA's are known as *primary standard metropolitan statistical areas* (PMSA's). To provide meaningful data for the very largest cities, it is necessary to have two sets of data. For example, it is possible to examine population and economic data related to the CMSA of New York, or any of the PMSA's included in the New York CMSA.

Geographic variables are used extensively by the print and broadcast media to define and describe their readers and audience. It is also vital to know from which geographic areas your business comes. For example, nearly 50 percent of all of the room nights in the hotel industry are generated by the top twenty-five CMSA's, PSMA's and MSA's. Segmenting a hotel's market based on the zip code origin of the guests is a very useful way to identify those areas that deserve the heaviest concentration of advertising, promotion, and personal solicitation.

Demographic Variables.   Markets are often segmented according to demographic variables. Demographic segmentation is based on statistical data related to such factors as age, sex, annual income, family size, stage in the family life cycle, educational level achieved, occupation, ethnic factors, religion, nationality, and social class. When the hospitality industry is considered in light of these variables, certain trends emerge. For example, different age groups are more likely to patronize specific types of operations. Young singles may be heavy users of high-energy lounges and health clubs, while married couples in their 40s and 50s are much more likely to belong to country clubs. As annual income increases, this normally is correlated with increased expenditures for travel and dining outside the home. Family size and stage in the family life cycle also influence dining habits. As family size increases, the number of times per week that the family dines outside the home decreases. As individuals and couples progress through the family life cycle, dining habits will change substantially. For example, couples with young children dine out less frequently than do other groups, such as older married couples without preschool children.

Segmentation by demographic variables is very common. It allows marketing managers accurately to describe the type of clientele desired. It is easily understood by nonmarketing managers as well. Demographic classifications are also widely used by various media to describe viewers, listeners, and readers. In this way a hospitality marketing manager can easily match the desired market segment with the most heavily used media, thereby increasing advertising effectiveness.

Psychographic Variables.   Psychographic variables are also commonly used to segment markets. *Psychographics* refer to segmentation based on life style, attitudes, and personality. Psychographics have the following characteristics:

☐ Generally, psychographics may be viewed as the practical application of the behavioral and social sciences to marketing research.

☐ More specifically, psychographics are quantitative research procedures that are indicated when demographic, socioeconomic, and user/nonuser analyses are not sufficient to explain and predict consumer behavior.

☐ Most specifically, psychographics seek to describe the human characteristics of consumers that may have bearing on their response to products, packaging, advertising, and public relations efforts. Such variables may span a spectrum from self-concept and life style to attitudes, interests, and opinions, as well as perceptions of product attributes.

Psychographics are used primarily to segment markets, but they can be used for other purposes as well. Psychographics are useful when selecting advertising vehicles, as the vehicle(s) selected can be matched with the interests, attitudes, and personalities of the target market segment. Psychographics are also helpful when designing the advertising itself. Illustrations, pictures, and the actual copy can be designed with the needs of a specific market segment in mind. By pinpointing the target market in this manner, the advertising and promotional efforts are likely to be more effective, thereby increasing sales and profits.

The division of the markets into segments is not based solely on easily quantified variables, such as age, sex, or income. Rather, the division is based on less easily defined factors, such as life style, attitudes, and personality.

Behavioral Variables.   The fourth segmentation variable is the behavioral variable. Behavioral segmentation focuses on the behavior that consumers exhibit in the marketplace. For example, what benefits do different consumers seek when dining out—economy, prestige, or convenience? How loyal are hospitality consumers? Are they easily swayed by the advertisements of competitors, or are they very loyal repeat patrons? How frequently do they dine out? Would they be considered light, medium, or heavy users of various types of hospitality facilities? What are their most commonly cited reasons for dining outside the home? When they travel on business, at what types of lodging facilities do they stay? When they travel for pleasure, do they stay at the same types of lodging facilities as when they travel on business?

One of the best uses of the behavioral variables is to identify those individuals who are heavy users—that is, to identify those who dine out very frequently or stay in hotels many more nights per year than the average person. If these individuals can be identified, then a plan can be formulated to aim more advertising and promotion in their direction. This is basically the strategy used by the airlines and hotels when they develop frequent flyer and frequent hotel guest programs. If the frequent traveler can be influenced to develop brand loyalty, the benefits to the hospitality organization can be tremendous.

Each year, more and more research is undertaken to understand more fully the field of consumer behavior. Potentially, behavioral variables represent an excellent segmentation tool, for as data are collected concerning the manner in which consumers actually behave in the marketplace, the information will allow hospitality managers to gain a better understanding of consumer behavior. As marketing managers better understand consumers, this will facilitate the development of product-service mixes that will better satisfy the needs of consumers. Selected aspects of consumer behavior are discussed in greater depth in Chapter 8.

Benefit Variables.   Finally, market segmentation can be based on the benefits that consumers are seeking. These benefits are expressions of the needs and wants of consumers. If management is fully able to appreciate and understand these needs and wants, then advertising can be pinpointed to discuss and to stress the benefits that the targeted market seeks. In this manner, consumer behavior can be influenced. Market research can identify the benefits that are important to various types of consumers. This marketing information allows management to segment the market based solely on benefits sought rather than on demographic, psychographic, or other variables. For example, those who value a fun-filled dining atmosphere as the most important benefit when dining out would be grouped together as a separate and unique market segment, regardless of other segmentation criteria. The challenge for the hospitality manager who uses this segmentation method is to link the benefits sought with the media used.

Criteria for Effective Segmentation

As hospitality marketing managers attempt to segment a given market, they have many methods from which to choose. As the segments are divided, however, how is a marketing manager to know whether a given segment holds significant potential? When any segmentation activities are undertaken, three criteria should be used to evaluate the market segments:

☐ Substantiality

☐ Measurability

☐ Accessibility

First, the size of the segment must be reasonably substantial. As the market is segmented, the hospitality manager manipulates the elements of the marketing mix, product-service mix, presentation mix, and communication mix to meet the needs of the individual segments. The size of each of these segments must be large enough to warrant this special attention. For example, segmenting the market into segments based on marital status and number of children seems logical because a substantial number of individuals would fall into each category. Segmenting a hospitality market into two segments for college graduates who had obtained master's degrees and those who had doctoral degrees would not be logical because the number of individuals in each of these categories would not be substantial.

Second, each of the segments should be measurable. The overall size of all segments should be measured in numbers as well as in purchasing power. Minimum cut-off points should be established relative to the size of the segments. If the number of consumers within a given segment falls below the cut-off point, segments can simply be combined.

Third, the segments must be accessible. It must be possible to reach the target market segments through advertising, promotion, and personal selling. Without accessibility, there is very little point to segmenting the market at all, as a major purpose for segmenting the market is to isolate viable segments of potential business and expose these segments to advertising, promotion, and personal selling related to specific aspects of the product-service mix. Without accessibility, this is not possible, and segmenting the market is of little value.

MEASURING DEMAND

Evaluating Market Segments

Determining the sales potential of a given market segment or an entire market for any given product-service mix is an extremely difficult task. Computer models and statistical approaches have facilitated the process somewhat, but it is still very difficult to account for all of the variables that can influence consumer demand. Even the best of forecasts may be subject to a margin of error of several percentage points in either direction. Obviously, other forecasts may be off the mark by a much greater margin, but management must have some knowledge of the level of market demand in order to plan for short- and long-term contingencies as well as day-to-day operations. Without reasonably accurate forecasts, management must operate "by the seat of the pants." The demands of the competitive situation in the hospitality industry today will not permit this casual approach.

Market demand can be defined as potential consumers having both purchasing power and motivation. This definition makes it easy to see that many variables can affect the demand within any given segment. Such variables as consumer motivation are often difficult to quantify. Market demand for a product or service is the total volume that would be bought by a clearly specified customer group in a defined geographic area in a defined period. Only when clear definitions are available for each of these variables can market demand be calculated precisely.

Forecasting Methods

It is not the purpose of this chapter to provide a complete discussion of forecasting methods. Rather, an overview will be provided. Additional information about forecasting demand will be presented in Chapter 13. Hospitality managers should be able to study a forecast and understand the basic methodological approach used.

The most common method used to forecast market demand is to base the expected future demand on the past sales histories. Guest histories and other historical information, as discussed in Chapters 5 and 6, serve as the foundation for accurate forecasting. This information asks such questions as "Where do our guests come from? How much do they spend? How often do they dine or stay with us? What types of specific advertising and promotions have the greatest appeal?" Forecasts based on this type of information are usually trend-line analysis.

Market demand for a new product-service mix is much more difficult to determine with any degree of certainty. The total potential market for any product or service is based on three factors:

1. The number of customers, given certain assumptions about the marketplace

2. The number of times the average customer will dine in the particular restaurant or stay in a particular hotel during a specified period of time

3. The average expenditure per person

For example, suppose that the total number of expected guests is 50,000, the average number of times per year in which a customer dined in a particular restaurant per year is four, and the average expenditure per person is $8.50. The total market demand would be $1,700,000, as shown in Figure 7.5.

Consumer surveys related to purchase intentions are also commonly used to determine market potential. These surveys are typically based on information related to past and anticipated consumer behavior. Consumers

Total market demand	=	Number of customers in market	×	Frequency of dining out in the specific foodservice operation	×	Average check per person
	=	50,000	×	4	×	$8.50
	=	$1,700,000				

FIGURE 7.5
Calculation of Total Market Demand

indicate how they have behaved in the past or what their purchasing intentions are for the future. While this method has the advantage of gaining information directly from consumers, it also has its drawbacks. For example, consumers may not accurately recall some of their past purchasing behaviors, or they may not actually behave in the manner they anticipate in the future. Also, they may not be entirely truthful—that is, they may respond by saying how they would like to behave, not how they actually will behave. If this occurs, the accuracy of the forecasts would be subject to error, and this is especially likely for hospitality customers. Purchasing decisions related to hospitality consumption are often impulse decisions without the amount of consideration that most consumers give, for example, to the purchase of an automobile. Because hospitality customers' decisions are often made "on the spur of the moment," it may be difficult for consumers to identify their future purchasing behavior accurately.

Expert opinion has a place in forecasting market demand. The opinions of experts are often the result of detailed study of such variables as economic effects and level of competition. Each year, forecasts are prepared by the leading hospitality industry trade journals, accounting firms, and professional associations. These forecasts make projections for specific geographic regions of the country and for the entire industry. These forecasts can be used as a gross estimation of future demand. Expert opinion may also be available through workshops and seminars. Expert opinion can be collected fairly quickly and at a relatively low cost. Data of this type may, however, be subject to error. Such data are more reliable for aggregate forecasting rather than for forecasts related to geographic areas and specific hospitality operations.

Another commonly used method for developing sales forecasts is test-marketing. This method allows management to gauge consumer purchasing behavior on a limited basis within a small-scale test area. The design of the test-market study can be very complex, so it must be well planned. The following are questions to consider when planning test-marketing:

☐ *How many test sites should be selected?* As more sites are used, the accuracy of data will increase, but the time and expense of establishing test-market sites should be weighed carefully.

☐ *What sites should be selected?* No one site is perfect, but the sites selected should represent the larger market.

☐ *For how long should test marketing be conducted?* To measure accurately not only initial purchase rates but also repeat patronage, the test-market study will need to be run for a reasonable length of time.

☐ *What information is desired?* As with any research study, clearly defined objectives are needed before initiating the study.

☐ *What action should be taken?* Data supplied by the market test should give some clue as to the market potential of the product or service. Rates of initial purchase and repeat patronage are useful, as are other forms of data. Management must, of course, still make the hard decisions.

Test-marketing is a very useful tool to forecast total market demand based on a small-scale setting. Many extraneous and often uncontrollable variables, however, can influence the test-marketing activities of the organization. These variables might, for example, include any of the variables present in the environment—economic, social, technological, or competitive trends.

Finally, a wide variety of statistical approaches can be used. These methods include many sophisticated approaches using computer resources, and they allow management to isolate single variables and determine the impact that changes in each variable will have on total market demand.

Determining total market demand is an important marketing function because so many other assumptions are based on its forecast. Hospitality managers should be able to examine forecasts for market demand and understand their uses and limitations.

TWO CONSUMER MARKETS WITH EXCELLENT GROWTH POTENTIAL

Until recently, the marketing efforts of many hospitality organizations were based on the assumptions that (1) the primary target markets are under 40 years of age, (2) marketing efforts should be aimed at males, and (3) the emphasis should be on youth and the image of youth. For many operations, these assumptions are normally successful, but the hospitality industry has, for the most part, ignored two potentially important markets. These are (1) working women and (2) those individuals over the age of 55.

Working Women and Women Business Travelers

It is very easy to fall into the trap of stereotyping individuals—placing people in categories based on personal attitudes and perceptions and assuming that individuals fit into a mold. Stereotypes can be very dangerous to the marketing manager, for they often cloud perceptions of reality and cause major errors in judgment.

Within the American lifestyle, a quiet revolution has taken shape. Women are working outside their homes in greater numbers each year, and this is having a major impact on the hospitality industry. Comparing the number of women working outside the home now with the number of homemakers points up a marked contrast with the early 1970s. In 1971, homemakers outnumbered working women, but now, more than 55 percent of women are working.

There are several reasons for the growth in the number of working women. Economic motivation is, of course, very strong. In lower economic groups, the economic motivation is simply to "make ends meet," or to survive. The working woman often heads a household or finds that two incomes are needed to maintain a standard of living. In higher-income groups, the woman's salary increases the standard of living, thereby allowing the household to engage in discretionary activities such as traveling or dining outside the home more frequently.

Personal motivation is also very strong for many women. Many women engage in employment simply to have a job, but an increasingly large percentage of women are engaged in career advancement. This is especially true of those individuals who are college graduates, as college-educated people are more likely to have a career orientation. In addition to a career orientation, personal motivation for many women is manifested through a desire for broadening horizons, contributing to self-image, and gaining a sense of satisfaction.

In addition to more women being active in the labor force, another trend is an increase in the number of women who are traveling as a part of their job requirements. As recently as the 1970s, women business travelers represented less than 1 percent of the business travelers; today they make up over 30 percent of the business travel market segment.

Various hotel chains have tried different approaches to appeal to the female traveler, including special rooms or floors for female travelers and providing extra amenities for women.

Research conducted by Beattie and Beggs, reported in *The Practice of Hospitality Management II*, indicates that the needs of this group do not differ from those of business travelers in general. Rather, providing the basics in both product and especially service will meet their needs. It is interesting to note the factors that they consider to be important when selecting a hotel: (1) service, (2) physical attributes of the room and bath, (3) reservation system, (4) security inside the hotel, (5) quick check-in/check-out, (6) image, and (7) price/value relationship.

It is also interesting to note the attributes that female travelers considered to be among the least important. They include (1) separate guest floor for business women only, (2) separate business section of the hotel, (3) availability of special business services such as secretarial or telex services, (4) special check-in desk for business travelers, (5) VIP or luxury rooms, (6) special female amenities such as skirt hangers, curling irons, and makeup mirrors.

The female business traveler segment is growing at a rate that is much greater than that for travel in general or even business travel. Those who seek to gain a greater share of this growing market should make efforts to extend to all business travelers the same products and services. It would appear that those who have tried to provide specifically for the needs of female business travelers have not been as successful as those who strive to deliver the basics of a high quality and consistent product and service to the broader segment of business travelers.

Individuals over 55

A second major market with tremendous growth potential for the hospitality industry consists of those individuals over the age of 55. The so-called greying of America is now well under way. Each year, those individuals over the age of 55 make up an ever-increasing percentage of the total population. These individuals represent a market segment that is growing roughly 2.5 times faster than the youth market.

Three major factors will influence the attractiveness and potential of this market: (1) economics, (2) available time, and (3) satisfactory health. As long as this group is able to satisfy these three factors, it will represent a very significant target market. Several characteristics of those over 55 should be considered by the marketing manager:

☐ Individuals over 55 are normally still actively working and have reached the highest levels of their working careers. After twenty to thirty years in the work force, they have "made it." This results in higher salaries and increased status, which allow for more travel and dining outside the home.

☐ Often, individuals over 55 have seen their children become more independent and/or leave home. They now have more free time than those with younger children. This increase in available time makes this market an excellent prospect for the hospitality industry. After many years of providing for their children, those over 55 who no longer have this responsibility often indulge themselves. They have a very high level of discretionary income.

☐ Finally, those over 55 should not be viewed as social and economic outcasts, for they often have adopted the values and life styles of younger target markets.

Those individuals who have retired make up another viable part of this growing market. While they may not be as flashy as other segments, such as the business expense account traveler, this segment represents some very solid growth and financial potential. There are several important characteristics to consider.

First, senior citizens do not represent "big spenders." Rather, they will make up in volume for this. They tend to stay at one location longer and will also travel during times when business might otherwise be slow. This can be particularly helpful during the shoulder travel seasons which precede and follow the peak travel seasons.

Second, senior citizens are quite loyal to a particular brand of product or service. In this day of limited brand loyalty, it is nice to know that once you have won this group over, they will continue to stay and dine with you.

Third, they tend not to be on the leading edge of trends and new concepts. This can be particularly important in the foodservice segment of the business. They will stick with a known concept and not be as tempted to run off to something new just to try it.

Finally, they have a tremendous potential to spend money within the hospitality industry. They have few financial obligations such as mortgages and they have a great deal of discretionary income to spend. They tend to be frugal, and will seek out those who provide a high level of perceived value.

Hospitality managers should look beyond traditionally targeted markets to achieve the highest degree of success possible. Such markets as women business travelers and individuals over 55 need to be explored to the fullest possible extent. Each hospitality operation must find a market niche in which to achieve success, for attempting to appeal to vast market segments is not likely to lead to success. A simple process that allows a hospitality manager to reformulate targeted markets follows:

☐ *Step 1: Reexamine the assumed market.* A manager would be wise to look closely at the market segments to which the hospitality operation is addressing its efforts. Attention should be paid to changes in values, attitudes, and life styles. Both primary and secondary data should be examined.

☐ *Step 2: Evaluate the market potential of new target markets.* All potentially target markets should be examined objectively to determine whether the potential is significant enough to warrant active solicitation.

☐ *Step 3: Develop a fresh perspective.* Old ideas and thought patterns may need to be discarded so that new ideas and outlooks may be adopted. An organization needs to develop a fresh perspective if it is to succeed.

☐ *Step 4: Explore the attitudes and needs of the new group.* This involves data collected from specially target markets, as discussed in Chapter 4.

☐ *Step 5: Redefine marketing targets.* Based on the appraisal of potential markets and the performance of existing markets, a shift in focus may be justified. Two cautions need to be considered: (1) "He who hesitates is lost," meaning that failure to move toward new markets may result in a lost opportunity; and (2) abandoning a successful target market for other potential markets may also result in failure, or "A bird in the hand is worth two in the bush."

Successful management of a hospitality operation, like the management of any business concern, requires decision making in an uncertain world. It is impossible to comprehend all the aspects of consumer behavior, but to make consistently high-quality decisions, management needs to use information, experience, and intuition.

POSITIONING THE PRODUCT-SERVICE MIX

Positioning Defined

What does it mean to position the product-service mix? Of what value is positioning to hospitality managers? Positioning the product-service mix involves two important considerations: (1) the consumer's perception of the major subjective attributes of the product-service mix, and (2) the distinction, if any, between this perception and reality. Unlike tangible physical products, such as automobiles and washing machines, which are "owned," the product-service mix of a hospitality organization is purchased and consumed simultaneously. It is a blend of both tangibles and intangibles, but the mix itself is largely intangible.

Three key elements should be considered when positioning decisions are made. They are (1) the perceived image of the organization, (2) the benefits offered by the organization, and (3) the product-service mix differentiation. First, positioning a hospitality organization entails establishing and measuring the consumers' perceived image of the organization. This image can be either positive or negative. It can accurately reflect the nature of the organization's product-service mix, or it may be inaccurate. The most important thing for hospitality managers to remember is that in order to position the operation's product-service mix successfully, a clearly perceived image must be established in the consumer's mind. Another aspect of the positioning of the product-service mix that management should consider is that the perceived image alone does not lead to purchasing behavior. Consumers simply hold a perception of the organization, and this image, no matter how positive, will not by itself lead to increased sales.

Second, management should carefully inventory all of the benefits offered by the organization. Because one of the methods used to segment a market concerns the benefits sought by consumer, it is the benefit dimensions that are the key to increasing sales, although perceived image, the first element, is important. Simply stated, consumers look at any hospitality organization's product-service mix and ask, "What will this hospitality operation do for me? Why should I select this hotel instead of another?" All consumers have needs and wants that they seek to satisfy, and they select hotels and restaurants with the expectation that these needs will be satisfied. The important thing for hospitality marketing managers is to package the benefits offered clearly, to demonstrate to sometimes-wary consumers that the organization can and will satisfy their needs and will meet or exceed consumer expectations. All advertising should emphasize these benefits and offer support. This support must convince consumers that they will indeed receive the stated benefits. The hospitality marketing manager must also work closely with the managers responsible for operations to ensure that the product-service mix and benefit package are delivered as promised. Nothing will undercut the efforts of a hospitality marketing effort more quickly than failure to deliver the product-service mix as promised through advertising and promotion. In fact, it is best to underpromise and over deliver.

This situation is clearly demonstrated within large hotels. Suppose that the sales and marketing staff makes a promise or a commitment to a meeting planner to provide a specific service to the convention group. The meeting planner assumes that the promise will be fulfilled, and likely communicates to the larger group about how the hotel will be providing something extra special just for them. Imagine how disappointed they will be if the hotel fails to deliver on its promise. It is vital that the communications link between the sales and marketing and operations staffs be maintained at peak efficiency. No hotel or restaurant can afford to have even small lapses in communication when it is trying to satisfy the needs of guests.

Third, the positioning statement should differentiate the organization's product-service mix from that of direct and indirect competition. For many years, hotels and restaurants have advertised and promoted "fine food," "prompt, courteous service," "elegant atmosphere," "first-class accommodations," and "top-flight entertainment." As might be expected, these promotional approaches are not as effective as they might be. Consumers usually do not believe these statements because they have heard them many times before and have often been disappointed when they patronized the properties that had advertised. Also, these statements do little to separate the organization's product-service mix from that of the direct and indirect competition. If other hospitality organizations are promoting "fine food" or similar benefits, then all the advertising is basically the same. The key to success in positioning is to establish some unique element of the product-service mix and promote it. This allows management to differentiate the product-service mix from that of the competition and thereby gain a competitive advantage. This approach is known as establishing a unique selling proposition, or USP. With a USP, every effort should be made to link the benefits with tangible aspects of the product-service mix. In this way, consumers have something tangible with which to associate the hospitality operation.

Three examples of this approach are shown by advertising campaigns run by Miller Lite Beer, Burger King, and Wendy's. Miller introduced a light beer product into the national marketplace, but they faced a real challenge. How do you market a low-calorie beer when there doesn't seem to be any real market for it? They sought to position the product as unique, with the positioning statement "Everything you've always wanted in a beer. And less." Those few simple words said it all. Success and the market share lead in the light beer market soon followed.

Burger King and Wendy's took similar approaches in successfully attacking McDonald's. Both of these companies felt that they had a superior product and sought a way to differentiate themselves from others in the fast-food segment. Both sought positioning statements that would allow them to do so. Wendy's used the now-famous Clara Peller to bellow, "Where's the beef?" Burger King used the Burger King challenge, with the positioning statement that "Broiling Beats Frying." Since their advertising campaigns, McDonald's has asserted itself more forcefully and remains the market leader.

A useful approach to take when trying to determine what the USP or differentiation should be is to construct a matrix, as shown in Figure 7.6. When the relative strengths and weaknesses of each of the major competitors are closely examined, the benefits or attributes that may be used to successfully differentiate may become more evident.

Positioning is a very important aspect of the marketing efforts of any hospitality organization. The positioning statement, and thus the advertising message, should clearly reflect image, benefit package and support, and differentiation of the product-service mix. Only when all three of these elements are reflected in the advertising and promotion of the organization can the full potential of the organization be realized. The positioning

Potential Benefits	Own Operation	Competitor A	Competitor B
Price			
Physical facilities			
Service			
Quality of rooms			
Quality of food			
Quality of beverages			
Entertainment			
Recreation			
Location			
Amenities			
Total meeting space			
Break out rooms			
Board rooms			
Audiovisual equipment			
Other attributes			

FIGURE 7.6
Benefit Matrix of Competition

statement should be supported with tangible clues, rather than the intangible and ineffective "fine food" or "excellent service," for this will add credibility to the advertising message.

Constructing the Space of the Product-Service Mix

A technique that has enjoyed wide acceptance is the use of spatial models or maps to represent the product space. These maps, based on statistics such as multiple discriminant analysis, represent a graphic representation of the various product-service mixes perceived by consumers. These consumer perceptions can be based on a wide variety of criteria or variables. The purposes for using spatial product-service maps follow:

- ☐ To learn how the strengths, weaknesses, and similarities of the different product-service mixes are perceived

- ☐ To learn about consumers' desires and how these are satisfied or not satisfied by the current products and services in the market

- ☐ To integrate these findings strategically to determine the greatest opportunities for new product-service mixes and how a product or service's image should be modified to produce the greatest sales gain

Figure 7.7 provides a hypothetical example of a product-service market map. This market map has been constructed based on two variables: the perceived quality of the product-service mix, and the perceived value provided by the product-service mix. A considerable amount of consumer research must be done before a map of this type can be constructed. The following are questions for which marketing managers typically seek answers:

- ☐ How do consumers perceive the existing product-service mixes available in the marketplace? These product-service mixes can be evaluated for a wide variety of variables, including price, value, atmosphere, product quality, service quality, entertainment, and level of prestige.

- ☐ How does my product-service mix compare to the product-service mix of direct and indirect competitors?

- ☐ What benefits are consumers considering when judging the similarities and dissimilarities among the various product-service mixes?

- ☐ How does my product-service mix compare with the consumers' perceptions of the "ideal" product-service mix?

- ☐ Are there areas within the product-service map for which there is significant consumer demand but no real offering in the prod-

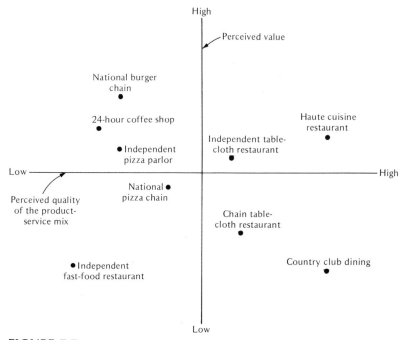

FIGURE 7.7
A Marketing Map for a Product-Service Mix

uct-service mix? This would indicate significant demand for which no product-service offers were available.

Several methods can be used to construct a product-service marketing
map. Among the most common methods are similarity/dissimilarity data,
preference data, and attribute data. Similarity/dissimilarity data are concerned
with consumers' perceptions of the attributes of the product-service mix.
Consumers are asked to compare and contrast a variety of product-service
mixes. For example, consumers might be given the names of three restaurants
and asked to select the two that are most similar.

Preference data involve asking consumers to indicate their ideal facilities
or preferences for specific types of hospitality operations. They might be asked
to rank-order a list of restaurants or rate a specific restaurant on a 1–10 scale.

Attribute data involve the marketing manager's determining in advance
the attributes of the product-service mix that consumers value (a judgment
normally based on previous research). The marketing manager might then
ask consumers to rate a given restaurant based on a series of attributes.

These approaches enable the marketing manager to understand the
various market segments more fully. The techniques used require statistical
techniques, such as multiple discriminant analysis, multidimensional scaling,
and factor analysis.

What are the managerial implications of using product-service market maps? Management can use these maps in several ways. First, market maps are used to determine the position in the market that will produce the largest dollar volume of sales and profits. Second, market maps are often used to help management decide how the product-service marketing mix might be changed or modified to improve the level of consumer satisfaction and to increase sales and profits. Third, these maps are used to indicate marketing opportunities where consumer needs are not currently being satisfied by competitors. This approach assists management in developing new product-service mixes.

Developing the Positioning Statement

It is quite easy to look at the positioning statements developed by other companies and evaluate whether they are excellent, very good or not so good. This is especially easy when we are able to do this from a hindsight perspective. We can see whether they were as successful as their creators had hoped that they would be. Actually developing the positioning statement is a very difficult task. It requires a very keen mind, a great deal of insight and creativity, and an excellent perspective of the competitive marketplace.

Perhaps the best set of guidelines for generating a positioning statement has been developed by Al Ries and Jack Trout in *Positioning: The Battle for Your Mind*. They have formulated six questions that are used to guide thinking.

1. *What position do you own?* It is critical that you look at the marketplace and your image from the consumer's point of view. How do consumers view you? What image do you have in their minds? Keep in mind that you must be honest, and must look at it from their perspective, as they see you and not as you would like to be seen.

If you don't know what image the consumer holds, an investment for marketing research would be well spent. Before you begin to develop a solid positioning statement, it is imperative to know the image that consumers have of you.

2. *What position do you want?* Remember that those who are most successful tend to carve out a niche of the broad market. Those who attempt be all things to all people often are not successful. Keep in mind what is within your capabilities. You must be able to "own" the position, even if that means displacing someone else who occupies the place now. Being the best or the finest may not be the best positioning statement. Both Avis and 7-Up developed very successful advertising campaigns around a position other than being the market leader.

3. *Who must you outgun?* No positioning statement is created in a vacuum. You must clearly visualize the positions held by the major competitors. Do they have a firm lock on their positions, or are they vulnerable? It is wise to avoid a direct frontal attack if they are strong; it's better to go around them.

4. *Do you have enough money?*   Establishing and maintaining an image in the consumers' mind is no small task. Every day we are exposed to hundreds of advertising images. If a change in positioning strategy is planned, then the necessary marketing resources must be appropriated if the change is to be successful.

5. *Can you stick it out?*   A key to successful positioning is to stick with a position that is successful. The most successful companies don't change their position, only the short-term tactics they use to communicate the position.

6. *Do you match your position?*   Creativity and flair are great, but it is critical that the exact positioning statement be communicated in the advertising and promotions that follow. The style of the advertising and promotion needs to follow the positioning statement. It is also critical that the operation of the hotel or restaurant match the positioning statement that the organization uses. If they don't match, the consumers will end up being confused and will likely take their business elsewhere.

SUMMARY

This chapter focuses upon market segmentation and positioning. Market segmentation involves considering several segmentation variables as well as segmentation criteria. Segmentation variables include geographic, demographic, psychographic, behavioral and benefit. Criteria for effective segmentation are (1) substantiality, (2) measurability, and (3) accessibility.

Positioning of the product-service mix involves consideration of three separate elements: (1) the perceived image of the organization, (2) the benefits offered by the organization, and (3) the differentiation of the product-service mix. Constructing the space of a product-service mix involves market maps, which allow management to visualize the market. Maps can be used to pinpoint marketing opportunities, and they carry many other managerial implications.

The measurement of market demand includes several methods used to forecast market demand. Today's marketing managers should also consider markets less often targeted when reviewing forecasts and determining marketing strategy. Marketing managers often find success by carving out a small market niche in which the intensity of competition is reduced.

KEY WORDS AND CONCEPTS

- ☐ Segmentation variables, geographic, demographic, psychographic, behavioral, and benefit
- ☐ Metropolitan statistical areas (MSA's)
- ☐ Segmentation criteria, substantiality, measurability, and accessibility
- ☐ Forecasting
- ☐ Test-marketing
- ☐ Women business travelers
- ☐ Shoulder season
- ☐ Off-season
- ☐ In-season
- ☐ Greying of America
- ☐ Positioning
- ☐ Product-service mix differentiation
- ☐ Unique selling proposition (USP)
- ☐ Benefit matrix
- ☐ Positioning statement

Questions for Review and Discussion

1. What is market segmentation?
2. Of what value is market segmentation to management?
3. Cite and discuss the criteria for effective segmentation.
4. Cite examples for each of the segmentation variables.
5. Is it possible to oversegment a market? Why or why not?
6. Define positioning. Use examples of hospitality firms to illustrate your point.
7. Of what value to management are product-service market maps?
8. By what methods can management measure market demand?

CHAPTER 8

Understanding the Behavior of Hospitality Consumers

Marketing managers in other industries have for many years understood their consumers very clearly. A great deal of in-depth research has allowed those responsible for marketing tangible products such as automobiles, toothpaste, laundry detergent, and most other products and services to understand the consumers who purchase these products. More recently, marketers have begun to better understand the subject of consumer behavior as it relates to the consumption of services. This knowledge enables marketing managers to develop sophisticated marketing programs aimed at very specific targeted market segments.

One of the most perplexing problems confronting hospitality managers is trying to understand why hospitality consumers behave as they do. This chapter explores several important aspects of consumer behavior.

The chapter is divided into the following major sections:

INTRODUCTION

A CONTEMPORARY CONSUMER DECISION-MAKING MODEL
☐ Extrinsic Influences on Consumer Behavior
☐ Intrinsic Influences on Consumer Behavior
☐ Understanding Consumer Decision Making

MODELS OF CONSUMER BEHAVIOR
☐ Seeking Innovators and Early Adopters
☐ The Uses of Models
☐ Marshallian Economic Model
☐ Pavlovian Learning Model
☐ Veblenian Sociopsychological Model
☐ The Howard-Sheth Model of Buyer Behavior
☐ The Nicosia Model

CONSUMER SATISFACTION IN THE HOSPITALITY INDUSTRY
☐ Techniques to Assess Consumer Satisfaction
☐ The Most Common Reasons for Consumer Dissatisfaction
☐ Foodservice Dissatisfiers
☐ Lodging Dissatisfiers

SUMMARY

KEY WORDS AND CONCEPTS

QUESTIONS FOR REVIEW AND DISCUSSION

INTRODUCTION

Understanding the behavior of those consumers who consume hospitality products and services is among the most important challenges that management faces. It is critical that managers be in close touch with those who consume the products and services, and keep a finger on the consumers' pulse so that they will be ready to change the product-service mix when the consumers' tastes shift in another direction.

The study of consumer behavior is really the study of humans when they purchase products or services. This behavior takes place within the larger context of society. Therefore, in studying consumer behavior we must closely examine the role and influence that others have on the behavior of consumers. Contrary to what some may think, the behavior of consumers is not random. Their behavior can be described and to some extent it can be predicted. Certainly, the study of consumer behavior is based to a large extent on theory. However, this theory can be used to understand and predict the future behavior of consumers.

Human behavior is influenced by several factors, including the following:

☐ *The social setting.* All consumers make decisions and take actions within the larger social setting. In doing so, their actions are influenced by others and they in turn will influence the actions of other consumers. Social settings will vary greatly. For example the social setting of a consumer living in New York City is much different from someone living in Ames, Iowa.

☐ *Social forces.* Forces within the society set the standards of acceptable behavior. These rules are both written and unwritten. These rules are established by those within the society with the most influence.

☐ *Roles.* A role is a pattern of behavior associated with a specific position within a social setting. Each of us assumes a variety of roles, some professional and others personal. Each of these roles brings with it a set of expectations for behavior.

☐ *Attitudes and knowledge relative to roles.* Within each of the roles that we play there are attitudes and knowledge that we gain about the setting. Attitudes are defined as predispositions about objects, while knowledge is facts about objects. Attitudes and knowledge are directly tied to a consumer's needs. These needs, which are the cause for all consumer behavior, are linked to an individual's attitudes and knowledge.[1]

Why study consumer behavior? The study of consumer behavior is critical to the future success of all hospitality consumers. Each and every day, a manager in the hospitality industry comes into direct contact with many consumers. One of the primary goals for each of these managers is to create and foster satisfied consumers. Without a working knowledge of the wants and needs of these consumers, it will be much more difficult to satisfy them. Keep in mind that the sole reason for being in business is to create and foster satisfied consumers.

Second, if a company is to grow and prosper it must anticipate the future needs and wants of consumers. For example, if a hospitality company is considering whether to build a new hotel, it must look into the future and anticipate the demand for hotel rooms, meeting space, and food and beverage for a particular location for several years. One of the ways to help make a better decision in this case is to more thoroughly understand the current and perhaps future behavior of consumers.

A CONTEMPORARY CONSUMER DECISION-MAKING MODEL

When consumers make decisions concerning the purchase of goods and services, a very complex decision-making process takes place. Numerous variables influence this decision-making process, as the many models of consumer behavior demonstrate. Figure 8.1 draws together several theories into a contemporary model that shows both extrinsic and intrinsic influences on consumer behavior.

This model illustrates the two major components of the decision-making process—*extrinsic influences,* or those external to or outside the individual, and *intrinsic influences,* or those internal to the individual.

Extrinsic Influences on Consumer Behavior

Culture is the first of four major extrinsic influences. It is defined as those patterns of behavior and social relations that characterize a society and separate it from others. It is important in viewing culture to draw legitimate generalizations about a given culture or subculture without resorting to stereotyping all its members. An individual's culture serves to provide a frame of reference concerning acceptable behaviors, and as such, culture is a learned set of arbitrary values. The dominant culture in the United States today stresses equality, use of resources, materialism, individualism, and youth.

In addition to the general culture of the United States, marketing must also be concerned with subcultures. Subcultures might include the black subculture, the Jewish subculture, the youth subculture, and the Chicano

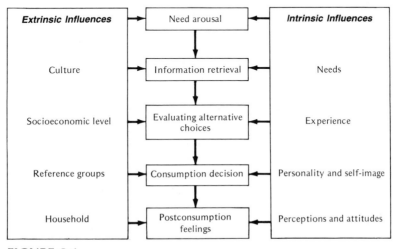

FIGURE 8.1
A Contemporary Consumer Decision-Making Model

subculture. One example illustrates the importance of subcultures in marketing. All of the fast-food chains are patronized by families, and parents pay the bills for the family. Much of the advertising for these chains, however, is aimed not at the parents who pay the bill but directly at the youth subculture. Research has shown that it is often the children who decide where the family will go to eat, once the adults have decided to dine out.

Second, socioeconomic level is a large influence in consumer decision making. Marketing managers have long attempted to correlate socioeconomic class with dining-out habits and travel patterns. Hospitality managers must identify the relative socioeconomic groups to which the operation appeals and must then appeal directly to those groups with elements of the product-service mix.

Third, reference groups exert tremendous influence on consumers' hotel and restaurant purchase decisions. Every individual is influenced directly and indirectly. Marketing research has identified three types of reference groups: comparative, status, and normative. Individual consumers use reference groups to compare their own feelings and thoughts with those of others. For example, an individual may have gone to dinner at a restaurant and felt that the food and service were excellent. Before these perceptions are internalized, however, a reference group is often consulted to validate the perceptions.

Reference groups also serve a status function. For example, when an individual seeks to become a member of a group, his or her actions are likely to emulate the group members' behaviors. Finally, reference groups serve to establish norms and values that regulate the behavior of individuals. For example, consider a high school-age reference group dining out. The group norm may state that patronizing chain restaurant A is more desirable than going to locally owned restaurant B, yet objective analysis indicates that restaurant B's product-service mix is superior. The group's norms and values might still point toward the established chain restaurant.

A hospitality manager can also influence consumer behavior through the use of opinion leaders. Opinion leaders are the formal and/or informal leaders of reference groups, and their opinions normally influence opinion formation in others. Common opinion leaders are leaders within the community, such as doctors, lawyers, and politicians.

Hospitality managers often strive to create their own reference groups and opinion leaders within the operation. Frequently, repeat customers can be rewarded with complimentary samples of new menu items or perhaps a complimentary flambé dessert. The flambé dessert creates excitement and is very likely to increase sales, as individuals sitting at other tables want to become part of the excitement and often order one for their own table. The desired result is of course a snowball effect among many tables, which results in increased sales.

The fourth extrinsic influence is the household. A household is defined as those individuals who occupy a single living unit. There are over 70 million households in the United States, and within every household are certain characteristics, leadership, and norms. Leadership is normally rotated among members of the household. For example, the children may decide which breakfast cereal to eat or which fast-food restaurant to patronize, while the mother and father jointly select the type of living accommodations. Hospitality market research points out that leadership is often shared. For example, the parents normally decide when the household will go out to eat, but it is the children who decide the place to go.

All extrinsic influences affect the decision-making process of a consumer whenever a choice among hospitality operations is made. The culture, socio-economic level, reference groups, and household influence both directly and indirectly, consciously and unconsciously, the dining habits of all consumers.

Intrinsic Influences on Consumer Behavior

In addition to their extrinsic influences, consumers are influenced by personal needs, experience, personality and self-image, and perceptions and attitudes. The first intrinsic influence, needs, is very difficult to understand. Despite many years of research into consumer behavior, no one has been able to explain all consumers' needs successfully. Figure 8.2 illustrates the role of needs in consumer behavior. Simply stated, needs lead to motivation, which leads to behavioral intentions, which finally lead to behavior.

Following behavior, feedback affects and may change a consumer's motivation. Maslow identified five needs arranged in the following hierarchy: physiological needs, safety needs, love needs, esteem needs, and self-actualization needs. Maslow's theory holds that individuals strive to satisfy unmet needs. As lower-order needs (physiological needs and safety) are satisfied, they no longer motivate, and as a result, the individual moves up the hierarchy, attempting to satisfy unmet needs at a higher level. When a hospitality operation is marketed, efforts should be made to aim promotional efforts at several levels of need. For example, four-color photography with rich descriptions may appeal directly to the physiological need of hunger. Another appeal to needs is the promotion of cleanliness and sanitation in appealing to the safety needs of consumers; early promotional efforts by

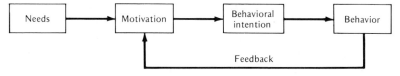

FIGURE 8.2
Needs Related to Consumer Behavior

fast-food chains emphasized this. Finally, higher-priced restaurants often emphasize service and atmosphere in appealing to the esteem needs of consumers. It is important that hospitality operators be aware of the various consumer needs and design marketing programs that address unmet needs.

McClelland[2] identified three social motives: achievement, affiliation, and power. Numerous advertising and promotional programs have been directly aimed at these motives.

Experience is also a major intrinsic influence on consumer behavior. As individuals confront novel situations, such as dining in a restaurant for the first time, they integrate their perceptions into an experience framework that influences future decisions. The old phrase "first impressions are important" applies directly to the hospitality industry, for if consumers are "turned off" the first time that they walk up to the front desk or meet the host at a restaurant, they are not likely to return. Hospitality managers must remember that consumers are in large part a product of their environments. Each new experience is integrated into a "frame of reference" against which novel situations are evaluated. This frame of reference includes beliefs, values, norms, and assumptions.

A third intrinsic influence is personality and self-image. Each individual consumer develops a unique personality and self-image over a period of time. For marketing, personality types can be grouped into various classifications: swingers, conservatives, leaders, and followers. The important thing for hospitality managers to remember is that no hospitality operation can be all things to all people. Each operation must single out a segment of the total market and then appeal directly to these consumers. These groups are known as target market segments. Many hospitality organizations experience difficulty when attempting to appeal to too wide a segment of the population or total market. The result is quite predictable: failure to satisfy any of the target market segments, which results in poor financial performance and often failure.

One example of this type of thinking involved a restaurant that featured a beef and seafood menu, with moderate to high prices and semiformal atmosphere. This restaurant had been fairly successful, but the owners and managers felt that more profits should and could be generated. In an attempt to broaden the target market, the atmosphere was made more informal, and the menu was changed to include hamburgers, snacks, sandwiches, and pizza as well as steaks and seafood. Thirty days after the change was made, volume had increased by 15 percent. Within three months, however, volume had fallen by 38 percent, and what had once been a profitable operation was now running in the red. Following careful examination of the performance of several hospitality organizations, one finds that it is normally those with well-defined target markets that are the most successful. Those attempting to be "all things to all people," however, often fail.

The final intrinsic influence is perception and attitudes. Each day, consumers are exposed to thousands of stimuli. Some of these stimuli are consciously received, resulting in a thought process, while others are simply ignored. The process by which stimuli are recognized, received, and thought about is termed *perception*. Each individual consumer perceives the world differently. Perceptions are manifested in attitudes. For example, some individuals' attitudes are that fast-food meals are very good because they are of high quality and low cost and offer fast and courteous service. Other individuals' attitudes are that fast-food meals are of low nutritional value and poor culinary quality and are not visually attractive. Both types of individuals hold attitudes based on their perceptions. Their perceptions may or may not be valid, but it is important for the marketing manager to remember that perceptions are the way an individual sees the world. In the mind of the individual consumer, the perceptions and resulting attitudes are correct and valid.

Understanding Consumer Decision Making

Because both extrinsic and intrinsic variables influence the decision-making processes of consumers, hospitality managers need to develop awareness of the specific influences most important to their particular target market segments. Figure 8.1 shows five key elements in the decision-making model: need arousal, information retrieval, evaluating alternative choices, consumption decision, and postconsumption feelings. Each of these elements is affected by extrinsic and intrinsic influences.

The decision-making process begins with need arousal. Thousands of different stimuli can trigger the awareness of a need. For example, if one feels hungry when driving down an interstate highway, this may trigger a need to seek a restaurant to satisfy the hunger need. In another situation, the need to feel important and be treated with the utmost of respect may lead a consumer to seek an upscale hotel with a concierge floor when making a reservation. The need may not begin within the individual; for example, if a couple comes home after both have worked all day, and one says to the other, "Let's go out tonight; I'm too tired to cook," this manifests a joint need that only one of the two individuals may have felt. Hospitality marketing managers should recognize the wide variety of needs that consumers are attempting to satisfy when they dine out.

Once the need is raised to a conscious level, the model holds that consumers seek to retrieve information. This information can come from a variety of sources, including reference groups and members of the immediate household, as well as the mass media in the form of advertising. If the felt need is as basic as the need to eat because of hunger, the information-retrieval process is likely to be brief; the restaurant facility selected in this case is likely to be chosen primarily because of convenience, and the number of sources of information consulted is likely to be quite small. In other situations, the number of sources consulted could be much larger. Consider the professional association meeting planner who is coordinating the annual meeting for the association. This individual is likely to consult several sources of information before selecting an appropriate hotel for this important event. The important thing for the hospitality marketing manager to remember is that consumers rely to a certain extent on the mass media for information.

Once the consumer has gathered a sufficient amount of information, the third element in the decision-making process is to evaluate alternative choices. Consumers who ask, "At which one of several possible restaurants should I dine tonight?" go through a cognitive process in answering this question, whereby they weigh the positive and negative aspects of each alternative. They also examine the attributes of the product-service mix of each restaurant. Consumers consider the relative importance of each attribute of the product-service mix by asking themselves how important each particular attribute is.

Marketing managers in other industries have long recognized this cognitive process and have used it to advantage in advertising and promoting their products and services. Rather than simply discussing their products or services as if these existed in a vacuum, they make direct comparisons with the competition. This assists the consumer's cognitive process of evaluating alternatives. Of course, every advertiser makes certain that its product or service compares favorably with those of the competition based on the criteria selected.

The fourth stage in the consumer decision-making model is the consumption decision. It is at this point that the individual actually makes the decision. All extrinsic and intrinsic variables come together to produce a decision. This decision is made based on the perceived risk associated with each alternative and the willingness of the individual to take the risk. This risk factor offers a tremendous competitive advantage for hospitality chains. When consumers step through the front door of a McDonald's, Burger King, Steak and Ale, Red Lobster, or any other nationally recognized chain, they are taking a much smaller risk than if they entered an independent restaurant about which they knew very little. There is little or no risk with the chain operation because the product-service mix is well known to them. Independent hospitality operations must work very hard to establish themselves and thereby reduce some of the risk consumers associate with patronizing a restaurant where the product-service mix is not well known.

Following the product-service mix consumption, the final stage is postconsumption feelings. How did the actual experience compare with the perceptions prior to purchase? Was the product-service mix better than or not quite up to the standards anticipated? Postconsumption feelings are based on two factors: the consumer's expectations and the actual performance by the hospitality operation. For this reason, it is very important for any hospitality operation to deliver the product-service mix promised in advertising, promotion, or personal selling. Failure to perform at or above the level anticipated by the consumer is likely to lead to negative postconsumption feelings. These negative feelings produce dissatisfaction and reduce the level of repeat patronage. From a management perspective, it is important to under-promise and over-deliver.

Consumer decision making is extremely complex. Marketing managers constantly strive to learn more about the way consumers reach decisions. As with other forms of human behavior, consumer behavior may never be totally understood.

MODELS OF CONSUMER BEHAVIOR

Hospitality consumers today are demanding more sophisticated dining and lodging experiences. Consumers are better educated, earn more money, and are more confident when they travel and dine outside the home. Today's hospitality consumer is seeking products and services tailored to meet their specific needs. They are more concerned about nutrition and safety, and they know more about value. Today's consumer is rejecting the following:

☐ The Protestant concept of self-denial in favor of instant gratification

☐ Feeling responsible in favor of feeling terrific

☐ Planning in favor of improvising

☐ Complexity in favor of simplicity

☐ The nuclear family in favor of more individual living arrangements

☐ Study in favor of instant creativity

☐ Egalitarianism in favor of a return to class-consciousness or status

Seeking Innovators and Early Adopters

Individuals have been classified according to willingness to change. Some are not upset by change, while others resist change in any form. Figure 8.3 illustrates how researchers have grouped individuals according to how they view change or innovation. When a new hospitality operation is opened, it is very important that those individuals representing the "innovators" and "early adopters" are reached by marketing efforts. These individuals offer excellent potential as early guests, for if they are satisfied, they will tell friends and associates, and these people in turn may become customers. People falling into the "early" and "late majority" categories will not usually try a new hospitality operation until they have heard positive comments from others.

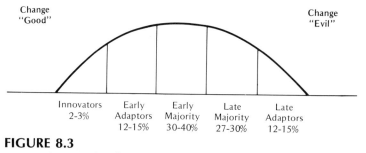

FIGURE 8.3
Innovations and Adoption

This process of influencing the innovators and early adopters is called *diffusion and adoption.* The key is to get those consumers most likely to try new products and services to make a trial purchase—that is, dine at the restaurant or stay in the hotel. If they are satisfied with the products and services received, they will then help to spread the positive word to others, and other consumers will follow.

The Uses of Models

Models of consumer behavior are not new; they have long been used to try to better understand the decision-making process of consumers. There are numerous models in the consumer behavior literature. This section will present several models with applicability to consumer behavior. Models are used for a variety of purposes by marketers, including these:

☐ To provide a framework for solving marketing problems

☐ To play an explanatory role in relationships and reactions

☐ To provide an aid in making predictions

☐ To help in the construction of a theory

☐ To stimulate the creation of hypotheses that can then be validated and tested[3]

Researchers have for many years attempted to categorize, classify, and more thoroughly understand the behavior of individuals in the marketplace. Literally thousands of research projects have been undertaken, and these have led to many models.

Marshallian Economic Model

This model views consumers as very rational and holds that consumers carefully calculate the maximum use of their money to provide them with individual happiness. It is not based solely on economic motivation, for if it were, the model would not explain why consumers dine away from home at all, since for the vast majority of people it is more expensive to dine out. Instead, the Marshallian model holds that utility factors, such as time and happiness, overcome the economic shortcomings of dining away from home. As a result, the individual chooses to dine out.

The Marshallian model advances several other hypotheses of consumer behavior in relation to a single product:

☐ As the price of a product or service is reduced, sales will increase.

☐ As the prices of competing products or services are reduced, sales of this product or service will decrease. For example, if the directly competing hotels reduce their room rates, it is anticipated that sales at your hotel would decrease and occupancy would decline as individuals elected to take their business to the competing properties.

☐ As the prices of complementary products or services are reduced, sales of this product will increase. For example, if a fast-food chain lowered the selling price of french fries, this model would predict that sales of both hamburgers and french fries would increase.

☐ As advertising and promotional expenditures increase, sales will increase.

Pavlovian Learning Model

This model finds its origins in the experiments of Pavlov, a Russian psychologist. The model proposes that consumer behavior is learned through association. Behavior is conditioned by drives, cues, responses, and reinforcement.

Drives are defined as strong internal stimuli that may lead an individual to act. For example, within every person is the drive to eat. *Cues* are weaker stimuli found in the individual and the environment. These determine when, where, and in what manner an individual responds. For example, an individual may be driving a car and hear a radio advertisement for a fast-food restaurant. This triggers the drive to eat, and the individual may respond by seeking the hospitality establishment mentioned in the advertisement.

A *response* is an individual's overt reaction to the configuration of cues received. In the previous example, the individual's response may have been to seek out the fast-food restaurant mentioned in the advertisement. Finally, *reinforcement* is anything that either positively or negatively influences, or strengthens or weakens, a response. It results in the likelihood that the response will be repeated or avoided, depending on positive or negative reinforcement, given a similar set of cues in the future. For example, if the response of seeking and patronizing a particular hotel or restaurant has been rewarded with a satisfying experience, then the next time an advertisement is heard, the response is likely to be positive. On the other hand, if the experience was unpleasant, each time the advertising stimulus is received, the individual remembers the unpleasant experience and responds negatively. Hence, it is very important that high-quality products and services be provided as reinforcement. If they are not, the individual presented with a marketing stimulus will respond negatively each time.

The Pavlovian model also holds that very strong cues must be used to overcome strong brand loyalties. For example, if a new hospitality operation is opening in an area where the consumers are very loyal to the direct competition, high levels of advertising would be necessary to induce patronage. In addition, the quality of the products and services offered would have to be perceived as superior to those of the direct competition in order to induce repeat patronage.

Veblenian Sociopsychological Model

This model takes into account the influences on an individual of the social environment. Consumer behavior is influenced more strongly by social pressures and less so by economic and internal needs. This model holds that an individual's culture, subculture, social class, reference groups, and peer groups hold primary influence in consumption decisions.

This model is supported by the evidence. Many consumers will not patronize a new hotel or restaurant until they receive positive feedback from others. Many individuals consciously avoid novel situations, such as dining out at a new restaurant, instead relying on the experiences of others as a basis for decision making. The Veblenian model illustrates why it is important to reach those individuals who are leaders of formal and informal groups, for directly and indirectly they influence the behavior of many others. The use of reference groups is also important. Most individuals aspire to be members of groups that are higher in socioeconomic status, and they use the members of these groups as role models. Therefore, inducing the patronage of one group should lead to patronage from others.

The Howard-Sheth Model of Buyer Behavior

This model, shown in Figure 8.4, seeks to explain consumer behavior when the consumer is presented with several brands from which to choose. The model consists of four fundamental parts: stimulus input variables, exogenous variables, sequential output variables, and the internal state of the buyer.

The inputs of this model include various dimensions transmitted by the brand, promotional efforts for the brand, and the buyer's social environment.

The exogenous variables are the "givens," over which the buyer has

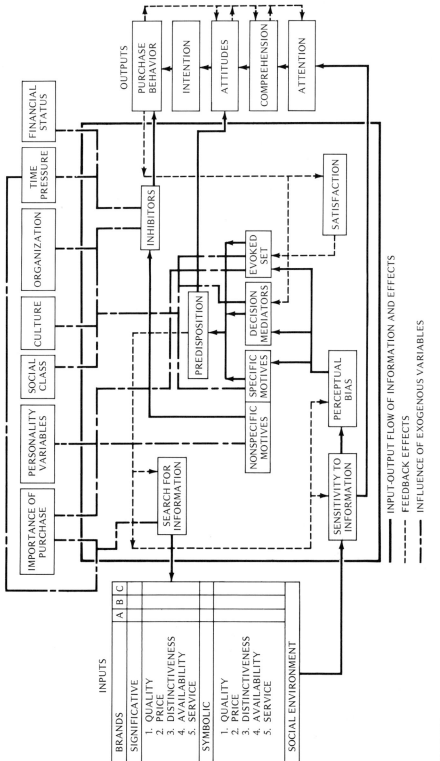

FIGURE 8.4
The Howard-Sheth Model

Source: John A. Howard and Jagdish Sheth, *The Theory of Buyer Behavior* (New York: John Wiley and Sons, Inc., 1969), pp. 22–49. Reprinted with permission of John Wiley & Sons, Inc.

little or no control. These include such things as personality, social class, culture, and time pressure. These variables will exert some influence on the purchase behavior, but the buyer will not be able to control them to any great extent.

Outputs of this model include more than the purchase-no purchase output of many models. Five steps are outputs—attention, comprehension, attitudes, intention, and purchase behavior.

Constructs that help form the sequential outputs are perception and learning. Perception consists of the search for information, sensitivity to information, and perceptual bias. The learning construct consists of specific and nonspecific motives; the evoked set, a list of brand alternatives a consumer will consider when making a purchase; decision mediators; inhibitors; and satisfaction.

The Nicosia Model

This model, illustrated in Figure 8.5, consists of four fields, the first being the output message from the firm. This is contrasted with the consumer's predispositions. The consumer then evaluates the received messages against

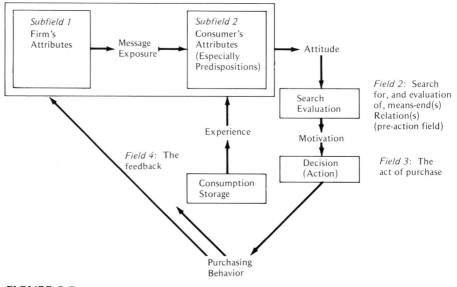

FIGURE 8.5
The Nicosia Model
Source: Francisco M. Nicosia, *Consumer Decision Processes: Marketing and Advertising Implications* (Englewood Cliffs, NJ: Prentice-Hall, 1966), p. 156.

his or her own attributes, and attitudes are formed. This attitude then forms the basis for the consumer's search and evaluation, which then lead to action and decision. The fourth step is feedback, which can take three forms: use and/or storage of the product, supply of sales results to the business, and storage of the consumer's recollection of the experience in his or her memory.[4]

CONSUMER SATISFACTION IN THE HOSPITALITY INDUSTRY

Management's ability to attain a high level of guest satisfaction has a direct and almost immediate impact on the sales volume of a hospitality organization. The management of each organization undertakes those activities that managers believe will contribute the most to overall guest satisfaction and profitability. How successful are these planned activities? What techniques are used in assessing guest satisfaction? How do organizations follow-up complaints or compliments? What operational characteristics have the greatest positive or negative impact on the guest?

Techniques to Assess Consumer Satisfaction

First, nearly all hospitality organizations seek to measure guest satisfaction through comment cards. While these cards sometimes do provide adequate information, far too often the information reflects the feelings of atypical consumers, for those individuals who complete comment cards often do not adequately reflect the feelings of the total clientele of a hospitality operation. All too often the information supplied by comment cards represents the feelings of the highly motivated guest, whose reaction may be either positive or negative. In the majority of cases, the feelings are negative. Figure 8.6 illustrates how those with either strong positive or strong negative feelings toward a hotel or restaurant are most likely to complete comment cards. While comment cards have a distinct place in any organization's program to assess the satisfaction level of consumers, they should be viewed with some degree of caution because they often do not reflect the opinions of the vast majority of consumers.

Those completing comment cards represent an atypical segment of the targeted market. A vast middle ground of typical consumers fails to use the comment card. In addition to comment cards, other measures of guest satisfaction often include the following:

☐ *Spoken complaints and compliments.* These have the same drawbacks as comment cards in that most consumers will voice opinions only if they are highly motivated either positively or negatively. For example, many consumers who are dissatisfied with a meal will respond positively to both the

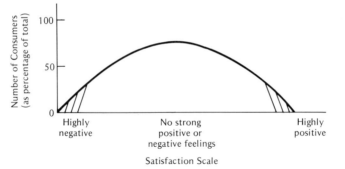

FIGURE 8.6
Comment Card Respondents Representing the Atypical Consumer

service person and the cashier when asked, "Is everything OK?" As soon as these consumers leave the operation, however, they cannot wait to tell their friends what a terrible experience they had at XYZ restaurant. The result is negative word-of-mouth advertising, yet a positive measure of guest satisfaction because no complaints were registered. A study that focused on consumer satisfaction in the hospitality industry noted that fewer than 60 percent of those who are not satisfied are likely to complain in person to a manager. When the consumers were asked about their preferred method to use to register a complaint, fewer than 5 percent said they would prefer to speak with someone directly at the time of the incident. Figure 8.7 illustrates the complaint behavior of hospitality consumers in a recent study.[5]

☐ *Following-up complaints and compliments.* Many hospitality managers have found it advisable to follow-up either by telephone or letter both the positive and the negative comments. This may be done for every comment or through a system. In this way, management attempts to overcome negative feelings and promote repeat patronage even when a guest may have had a poor experience.

It is imperative that management take the steps necessary to assure that

Likely to tell others outside the family about complaint, regardless of resolution	62%
Number of people told on average	12
Likely to tell others when complaint was *not* resolved	73%
Likely to tell others not to use hotel, regardless of resolution	43%
Number of people told on average	8
Likely to tell others when complaint was resolved	71%

FIGURE 8.7
Complaint Behavior of Hotel Guests
Source: Robert C. Lewis and Susan V. Morris, "The Positive Side of Guest Complaints," *The Cornell Hotel and Restaurant Administration Quarterly,* Vol. 27, No. 4, p. 14.

complaints by guests are resolved. It has been shown that the average guest will tell twelve other individuals about any problems that they might have encountered. This type of situation calls for positive action. Among the best responses that management can take are training, hotlines, responding to comment cards and letters, and increasing the emphasis on guest service and satisfaction.

All managers and employees need to develop an increased awareness and sensitivity toward guests who may be dissatisfied with some aspect of the product-service mix. Rather than trying to avoid unhappy guests, which is what many managers and employees do, the opposite approach is called for. The complaint should be caught at the point of origin and the guest must be shown that the company is prepared to take the complaint seriously and take action to resolve the problem.

Guest service hotlines have been established by some hotel companies and individual properties in an effort to more effectively deal with guests who are not satisfied. These hotlines are established with the goal that guest's complaints will be identified and resolved quickly. This avoids the situation in which the unhappy guest is shuffled from one person to another, often with the phrase, "You'll have to call Ms. XYZ in the Housekeeping Department for that." With the use of hotlines and hotline log books, managers are able to see the nature of complaints and identify trends that, if they are not handled properly, can result in reduced guest satisfaction.

☐ *Number of repeat guests.* This can be a very accurate indicator of the degree to which a hotel or restaurant is satisfying its consumers. Information maintained in a marketing information system should provide the percentage of total consumers who are repeat guests. Many hospitality operations have developed standards that they attempt to achieve. For example, one manager's target is to have 80 percent of all guests be repeat guests. If the percentage falls below 80 percent, immediate management action is undertaken to increase the percentage of repeat patronage.

☐ *Sales trends.* As long as sales trends are increasing, one might assume that guest satisfaction is also high and that the increasing sales are at least partly the result of positive word-of-mouth advertising. A hospitality manager must be careful, however, not to be lulled into thinking that volume is increasing simply because the dollar amounts of sales are increasing. It is possible in times of rapidly rising prices to have increasing dollar sales yet decreasing customer counts or occupancy. Therefore, attention should be paid to "real growth," in excess of price increases. If a hospitality operation records three months of negative real growth, this should signal that immediate actions need to be taken by management.

☐ *Market share trends.* This is a useful measure for larger hospitality organizations. It measures the percentage of a particular market that the organization has captured. A declining market share often indicates poor guest satisfaction. It can also be a symptom of other, larger problems.

□ *Shopping reports.* Many consulting organizations offer services known as "shopping." These are anonymous evaluations of the operation and include evaluations of all aspects of the product-service mix and other qualities of the operation. They can serve a very useful function if properly performed. Before a hospitality manager contracts with a company offering shopping services, a thorough check should be done to ensure the professional quality and reliability of the service.

The Most Common Reasons for Consumer Dissatisfaction

Guest satisfaction as it pertains to marketing is not a difficult subject to understand; it revolves around the basics of sound management. Why, then, do so many hospitality operations fail to achieve success? No amount of professional marketing effort or intense advertising will draw consumers to a hospitality operation that is perceived to be low quality. What is it that turns people off?

Foodservice Dissatisfiers

A look at the basics shows that eliminating the major sources of guest complaints would be a major marketing advantage. National Restaurant Association studies indicate that the most frequent complaints are poor food quality, poor service, overexpensive meals, improperly prepared meals, poor sanitation, overcrowded foodservices, overly noisy foodservices, rude service personnel, too small portions, and limited parking.[6]

The vast majority of problems with guest satisfaction relate to "people problems" involving poor treatment by the staff. Such practices as keeping guests waiting in the lounge even though tables are available, and failure of a service person to smile and make the guest feel genuinely welcome are to be avoided at all costs. Special attention must be paid to the development of "people skills" and "hospitality skills" for all personnel. First-class treatment by the staff can turn even an average meal into a memorable and positive experience. Poor treatment, however, can make even the finest of cuisine seem second-rate. Surely, everyone can think of numerous examples to support this.

Lodging Dissatisfiers

In a study conducted by Stephen Hall and Associates for the American Hotel and Motel Association, the most common dissatisfiers were identified and the costs associated with these were estimated.[7] The study focused on quality assurance, with the goal of increasing the level of service quality provided to guests. Just as manufacturers in America have been criticized by consumers for providing products of inferior quality to those from other countries, so too has service in the United States been disparaged as well, especially in the critical area of employee attitude.

Consumers were asked to provide their three greatest reasons for dissatisfaction with the products and services provided by the American lodging industry. Figure 8.8 lists the ten most frequently mentioned reasons and Figure 8.9 lists the most common errors by functional area. It is worth noting that fully 70 percent of those responding listed employees as being among their three major criticisms of the lodging industry. It is often boasted that the hospitality industry is a "people business", one where top-quality employees treat guests in a restaurant or a hotel as if they were guests in their homes. However, this it not always the case. Improving the level of service provided by employees is perhaps the greatest challenge that service industry managers face in the next five to ten years.

Frequent travelers were also asked to indicate the frequency with which specific problems occurred in their travels, and how frequently these prob-

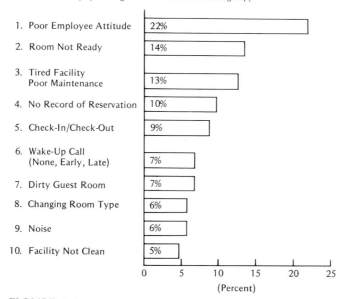

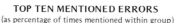

TOP TEN MENTIONED ERRORS
(as percentage of times mentioned within group)

1. Poor Employee Attitude	22%
2. Room Not Ready	14%
3. Tired Facility Poor Maintenance	13%
4. No Record of Reservation	10%
5. Check-In/Check-Out	9%
6. Wake-Up Call (None, Early, Late)	7%
7. Dirty Guest Room	7%
8. Changing Room Type	6%
9. Noise	6%
10. Facility Not Clean	5%

(Percent)

FIGURE 8.8

Problems Most Frequently Mentioned by Frequent Travelers in the United States

Source: Stephen Hall and Associates, *Quest for Quality*, p. 8.

(As a Percent of Total Mentions)

FRONT DESK
Room not ready, no record of reservation, check-in/check-out,   32%
overbooked, room not held, changing room type, high rates,
message not delivered

MANAGEMENT
Employee attitude, poor service, perceived poor management,   23%
slow service, misleading advertising, poor response to complaints

HOUSEKEEPING
Dirty, not enough linen, noisy maids, maids who enter too early   16%
or too late, condition of linen, dirty bathroom, smoky/stale, tired
room

OVERALL FACILITY
Noisy, tired facility, dirty, security, small rooms, safety, lack of   13%
facilities

ROOM/MAINTENANCE
Shoddy maintenance, TV/radio out of order, temperature control,   11%
plumbing, heating, general mechanical problems, slow elevators

FOOD & BEVERAGE
Poor food, slow service, inadequate outlets, expensive   4%

PARKING
Cost and unavailability   1%
   ————
   100%

FIGURE 8.9
Frequent Errors by Functional Area
Source: Stephen Hall and Associates, *Quest for Quality*, p. 9.

lems would cause them to change their travel plans the next time they visited a particular location. The results are shown in Figure 8.10.

Other interesting results that should be noted include the following:

☐ Males seem to encounter a slightly greater number of problems when traveling, but their discontinuance rate is lower than the rate among women (24 percent versus 31 percent). This would indicate that women are less tolerant of errors, a trend that will become increasingly important as the percentage of women business travelers continues to increase.

☐ There seems to be little brand loyalty in the marketplace. Results of the study indicate that men will change facilities once every 4 trips,

OCCURRENCE FREQUENCY AND DISCONTINUANCE RATE
(by Sex)

| | MALE | | FEMALE | |
	FREQ.	DISC. RATE	FREQ.	DISC. RATE
Unsatisfactory food service	19%	20%	13%	18%
Tired facility—poor maintenance	18	27	13	35
Slow check-in, check-out	18	15	18	31
Employees not friendly	12	32	9	48
Room not ready upon arrival	10	11	13	15
Poor overall service	9	48	10	58
Requested room type N/A	7	14	7	16
Morning wake-up call not made	5	14	3	19
No record of reservation	4	31	5	27
Overbooked—guest walked away	2	59	1	81

Overall:		
Frequency rate per trip	1.035	0.909
Discontinuance rate	24%	31%
Trip per discontinuance	4.0	3.5

FIGURE 8.10

Consumer Perception Study: Frequency of Guest-Encountered Errors and the Rate of Discontinuance (Percentage of times in which the guest would change his or her travel plans on a return visit to the same location)

Source: Stephen Hall and Associates, *Quest for Quality*, p. 10.

while women will change once every 3.5 trips to the same destination.

While the *Quest for Quality* study was a limited-scale exploratory study, it is worth noting that consumers perceive some definite service problems that managers must face head on. Figure 8.11 provides a summary of how consumers perceived service in the United States in comparison with the rest of the world. Managers in the hospitality industry really have some clear service challenges ahead.

SUMMARY

This chapter provides a broad overview of the complex subject of consumer behavior. Management must constantly strive to learn more about consumer behavior, for this will allow managers to better serve the needs of guests. In

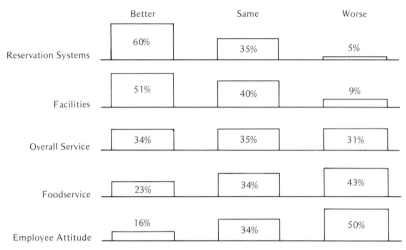

FIGURE 8.11
Consumer Perceptions of Service in the United States and the World

this way, sales and profits can be increased and a competitive advantage will be gained.

Several techniques are commonly used to assess consumer satisfaction. These include comment cards, oral comments, the number of repeat guests, sales trends, follow-up comments, market share trends, and shopping reports. Results are presented for both the foodservice and lodging segments of the hospitality industry concerning those factors that most frequently cause consumers to feel unhappy.

A total of seven models of consumer behavior are presented and discussed in the chapter. These models attempt to explain the reasons behind the purchase decisions that consumers make. A contemporary consumer decision-making model is presented. It introduces a five-step process involving need arousal, information retrieval, evaluating alternative choices, consumption decision, and postpurchase consumption feelings. Each of these stages in the decision-making process is influenced by several intrinsic and extrinsic influences.

KEY WORDS AND CONCEPTS

☐ Consumer behavior models

☐ Extrinsic influences

☐ Intrinsic influences

☐ Culture

☐ Reference groups

☐ Opinion leaders

☐ Individual needs

☐ Consumer decision-making process

☐ Diffusion and adoption

☐ Consumer satisfaction

☐ Shopping reports

☐ Quality assurance

☐ Brand loyalty

Questions for Review and Discussion

1. Briefly review the seven consumer behavior models presented in this chapter.
2. How would you compare and contrast the consumer behavior models presented?
3. What are the leading dissatisfiers in both the food service and lodging segments of the industry?
4. How can management monitor consumer satisfaction?
5. Which of the techniques pertaining to the previous question is the one you would consider to be the best? Why?

PART IV

ADVERTISING AND PROMOTION

CHAPTER 9

Advertising Management

As the marketing environment in which hospitality organizations function becomes more competitive, the importance of advertising and other forms of promotion increases. This chapter focuses on advertising management and lays the foundation for the next chapter, which focuses on advertising media. Emphasis here is on defining commonly used advertising terms, relations with an advertising agency, advertising budgets, positioning and strategy, and planning and evaluating advertising campaigns.

The chapter covers the following topics:

INTRODUCTION
☐ Functions of Advertising
☐ Criticisms of Advertising

DEFINITIONS OF ADVERTISING TERMS
☐ Advertising and Promotion
☐ National and Local Advertising
☐ Cooperative Advertising
☐ Advertising and Promotion Throughout the Life Cycle

RELATIONS WITH AN ADVERTISING AGENCY
☐ Advantages and Disadvantages of Working with an Agency
☐ The Role of an Agency and the Types of Agencies
☐ Selecting an Advertising Agency
☐ Agency Compensation

ESTABLISHING ADVERTISING BUDGETS
☐ Functions of Advertising Budgets
☐ Advantages and Disadvantages of Advertising Budgets
☐ Budgeting Methods
☐ A Budgeting System
☐ A Rolling Advertising Budget

ADVERTISING POSITIONING AND STRATEGY
☐ Developing Strategy
☐ Developing a Central Appeal
☐ Keys to Successful Advertising

PLANNING AND EVALUATING ADVERTISING CAMPAIGNS
☐ Types of Advertising Campaigns
☐ Campaign Checkpoints
☐ An Advertising-Planning Model
☐ Evaluating an Advertising Campaign

SUMMARY

KEY WORDS AND CONCEPTS

QUESTIONS FOR REVIEW AND DISCUSSION

INTRODUCTION

Functions of Advertising

The terms *advertising* and *promotion* evoke many different responses from hospitality managers. Some smile, remembering a successful advertising campaign from the past. Others simply view advertising as a waste of time. They claim that advertising and promotion are things that should be used to sell automobiles or laundry detergent, but not hospitality operations. These individuals usually champion word-of-mouth advertising, claiming that good food and service will produce satisfied consumers, who in turn will produce more consumers. While this argument has some truth to it, those managers who fail to engage in a significant advertising program may be missing a unique opportunity to increase both customer counts and total sales. Advertising is not something to be limited to the chain operations, such as McDonald's and Wendy's, nor is it only something a manager does when business is poor and needs a shot in the arm.

Advertising and promotion are marketing functions that need to be managed along with other functions. They demand management's time and attention if they are to be successful, for advertising must be planned, implemented, coordinated, and evaluated with care if it is to achieve increased sales. What can advertising and promotion do? First, advertising and promotion present information to the consumer. They tell about new products, new services, new decor, and other items of potential interest. Second, they reinforce consumer behavior by communicating with those individuals who have patronized a particular hotel or restaurant in the past. Exposing these consumers to a continuous flow of advertising is likely to induce repeat patronage by reinforcing their positive experiences. Brand loyalty is very difficult to establish, but advertising is one weapon to use in this effort.

Third, advertising induces first-time patronage. If consumers are exposed to a continual flow of advertising, their curiosity is aroused and this often results in patronage. If a first-time guest is rewarded with a pleasant experience, the foundation for repeat patronage has been successfully established. At least a portion of the advertising must be directed toward individuals who have not already patronized the operation. Some managers believe that the key to success is to build a steady group of repeat guests, and while this is one good aim of an advertising and promotional strategy, other efforts must be directed at those who have not previously been guests. Fourth, advertising enhances the image of hospitality operations. Advertising does not always seek to promote a specific product or service; it can instead seek to create and reinforce an image for the consuming public. Words and phrases often contribute to this image building; for example, Westin Hotels and Resorts' "Caring, Comfortable, Civilized" seeks to establish and maintain a specific image that has been created in the mind of the consumer.

Still, a significant number of hospitality owners and managers do not believe in advertising. Some will argue that the only good form of promotion is by word-of-mouth; "Let our guests speak good words about us, and we'll succeed," they claim. Some operators refer to this as word-of-mouth advertising, but it is not advertising; rather it is a form of public relations. Unfortunately for these individuals, this point of view does not always hold true. Many independent operations, especially those in the foodservice segment, are simply being squeezed by larger national and regional chain advertising, while many managers withdraw from all advertising, rationalizing that they cannot compete with the big chains. The result is the all-too-often predictable bankruptcy!

Advertising and promotion are necessarily a vital part of the marketing program of all types of hospitality operations. But just what should advertising do? What should it accomplish? Generally speaking, advertising should set out to accomplish three goals: (1) to establish awareness in the minds of consumers, (2) to establish positive value in the minds of consumers, and (3) to promote repeat patronage and brand loyalty among consumers.

Awareness must be created among those consumers who have not heard of a particular hotel or restaurant establishment. This awareness should create sufficient interest so that patronage results. Next, to induce both first-time and repeat patronage, a positive perceived value must be established and reinforced in the minds of consumers. All consumers have limited resources chasing after unlimited wants; hence, only those products and services offering a high level of perceived value will be rewarded with patronage. A hospitality operation might have the very finest to offer in rooms, food, and service in a given market segment, but if it offers a low perceived value, the number of consumers served is likely to be small. Finally, advertising should strive to promote brand loyalty and repeat patronage among the highest possible percentage of consumers. Very few hospitality operations can survive on one-time patronage only. Repeat business must be encouraged and promoted. Even better than repeat patronage is brand loyalty, wherein consumers begin to prefer one brand of hotel or restaurant over and above the direct competition. This is, of course, a very lofty goal.

Criticisms of Advertising

Many critics of advertising raise questions about whether a hospitality operation should advertise. Several typical questions and responses follow.

Doesn't a lot of advertising contain misleading information? Advertising is indeed a powerful force in the marketplace, and occasionally, it may be used by a dishonest manager to deceive. This type of logic would hold, however, that because one apple in a box was rotten, the entire box should be thrown out.

The government has gone to great lengths to protect the consumer. Many other groups, including the Better Business Bureau and the National Advertising Review Council, strive to limit the amount of false and misleading advertising. Also, it simply is not in the long-term interests of any hospitality operation to deceive its consumers. Advertising seeks to induce first-time and repeat patronage by promising consumers specific products and services. Failure to deliver as promised hurts the advertiser's credibility and sales.

Doesn't advertising result in a vicious circle of spending among competitors?

Some believe that if two hospitality operations (A and B) are in direct competition, A's spending more on advertising means that B will increase expenditures to counteract the efforts of A. A in turn will increase expenditures to regain the advantage over B, and so on. This is not normally the case. However, in recent years, there has been a significant increase in the advertising expenditures by companies in the hospitality industry, especially those in the fast-food segment. During the 1980s, advertising expenses have increased at an annual rate of over 20 percent, a rise that far outpaces the growth in sales. This increase simply is a reflection of the increasing competitiveness of the fast-food segment. It is not the dollar amount spent but the effectiveness of the advertising that counts.

Why should the consumer have to pay for advertising? Doesn't this result in higher prices? Yes, the consumer pays for advertising. Consumers bear the cost of raw materials, labor, and all other variable and fixed expenses. Consumers do not, however, necessarily pay a higher price as a result of advertising. Very often, advertising features lower prices in the form of specials, coupons, and combining several menu items at a price that is lower than if they were purchased separately.

Economy of scale is also possible through advertising. All hospitality operations have certain fixed expenses that must be paid whether zero, one, or one thousand consumers are served. As more consumers are served, the cost per consumer for fixed costs is reduced, and these reductions can actually lower rather than raise prices. Increased volume also allows a manager to purchase all supplies in larger quantities, often lowering the price further. Yes, the consumer does pay for advertising, but this price is not necessarily higher.

Doesn't advertising give the larger chains an unfair advantage? Yes, large chains do have very definite advantages over smaller firms, simply because of a broader financial base and depth of resources. This is a part of business life and should not be tampered with. Mere size does not necessarily mean monopoly, as there are many thousands of small, independent hospitality establishments in operation. Several years ago, some people believed that McDonald's was beginning to establish a virtual monopoly in the fast-food segment of the industry. These people held that McDonald's would drive the independent operations out of business and would then consume many of the smaller regional chains. This has not been the case. McDonald's does hold a very commanding lead in annual sales, but there has been room for growth by other chains such as Domino's Pizza and Hardee's. Large chains do enjoy certain advertising advantages, but these advantages hardly create a monopolistic marketplace.

Doesn't advertising make consumers purchase things they do not want or cannot afford? In some cases, yes. Advertising seeks to persuade consumers to purchase specific products and services from the advertiser. No one is forcing consumers to purchase these products and services. Some would argue that an expensive dining experience or a night in a luxury hotel is unnecessary when a more simple substitute would adequately satisfy requirements. Most dining out and travel is an acquired taste, and once acquired, it needs to be satisfied just as other needs do. Consumers are the ones who make the final decision concerning how their limited resources will be allocated. Advertising simply makes them aware of choices and attempts to encourage patronage.

DEFINITIONS OF ADVERTISING TERMS

Advertising and Promotion

The American Marketing Association defined advertising as "any paid form of nonpersonal presentation and promotion of ideas, goods, or services by an identified sponsor." This definition is uniformly accepted throughout the business community. It can be broken down into four component parts:

1. *Paid form*. Any advertising is paid for and controlled by the individual or group that is the sponsor. Because someone is paying for the space (newspaper, outdoor) or time (radio, television), this individual or group has complete control over what is said, printed, or shown. Any promotion that is not paid for is called *publicity*. Because the individual or group is not paying for the time or space, those involved do not have complete control and hence are at the mercy of the writer or producer. A common form of publicity is a review of a restaurant in a dining or food section of a local newspaper. Publicity can obviously be either favorable or unfavorable.

2. *Nonpersonal.* Advertising is done through the mass media without personal contact or interaction between the seller and the potential buyer. Advertising relies strictly on nonpersonal promotion of goods, services, or ideas.

3. *Promotion related to ideas, goods, or services.* Advertising need not be restricted to the promotion of a tangible physical product or good. It may try to influence individuals to change their ways of thinking or their behavior. The "Ours Is a Special World" campaign launched by the National Restaurant Association and other professional associations was an attempt to draw attention to the tremendous career opportunities in the hospitality industry.

4. *Identified sponsor.* All advertising has an identified sponsor.

Promotion is a broader-based term denoting efforts undertaken to induce patronage. It includes personal selling that is face-to-face communication between the seller and the prospective buyer as well as other efforts designed to increase sales. Simply stated, advertising is a form of promotion, but all forms of promotion are not necessarily advertising.

National and Local Advertising

Advertising can be divided into two broad categories, national and local. National consumer advertising is aimed at a national audience by using network television and radio, or national print media such as magazines. This form of advertising normally promotes the general name of the chain, not individual locations or stores.

Local advertising is used not only by the major hospitality chains but also by second-tier chains, regional chains, and independent operations. Local advertising using television, radio, print, and other media is used extensively in the hospitality industry. This is the level where the action really lies, and to coin a phrase, the battle of market share is won or lost in the trenches of local advertising.

Cooperative Advertising

A simple fact of business life for many managers is that specific advertising media are too expensive for the organization to use. For many managers, cooperative advertising is an excellent alternative. Cooperative advertising, as the name implies, involves having two or more parties work together as sponsors of an advertisement that provides benefit to all parties involved. For example, a group of hospitality operations located in a given geographic area may join together and promote dining in the area without promoting any one operation specifically. By joining together and sharing the expenses, managers are able to advertise in more expensive media and reach new audiences. Cooperative advertising is an area of tremendous promise because it allows a manager to expand the advertising media selection. Caution should be exercised, however, to ensure that all cooperative advertisers are represented fairly and equally. Herein lies the major drawback of cooperative advertising.

Cooperative advertising is often favored by national advertisers as a way to improve relations with local store owners. For example, if a national hospitality chain wanted to place a series of advertisements in local newspapers or on a local radio station, it would pay what is known as the "national rate," or the highest rate for the advertising space or time. If, however, a local store owner placed orders for the same amount of space or time, the store owner would pay the local rate, which is lower than the national rate. Cooperative efforts between the national chain and the local store owner benefit both parties. The national advertiser will generally pay no less than 50 percent of the advertising costs and in some cases will pay up to 100 percent. The most common arrangement is for the two to split the cost of the advertising, with each normally paying 50 percent of the cost. The local store owner is then able to purchase a good deal more advertising than would have been possible without the assistance of the national chain. The national chain, on the other hand, is able to purchase the space through the local store owner at the local advertising rate. Thus, the national chain is able to purchase the same amount of advertising space at a reduced cost, and the local chain is able to get more advertising time and space for the same dollar investment. The national chain can also build improved relations with the local store owner because they worked together.

Those companies that have cooperative advertising programs will often provide advertising shells into which the local advertiser can insert localized information.

Advertising and Promotion Throughout the Life Cycle

As discussed in Chapter 3, all hospitality organizations progress through a distinct life cycle, as shown in Figure 9.1. As an organization moves through the stages of the life cycle, different advertising approaches must be used, as the Table 9.1 indicates.

Introductory Stage. Rarely does a new hotel or restaurant open without creating some interest in the local community. The goal of all hospitality managers should be to capitalize on this natural curiosity and make it work to the advantage of the new hospitality establishment. Two broad-based philosophies are often used. One promotes solely the quality and desirability

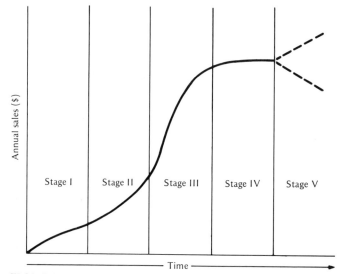

FIGURE 9.1
The Life Cycle of Hospitality Organizations (Stage I = introduction;
Stage II = conservative expansion; Stage III = rapid expansion;
Stage IV = plateaued maturity; Stage V = decline or regeneration)

TABLE 9.1
Advertising Strategies for Stages in the Product Life Cycle

Life Cycle Stage	Advertising and Promotion Strategy
Introduction	Aimed at need and wants of innovators
Conservative expansion Rapid expansion	Make target markets aware of products and services
Plateaued maturity	Used to differentiate among major competitors
Decline or regeneration	Emphasize low price to increase volume

of the one hospitality facility; the other involves direct comparisons with major competitors (comparative advertising), indicating that the products and services offered by the advertiser are superior to those offered by the competition. Both of these philosophies have been implemented with success by many different types of operations. One brief word of caution deserves mention, however: If a direct comparison to other operations is made, every effort must be made to deliver the products and services as promised. Failure to do so will result in a marked drop in credibility and effectiveness of subsequent advertising. Once deceived, the consumer is wary! The principal goal during this phase is to build volume within the operation by reaching those individuals who are innovators and are most likely to patronize a new operation. This approach is very critical to the independently owned operation. Every effort must be made to reach potential consumers and encourage first-time patronage. All potentially targeted segments should be identified and specific strategies developed to reach these markets.

It is very desirable to bring all management personnel with marketing responsibilities together to generate ideas for possible promotion. These idea-generating sessions should produce a wealth of potential promotions, leading to a schedule of what is to be done and when it is to be accomplished. The list of possible promotional ideas is endless; a few examples follow:

☐ Signs can announce "Coming Soon" for a new hospitality operation and perhaps indicate the number of weeks until the grand opening.

☐ Press releases can indicate the where, what, when, and why of the new operation.

☐ Mailing lists can be developed from a guest book signed by first-time consumers. This list can then be used later as a mailing list for direct-mail campaigns.

☐ Numerous media can, of course, be used. One rather novel approach involved advertising in the classified section of the newspaper and on radio for high-quality personnel for a new restaurant. The results were not only surprising, but very successful. Hundreds of individuals applied for jobs, making the restaurant "the place" to work. In addition, the advertisements described in some detail the atmosphere, menu, and image of the restaurant, thereby informing the general public of the existence of the restaurant. The result was high-quality personnel, high guest counts, and very satisfied management.

☐ Community opinion leaders, such as doctors, lawyers, and restaurant reviewers, can be invited to opening-week parties and the like, all designed to enhance the image of the hospitality operation. The goal, of course, is to present a positive image and influence those who can in turn influence others.

☐ Numerous door prizes, contests, and raffles can be used to encourage patronage. The American consumer seems infinitely willing to take a chance on getting something for nothing, or something for next to nothing. Consider the success of Las Vegas and Atlantic City gambling. This approach is simply an application of psychologist B. F. Skinner's variable-interval reinforcement schedule. Individuals will continue to take chances, even though the probability of winning is very small.

☐ Handbills or flyers represent an inexpensive yet effective method for introductory promotion. These can, of course, be used as direct-mail pieces, or they may be distributed by other means. One new restaurant located near a large shopping mall and several office complexes distributed handbills offering a variety of discounts and freebies at these locations. In addition, they invited the secretaries of the high-ranking management personnel to a complimentary lunch and formed a secretaries' club that provided incentives and rewards to those secretaries who provided the restaurant with the largest number of reservations. The results were predictable: very high volume and the satisfaction of all parties involved.

The list of potential introductory advertising and promotional ideas is endless. Each management group must determine a sound strategy for the introductory stage of advertising and promotion.

Conservative and Rapid Expansion Stages. During both the conservative and rapid expansion stages, advertising is based on building name recognition and awareness among consumers. If the introductory stage has been successful, a solid core of consumers has been established. With this core, expansion advertising must take two approaches: (1) to reinforce and remind those consumers who have patronized the hospitality establishment, to induce repeat patronage; and (2) to reach those consumers who have not patronized the operation, thereby expanding volume with a significant number of first-time consumers.

The expansion stage marks a well-established image within the marketplace. During this stage, the mention of the name of the hospitality establishment brings a distinct image to the consumer's mind. Expansion advertising should therefore seek to reinforce the most positive aspects of this image. Hospitality operators who successfully reach the expansion stage of advertising are seeking to retain current consumers and entice new ones. The strategies used include comparative advertising and stressing the special advantages offered by the product-service mix of the operation.

One promotional technique that has grown in popularity has been the use of coupons. These are normally distributed in one of three manners: through a variety of print media, by direct mail, or by service personnel at the time the bill is paid. Coupon promotions are generally most effective in increasing consumer counts. A word of caution should be offered, however: as couponing has become more popular, the potential consumer may not be brand loyal. Rather, the consumer uses coupons as the method to shop for the best deal at any given point. If a large number of hospitality operations in a given geographic area offer coupon discounts, consumers can become conditioned to coupons as a way of life, and the result is that they will patronize only those hospitality operations that offer such discounts.

Plateaued Maturity.   Only the largest and most successful hospitality organizations achieve this stage of the advertising life cycle. The firms that achieve this level are very well established and have the tremendous advantage of nearly universal name recognition and reinforcement. The best example is McDonald's; a McDonald's advertisement need not even mention the product or service in order to be successful. Simply by using the word *McDonald's* or showing the restaurant and the people who patronize it, the advertisement serves to reinforce the image and quality of the organization in the minds of the consuming public. The primary goal of an advertiser at this stage is to use the organization's size and brand recognition to differentiate it from the competition. This can be seen within the fast-food segment, as each of the largest competitors (McDonald's, Burger King, Wendy's, and Hardee's) attempts to differentiate itself from the others.

Regeneration Stage.   The goal of any firm that reaches this stage of its life cycle and the stabilization stage of the advertising life cycle is to use its competitive advantage to launch new products and services that will further strengthen the organization. By adding to the product-service mix, the firm can attract new consumers and will further strengthen its market standing. McDonald's again serves as an excellent example, as it has repeatedly used its number one position in the fast-food segment to launch new products and services, most notably a variety of breakfast items and such new hamburgers as the McDLT™. These products contribute to the wealth of the organization and serve to broaden the market appeal. All have, of course, been test-marketed prior to being introduced into the system. They serve as examples of ways an organization can market new products and services from a position of strength and, as a result, become stronger still. Granted, no other hospitality organization enjoys the strength of McDonald's, but the same concept can be applied on a smaller scale at the regional or local level.

RELATIONS WITH AN ADVERTISING AGENCY

Advantages and Disadvantages of Working with an Agency

Should a hospitality organization use the services of an advertising agency? With the exception of small motels or restaurants, which because of their size, do not devote a large amount of money to external advertising, all operations should consider the use of an agency. The final decision is certainly for each organization to make, but agencies offer several advantages. First, an agency can increase the effectiveness of advertising; its work is more professional, and its use of media is better. Second, agencies can be especially helpful, if not necessary, in overcoming the special production requirements of radio and television advertising. Third, using an advertising agency is like maintaining on staff several part-time specialists—copywriters, artists, and layout professionals. Fourth, agencies are able to maintain closer contacts with media representatives than can a single advertiser. Finally, some advertising agencies are able to offer consultative services related to such advertising and marketing projects as test-marketing.

Management must, however, consider the negative aspects of using an agency. First and foremost is, of course, the question of money. "There is no such thing as a free lunch," and top-quality professional assistance will cost money. Furthermore, if the hospitality organization has access to adequate free-lance talent and assistance, the services of an agency may not be required.

Managers have to make decisions about how advertising will be handled. These decisions should be based on the following factors:

☐ The amount of available time to devote to advertising

☐ The sizes of the target market segments

☐ The specific media that are being considered or have been selected

☐ Management's knowledge of and experience in advertising

☐ The amount of money to be spent on advertising

The Role of an Agency and the Types of Agencies

What is an advertising agency, and what services can it provide? An agency is an independent business that works for the client that is purchasing the advertising. Agencies come in all shapes and sizes, from one-person operations to large agencies employing hundreds of individuals. Generally, a small advertiser should avoid the very large agencies because these often are not able to give the personal attention that the small advertiser needs and wants. Agencies that push out advertising in huge quantities may lack creativity and may resort to a production-line approach.

Figure 9.2 illustrates the typical organization of a large advertising agency. Most hospitality advertisers have little contact with the agency beyond the account executive and perhaps the creative staff. The relationship between the account executive and the client is critical and should be of primary concern when selecting an agency. A manager should remember that this individual will be in charge of the account and that the management of the hospitality operation will need to work closely with the account executive. The account executive and hence the agency should be selected with the same careful screening that any other member of the management team would receive. The management of the hospitality operation must establish a positive working environment with the account executive if the relationship is to be successful.

The agency is staffed by both creative and business professionals who are specialists in various areas. First, they apply both art and science to advertising. An agency develops and implements an advertising plan tailored

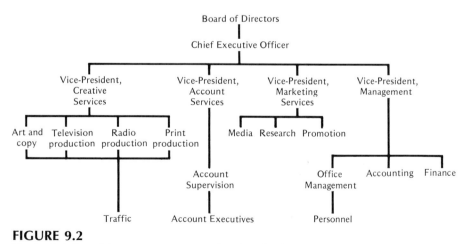

FIGURE 9.2
Typical Advertising Agency Organizational Chart

to the needs of the individual client. Second, they coordinate the various functions that must take place if an advertising campaign is to be successful. They do this by coordinating the creative staff, which develops the advertisements, and the business staff, which secures the advertising time and space in the various media. An agency can actually save the client money, because the fees earned by the agency are paid as commissions by the medium in which the advertisements are placed.

There are several types of advertising agencies. They can be classified based on two criteria: the type of business they handle and the range of services they offer. Agencies may serve a broad range of consumer products, or they may specialize in one field such as consumer goods, industrial products, financial services, retail sales, or real estate. Needless to say, it is wise to select an agency with a proven track record in working with services or with hospitality industry clients. An advertising agency may offer specific functions such as media buying services or creative services, or it may be a full-service agency. Full-service agencies will handle not only the advertising that the client elects to purchase, but also nonadvertising activities such as sales promotional materials, trade show exhibits, publicity, and public relations.

Advertising agencies are able to provide a wide variety of professional services, including campaign planning, market research, media selection and production, public relations, and campaign evaluations. The following represents a list of most of the services that an agency should be able to provide.

- [ ] Studying the client's product-service mix to determine strengths and weaknesses and the client's relation to the competition

- [ ] Conducting an analysis of the current and potential market segments to determine future potential

- [ ] Providing direction and leadership with regard to selecting available media and the best method to advertise and promote the product-service mix

- [ ] Formulating a detailed plan to reach the stated advertising and promotional objectives

- [ ] Executing the plan by coordinating the creative process (writing and designing the advertisements) and the business process (securing the desired advertising time and space)

- [ ] Verifying that the desired advertisements have been run in the media selected

- [ ] Evaluating the effectiveness of the advertising campaign and submitting a report to the client

Selecting an Advertising Agency

The agency-client relationship is very important, so the agency should be selected with great care. How should a hospitality manager go about selecting an agency? Entering into an agency-client relationship is not a move to be taken lightly, but it can be based on a rational process. A few recommendations follow.

First, make a list of the needs that an agency must satisfy. It is also wise to make a list of the major problems or symptoms unique to the character of the specific hospitality client. Begin a list of questions to ask in selecting an agency, such as "What is the reputation of the agency?" "What experience does the agency have with hospitality accounts?" "How much depth of talent does the agency have?" Other needs and criteria should be listed, but these will depend on the needs of an individual hospitality organization.

Second, make a list of prospective agencies. This will involve checking the track records of several agencies as well as informing them of the organization's interest. Some managers prefer to use an agency questionnaire to gather preliminary data from prospective agencies. An example of such a questionnaire is shown in Figure 9.3. Using this type of questionnaire offers both pros and cons. It allows management to gather information from a variety of agencies and then use that information in initial screening. It does, however, occasionally "turn off" an agency, making the agency feel that the prospective client is asking for too much information before the agency-client relationship has been established.

Third, after a list of prospective agencies has been developed, it must be narrowed to a few viable agencies. At this point management should be prepared to meet with agency representatives, review samples of their work, listen to ideas, and evaluate the agency against the organization's needs and criteria.

Agency Compensation

How are advertising agencies compensated? Typically, agencies receive payment in several ways: (1) commissions from media, (2) fees or retainers paid by client, (3) service charges for creative and production work, (4) markups on outside purchases, and (5) trade-outs.

Commissions of 15 percent are normally paid to the agency by the media. For example, if an advertisement costs $1000, the agency would collect $1000 from the client but would pay the media $1000 minus $150 (15 percent), or a total of $850. Agencies often do not generate sufficient revenue from small advertisers to cover production and creative costs, and therefore they charge other fees. Such fees are often monthly retainers and hourly charges for creative work.

1. _____
             Name   *Phone*
   _____
     Street and number   *City*   *State*   *Zip*

2. Proprietorship ___ Partnership ___ Incorporated ___

3. Who has control? _____

4. Media recognition? _____

5. How long have you been in business? _____

6. Billings: Now ___ two years ago ___ five years ago ___

7. Present accounts (Attach list showing name and address, type of business, and number of years with your agency.)

8. Three largest active accounts:

Name	Percentage of your total billings
_____	_____
_____	_____
_____	_____

9. Percentage of total billings you place with each medium:
   Newspapers ___   Consumer magazines ___   Directories ___
   Business papers ___   Radio ___   Direct mail ___
   Farm papers ___   Television ___   Other ___
   Business magazines ___   Outdoor ___   (Explain)

10. Accounts lost during last five years. (Attach list showing name, type of business, dates with your agency, and reason for termination.)

11. Number of full-time salaried employees:
    Executive and professional _____
    Clerical   _____

12. Account executive who would be assigned: _____
    Experience and other qualifications: _____
    _____

FIGURE 9.3
Advertising Agency Questionnaire
Source: Harvey R. Cook, *Selecting Advertising Media: A Guide for Small Business,* 2nd ed. (Washington, DC: Small Business Administration, 1977), p. 93.

Charges are also levied for such production work as photography and typesetting. These are usually billed at a rate of cost plus 17.65 percent. If services are performed for the agency by a third party, the agency may add a markup to the amount billed by the third party. This markup would cover the costs of securing the services and coordinating the services of several third-party providers. Charges are made for advertising on which commissions are not paid, such as direct mail and local newspaper advertising.

Agencies may also accept trade-outs as a form of compensation. Trade-outs consist of trading services for services. The agency performs services for the hotel or restaurant in exchange for services in the form of food and beverages or guest rooms that are provided on a complimentary basis up to the retail value of the services provided by the advertising agency. This method is widely used by hotels and restaurants for it increases the purchasing power of each dollar spent.

Establishing a positive agency-client relationship is of critical importance. Management should be willing to work closely with the agency and be honest and open in communication. A manager should be critical of the agency's work but should not nitpick each advertisement. Attention should instead be focused on the broader overall strategy. Taking an active interest in the relationship is a very positive step in making the relationship a good one.

ESTABLISHING ADVERTISING BUDGETS

Functions of Advertising Budgets

Budgets should predict and monitor revenues and expenses. Major expenses such as labor are tangible and more easily predicted and monitored. Advertising is also an expense that must be carefully planned, monitored, and controlled. Compared with major expense items, advertising may not seem like a large percentage, but because advertising is not tangible, careful planning and control must be implemented.

Management must carefully establish the advertising budget in order to maximize the productivity of the dollars spent. Advertising is not something that should be handled in a "seat of the pants" manner, with funds allocated solely on the basis of managerial whims. Some managers advertise when business volume is slow, thereby hoping to increase volume. Others attempt to reduce expenses by cutting back on advertising when a decline in volume occurs. Both approaches are subject to error because they are based on whim rather than on a rational decision-making and budgeting process.

Advertising budgets serve several useful and important functions: (1) to provide a detailed projection of future expenditures, (2) to provide both short- and long-range planning guides for management, and (3) to provide a method of monitoring and controlling advertising expenses by comparing actual expenses against projections.

Advantages and Disadvantages of Advertising Budgets

Numerous executives debate the pros and cons of budgeting advertising expenses. These are summarized as follows.

Advantages of Advertising Budgets

☐ Developing budgets forces management to look into the future. Although both the past and the current conditions certainly need to be considered, the future is the key. All management personnel must develop the ability to project future trends, revenues, and expenses. Failure to do so can easily lead to "management by crisis."

☐ Budgets serve as reference points. Advertising budget projections need not be solid figures cast in stone. Budgeted figures and media plans are, of course, subject to modification if the marketing situation changes dramatically. The budget, however, is important as a point of reference, a goal, and a standard against which actual performance can be compared.

☐ When advertising budgets are developed, all management personnel with marketing responsibilities should be involved in their preparation. This involvement fosters improved communication among individuals. In addition, as all managers have input into the development of the plan, support for the plan increases as each manager "owns a piece" of the plan. Once individuals identify with the budget as it is developed, this will increase their personal motivation to see that it is implemented successfully.

Disadvantages of Advertising Budgets

☐ Time is money. To prepare an advertising budget properly, a considerable amount of management time is necessary. Because the highest-paid management personnel engage in planning the advertising budget, the cost to the organization can be considerable. This represents time that some say could be spent more profitably performing other functions. The question to raise is "How much is it worth to the organization to have well-developed budgets and plans?"

☐ What events will shape the future? Certainly, the future is always going to be somewhat uncertain, but astute managers should be able to foresee trends and adapt to take full competitive advantage of these trends. Businesses often fail because management does not foresee changes and, as a result, is unable to adapt in a timely manner. Successful management must develop a proactive rather than a reactive posture; it must foresee change before it occurs and adapt to allow the organization to benefit from the change. A reactive posture means that management simply awaits changes and tries to adapt as best it can. Continual adaptation can easily result in management without direction and management by crisis. Clearly, a proactive approach is superior to reactive management as an advertising and marketing strategy.

Budgeting Methods

Advertising budgets are normally either fixed or contingency. Fixed budgets, by definition, are those based on a given prediction of sales volume and expected advertising activity. Projected expenditures are normally held firm, even if the assumptions on which the budget was based prove to be incorrect. Contingency budgets, on the other hand, are developed based on several sets of assumptions. This development means that if situation A happens, then implement plan A; if situation B occurs, then implement plan B; and so on. This type of budget draws its name from being based on a number of contingencies, or plans developed to be appropriate for several possible outcomes.

The development of weighted projected annual revenue figure or a similar approach is used in the development of a contingency approach to an advertising budget. Recall that three different budgets are developed based on optimistic, moderate, and pessimistic levels of sales. Based on actual sales trends, the advertising budget developed for that contingency is then implemented.

There are perhaps twenty to thirty methods to use in developing an appropriation for advertising. All of these methods are, however, variations on three basic methods: (1) the percentage of sales method, (2) the desired objective method, and (3) the competitive method.

The percentage of sales method has found very wide use in the hospitality industry. The method offers relative simplicity; sales are forecast, and a given percentage of this forecast is allocated to advertising. Within the hospitality industry, the amount of money spent for advertising is typically between 2 and 8 percent of gross sales. This method offers several advantages:

☐ It is very simple and straightforward.

☐ Some managers prefer to view all expenses as a percentage of sales, including advertising.

☐ It works well if sales can be forecasted accurately and market conditions are stable.

There are drawbacks as well:

☐ This method holds that if sales decline, so too will advertising expenditures. This is not a valid argument; instead, in this situation it would be wise to increase advertising expenditures.

☐ Increased advertising should result in increased sales, yet this method holds that an increase in sales results in an increase in the advertising budget.

The desired objective method involves developing an advertising budget based on well-defined objectives. Management must plan precisely what it wishes to accomplish through advertising. Based on these objectives, management must then decide what type and what amount of advertising will be necessary to achieve the objectives. Many factors must be considered, including projected sales, previous advertising, financial position of the firm, and competition within the marketplace. Advantages to this method include the following:

☐ Rather than simply allocating a fixed percentage of sales for each budget period, management must critically evaluate advertising expenditures.

☐ Advertising efforts are tied to specific measurable objectives, thereby making evaluation easier.

☐ Several variable factors, such as competition within the marketplace, are considered.

Two major disadvantages, however, must be considered:

☐ It is difficult to determine the precise mix of advertising that will accomplish the objectives satisfactorily.

☐ Engaging in this type of budget preparation is very time-consuming, especially when one considers that advertising and promotion represent only one line item on an income statement and only one aspect of the marketing mix.

The competitive method for establishing an advertising budget involves direct comparison with the advertising efforts of major competitors. Based on the type and amount of advertising done by the competition, management then establishes a budget that will roughly match the activities of the major competition. Advantages include the following:

☐ A relative level of equilibrium is established with regard to the competition.

☐ The method is simple and straightforward, especially if an industry average is used.

Disadvantages of the competitive method include the following:

☐ Relative advertising budgets and media decisions made by one firm usually are not applicable to other firms. How can management be assured that the competition's advertising is appropriate for its hotel or restaurant?

☐ Basing future advertising plans on the past performance of others is shortsighted in that it does not focus attention on the future.

A Budgeting System

Those exposed to the budget-preparation process for the first time are often overwhelmed. Images of political in-fighting sometimes develop until the process has been experienced and understood. Figure 9.4 illustrates the budget system in a manner that encapsulates the process in an easily understood format. Initially, upper management must determine future objectives. At the same time, the desired future performance for advertising is projected by taking into consideration trends, future influential factors, past performance, and input from subordinates. A preliminary budget is prepared and is then compared with the short- and long-range objectives of upper

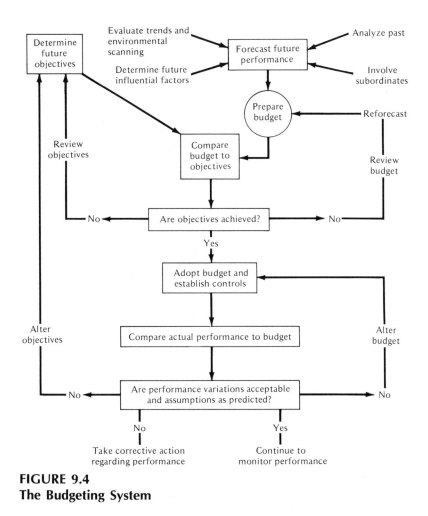

FIGURE 9.4
The Budgeting System

management. If the budget appears to satisfy the objectives, it is adopted, and controls are established. If the budget fails to meet the objectives, then the objectives and/or the budget must be revised to bring the two into harmony.

Once the budget is implemented, a simple control process is used. If the advertising performs as planned, the monitoring process continues. If, however, evaluation shows that the advertising is not successful, several avenues can be taken:

☐ The advertising can be changed to increase the probability of satisfying evaluation standards.

☐ The budget can be modified based on changing market conditions.

☐ The short- and long-range objectives can be changed based on new available information.

A Rolling Advertising Budget

One of the drawbacks to a traditional annually prepared budget is the amount of preparation time. Many personnel hours are required to solicit input from subordinates and combine it in a finished and workable budget. For this reason, a rolling budget may be implemented. A rolling budget begins with an established twelve-month budget. At the end of the first month (January, for example), actual figures are compared with budgeted figures, and based on this and other input, a budget is formulated for January of the next year. At the end of the next month (February), actual figures are compared with those budgeted, and a budget for the following February is formulated. In this way, the budget is prepared in a piecemeal fashion, yet each month is examined while the results are still fresh in everyone's mind. By formulating a budget in this manner, a manager always has a budget projection for a full twelve months in advance. By considering each month separately, management avoids rushing to complete a full twelve-month budget in a short period of time.

Advertising is not an expense to be taken lightly. It must be carefully planned, and its results should be monitored. With careful planning, a modest investment in advertising can produce satisfactory results. Without careful planning, a large investment may produce dismal results. The amount of money spent is not nearly as important as the way it is spent. Whatever method is used to establish as advertising budget, the level of advertising activity is important. Management should be aware of a distinct relationship between the number of advertising exposures and the consumers' purchasing response. This relationship is shown in Figure 9.5.

With a relatively small number of advertising exposures, the impact on

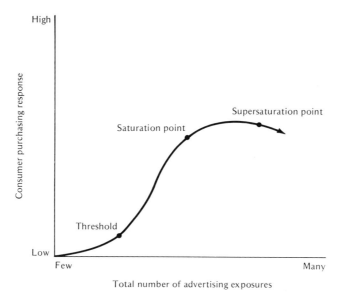

Total number of advertising exposures

FIGURE 9.5
Relationship Between Consumer Purchasing Behavior and the Total Number of Advertising Exposures

consumer purchasing behavior will be minimal. A very low level of advertising activity will not have an impact on consumers because they are exposed to many other advertisements each day, and any advertising needs to overcome the "noise" or "clutter" in the advertising media. Raising the level of advertising to reach a threshold point—the point at which consumers become aware of the advertisements—begins to affect the purchasing response. For example, if a single consumer is exposed to a radio advertisement once, the effect of this single exposure will be minimal. If this same consumer is exposed to the advertisement five times, however, the threshold point may be reached, and the combined frequency of exposures will begin favorably to affect purchasing behavior.

Once the threshold point is reached, any increases in the level of advertising exposure will also result in a favorable response in consumer purchasing, although this relationship is subject to the law of diminishing returns. Beyond the saturation point, any increases in the total number of advertising exposures will not result in similar increases in consumer purchases. In fact, if the total number of advertising exposures is increased further, to the supersaturation point, consumers will actually turn against the advertiser and reduce the level of patronage. The precise levels at which the threshold, saturation, and supersaturation points occur will vary greatly, depending on several variables. Only through experimentation with different levels of advertising can the optimal level of advertising exposures be established and maintained.

ADVERTISING POSITIONING AND STRATEGY

Advertising terms and jargon often sound like the language of war. Campaigns are *launched* and advertisements are *aimed* at *target* markets. Advertising need not be anything like war, but successful advertising is the result of carefully planned strategy.

A manager must first decide how to position the produce-service mix. Positioning is the manner in which the consumer views the product-service mix, and each hospitality operation is positioned differently, as discussed in Chapter 7. Before any advertising decisions are made or strategy is plotted, the proper market position must be determined.

Developing Strategy

Successful advertising does not result from haphazard planning and execution. A single advertisement may be very good, but successful companies produce consistently superior advertising. One of the keys to successful advertising is repetition. Long-term advertising success does not result from an occasional advertisement. An company must strive constantly to place its name in front of consumers, and it must also position itself in the proper manner.

Advertising succeeds when good strategy is developed. Strategy is not a magic, secret formula. According to advertising experts Kenneth Roman and Jane Maas, strategy development revolves around five key points:

1. *Objectives.* What should the advertising do? What goals does management want to achieve? For example, a new hospitality operation may set recognition among local residents as an objective, while another hospitality operation might seek to increase sales on slow nights. For the latter operation, most of the money would concentrate on promotions designed to increase volume on these nights.

2. *Targeted audience.* Who is the customer or potential customer? Advertising is not a success when used in a hit-or-miss manner. Successful advertising addresses a specifically targeted market and talks directly to that market. Many advertising programs fail because they attempt to appeal to too broad a targeted market. Figure 9.6 illustrates an advertisement that was targeted towards corporate meeting planners, with the purpose of introducing a new resort property.

3. *Key consumer benefit.* Consumers can be skeptical and often need a benefit, or a reason to buy, before they are persuaded. This is the pitch to the consumer. What key ideas or benefits should be promoted? Why should the

FIGURE 9.6

An Example of a Print Advertisement Targeted Toward Corporate Meeting Planners

Courtesy: Virginia Beach Resort and Conference Center, Virginia Beach, VA

consumer come to this operation instead of another? True differences between hospitality operations are rare, but a list of products and services the operation offers should stress those different from or superior to those offered by other hospitality facilities.

4. *Support.* To have a successful advertising campaign, the key benefit must be supported in some manner. Consumers are skeptical of advertising claims; who can blame them? Included in any advertisement should be a reason for the consumer to believe in the benefit. Consumer testimonials or test results showing superiority are often used for this purpose.

5. *Tone and manner.* The advertising strategy must have a "personality." This personality should blend with the image and positioning of the hospitality operation. McDonald's has been extremely successful with Ronald McDonald when advertising to children. This figure makes McDonald's seem like a fun place to be. Wendy's famous "where's the beef?" advertising campaign also featured a strong personality in the form of Clara Peller. The tone and manner selected should blend with the overall theme that management is trying to create and should show the potential customer the nature of

FIGURE 9.7
An Example of Using the Personality and Background of the General Manager to Create a Personality for the Hotel
Courtesy: Ramada Renaissance Hotel, Richmond, VA

the operation.[1] Figure 9.7 provides an example of how the personality and background of one individual can be used effectively to provide a personality for an intangible service such as a luxury hotel.

Developing a Central Appeal

Developing a central advertising appeal is not an easy process. Considerable time and thought must be devoted to the creative process before a viable appeal is found. Several rules of thumb exist for the development of this appeal:

☐ *A central appeal must offer some value to the consumer.* If the central appeal does not speak directly to the needs of the primary target market, the chances for success are greatly reduced. A well-developed marketing information system should provide specific data about the marketplace, enabling management to be in tune with the values of consumers.

☐ *The appeal must be distinctive.* All advertising must compete not only with all other hospitality organizations that are advertising but also with all consumer advertising, for everything from automobiles to washing machines. For the advertising to be effective, the appeal must offer something that separates it from everything else. Distinctive and unusual appeals are needed.

☐ *The appeal must be believable.* Claims made for the product-service mix must be backed up if the appeal is to have credibility. Because some consumers are more skeptical than others, the appeal should be believable to those who might at first have doubts.

☐ *The appeal should be simple.* Consumers are confronted each day with hundreds of advertising stimuli, and if one is to be recalled, it must be simple and straightforward. Effective and simple appeals that have been used successfully in the past include "We Do It All for You," "You, you're the one," "It's a good time for the great taste" (McDonald's), "The Burgers Are Better At Burger King," "Broiling beats frying" (Burger King), "America's Business Address" (Hilton Hotels).

Keys to Successful Advertising

To be successful, advertising needs to be approached in a systematic manner. The following are several suggestions on how to improve advertising efficiency.

☐ *Time.* Advertising should not be considered a necessary evil. Sales and operations are equally important and require time for an advertising program to generate satisfactory results.

☐ *Budgets.* These should be developed for the needs of each operation. It makes little sense to base an advertising budget on figures and percentages that represent the national average. Generally, a manager must have the courage to spend enough to produce successful results.

☐ *Study.* A manager needs to analyze the operation and determine the operation's advantages as compared with those of the competition. Disadvantages also need to be identified so that they may be minimized or eliminated completely. This evaluation must be done constantly so that any changes in the competitive situation are noted and adjustments are made quickly.

☐ *Analysis of market segments*. Each year, many people change jobs and move, and as people change jobs, their life styles change too. No market segment is constant; they are always changing. For this reason, management must know the patrons of the hospitality operation. By doing this, management can modify the operation to meet changing consumer demands.

☐ *Media*. Media must be selected very carefully to be effective. Media used must match the intended targeted markets. Each type of medium offers advantages and drawbacks, which are discussed in Chapter 10.

☐ *Formulation of a plan*. Advertising cannot be successful if it is approached in a haphazard manner. It is important that continuity be established among all forms of advertising so that advertising gains momentum. Continuity can be established through the consistent use of logos, distinctive type styles, music, or any creative touches to make the advertising stand out from other advertisements. Managers should not be afraid of advertising and should draw up plans designed to produce results. Nothing is worse than spending too little money on advertising, so advertising expenditures should not be cut. To be successful, advertising must be used regularly, not intermittently. Successful advertising is based on repetition.[2]

Embassy Suites has established itself as the market leader in the all-suite hotel market. One of the reasons behind their success has been their ability to develop a unique advertising campaign. They have been successful in creating an image in the consumer's mind and have developed a strong identity with the cartoon character Garfield. Figures 9.8, 9.9, 9.10, and 9.11 illustrate several of the print advertisements that are part of the total campaign.

PLANNING AND EVALUATING ADVERTISING CAMPAIGNS

Single advertisements may be creative or humorous and may convey a message, but by themselves, they are not able to achieve the necessary degree of advertising effectiveness. Many independent hospitality advertisers purchase print advertising or a few radio spots only at certain times of the year, particularly when business is slow. This type of advertising is not likely to be as effective as it could be, because continuity between the advertisements is lost. Such advertisements are not packaged as a campaign but are instead a hit-or-miss approach. An advertising campaign includes all forms of advertising held together by a single message or overall theme. A campaign is the

FIGURE 9.8
An Example of Embassy Suites Print Advertising Campaign
Courtesy: Embassy Suites, Irving, TX.

overall plan or strategy that guides the development of all forms of advertising.

Campaign planning is initiated by considering the competitive situation, currently targeted markets, potentially targeted markets, and market positioning. An astute manager should always be aware of the advertising activities of major competitors. This, of course, is not to say that the competition should dictate advertising activities, but awareness of competitors' activities may indicate trends. For example, what product-service attributes is the competition stressing? Is it food quality, service quality, physical facilities, extra amenities, guest room atmosphere, or something else? Awareness of the efforts of direct competition may allow a manager to counter the competition's benefits and gain a competitive advantage.

Both the current target markets and the potential new markets must also be evaluated. How can management best reinforce the current markets to promote repeat patronage? What type of message will reach these markets

FIGURE 9.9
An Example of Embassy Suites Print Advertising Campaign
Courtesy: Embassy Suites, Irving, TX.

most effectively? In addition, what new markets should be explored? What is the best type of message to use to overcome uncertainty and resistance and thereby promote first-time patronage? Can these two messages be combined, or are they best kept separate? The market positioning must also be considered. How is the operation perceived by repeat consumers and by potential consumers? Is this the same perception that management wishes to project?

Types of Advertising Campaigns

Advertising campaigns come in all patterns and sizes, depending on the resources and needs of the individual hospitality organization. Generally, campaigns are organized geographically on a national, regional, or local level.

FIGURE 9.10
An Example of Embassy Suites Print Advertising Campaign
Courtesy: Embassy Suites, Irving, TX.

Each is self-explanatory and will differ in sophistication and media selection. Local campaign planners often feel that they are at a distinct disadvantage because they have smaller advertising budgets and less marketing expertise. This need not be a disadvantage; instead, it is often just the opposite. The use of local radio spots and local print and/or television advertising allows the advertiser to speak directly with the local clientele. Often the local advertiser has a much clearer understanding of the target market and is thereby able to achieve a competitive advantage over regional and national advertisers.

Campaign Checkpoints

When developing the theme for a campaign, Roman and Maas suggest that the advertiser consider four checkpoints:

FIGURE 9.11
An Example of Embassy Suites Print Advertising Campaign
Courtesy: Embassy Suites, Irving, Texas.

1. *Maintain visual similarity.* This similarity applies to the visual media. Most common of all approaches is the use of a well-defined logo or the same layout and type style in all advertisements. Are advertisements easily recognized without a look at the organization's name? If not, perhaps the visual similarity needs further attention. In national fast-food advertising, visual similarity is maintained by the McDonald's golden arches.

2. *Maintain verbal similarity.* Phrases and statements are repeated in all advertisements, reinforcing the advertiser's image and message.

3. *Maintain similarity of sound.* With the increased use of television and radio advertising, maintaining similarity of sound is also important. The use of the same announcer and/or the same musical logo can aid in maintaining this similarity. Almost everyone could hum or sing the McDonald's song, indicating superior similarity of sound.

4. *Similarity of attitude.* Projecting consistent attitude and positioning is critical to the success of an advertising campaign. All media advertisements should project a consistency of attitude in order to establish continuity.[3]

The examples shown earlier in the chapter illustrate the points discussed above. In addition, Figures 9.12 and 9.13 provide excellent examples of visual similarity.

An Advertising-Planning Model

For many managers, one of the most difficult aspects involved in managing the advertising and promotional function is the detail of planning, implementing, and evaluating an advertising campaign. Figure 9.14 illustrates an advertising-planning model. This visual format makes it easier to concep-

FIGURE 9.12
An Example of Visual Similarity
Reprinted with the permission of Holiday Inns, Inc.

FIGURE 9.13
An Example of Visual Similarity
Reprinted with the permission of Holiday Inns, Inc.

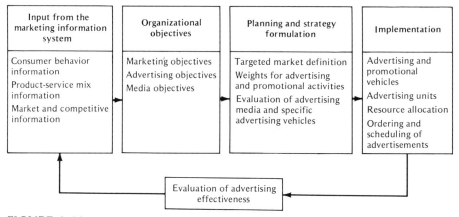

FIGURE 9.14
An Advertising-Planning Model

tualize all aspects of the process and should provide a novice planner with a structured framework from which to work. The model contains five components: input from the marketing information system, organizational objectives, planning and strategy formulation, implementation, and evaluation of advertising effectiveness.

The first component, input from the marketing information system, includes information from three separate areas. First, relevant information concerning consumer behavior should be reviewed and analyzed. What are the trends in consumer behavior? How are dining habits changing? How are the travel patterns of the key market segments changing? What hospitality concepts are "hot," and which ones are "not so hot"? Input concerning the product-service mix is also important. What are the sales trends for the various products and services offered? Information concerning the activities of direct and indirect competition is also of value in planning the advertising campaign. The use of this type of marketing information is discussed in Chapter 5.

The second component, organizational objectives, should be established in three separate areas: marketing, advertising, and media. Marketing objectives focus on such things as market share, producing a specified percentage of increase in sales volume or a specified percentage of increase in repeat patronage. Advertising objectives focus on such topics as increasing consumer awareness and drawing consumers away from the competition with advertisements demonstrating the superiority of the organization's product-service mix. Media objectives focus on the selection of the individual media to achieve the marketing and advertising objectives. For example, an objective might read, "to plan media selections so that 90 percent of the target market segments are exposed to at least two of the advertisements."

The third component, planning and strategy formulation, involves the formal definition of the specific target markets. Given the limited resources available, it is virtually impossible to reach the saturation point with all target market segments. Therefore, what specific target market segments are most important? Weights should be established for all of the desired advertising and promotional activities. For example, what proportion of the resources available should be allocated for radio, print, direct mail, and all other activities? Finally, each advertising medium and its individual vehicles are evaluated based on effectiveness and cost efficiency in reaching the target market segments.

Fourth, the advertising plan is implemented. This component includes working with each of the selected advertising vehicles, determining the advertising units (for example, half-page print advertisements or 30-second radio spots), allocating resources to pay for the advertising time and space, and finally ordering and scheduling the time and space with each individual vehicle.

The fifth and final component is evaluation of advertising effectiveness.

Without engaging in some form of evaluation process, how will management know to what degree the advertising efforts have met with success? There are three important explanations of why some form of evaluation procedure should be undertaken:

1. *To come to understand the consumer.* This involves learning what consumers want, why they want it, and how best to serve these wants.

2. *To avoid costly mistakes.* When advertising effectiveness is tested, errors that might have gone undetected are noted, and adjustments can be made. In this way, both the effectiveness and cost efficiency of advertising is increased.

3. *To add structure.* Rather than viewing advertising as a business expense whose impact is impossible to measure, management can measure the impact of advertising. If sales increase by 10 percent, what is the reason for this increase? What types of advertising and promotion have had the greatest impact on sales?[4]

Evaluating an Advertising Campaign

Several years ago, the president of a large retail chain was discussing the firm's advertising efforts with a group of business people. When one person posed a question about evaluating advertising, the president responded, "I suspect that half our advertising is wasted. The only problem is that I don't know which half." This story may bring a smile to one's face, but it is often an accurate assessment of the situation. Large hospitality organizations engaged in national and regional campaigns normally have the resources to evaluate advertising effectively. Smaller advertisers and local advertisers often are not able to evaluate advertising effectiveness.

Advertising effectiveness can be measured for both its short- and long-term impact. Short-term measurements are usually given most attention because they reflect directly the income statement and the financial position of the organization. In addition, managers' tenure and bonuses are normally based on short-term performance. The long-term effects of advertising, however, should not be overlooked. Long-term effects are reflected by repeat patronage, brand loyalty, and an asset called "good will." It is difficult, however, to measure the long-term residual effects of advertising within a reasonable margin for error. In the last several years, econometric techniques have advanced to the point where measuring advertising effectiveness is more precise.

Advertising can be evaluated subjectively by the management of a hospitality operation, either alone or in conjunction with an advertising agency. Experienced management plays a key role in this type of evaluation.

If management has successfully directed advertising campaigns, subjective evaluation may indeed be adequate. This is especially true of agency executives, as they often have a wealth of experience that allows them to gauge quite accurately the overall effectiveness of advertising efforts.

It is also wise to maintain a file of all advertisements. These can then be available for easy reference and reviewed periodically for "winners" and "losers." Subjectivity does have a place in the overall evaluation of advertising effectiveness. The experience and expertise of agency personnel and hospitality managers should not be discounted. These resources are best used in combination with objective methods.

It is almost impossible to measure advertising effectiveness objectively unless well-defined objectives have been formulated prior to initiating a campaign. How would management know whether they were successful if they were not able to compare actual performance with specific objectives? As stressed in Chapter 4, clearly defined, quantifiable objectives are very important. Variances between actual performance and objectives are noted and corrective action taken. In the event that the advertising proves more successful than expected, this too should be evaluated so that the success might be repeated.

Objective testing of advertising is time-consuming and expensive. Not all operations can afford or will want this type of testing. Testing is invaluable if undertaken with care and is cost-effective if used occasionally. Following is a brief review of commonly used techniques, although not all are suitable for all types of operations:

1. *Copy testing.* This involves pretesting the copy of an advertisement prior to running it in the media. Several advertisements are normally shown to a group of consumers, and questions are asked of the group, typically, "Which advertisement would interest you most?" "Which advertisement is most convincing?" "Which advertisement is most likely to cause you to patronize the hospitality establishment?" These questions can be asked of an entire group assembled to review a series of advertisements, or personal interviews can be conducted.

2. *Inquiry and sales.* Direct mail advertising lends itself to the inquiry and sales method. This involves keeping a tally of each inquiry and sale. For example, if a series of advertisements were run to promote banquet business, how many people phoned or contacted the operation? How many of these inquiries were converted into sales? From these tallies, it is easy to compute a cost per inquiry and a cost per sale for this type of advertising.

3. *Coupons and split runs.* Coupons can be tallied to evaluate the effectiveness of one promotion against others. For example, did the sundae special sell more than the special french fries promotion? Coupons are used extensively by the hospitality industry because they allow for easy evaluation.

Coupons can be carried one step further and used to compare one medium against another. For example, suppose that management had a choice among three print media in which to place advertisements. Which one will reach the target market most effectively? The same advertisements and coupons could be run in the three media, with each coupon coded so that a tally could be made of the number of coupons from medium A, B, and C. In this way, a relative ranking of effectiveness is possible.

4. *Sales tests.* The level of gross sales or sales of specific items can be monitored following a specific period of advertising aimed at increasing one or the other. It is often difficult to take into account all the variables that affect sales both positively and negatively and thereby establish a cause-and-effect relationship.

5. *Consumer testing of awareness, recall, and attitude.* Through assembled groups, telephone surveys, direct mail surveys, and personal interviews, consumers can be tested to determine their relative awareness concerning a specific hospitality operation. Have they heard of the operation? Do they patronize it? If so, how frequently? Do they recall seeing any advertisements? Which ones do they recall? When shown certain advertisements, do they recall seeing these? (This is known as *aided recall.*)

SUMMARY

This chapter reviews advertising and promotion function as applied to hospitality marketing, providing a broad-based overview of a process that includes promotion, national and local advertising, and cooperative advertising.

Relationships which are developed with an advertising agency are critical. The chapter provides an overview of the advantages and disadvantages of working with an agency, the role of the agency, the types of agencies, methods that can be used to select an agency, and methods for compensation.

An advertising life cycle can be defined to correspond with the product life cycle discussed in Chapter 3. It consists of five major stages: introduction, conservative expansion, rapid expansion, plateaued maturity, and regeneration or decline. Each stage calls for a unique approach to advertising and promotion with goals appropriate for the life cycle position of the organization.

To reach the highest level of success, management must engage in various advertising efforts. Generally, advertising seeks to satisfy three goals: (1) to establish awareness in the minds of consumers, (2) to establish a positive perceived value in the minds of consumers, and (3) to promote repeat patronage and brand loyalty among consumers.

The chapter's discussion of advertising budgets includes their functions, advantages and disadvantages to budgeting, types of advertising budgets, methods for developing advertising budgets, the budgeting system, and rolling advertising budgets. Advertising budgets perform several functions: to provide a detailed projection of future expenditures, to provide both short- and long-range planning guidelines for management, and to provide a method of monitoring and controlling advertising expenses by comparing actual expenses against projections. Advertising budgets are usually either fixed or contingency, and they are developed using three major methods: (1) the percentage of sales method, (2) the desired objective method, and (3) the competitive method.

A budgeting system provides an easily understood presentation of budget development. Advertising positioning and strategy include formation of an objective, a target audience, key consumer benefits, support for the benefits, and an appropriate tone or manner. The development of an advertising appeal includes six keys to successful advertising.

Finally, planning and evaluating advertising involve noting campaign checkpoints. A five-component advertising planning model includes input from the marketing information system, organizational objectives, planning and strategy formulation, implementation, and evaluation of advertising effectiveness.

KEY WORDS AND CONCEPTS

- ☐ Goals for advertising
- ☐ Criticisms of advertising
- ☐ Definition of advertising
- ☐ National and local advertising
- ☐ Cooperative advertising
- ☐ Advertising agencies
- ☐ Advertising agency compensation
- ☐ Advertising budgets; percentage of sales, desired objective, and competitive methods
- ☐ Rolling advertising budget
- ☐ Steps to advertising strategy formulation
- ☐ Advertising central appeal
- ☐ Visual, verbal, sound, and attitude similarity
- ☐ Evaluation, copy testing, inquiry and sales, coupons and split runs, sales tests, and consumer testing of awareness, recall, and attitude

Questions For Review and Discussion

1. What are the major advantages and drawbacks to advertising?
2. Define the following: (1) advertising, (2) promotion, (3) national advertising, (4) local advertising, and (5) cooperative advertising.
3. Cite and discuss in some detail the advertising life cycle. How is this life cycle integrated with the organizational life cycle? What advertising strategies are appropriate for the different stages in the product life cycle?
4. Develop a planned and rational argument both for and against hospitality advertising.
5. What are the three major goals of advertising?
6. How would you respond to the charges raised by advertising critics?
7. What are the pros and cons of using an advertising agency? Would you use the services of an agency?
8. How are agencies compensated for their work?
9. How would you go about selecting an agency?
10. How are advertising and promotion integrated with other marketing functions?
11. Of what value are advertising budgets?
12. Cite and discuss the methods of developing an advertising budget.
13. What is a rolling advertising budget? How is one developed?
14. What is meant by *positioning?*
15. How might advertising strategy be developed?
16. Critique the six keys to successful advertising.
17. What is an advertising campaign?
18. What factors should be considered when planning a campaign?
19. Cite and discuss the major campaign checkpoints.
20. Do you believe that advertising is wasteful? Why or why not?
21. How might advertising be made more effective?
22. What techniques are used to evaluate advertising effectiveness?

CHAPTER 10

Advertising and Promotional Media

This chapter examines the most visible of all advertising and promotion, the external advertising media, as well as brochures and supplemental media. Each of the major media are examined in considerable detail. The techniques that make successful use of the individual media are reviewed, and the relative strengths and weaknesses of each are introduced.

The chapter is divided into the following sections:

INTRODUCTION

MEDIA SELECTION
☐ Factors Affecting Media Selection
☐ Developing Media Plans
☐ Media Scheduling

PRINT ADVERTISING
☐ Techniques for Successful Print Advertising
☐ Developing Copy for Print Advertising
☐ Print Advertising Terms

RADIO ADVERTISING
☐ Techniques for Successful Radio Advertising
☐ Types of Radio Stations
☐ Selecting Radio Spots
☐ Producing Radio Commercials
☐ Radio Advertising Terms

TELEVISION ADVERTISING
☐ Techniques for Successful Television Advertising
☐ Types of Television Commercials
☐ Classes of Television Advertising
☐ Television Advertising Terms

DIRECT MAIL ADVERTISING
☐ Techniques for Successful Direct Mail Advertising
☐ Mailing Lists

OUTDOOR ADVERTISING
☐ Techniques for Successful Outdoor Advertising
☐ Types of Outdoor Advertising
☐ Outdoor Advertising Terms

BROCHURES
☐ Creating Effective Brochures

SUPPLEMENTAL ADVERTISING MEDIA

SUMMARY

KEY WORDS AND CONCEPTS

QUESTIONS FOR REVIEW AND DISCUSSION

INTRODUCTION

No one questions that advertising and promotion are extremely powerful forces in the hospitality industry. They must be managed with care and used to the maximum advantage of the organization. External advertising and promotion constitute a major area of marketing effort for most hospitality organizations, as numerous media are employed in an effort to communicate with selected target markets. The success of these advertising efforts rests to a large degree on the media and the manner in which they are used. Many times, advertisers spend large amounts of money without achieving the desired results. In other cases, advertisers spend only a relatively small amount, yet the results are dramatic. It is useful to remember that it is not how much is invested, but how it is invested. The word *investment* is what advertising is—an investment. Dollars allocated to advertising are expected to generate increased sales; a positive return on an investment is expected.

External advertising is important because it can make the difference between success and failure. Management must ask three simple questions in initial advertising planning:

1. *To whom should the advertising be directed?* Specifically, what target markets have been identified as primary and secondary markets? Which individuals represent opinion leaders and reference group leaders?

2. *Where do these people live?* Once the target markets are identified, it is imperative to determine where these individuals live and work. What are the best methods to reach them through advertising? In many cases, this will be as easy as determining the leaders of the business community in a small town. In other instances, determining where these individuals live and work will prove quite difficult. Suppose, for example, that a tablecloth restaurant operated in the suburbs of a major city. Where should the restaurant advertise? How should the target markets be reached? Where do these people live and work? These questions may not have self-evident answers, and a considerable amount of research and discussion may be necessary before the answers are determined.

3. *What media should be used?* Would it be best to use print advertising? Perhaps radio or television should play a major role? What about outdoor, direct mail, or supplemental advertising? Should directories, such as the yellow pages, be considered?

MEDIA SELECTION

Selection of advertising media is one of the most critical decisions facing management. The product-service mix must be positioned in such a way that maximum effectiveness in each medium is achieved. Consideration must also be given to the types of media to be used and the allocation of resources among the selected media. Finally, contracts must be arranged with each medium, a time-consuming process if managers do this themselves.

Factors Affecting Media Selection

First and foremost when selecting media is the nature of the target market segments. A medium should be selected based on its ability to reach the maximum number of potential consumers, at the lowest cost per thousand consumers (C.P.M.).

Second, the objectives of the overall campaign must be considered. Is the advertiser seeking maximum impact, or is continuity with previous and future advertising more important? For example, if a well-established restaurant had used a refined and sophisticated approach in newspaper and magazine advertising, it would not make sense for it to advertise using a high-volume, high-energy advertisement, for this would break up the continuity among advertisements in different media.

Third, consideration must be given to the amount of coverage desired. The relative costs of the various media must be weighed when decisions are made. The sizes and frequency of advertisements should be analyzed carefully.

Fourth, the activities of the direct competition should be reviewed and trends identified. This is not to say that media should be selected based on a "monkey see, monkey do" philosophy, but it is sound management to keep close tabs on the advertising efforts of major competitors.

Howard Heinsius, President of Needham and Grohmann, Inc., suggests several essentials in media selection:[1]

☐ *Market focus.* Carefully examine your market by product-service mix category or brand and by target market segment. How does your hotel or restaurant fit in? What are the specific attributes you want to advance?

☐ *Media focus.* Keep an open mind and listen to all media sales representatives in your area. Make note of changes, events, new programs, and the opportunities they might offer. Media time and space is perishable; keep an alert eye for special purchase opportunities.

☐ *Periodic media update.* Keep current information about rates and other important information such as cost per thousand and circulation. The situation can change rapidly. Be sure to stay on top of it.

☐ *Establish media effectiveness guidelines.* Keep tangible guidelines in mind as you examine each of the media options. This will help you to make better media selections.

☐ *Advertising by objective.* If specific advertising objectives have been established such as sales targets or consumer awareness levels this will aid in determining the best media combination.

☐ *Coordinate advertising with marketing campaigns.* Advertising is but one part of the total marketing mix. Be sure that it is coordinated with the other efforts in the areas of personal selling, promotion, and public relations.

☐ *Develop a sound advertising budget.* Start with an amount that is within your means and then allocate it by target markets. It is important to not try to do too much with very limited funds.

☐ *Plan around media pollution.* All forms of media are oversaturated at times. Try to select the best times to get your message across and how to rise above the pollution of other advertisements.

☐ *Coordinate the local efforts to match the national advertising efforts.* When a national campaign is being run, try to take advantage of this by running a local campaign that will follow.

☐ *Use a variety of media.* Within the limits of budgets, try to use different combinations and levels of different media to determine which is most effective.

☐ *Keep accurate files.* It is important to be able to review the results of each advertising campaign. Maintaining accurate records of budget, media schedules, and sales results is critical.

Developing Media Plans

The development of media plans involves planning the media to use, and determining when specific media will be used and how a specific combination of media will allow the organization to achieve its advertising objectives. Media plans must involve answers to these questions: (1) What specific target markets are to be reached? (2) When does management want to reach these target markets? (3) Where do these target markets live and work? (4) What ways are best to reach these target markets? and (5) Why?

It is important to clearly identify those individuals the advertising should reach. Demographics are perhaps the easiest way to define markets. For example, all advertising might be aimed at men and women between the ages of 25 and 35 with annual incomes above $25,000. Advertising might be slanted toward women such that a 60-to-40 ratio of female-to-male exposures is achieved.

When is the best time to reach these target markets? Are there specific times of the year when management wants to concentrate advertising, such as the fall in preparation for Christmas banquet business or the winter months, to increase business? What time of the day does management want to reach the target markets?

Where do these individuals live and work? If management truly wants to make maximum use of advertising expenditures, this information will prove useful. What is the best way to reach target markets? This is the question that separates successful advertising from the less than successful. Specifically, which media will be most effective?

Finally the question why: A solid rationale for each decision is essential. Decisions based on intuition or "gut feelings" may be huge successes, but in the long term, objective decisions are usually superior. Management must review the plan with some degree of skepticism, constantly questioning why a certain course of action is best for the organization.

Media Scheduling

Each hospitality organization must tailor the scheduling of media to fit its individual needs. Generally speaking, however, there are three approaches to scheduling, as shown in Figure 10.1. *Continuous advertising* involves keeping the amount of advertising relatively constant over time. This type is appropriate for those hospitality operations with very stable volumes. *Flighting media scheduling* involves a schedule set up in spurts and stops. Periods of blitz advertising are used, with no advertising between blitzes. *Pulsing advertising* balances the previous two approaches in that it provides a constant low-level flow of advertising with intermittent periods of blitz advertising. Ideally, high levels of continuous advertising are normally thought to be superior, but economic considerations may necessitate the adoption of either flighting or pulsing media scheduling.

PRINT ADVERTISING

Print advertising includes newspapers and magazines. Print advertising is used more frequently by hospitality advertisers than other media because it offers several advantages:

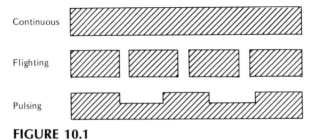

FIGURE 10.1
Approaches to Media Scheduling

☐ *Ease of scheduling.* If a manager decides to run an advertisement on one day's notice, it can normally be scheduled in the next day's newspaper.

☐ *Relatively low cost.* A local advertisement in a newspaper is usually low-cost.

☐ *Flexibility of advertising copy.* Copy can easily be changed, allowing advertisements to be tailored to fit ever-changing market conditions.

☐ *Broad appeal.* Newspapers reach all demographic segments in a geographic area.

☐ *Coupons.* Newspapers allow for the use of coupons, which can increase volume and are also valuable in evaluating advertising effectiveness.

Newspaper advertising has its drawbacks:

☐ *Short life span of the advertisement.* Newspapers are read one day and put in the trash can the next day.

☐ *Difficulty of pinpointing the target market.* This causes a good deal of wasted circulation and raises the cost per thousand potential consumers.

☐ *Competition within the newspaper.* It is easy to have an advertisement buried amid other advertisements, decreasing readership and effectiveness.

☐ *Poor reproduction of photographs.* Newspaper production and printing does not reproduce photographs with clarity. Drawings are usually a better choice.

Magazines offer these advertising advantages:

☐ *Superior reproduction of artwork and photographs.* Color photographs reproduce particularly well.

☐ *Longer life span of advertisement.* Through pass-along readership, magazine advertisements are seen by more people and have a longer life span than that of newspapers and other media.

☐ *Audience selectivity.* Some magazines are aimed at the general population, but through the use of regional and metropolitan editions as well as selective market magazines, advertisers can pinpoint specific target markets. This is especially true of city magazines.

Drawbacks to magazine advertising include the following:

☐ *Lack of timeliness.* Magazine publishers require advertisers to adhere to closing dates far in advance of the distribution date. This does not allow for immediate changes of layout and copy if market conditions change rapidly.

☐ *High production costs.* Costs associated with magazine advertising are generally substantially higher than those for newspapers.

☐ *Magazines not suited for local market.* Magazines are generally either regional or national in scope and are often of limited value to local hospitality operators. Their maximum advantage is derived by regional and national chains. City magazines do, however, overcome this drawback. In addition, city magazines generally reach a more highly educated and higher-income reader than general interest magazines.

Techniques for Successful Print Advertising

As with all types of advertising, no hard and fast rules exist; only guidelines can aid in management decisions. The following guidelines, developed over time, are generally accepted within the advertising community.

First, every effort should be made to attract the consumer's attention with the headline. Many print advertisements are ineffective because a large percentage of consumers skim through the pages and never read the entire advertisement. The headline must therefore get the attention of the reader and deliver the message.

Second, print advertising is more effective if visual components, such as artwork and photographs, are used. Although photographs do not generally reproduce well in newspaper, simple drawings can be used very effectively to increase readership. Photographs and artwork are both effective in magazines.

Third, every effort should be made to keep the layout and copy simple and straightforward. Print readers are less likely to read an advertisement that looks crowded and contains many ideas. Instead, the advertisement should have one or perhaps two points and no more. Print advertising is one place where "less is more," and this means more effectiveness.

Fourth, print advertising lends itself to the use of coupons. Coupons serve to increase volume and can be very valuable in assessing the effectiveness of print advertising media. Coupons should be designed so that they are really mini advertisements that can be clipped out and will convey the message without the need for the consumer to save the rest of the advertisement. Placement of coupons is important both within the advertisement and on the page on which the advertisement appears. They should be placed at the edge of the advertisement, and the advertisement at the edge of the page to make it easier to clip them out. Simple things like coupon placement can increase advertising effectiveness dramatically.

Finally, when a given print advertisement has been effective, management should not hesitate to repeat it. The advertisement may seem old hat to the management of the hospitality operation, but many potential consumers have not seen the advertisement or do not recall it. Therefore, what has proven successful in the past should be repeated.

Developing Copy for Print Advertising

For some individuals, developing advertising copy is simple and easy; for others it is painful and frustrating. This section offers a few ideas and clues to make the task easier. Copywriting does not require the brains of a genius or the writing skills of a Pulitzer Prize winner. It simply requires looking closely at the consumer and the hospitality product-service mix.

The first step is to take a close look at the product-service mix. What does the hospitality organization's product-service mix offer that is appealing to the potential consumer? It is important to avoid generalizations, such as "good food," "luxurious guest rooms," and "fine atmosphere." These phrases may be true, but what will they do for the consumer? Those items that could separate the operation from others and give it a real competitive edge should be listed. Emphasis should be placed on the tangible aspects of the product-service mix, such as the decor or service personnel. It is very important to try to make the intangibles seem more tangible. This will help the consumer remember the advertisement.

Second, it is important to talk directly with the potential consumer and discuss the benefits of the hospitality operation. What is the operation going to do for the consumer? What specific benefits are offered? What specific needs are satisfied? For example, a tablecloth restaurant appealing to the business community might advertise a "lightning lunch" or "express lunch" featuring a selection of menu items that could be served immediately. It is important to back this claim with a guarantee such as "if the menu items are not served within 15 minutes, the lunch is free."

Third, the consumer benefits should be listed in priority order. Perhaps it is best to develop two or three advertisements around the top three benefits and translate these consumer benefits into headlines. Headlines can take many forms, as shown in Table 10.1.

TABLE 10.1
Examples of Print Headlines

Type of Headline	Example
Direct-promise headline	You'll love our 42-item salad bar.
	Your room will be perfect or you won't pay for it.
News headline	Grand Opening—July 1st
Curiosity headline	Who says you can't get something for nothing?
Selective headline	To all single women
Emotional headline	Mother's Day—What have you done for your Mom lately?

Once the headline is developed, the copy for the remainder of the advertisement is written. It should reflect and support the headline and should be brief. This is not to say that long copy can never be successful. Instead, each work, each sentence, and each paragraph must say exactly what the copywriter wants it to. All the words must count and must drive home and support the benefits to the consumer. Writing, rewriting, and further editing are the key elements in developing copy that sells. Copy should be clear; nothing is worse than vague advertising copy. When a vague phrase such as "fine food" is used, it is meaningless to the consumer. Copy should instead explain what this food will do for the consumers and how it will make them feel. It is important to make the intangibles more tangible and to talk to the consumer in terms of how the product-service mix will provide benefits that are important to the potential buyer.

Print Advertising Terms

Following are terms commonly used in print media, although some apply to other media as well:

☐ *Agate line.* A measurement by which newspaper and some magazine advertising space is sold, regardless of the actual type size used. There are 14 agate lines to the inch. Therefore, if a manager wanted advertising space two columns wide and three inches deep, the firm would be charged for 84 agate lines.

☐ *Base rate.* The lowest rate for advertising in print media. This rate is for run of paper (R.O.P.) and means that the medium, at its discretion, puts advertisements wherever there is space.

☐ *Bleed.* An advertisement that extends into all or part of the margin of a page. Rates for bleeds vary with the medium used. Most media usually charge extra for bleeds.

☐ *Circulation.* The number of copies distributed. Primary circulation includes those who subscribe, while secondary circulation includes those who read pass-along copies. It is very difficult to measure secondary circulation.

☐ *Controlled circulation.* For business publications, this is now usually called *qualified circulation.* It is nonpaid. Specific business publications are provided, often at little or no cost, to those individuals who qualify by engaging in a specific line of business. For example, meeting planners typically receive 2–3 publications targeted toward individuals who plan meetings. These publications are not available to the general public.

☐ *C.P.M. (Cost per thousand).* The C.P.M. formula is the oldest means for comparing media rates. For print, the cost per 1000 units of circulation is calculated on the basis of the one-time rate for one black-and-white page.

☐ *Frequency.* The number of times the same audience—listeners, readers, or viewers—is reached. It is expressed as an average, since some people may see or hear an advertisement only once, while others see it a dozen times. Frequency can be increased by advertising more often in the media used currently; adding more vehicles in a medium currently used, as in using two newspapers instead of one; and expanding into other media, such as radio as well as newspapers.

☐ *Milline formula.* This is used to compare the costs of advertising in different newspapers. It is customary to use the cost per line per million circulation, called the milline rate. (Line rate × 1,000,000/circulation = milline rate.) The reason for multiplying by 1,000,000 is that the larger figures are easier to compare. If the rates compared are quoted in column inches, this rate can be used in the formula instead of the line rate. The same rate—baseline or column inch—must be used for all newspapers compared.

☐ *Reach.* The number or percentage of people exposed to a specific publication. The reach is usually measured throughout publication of a number of issues. It is the net unduplicated audience.

☐ *Volume rate.* Also called a *bulk rate,* a volume rate may be for total space, time used, or total dollars expended during a contract period, usually twelve months. As more advertising is done, unit costs decrease. Newspapers generally quote their rates in agate lines or column inches. Rates get progressively lower as the number of lines increases.

RADIO ADVERTISING

Radio advertising finds extensive use in the foodservice segment of the industry, and in most cases, it is extremely effective. Radio is able to develop a distinct personality for a hospitality operation and it can reach consumers twenty-four hours a day. Radio advertising offers these advantages:

☐ *Personal quality.* Radio spots can be written so that they talk directly to the consumer.

☐ *Low relative cost.* The cost of radio is usually quite low for local advertising, especially when a package involving several spots is purchased.

☐ *Flexibility.* Radio copy can be changed quickly, should market conditions change rapidly.

☐ *Market saturation.* Through the use of several local stations, each appealing to specific target markets, it is possible to saturate an area with radio advertising. This saturation approach can be very effective for new operations or for those exploring new markets.

Drawbacks of radio advertising include the following:

☐ *Lack of visual appeal.* It is said that people "eat with their eyes," yet this is not possible on radio. Extra effort must be made when developing the copy and sound effects for a radio commercial to stretch the listener's imagination. The commercial must "sell the sizzle."

☐ *Broad target markets.* Just as this is an advantage when attempting to saturate a market, it is a disadvantage when attempting to appeal to narrowly defined target markets. To reach the potential target market, radio advertising is wasted on individuals who may not represent good prospects.

☐ *Nonlasting impressions.* Once the commercial has aired, it is gone. The listener cannot refer back to the advertisement to check the price, phone number, or hours of operation.

☐ *Advertising competition.* The airwaves are filled with advertisements for other hospitality operations and for every consumer product and service imaginable. Given this situation, called advertising "noise," it is often necessary to maintain higher levels of advertising to achieve the desired effectiveness.

Techniques for Successful Radio Advertising

It is important to recognize that those listening to the radio are also engaged in other activities. They may be cleaning house, driving their cars, or playing at the beach, but they are doing something besides listening to the radio. Because listeners are not devoting 100 percent of their attention to the radio, a commercial should be kept fairly simple, with benefits limited to support one or two major ideas. It is not effective to bombard listeners with several ideas in each commercial; they simply will not remember these points. It is also important to mention the name of the hospitality operation and the benefit early in the commercial. Many consumers "tune out" commercials, and an advertiser wants to make sure they hear at least part of the commercial.

Second, music should be kept simple, and complex lyrics should be avoided. Ideally, a jingle or short composition should trigger name recognition in the consumer's mind. Short and simple music aids in developing this recognition, especially if it is repeated as a musical logo in all radio commercials.

Third, the advertisement should suggest immediate action. Every effort should be made to get the consumer to act. Consumers will quickly forget the radio commercial, and unless the advertiser can encourage almost immediate action, the effectiveness of the advertising will be decreased.

Fourth, the advertisement should talk directly to consumers in a language and a tone that they will understand. The approach should be personal, much as if it were a conversation, albeit one-way. Many hospitality establishments, especially on the local level, have had success using live radio commercials. These can be particularly effective if a dominant radio personality does the commercials. These individuals often have very loyal listeners and can have a significant influence on them.

Finally, the copy for radio commercials should be written so that it makes the listener visualize the products and services.

Types of Radio Stations

The variety of choices in radio stations is very broad, both on the AM and FM bands. Stations are typically classified as progressive, contemporary, middle of the road (MOR), news-information-sports, talk, good music, classical, country and western, and ethnic.

Progressive stations, sometimes called album-oriented rock, or AOR, appeal to a young audience with contemporary musical tastes. Those who listen to this type of station tend to "think young" and listen to the less conservative music that this type of station offers its listeners.

Contemporary stations offer a milder selection of rock music featuring current hits and sometimes specializing in specific types of rock such as light "adult rock" or "golden oldies."

Middle of the road, or MOR, offers as close to a mass appeal format as is offered by radio. This segment was at one time dominant, but now the popularity of this format has declined. It appeals to the middle demographic segments.

News, information, and sports radio stations have proven to be very popular in the morning hours, when they attract those commuting to work. Talk-oriented stations appeal to an older audience and find their listeners in their homes during the day.

Good music stations offer a light type of music, sometimes called "background music." The sound is very relaxing and unobtrusive. This format has grown in popularity with the increase in the average age, which is the result of the aging of the baby boomers.

Classical-oriented stations are not numerous, but they do attract a very upscale audience, one that many hospitality industry advertisers would find attractive. Even within major markets, there is usually only one classical station, as the format does not enjoy wide popularity. Country and western formats are widely popular in certain geographic sections of the country, while they tend to be less popular in major cities.

It is not possible to provide a specific demographic profile of the type of listener that each of the above radio formats attracts. Rather, it is best for the individual hospitality manager to compare the listener demographics of the available stations with those the hotel or restaurant is seeking to attract. In this way, the best "fit" between the radio stations' listeners and the potential advertiser's target market segments can be achieved.[2]

Selecting Radio Spots

Radio spots can be purchased in a wide variety of lengths, ranging from ten seconds to one minute. Special attention should be paid to (1) the number of spots, (2) the days the spots are broadcast, and (3) the times of day the spots are broadcast.

The number of spots purchased is important in achieving effectiveness in radio advertising. Normally, the larger the number of spots, the better. Repetition is critical to success in radio, as it is in all advertising. The days of the week selected are also important, for they suggest when the hospitality advertiser is seeking to promote business. For example, for a tablecloth restaurant, is early-week advertising most important, or should the traditional weekend dining be advertised?

The time of day must also be considered. Radio should reach the consumer at a time when a decision is being made or when the advertiser is seeking to stimulate demand. Table 10.2 shows the time classifications used by radio stations. The most expensive times are morning and afternoon commuting times. A hospitality advertiser should seriously consider these times, despite the increased cost, because they are likely to prove the most effective, especially for restaurants.

Table 10.2
Radio Time Classifications

Classification	Time	Relative Cost
Class AA—Morning drive time	6 A.M. to 10 A.M.	High
Class B—Daytime	10 A.M. to 3 P.M.	Moderate
Class A—Afternoon drive time	3 P.M. to 7 P.M.	Moderate to high
Class C—Evening	7 P.M. to 12 A.M.	Low to moderate
Class D—Nighttime	12 A.M. to 6 A.M.	Low

Producing Radio Commercials

Figure 10.2 illustrates a time guide for producing a radio commercial. This guide can, of course, be modified, but generally a commercial should consist of introduction, commercial copy, recap of pertinent points, and musical logo. The introduction usually consists of music and copy written to gain the attention of the listener. It serves the same function as the headline in a print advertisement.

The copy of the commercial is the real heart of the selling proposition. A guide for gauging the pace of the copy is presented in Table 10.3. Copy should provide the benefit to the consumer, and the support for this benefit. The recap of pertinent points should repeat points that the consumer should remember, such as a special price or new hours of operation. Finally, a musical logo is often used to fade out the commercial. Many advertisements allow five to ten seconds at the end for the announcer to read a live segment of the commercial. Both of these approaches can be very effective.

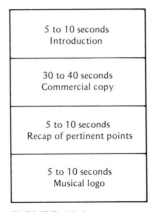

FIGURE 10.2
Production Guide for 60-Second Radio Commercial

TABLE 10.3
Radio Commercial Copy Length

Time	Number of Words of Copy
10 seconds	25 to 30
20 seconds	45 to 50
30 seconds	65 to 70
60 seconds	125 to 135

Radio Advertising Terms

The following are terms commonly used in radio advertising:

☐ *Advertising spot.* A short advertising message on a participating program or between other radio programs that an advertiser does not sponsor. This is what most people call a *commercial.* Advertising spots may be (1) fixed, broadcast at a time guaranteed by contract; (2) preemptible, broadcast at a certain time unless bumped by an advertiser willing to pay a higher rate; or (3) floating, broadcast when the station decides (run of station, or R.O.S.).

☐ *Drive time.* The early morning and late afternoon/early evening hours when radio has its largest audiences and highest rates.

☐ *Gross rating points.* Another way of comparing media vehicles and programs. The phrase is usually used for broadcast media, but the term has also been adopted by the outdoor industry. This rating can be calculated by multiplying the rating points (percentage of households, according to surveys, listening to a program or station at a particular time) by the number of times that program or station is heard or viewed during a given period (usually four weeks). Twenty percent of a potential audience equals twenty rating points.

☐ *Preemptible rates.* Charged for broadcast advertising spots that may be bumped to different time periods by advertisers paying higher rates. They vary in cost by the amount of notice the station must give the advertiser before moving an advertisement; the longer the notice, the higher the rate.

TELEVISION ADVERTISING

Each year, more and more hospitality organizations use television as an advertising medium. For some, the move into television brings increased sales and advertising success. For others, it is not such a bright picture. Television is a very demanding medium, one that delivers huge audiences but requires great skill in advertising. Before a hospitality organization decides to commit resources for television, very careful thought must be given to its impact on the remainder of the organization's advertising efforts.

Advantages to television advertising include the following:

☐ *Large audiences.* Television, even at the local level, is able to deliver large numbers of viewers. It does not allow selectivity of target markets, but market saturation is high.

☐ *High impact of message.* The combination of sight, sound, and motion holds the potential for tremendous impact on viewers. This combination helps viewers to perceive the hospitality operation accurately and allows the advertiser to demonstrate the product-service mix.

Drawbacks to television advertising include these:

☐ *Cost, cost, cost.* For the vast majority of hospitality organizations, particularly small independent restaurants, the cost of television is simply too high. Venturing into television advertising necessitates such a drastic reduction in other advertising efforts that the final result is often a reduction in overall advertising effectiveness. High costs are involved in both production and televising the commercials. This single disadvantage should be weighed with great care before television advertising is initiated.

☐ *Comparison with national advertisers.* Every time a local or regional hospitality advertisement is televised, consumers compare its quality against all other television advertisements. Do these local and regional advertisements look second-rate in comparison? Will television advertising adversely affect the image and positioning of the hospitality operation? It all comes down to this: Television advertising should be used only if the organization has the resources to do a credible job.

☐ *Nonlasting impressions.* Much like radio, once a television advertisement is televised, it is gone, and a potential consumer cannot refer back to it.

Techniques for Successful Television Advertising

First, the visual aspect of the commercial must convey the message to the consumer. The sound should add to and support the message, but the message should be able to stand on its visual impact alone. Television is a visual medium; the visual aspect is the key to successful television advertising. Messages that hospitality advertisers try to convey include the luxury and high living of upscale hotels, and the fun people have at a restaurant. This is done by showing people in the actual setting, not just showing the facilities or the food and beverages.

Second, television advertising must capture the viewer's attention immediately or it is doomed to failure. Facing facts, a manager must remember that consumers use commercial time to do other things, such as get snacks in the kitchen. If a commercial does not spark interest, they will not even watch.

Third, the advertisement should stay with one idea and repeat it within the time allocated. Television viewers see many commercials each day, and they cannot possibly remember all that they see and hear. Therefore, one key idea should be hammered home. For example, both Wendy's and Burger King achieved success with televising simple but very effective campaigns centered around the themes of "Where's the Beef?" and "Broiling Beats Frying," respectively. Certainly the commercials for both Wendy's and Burger King showed many visual images, but each one hammered home a basic and effective concept. Every effort should be made to trim commercials that talk too much. The age-old phrase "a picture is worth a thousand words" should be used as a guide when evaluating television story boards.

Fourth, television advertisements should accurately project the image of the hotel or restaurant to the consumer. Much time, effort, and money has been invested in the physical facilities and in staffing the operation, in order to create an image; advertising should not lower that image with poor television commercials. For example, one tablecloth restaurant operating in a major metropolitan area enjoyed a fine reputation and steady clientele. In an effort to increase sales during slow periods, management ventured into television advertising. After work with the creative staff, a story board and script were created, and production began. The result was a commercial that featured several still photographs of the restaurant depicting dining situations. These were well done, but the announcer was talking in a "hard sell" tone and at a very fast pace. This commercial cheapened the image of the restaurant and, in fact, hurt sales figures.

Types of Television Commercials

All television commercials fall into one of six types:

☐ *Demonstration.* Showing an actual part of the operation can be very effective. For example, preparing a certain menu item or banquet service in action within a hotel can help create an image.

☐ *Straight announcer.* This involves the use of only one announcer offering the benefit and support.

☐ *Testimonial.* This is a form of word-of-mouth promotion in which a series of satisfied consumers talk about elements of the product-service mix.

☐ *Problem solving.* This type of commercial offers a problem or series of problems and shows how a given hospitality operation can be the proper solution. For example, "What should you give your girlfriend for her birthday?" "How can you best celebrate your fortieth birthday?" "Why of course, come to the famous XYZ restaurant!"

☐ *Story line.* Some commercials tell a story in the thirty to sixty seconds available. For example, imagine the young boy sitting in a classroom at school daydreaming about a fast-food hamburger and french fries. The visual pieces and the sound discuss the benefits of the products, and when the commercial concludes, school is out, and the young boy is eating his favorite fast-food meal.

☐ *Musical.* Several successful television commercials have used the appealing visual effect of food products backed with appropriate music. If done well, this can be a very effective "soft sell."

Classes of Television Advertising

Just as radio stations divide the day into different time classifications, so too does television. These are shown in Table 10.4.

Television Advertising Terms

Following are terms commonly used in television advertising:

☐ *Dissolve.* One scene fading into the next with both showing simultaneously for a moment.

☐ *Dubbing.* Recording the sound portion of the commercial separately and then synchronizing it with the visual components.

☐ *Fade in/fade out.* The screen goes from black to the visual material, or the final visual shot is faded into black.

☐ *Fringe time.* The periods immediately before and after TV prime time, 4 P.M. to 8 P.M. and after 11 P.M. in all time zones except the Central time zone, where periods run an hour earlier.

☐ *Network.* A link of many stations by cable or microwave for simultaneous broadcast on all from a single originating point. The stations may be owned by or affiliated with the network. Major networks are ABC, CBS, NBC. However with the growth of cable television, the importance of the three major networks has declined. Other networks such as CNN and ESPN have increased their impact on the television market.

☐ *Prime time.* The time during which television has its largest audiences

TABLE 10.4
Television Time Classifications

Classification	Time	Relative Cost
Class AA	Daily, 8 P.M. to 11 P.M.	High
Class A	Daily, 7 A.M. to 8 A.M.; Sunday, 6 P.M. to 8 P.M.	High to moderate
Class B	Daily, 4 P.M. to 6 P.M.; Sunday, 2 P.M. to 5:30 P.M.	Moderate
Class C	Daily, 12 P.M. to 4 P.M.; Saturday, 6 A.M. to 4 P.M.	Low to moderate
Class D	Daily sign-on, 12 P.M.	Low

and highest advertising rates. In the Eastern, Mountain, and Pacific time zones it is from 8 P.M. to 11 P.M. In the Central time zone, it is from 7 P.M. to 10 P.M.

DIRECT MAIL ADVERTISING

There are those who refer to direct mail advertising as "junk mail." These individuals believe that direct mail advertising is of little value and is not appropriate for the hospitality industry. These beliefs simply are not true. Direct mail can and does work for many hospitality advertisers. It is often used to solicit group and banquet business. Most hotels routinely send direct mail pieces describing guest room and meeting facilities to potential meeting planners and then use inquiries and personal calls to generate leads from the mailing. Direct mail is also used to promote special events, such as holidays or special packages, often involving discounts.

Advantages to direct mail include the following characteristics:

☐ *Selective and personal.* With direct mail, an advertiser can be very selective with the target market segment and can include only the very best potential consumers on the mailing list. Direct mail need not be junk mail addressed to "occupant" or "home owner." The widespread use of personal computers has allowed even small hotels and restaurants to manage large data bases and address lists that can then be merged with personalized letters.

☐ *Easily evaluated.* It is easy to monitor the effectiveness of direct mail pieces by looking at inquiries and sales. Many firms include a postage paid postcard for the prospect to use to inquire about additional information. These can be easily evaluated.

☐ *Few restrictions and easy scheduling.* There are no time or space limits, as is the case with other media. There are no limits of size or shape. Therefore, one can be very creative. The manager who develops the direct mail piece has a great deal of control over the design, production, and distribution of the direct mail efforts.

Drawbacks to direct mail advertising include the following characteristics:

☐ *Poor image.* Direct mail suffers from a poor image in the minds of many consumers. Unless the piece is able to attract immediate attention, many consumers will not read it.

☐ *Increasing competition.* In recent years, there has been tremendous growth in the use of direct mail, especially in the area of direct mail marketing of retail items. Such well-known companies as L. L. Bean, Eddie Bauer, and others were at the forefront. However, the number of direct mail pieces that the typical consumer receives each day is increasing. It is becoming more difficult to design direct mail pieces that will carry your message across.

☐ *Expensive.* When all the costs associated with direct mail are added up, the total is often surprising to the advertiser. Included in these costs are mailing lists, printing, word processing and letter generation, envelope stuffing, and postage.

☐ *USPS regulations.* The United States Postal Service has a vast number of ever-changing regulations that apply to direct mail advertising especially bulk mail. A local post office can provide several publications that review the regulations.

☐ *Difficulty with mailing lists.* Maintaining mailing lists can be both time-consuming and expensive. Lists must be updated to avoid duplication and nonproductive names.[3]

Techniques for Successful Direct Mail Advertising

First and foremost, any direct mail piece that achieves success must capture the potential consumer's attention. Many consumers throw out direct mail advertising unopened; others open it but do not read it. This is obviously a waste of a firm's money. A tried and true approach to direct mail advertising is based on AIDA (attention, interest, desire, action). If the advertising fails to motivate the consumer to act immediately, chances are that the advertising will be set aside and eventually forgotten. Consumer action is the goal of direct mail advertising; action leads to inquiries, inquires lead to prospects, and prospects lead to sales. Examples of copy written to spur action include, "Act within 10 days and receive a free gift" or "Call today for reservations; only a limited number will be accepted for this special evening."

Special attention needs to be given to the layout and copywriting of direct mail pieces. Generally, the use of several long paragraphs of copy should be avoided because most people simply will not read them. The more personal the piece looks, the greater likelihood that the recipient will open and read it. Many firms doing small selective mailings will hand stamp and/or hand address the envelopes. Both of these techniques usually prove to be more effective than using bulk-rate postage and peel-off address labels.

If specific direct mail pieces prove successful, an advertiser should run them again. The piece may seem old to the management of the hospitality operation, but to consumers, it will be new and different. If something works, there is no reason to change merely for the sake of change.

Finally, direct mail efforts are often successful because of the creativity on the part of the advertiser. Taking a familiar object and putting it to a new use can create dramatic results. For example, one restaurant used brown lunch bags instead of standard envelopes. Printed on the outside of the bag was "Are you still brown bagging it?" Another restaurant used a piece that resembled a parking ticket and put them on the cars parked in specific areas. Printed on the top of the pseudoticket was "Here's your ticket to a great lunch." While this last promotion is not direct mail by strict definition, it was very successful and used a direct mail approach.

Mailing Lists

The maintenance of direct mail lists is critical to the cost-effectiveness and success of any direct mail advertising program. Only names that are truly potential consumers should be included, and names that are duplicated because several lists are used should be avoided as well. Both of these problems sound simple, and the solution is simple too, but it is easier said than done. Using computer lists with the capability of cross-checking for duplication is a distinct advantage in list maintenance.

Mailing lists fall into two categories: in-house lists and external lists. In-house lists are generated internally by the management. These lists should reflect those who have patronized the hotel or restaurant or who have the potential to generate a significant amount of business. Many restaurants use the guest book concept very successfully. They place a guest book at the entrance and ask each individual to sign it. Another approach is to keep a large bowl, often a fish bowl, at the host's stand into which guests may place business cards. The names and addresses provided by the guests become an excellent foundation on which to build a mailing list.

Within hotels, it is relatively easy to build a mailing list based on registration cards, as well as the contacts that are made by the sales and marketing staff. External lists are obtained from companies that sell mailing lists based on demographics, socioeconomic levels, geographic areas, and numerous other variables. Costs of these lists vary depending on selectivity and size. Lists purchased externally should be guaranteed to be current. Reputable companies will guarantee lists to be 90 to 95 percent accurate and current. In addition to mailing list and data base firms, mailing lists can also be purchased from clubs, associations, and other businesses.

One final word on direct mail advertising: Results may seem discouraging based on the total number of pieces mailed. Typically, the response rate of sales versus mailings is 1 to 2 percent. Anything more than 2 percent is very good, and more than 5 percent is outstanding. Consider a restaurant that sent a mailing to 20,000 potential consumers advertising a promotional item. A response rate of 1 percent would be 200, 2 percent would be 400, and 5 percent would be 1000. Even as few as 200 extra covers would normally make a substantial impact on sales.

OUTDOOR ADVERTISING

Outdoor advertising has widespread use among those hospitality operations located near interstate highways, but it can be effective in other locations as well. One hospitality organization in a large northern city allocated a substantial portion of its advertising to outdoor advertising. The outdoor displays were both creative and somewhat risqué; the results were very successful. The advantages of outdoor advertising include these characteristics:

☐ *Low cost.* The cost per thousand is extremely low.

☐ *Repetition reinforcement.* Consumers constantly using a given route will see the outdoor advertising again and again. This repetition aids in recall and retention.

Some drawbacks to outdoor advertising are these:

☐ *Poor target market segment selectivity.* While the cost per thousand is low, outdoor advertising does not lend itself to reaching small target market segments. It is a mass-market method.

☐ *Legislation.* Beginning with the Highway Beautification Act, all levels of government have discussed and often have enacted legislation to limit and tightly control the construction of outdoor billboards and signs. Legislation at all levels of government have made it more difficult for a hospitality organization to obtain the desired number of signs in the locations that are the most desirable.

☐ *Lack of timeliness.* It requires considerable planning to use outdoor advertising. Once outdoor advertising is in place, it is not subject to change without considerable effort and cost.

Techniques for Successful Outdoor Advertising

Three simple thoughts should influence all outdoor advertising. First, the copy should be kept brief and the print large. Those viewing outdoor advertising will be riding in buses, cabs, and cars or walking down the street. Their attention will be focused on the advertisement for only a few seconds; therefore, the message must be brief. A maximum of five to seven words should be used; the fewer, the better. Such information as the telephone number or hours of operation is not likely to be remembered and should not be included.

Second, a picture or illustration is often very helpful in gaining attention. The picture or illustration should convey the message and not be dependent on the copy for support. Finally, a logo or similar method is often used to provide clear name recognition. The best example is the McDonald's golden arches. It can be clearly seen on all outdoor advertising for McDonald's. The name recognition is instant and lasting.

Types of Outdoor Advertising

Standard outdoor advertising consists of posters and painted bulletins. Posters are blank boards on which the printed advertising is mounted. Painted bulletins are more permanent signs on which the message is painted. Both posters and painted bulletins are available in a wide variety of sizes, ranging from 6 feet by 12 feet, to 10 feet by 22 feet and larger. Painted bulletins are sold individually, while posters are sold by showings. Showings refer to market coverage within a thirty-day period. A 100 showing (explained below) is determined by the individual poster companies, known as plants.

When renting posters, circulation, or the number of people who will see the board, should be considered. The length of time a passer-by can see the poster clearly should be considered. Is the poster obstructed by buildings or trees? Not all locations are good ones. The physical condition of the posters and painted bulletins should also be considered. Nothing will reflect more negatively on an advertiser than a poorly maintained board or one with its lights burned out.

Outdoor Advertising Terms

The following terms are commonly used by outdoor advertisers:

☐ *Plant.* A company that buys or leases real estate (where it erects standard-size boards) or rents walls of buildings. It then sells to advertisers use of space at these locations.

☐ *Showing.* This refers to the coverage of a market, not the number of posters. A 100 showing is complete coverage of a market; a 50 showing is half of it, and so on. In some communities, 10 posters might be a 100 showing, while in much smaller places, two posters could be a 100 showing.

BROCHURES

Creating Effective Brochures

Brochures play a vital role in the advertising and promotional efforts of hotels, and they can be of benefit to restaurants as well. They can be used in a wide variety of situations.

It will not be possible to tell the entire story within a brochure, as there are space restrictions. The most important point to remember is to communicate your facility's positioning. It is imperative that you create and maintain an image in the consumer's mind. Once you have determined the type of positioning statement you want to communicate, then you can move on to the key benefits and support that the brochure will communicate.

Several guidelines will result in more successful brochures:

Brochure Cover.   First, the cover design is very critical. It should communicate where your property is located and your positioning statement. The cover is valuable space and it should be used to convey your primary selling message and the key consumer benefit. The photograph used on the front cover should grab the attention of potential guests, capturing their interest. Figure 10.3 uses an excellent photograph to capture interest and en-

Virginia Beach Resort And Conference Center

FIGURE 10.3
An Example of an Excellent Cover Photograph
Courtesy: Virginia Beach Resort and Conference Center, Virginia Beach, VA

courages the potential guest to open the brochure to learn more about the resort.

Photographs.   All photographs should help to stretch the potential guests' imagination. They should be able to see themselves in the setting. Photographs of activities are more useful than photographs of just the facilities. If you plan to use food in the photographs, use close-up photos of finished products, not just the ingredients. Avoid the use of standard types of photographs that are all too common in hotel brochures. These include the smiling chef standing beside the buffet table and service personnel serving food in a restaurant. Strive for a fresh appeal.

Information.   Potential guests need information that will help them to better understand things about your product-service mix. The use of maps and/or graphics on the brochure helps the reader to gain a better understanding of where you are located, as well as some specifics about the types of products and services offered. Basic information such as address, telephone, and chain affiliation should also be included. An example is shown in Figure 10.4.

Copy.   Just as with any type of advertising, the copy used in a brochure must talk to the consumer in his or her own words and must speak directly in terms of benefits which are important. The use of a professional copywriter may be useful. It is important to avoid the use of clichés, as these are overused and will actually turn off a potential guest.

SUPPLEMENTAL ADVERTISING MEDIA

In addition to the media hospitality advertisers use, supplemental advertising is any object bearing the advertiser's name that is given or sold to a targeted consumer. There are literally thousands of supplemental items, including pens, pencils, calendars, rulers, paperweights, jewelry, matches, programs, candy jars, travel bags, and T-shirts. Displays in the yellow pages are also a form of supplemental advertising, one that must be considered for hospitality operations.

Some advantages of supplemental advertising media include these:

☐ *High repetition.* If the item is of value or usefulness to the recipient, it is likely to be retained, and the advertising message is then seen repeatedly.

☐ *Something for nothing.* Everyone loves a bargain, and if the item has value in the eyes of the recipient, this creates a positive image. For example, only a few cents separates a common matchbook from one that consumers will save.

Some drawbacks of supplemental advertising media include the following:

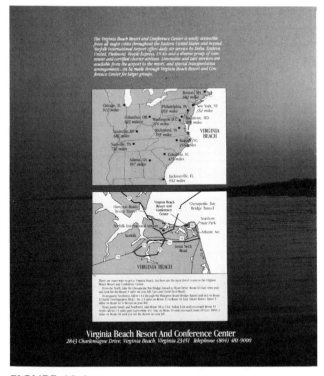

FIGURE 10.4
An Example of a Directional Map
Courtesy: Virginia Beach and Conference Center, Virginia Beach, VA

□ *Expense.* In some cases, the initial cost of producing an item may be high. It is therefore important to identify a specifically targeted market for those items of higher value.

□ *Message necessarily brief.* Most supplemental media allow only a few brief words. The advertising message must be made to count.

□ *Impossibility of evaluating effectiveness.* No evaluation methodologies can easily be used with supplemental media. Most of these media promote good will rather than absolute sales.

SUMMARY

This chapter covers the vast area of external advertising and promotional media. These media constitute an invaluable resource, which if managed properly, can generate increased sales and handsome profits. Managed poorly, these media will drain away advertising resources and leave little or nothing to show in return. As with all investments, management must evaluate advertising for its return on investment.

The relations between a hospitality client and an advertising agency involve both positive and negative aspects. Management should consider several factors when selecting an agency and should consider compensation practices within the industry.

Media selection involves several factors that influence the selection of media. These include the nature of the target market, the campaign objectives, the desired amount of coverage, and the activities of direct competition. Media plans must be developed to achieve maximum effectiveness. These plans must consider the target markets closely to blend the media to achieve the desired results. Media scheduling includes the following approaches: continuous, flighting, and pulsing advertising.

External advertising media include print, radio, television, direct mail, outdoor, and supplemental advertising. Each of these media has its appropriate use, advantages, drawbacks, and techniques that generally are successful. A knowledge of advertising terms allows a manager to communicate more intelligently with media and advertising agency personnel.

KEY WORDS AND CONCEPTS

- ☐ Cost per thousand (C.P.M.)
- ☐ Media plans
- ☐ Target markets
- ☐ Continuous, flighting, and pulsing media scheduling
- ☐ Coupons
- ☐ Agate line
- ☐ Base rate
- ☐ Bleed advertisement
- ☐ Circulation
- ☐ Controlled circulation
- ☐ Frequency
- ☐ Milline formula
- ☐ Reach
- ☐ Drive time

☐ Gross rating points

☐ Preemptible rates

☐ Demonstration

☐ Testimonial

☐ Dissolve

☐ Dubbing

☐ Fade in/fade out

☐ Fringe time

☐ AIDA

☐ Network

☐ Outdoor advertising plant

☐ Showing

Questions for Review and Discussion

1. What factors affect the selection of advertising media?
2. How would you develop a media plan?
3. What are the methods of media scheduling? Which one do you consider the best? Why?
4. Cite and discuss two advantages and two drawbacks of each of the following media: (1) print, (2) radio, (3) television, (4) direct mail, (5) outdoor advertising, and (6) supplemental advertising media.

CHAPTER 11

Promotions and Public Relations

This chapter focuses on the promotional mix elements of sales promotion and public relations. Many hospitality organizations devote more time and attention to advertising and personal selling, the more visible elements, but sales promotion and public relations can be very valuable tools.

This chapter is divided into the following sections:

INTRODUCTION

SALES PROMOTION
☐ Role of Sales Promotion
☐ Types of Sales Promotions
☐ A Closer Look at the Most Commonly Used Techniques
☐ Managing Successful Promotions
☐ Budgeting for Promotions

INTERNAL PROMOTION
☐ Missed Selling Opportunities
☐ Training Guest-Contact Personnel
☐ Entertainment
☐ Other Promotional Techniques

PUBLIC RELATIONS
☐ Public Relations Techniques

SUMMARY

KEY WORDS AND CONCEPTS

QUESTIONS FOR REVIEW AND DISCUSSION

INTRODUCTION

The hospitality industry is a people-oriented business. Hospitality operations promote hospitality, yet hospitality cannot be purchased, cannot be traded, and does not appear on the menu. Hospitality is intangible, yet it is absolutely necessary for success. When service personnel project the "spirit of hospitality," the results can be dramatic—increased sales, increased profits, increased consumer satisfaction, and, yes, increased employee satisfaction and motivation. Foodservice operations also sell atmosphere, convenience, entertainment, escape, and social contact. All of these are related to the spirit of hospitality and are equally intangible. All deserve consideration as promotable items.

The more visible forms of advertising are often used to help increase sales and profits. However, all of the elements of the promotional or communications mix are equally important. The basic elements include advertising, personal selling, sales promotion, and public relations. This chapter will focus on the last two elements. All four are defined here:

☐ *Advertising* is any paid form of nonpersonal presentation of ideas and promotion of ideas, goods, or services by an identified sponsor.

☐ *Personal selling* is an oral presentation in a conversation with prospective consumers for the purpose of making a sale.

☐ *Public relations* is a nonpersonal stimulation of demand for a product or service by providing commercially significant news about the product or service in a published medium, or obtaining favorable presentation in a medium that is not paid for by the sponsor.

☐ *Sales promotion* includes the marketing activities other than advertising, personal selling, and public relations that attempt to stimulate consumer demand and increase sales. Commonly, sales promotion is a direct inducement offering an extra incentive to take action, be it to buy the product or service or to inquire about further information.

In all forms of the promotional mix, it is critical that the intended message be delivered to the potential target markets. A model of communication is shown in Figure 11.1 to illustrate how this process takes place.

It should be remembered that both the sender and the receiver are humans, and are subject to the failings common to all of us. No one communicates as well as he or she would like. We simply do not speak as clearly and understandably as we would like to. Also, we do not listen as well as we should. With this in mind, all communication attempts with target markets should be kept as clear and concise as possible. In addition to the human failings, there are potential difficulties with the message, the channels that are used, and the noise level in the environment, and efforts should be made to overcome these difficulties. When management designs a new form of promotion, it is sometimes expected that the entire target market can be reached with a limited number of contacts. This is simply not possible, because the target market is being bombarded with other messages and as a result, sometimes your message is not received and retained above the noise in the environment. It is important to keep this communications model in mind when designing any type of communications with target markets. It will serve as a reminder of how great the challenge really is. It is also critical to review the feedback received, studying it carefully and looking for ways to improve.

SALES PROMOTION

Role of Sales Promotion

In recent years, most companies have devoted an ever-increasing percentage of their budgets to sales promotions and have reduced the percentage devoted

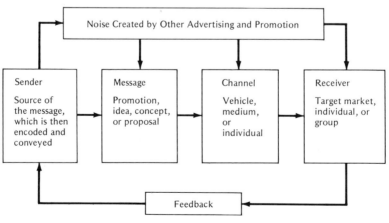

FIGURE 11.1
Communications Model

solely to advertising. Sales promotions seek to accomplish several broad objectives and can be used for several reasons:

☐ *To increase consumer awareness.* This is the first step in attracting new guests or customers. In order to create a guest, one must first stimulate interest and a desire to act. Advertising seeks to increase awareness as well, but sometimes it takes a special promotion to turn that awareness into consumer purchasing action.

☐ *To introduce new products and services.* Every hotel and restaurant launches new products and services. The best way to ensure that the target markets are aware of these products and services is to initiate a special promotion to draw attention to them. When McDonald's or Burger King launches a new product, you can be sure that they support the introduction with extra advertising and special promotions designed to promote trial of the new product. Merely introducing the new product or service to the target markets is not enough—you need to beat the drums, create interest, and stimulate trial purchases and future demand for the new products and services.

☐ *To increase guest occupancy and customer counts.* With increasing competition and tight supply and demand in many markets, one of the few avenues for market share growth is to take business away from the direct competition. In order to accomplish this, it is necessary to feature promotions offering consumers a "better deal" than they can receive elsewhere. Promotions are used to spread the word to potential guests.

☐ *To combat competition.* If the direct competition is gaining market share at the expense of your hotel or restaurant, you may be forced to match their promotion or to add one of your own with a new twist. For example, Marriott Hotels was among the first hotel companies to offer a frequent guest program. Their program proved to be so successful that other competing hotel chains were forced to offer frequent traveler programs to compete with Marriott.

☐ *To encourage present guests to purchase more.* By packaging or bundling different products and services at a total price that is less than their cost if purchased separately, total sales can be increased. Promotions can also be used to encourage guests to trade up to more expensive products and services by offering a discounted price on the more expensive product or service. The primary purpose is to increase sales by encouraging present guests to purchase more.

☐ *To stimulate demand in nonpeak periods.* All hotels and restaurants have periods when demand is weak. Promotions can be used to increase weekend business for a business-oriented hotel, or stimulate off-season and shoulder season business at a resort. Within the foodservice segment, promotions can be used to increase sales during periods of the day or days of the week when demand is slow. For example, many restaurants stimulate early evening business by offering a discount to senior citizens who dine between 5:00 and 7:00 P.M., when business is often slow. They take advantage of the fact that seniors usually try to dine earlier and are often more conscious of the price-value relationship. Early dining promotions directed at this target market are often quite successful.

As is the objective with all forms of promotion or advertising, the ultimate goal is to stimulate attention, interest, desire, and action (AIDA).

Types of Sales Promotions

Within the broad sphere of sales promotion two strategies are commonly used, push promotion and pull promotion. Push promotion is used when the marketing manager wants to "push" the product-service mix through the service delivery system or channels of distribution. This approach encourages increased purchases and increased consumption by consumers. Pull promotion, on the other hand, is aimed at stimulating the interest of the consumer and creating purchase action by the consumer. This in turn puts additional pressure on the retail outlets or hospitality facilities to supply the products and services most in demand by consumers. Listed below are some of the commonly used techniques for both push and pull strategies.

Push Techniques

☐ *Point-of-sale displays.* These displays, often seen at the counter of fast-food restaurants or as table tents in other types of restaurants, are designed to stimulate increased sales. Banners and other forms of point-of-sale displays are commonly used by hotels as well.

☐ *Cooperative advertising.* A national chain will often share the cost of placing advertising at the local level. The national chain's share is rarely less than 50 percent and in some instances may be as high as 100 percent.

☐ *Advertising materials.* To encourage the local property to run advertising, the national chain will supply camera-ready advertising materials as well as prepared radio commercials.

☐ *Collateral material.* This covers types of material often provided as brochures, flyers, or directories of hotel properties within the entire chain.

☐ *Convention and managers' meetings.* National chains use these meetings as a method to introduce new products and services to those who will be working in the individual units. These meetings are used for sales and service training.

Pull Techniques

☐ *Sampling.* This is a technique that can be used very effectively by foodservice managers. For example, samples of menu items can be distributed in the lobby area of a fast-food store, thereby encouraging trial of the new product. The goal is to convert this trial into regular use and repeat purchase. Within the lodging field, this technique is common as well. Meeting planners often visit the potential hotel meeting site to "sample" the product service before they make a final decision about the host hotel for the upcoming meeting.

☐ *Price reduction promotions.* Price reductions for a limited time can encourage trial and increase sales. A successful use of this type of promotion was Marriott Hotel's "Two for Breakfast Weekend" in which two guests could experience a get-away weekend at a heavily discounted price and also receive a complimentary breakfast for two. As with all promotions of this type, restrictions should apply and a definite time period should be stated.

☐ *Price reduction coupons.* These are certificates that entitle the consumer to receive a discount when presented at the retail outlet. They can be distributed in newspapers, magazines, face to face, or via direct mail.

☐ *Combination offers or bundling.* This involves combining two or more products or services and offering them for a price less than the price if they were purchased separately.

☐ *Premiums.* These are extra merchandise or gifts that the hotel or restaurant gives away free or sells at a very favorable price to guests. Examples include such items as hats, tote bags, glassware, and T-shirts with the logo printed on them. If the hotel or restaurant is able to cover the direct costs of the item, the premium is called self-liquidating.

☐ *Contests and sweepstakes.* The attraction of contests and sweepstakes is the highly desirable prizes that consumers can win. There is one minor difference between a contest and a sweepstakes. A contest requires some skill on the part of the participant, while a sweepstakes is based solely on chance. In all states lotteries are illegal. Lotteries consist of three elements: (1) the element of chance; (2) consideration, giving something in return (for example, having to make a purchase in order to enter the sweepstakes); and (3) a valuable prize. In order to avoid illegal activities in most localities, it is necessary to eliminate one of these elements. By simply having no purchase required to enter the sweepstakes, it is not classified as a lottery and is therefore legal in most localities. Contests, because they require some skill on the part of the participant are not considered to be lotteries because there is no element of chance involved.

A Closer Look at the Most Commonly Used Techniques[1]

Of all of the techniques discussed in the preceding section, four are used most frequently by companies in the hospitality industry. They deserve a more complete examination.

Coupons.   The primary objectives for coupons are to stimulate trial of your products and services by reducing the price, encourage multiple purchases, and generate temporary sales increases. Coupons offer several advantages:

- ☐ The coupon represents a tangible inducement, offering a savings or benefit.

- ☐ The price reduction is for a limited time and will not affect profit margins in the long term.

- ☐ Coupons can be used to accomplish specific objectives, such as boosting business in nonpeak periods.

- ☐ The maximum cost of the promotion can be calculated in advance. For example, if a certain percentage of the coupons are redeemed, the maximum total cost will be X dollars.

Coupons have disadvantages as well:

- ☐ Some employees will be tempted to defraud the business. It is possible for them to take cash and substitute coupons. The higher the value of the coupon, the closer the supervision necessary.

- ☐ Redemption rates are not easily predicted. Among the environmental factors that can affect the redemption rate include value of the coupon, timing, and competitive activities.

Sampling.   Encouraging trial of new products is the primary objective of sampling. If consumers will at least try the product, the thinking goes, they are more likely to purchase. Sampling also is an excellent way to persuade consumers to trade up to more expensive products and services. Sampling can also be tied in with other types of promotions. For example, airlines routinely offer upgrades to first class for frequent travelers as a reward for their frequent use of the airline. Not only is this a reward, but after flying in first class, travelers may decide to book themselves into first class for subsequent flights, thereby increasing sales and profits. Airlines help the traveler to rationalize this additional cost by awarding additional mileage points when the traveler flies in first class. Sampling offers these advantages:

- ☐ Getting consumers to try the product is superior to getting them to look at an advertisement. It provides the consumer with instant feedback.

☐ It represents value to the consumer. Many consumers like to think that they can get something for free. For example, including small portions of entree and appetizer items within the offerings for "happy hours" is an excellent way to stimulate dining room business.

Some disadvantages of sampling follow:

☐ Giving away products can become a major expense if it is done for an extended period of time.

☐ Samples of food products must be served when they are freshly prepared. If the products are to be held for any period of time, care must be taken to ensure that the quality can be maintained.

Premiums.   Premiums giving away something, are used to bring in new guests, to encourage more frequent visits by current guests, and to build positive word-of-mouth about the operation. Advantages include the following:

☐ Most consumers like to get something for nothing or for a good price. It helps to build good will for your business, especially if the premium is highly valued by the consumer.

☐ If the premium is clever to unique, it will build positive word of mouth as consumers tell others where they found the premium. When your logo is included on the premium, the message is always in front of the consumer.

Disadvantages of premiums include these:

☐ Storing and handling the premium items can be a challenge, if they are large or bulky.

☐ Employees and others may take the premiums for their own use or for families and friends.

☐ The quality of the premium must be equal or superior to the image of the hospitality facility. If the premium does not work properly or breaks, it will diminish the image the consumer has of the facility or organization.

☐ Anticipating demand for premiums is difficult. If they are to be advertised as being available, it is imperative that a sufficient inventory be maintained so that consumers are not disappointed. Raising expectations and then not delivering will result in negative consumer perceptions.

Contests and Sweepstakes.   These are being used with increasing frequency, especially within the more competitive segments of the industry such as fast-food. They are designed to increase the number of customers and build market share, often at the expense of the competition. Advantages of contests include the following:

☐ *Increased consumer involvement.* Because there is some element of skill and thinking involved, an opportunity to create and support a more lasting positive image in the consumer's mind is created.

☐ *Elimination of chance winners.* Those who enter have already shown an interest in your products and services and are more likely to purchase them.

Disadvantages of contests include these:

☐ *Difficulty of judging in some instances.* Often the criteria are subjective. Those selected to judge must take the responsibility seriously, because the contestants will be serious about the outcome.

☐ *Complicated rules.* Often the rules and guidelines for the contest are lengthy and may turn off potential participants.

The advantages of sweepstakes include the following:

☐ Entry is very easy; no purchase is necessary. The names and addresses of those who enter can be stored in a data base and used in future direct mail advertising efforts.

☐ Because the rules are usually quite simple, attention can be focused on the prizes in advertising.

☐ Sweepstakes will attract more participants than contests because it is easier to enter. There is no skill involved or time required to enter.

☐ Selection of the winner is easier and judging is not required.

Disadvantages of sweepstakes include these:

☐ The entry box may be stuffed. It is possible for a consumer to reproduce the entry blank and enter thousands of times. For this reason, the rules should prohibit the mechanical reproduction of the entry forms.

☐ An individual's chances of winning the large prizes are very small, and consumers may get discouraged and not enter.

Managing Successful Promotions

The hospitality industry trade journals are filled with terrific ideas for promotions. There is never a need to "reinvent the wheel." Rather, simply modify the ideas that others have used successfully before. With this in mind, an excellent source that managers might want to review is *Fifty Promotions That Work*, published by the American Express Company. This publication was an outgrowth of *Briefing*, a newsletter that they provide to restaurateurs across the country.

Like anything else managers do, planning a promotion calls for careful planning, execution of the plan, and finally evaluation. The steps to a successful promotion follow:

1. *Select the target market for the promotion.*   When the sales records are analyzed, the most likely targets for a special promotion can be identified, as those segments that offer the greatest potential for increased sales.

2. *Establish specific objectives for the promotion.*   Objectives should be very specific, detailing exactly what the promotion should accomplish. Expected results should be quantified.

3. *Select the promotional technique.*   Based on the situation and the advantages and disadvantages of each of the techniques, select the one best suited to the situation.

4. *Brainstorm about the potential offer.*   There are hundreds of excellent ideas. Make a list of those being considered and seek input from others. All potential offers should be examined carefully from two perspectives—the potential appeal to the target market, and the potential costs and expenses.

5. *Create the promotional theme.*   This is the area where one can be very creative. What will be the promotional copy line or tag line? Does it capture the interest of potential guests? Can it be used both internally and externally in the promotion? For a promotion to achieve the maximum potential, it needs to be carried forward both outside and inside the operation. Externally, it should build business. Internally, it should create excitement among the staff and build morale.

6. *Develop the promotional budget.*   A projection of the total anticipated costs should be prepared to include all internal and external costs. It is wise to project the impact on costs and revenues at several different levels of consumer participation.

7. *Select the advertising media and vehicles to support the promotion.*   Based on your knowledge of the media, those that will best support the total promotional campaign should be contacted. Advertising space and time should be secured.

8. *Develop an implementation timetable.*   Promotions require attention to detail so that all phases are integrated and implemented properly. To accomplish this, a timetable is required. Specific dates should be established for each task. Assigning responsibility for the completion of these tasks will increase accountability.

9. *Conduct internal training of the entire staff.*   Just prior to the implementation of the program, the entire staff should be briefed so that they are familiar with the details of the promotion. Items of interest to them are how

long the promotion will last, how the details will be handled by the different members of the staff, and what is expected of them.

10. *Work the plan.*   Put the promotional plan into action and follow the timetable.

11. *Monitor results.*   Feedback should be followed very carefully and should be compared with the timetable. Are things progressing as planned? Is the level of consumer participation within the projected ranges? Are the staff members working as planned? Attention to detail is very important. All information collected should be retained for future use in other promotions.

Budgeting for Promotions

Developing promotional budgets is not an easy task. Numerous variables that are not subject to management control can affect the budget. When a promotional budget is generated, two decisions must be made. The first involves determining the amount of money that will be allocated to the total promotional effort. The second revolves around how to allocate the resources among the promotional elements and the media.

The techniques for determining a promotional budget are the same as those for determining an advertising budget. These methods, discussed in Chapter 9, include the percentage of sales method, the desired objective method, and the competitive method.

Once the total promotional budget has been established, allocating the resources among different promotions can be accomplished in several ways. The first method is to allocate the resources by geographic area or region. For example, regions where the company enjoys higher market share and strong sales would receive a smaller percentage of the promotional budget than those areas in which sales and market share were viewed as being weak.

A second method is to allocate the resources based on products. These products might be any aspect of the product-service mix. Again, those elements of the product-service mix that are seen as weaker or offering the most growth potential would receive a higher proportion of the promotional budget.

Third, the budget can be allocated by market segment. Those types of guests with the potential to generate additional revenue would be targeted to receive a greater percentage of the promotional dollars.

INTERNAL PROMOTION

When the consumer comes through the front door of a hospitality operation, all the attention of management and the service employees should be focused on satisfying the consumer. Hospitality is not like the retail business; consumers do not come into hotels and restaurants to browse; they come in to buy. All too often, though, the service employees show about as much enthusiasm for selling as for changing a flat tire. Instead of performing as professional salespeople, they often serve as little more than order-takers. They saunter up to the table with a guest check in hand and ask unsmilingly, "Ya ready to order?" When asked a simple question such as how an item is prepared, the answer is often, "I don't know; I'll ask the chef." When they bring items to the table, they often ask, "Who had the roast beef?" while the plate is passed from one guest to the next. Sound familiar?

Missed Selling Opportunities

Lack of professional selling on the part of service employees results in lower sales and less satisfied consumers. All of this is simply a matter of missed opportunities. For example, consider the following situation in which four friends were planning to have dinner at a restaurant. They were seated by the host following this greeting: "Do you have reservations?" After they had waited about five minutes for a server to approach the table, Sally appeared, presented each guest with a closed menu, and asked, "Would anyone like anything from the bar?" Each responded "no," and Sally said that she would be back in a few minutes to take their dinner orders. She returned in a few minutes, asking "You ready to order?" When a guest inquired about any special items or recommendations, Sally responded, "There isn't a special today; I guess the chef just wasn't in the mood. Everything on the menu is good. Can I take your order?" The guests then placed their orders, which Sally took without speaking except to ask about the type of vegetable and salad dressing that each guest would like. What was wrong with this situation and who is at fault?

Clearly, Sally failed to sell; she merely took the orders. She failed to suggestive-sell a round of drinks, a bottle of wine, or a specialty of the house. Simply stated, Sally failed to do her job. Less clear is who is at fault. Management is at fault. Management has the responsibility to recruit, train, supervise, coach and counsel, and motivate the service personnel. If they fail to do their jobs, management must accept the responsibility. Figure 11.2 summarizes the loss of potential revenue from the table that Sally serviced. The total lost revenue is $45 for the party of four. Although it is doubtful that the party of four would have spent an additional $45, they might easily have spent an additional $10, $20, or $30. The point is that the service people are salespeople. They must be taught to suggestive-sell, to increase the check averages, to deliver additional profits, and to ensure satisfied guests. If employees suggestive-sell, they have a 50 percent chance of being successful. If they do not suggestive-sell and do not say anything, the chances of being successful are nearly zero percent. Suggestions for ways to effectively suggestive-sell are shown in Figure 11.3.

Sales of drinks	4 @ $3.00	= $12.00
Sale of wine	1 bottle	= 15.00
Trading up or suggestive-selling a more expensive entree or accompanying item	4 @ $1.50	= 6.00
Dessert or after-dinner drink sale	4 @ $3.00	= 12.00

Potential lost revenue = $45.00

Potential lost gratuity = $ 6.75
(15%)

FIGURE 11.2
Missed Opportunities

1. Develop a positive mental attitude. Not everyone will accept the suggestions, but all guests will appreciate the desire to serve and attend to their needs.

2. Do not try to manipulate the guest; simply make positive and upbeat suggestions.

3. Suggest favorite items or aspects of the product-service mix with which the employee is most familiar.

4. Use props to support suggestive selling. For example, it is relatively easy to turn down an offer for dessert, but if a dessert tray is brought to the table and the server offers the right suggestion, sales of desserts will increase.

5. Always make positive suggestions; always focus on the positive aspects of the product-service mix. If a guest makes a negative comment, acknowledge the comment, but try to turn the negative into a positive.

6. Always be attentive to guests' needs. Some will be very receptive to suggestive selling, while others will want speedy treatment with a minimum of extra conversation and suggestive selling. Do not use a "canned presentation" to suggestive-sell. Stay tuned to the guests' needs and vary the suggestive selling presentations.

7. Never make excuses for why suggestive selling will not or has not worked in the past.

FIGURE 11.3
Suggestions for Effective Suggestive Selling

This example was focused on a foodservice operation, but similar examples can be seen in the lodging segment of the business.

Training Guest-contact Personnel

Management has the responsibility to recruit and staff, orient and train, supervise, coach and counsel, and motivate the service personnel. This is no small task and it does not happen by accident.

When recruiting, it is imperative that management view the potential guest-contact employees as the lifeblood of the organization, for they can make or break the hotel or restaurant. Managers should seek individuals who "come alive in front of the guest." Recruiters and interviewers should look for enthusiasm, good organizational skills, obvious ambition, high persuasiveness, experience, verbal and communication skills, and a "can do" and "will do" attitude.

A wide variety of training methods can be used, but the overall focus should be on the following. Four basic aspects of training guest-contact and service personnel are product-service knowledge (cognitive aspect), physical skills (psychomotor aspect), attitude (affective aspect), and reassurance (affective aspect). Each of these is discussed in the following paragraphs.

Product-service Knowledge (Cognitive Aspect). This refers to the learned or memorized job knowledge, such as how specific menu items are prepared or presented, specific attributes related to guest rooms, or other ingredients of the product-service mix.

Physical Skills (Psychomotor Aspect). These are learned physical skills, such as how to prepare a tableside salad or how to present, open, and pour a bottle of wine.

Attitude (Affective Aspect). These are more difficult to teach because they are related to an individual's perceptions and beliefs, which are not easily changed. Attitudes affect the individual's behavior and motivation to provide service to the guest. Even if training in the first two areas results in exceptional employee performance, poor attitudes can and do result in unsatisfied guests. All employees must be trained, coached and counseled, and led by example in displaying the spirit of hospitality in serving guests. Bear in mind that in today's service economy, poor employee attitude is the number one criticism of consumers. Consumers will tolerate minor problems, but they will not and should not be expected to deal with poor employee attitudes. The focus of training employees should be that the operation will tolerate any employee mistake except rudeness to a guest.

Reassurance (Affective Aspect). The service person should be trained in how to reassure guests. This can take many forms—for example, if a guest in a dining room orders an item, the server might respond, "That's our most popular item, you'll enjoy it" or "All of our desserts are fresh baked, but that one is my favorite." Service personnel also need to be trained in how to effectively handle guest complaints. Some guests will complain no matter what you do to please them, but this group represents a very small minority. The vast majority of guests who complain have good reason, and every effort should be made to correct the error and make sure they are satisfied. It is wise to think of a guest's complaint as the tip of the iceberg, because for every complaint that you hear, there are likely to be others that you do not hear. It is imperative that employees receive specific training in how to handle guest complaints. Part of the training should also provide guidance in how an employee can get the manager involved in resolving the complaint so that the guest is satisfied.

Training service personnel is of critical importance if internal promotion is to be successful. An employee must be aided in developing product-service knowledge, physical skills, a positive attitude and the ability to reassure and effectively handle all guest situations.

Entertainment

Entertainment can generate increased sales and more satisfied guests. Entertainment during the last several years has taken on many new forms, including in-room movies, large-screen television, various forms of disk jockey and music video entertainment, comedy clubs, and other forms of media entertainment. Many forms of entertainment are suitable, but live entertainment has long been regarded as the most powerful entertainment form.

Live entertainment is not the best approach for all hospitality operations, but it should be considered. Several questions should be considered:

☐ What impact will the entertainment have on volume, both in sales and the number of guests?

☐ Is the physical layout of the facility suitable for live entertainment?

☐ How will the cost associated with live entertainment, such as payment to performers and increased advertising costs, be covered?

First, the impact that entertainment will have on sales volume should be analyzed closely. The breakeven point should be calculated. Different methods to cover the costs of entertainment are feasible; these include charging higher prices for food and beverage to offset the increased cost, instituting a cover charge or a cover charge and a minimum purchase, and covering costs through increased sales.

Second, the physical layout of the facility must be examined closely. Is the configuration of the facility suitable for live entertainment and perhaps for dancing? Many operators have discovered that their facilities were simply too small for live entertainment, but have discovered this after they had made the commitment.

When entertainment of any type is selected, the marketing concept should be a paramount concern. Management should focus on the needs and wants of the guests and attempt to satisfy the guests rather than themselves. If the guests want rock music, yet the management prefers jazz, there should be no question as to which type of entertainment is selected.

Other Promotional Techniques

Many other techniques should be considered for promoting your hotel or restaurant. These include brochures and meeting planner guides, directories, flyers and in-house signs, and tent cards. All of these techniques offer a great deal of potential when they are used properly and directed toward the appropriate target audience.

Brochures are not as easy to design as one might think. When hotel brochures are placed in a rack with others, it becomes clear how difficult it is to design a brochure that will stand out from the others, capture the potential consumer's interest, and spark further inquiry or action. If a brochure is able to accomplish this, it truly is successful. Nykiel[2] offers several suggestions for designing an effective brochure:

☐ *Identification of the facility, including logo.* It is important to emphasize the chain affiliation if one exists.

☐ *Descriptive facts on the facility.* Too many brochures use pretty faces and flowery copy and do not provide enough description of the facts related to the facility.

☐ *Map and directions for how to get to the facility.* This is particularly needed if the facility is not as easily reached as the competition. It needs to be strongly emphasized that you can reach the facility. A map showing travel mileage and times from major cities or other attractions is also useful.

☐ *Basic information.* Be sure to include address, telephone number, and other pertinent information, such as hours of operation if that applies.

☐ *Person or individual to contact for further information.* This might be the director of marketing, catering, or another department, depending on the purpose and intended target audience for the brochure.

☐ *Products, services, and amenities offered by the facility.* It is important to emphasize those aspects of the facility that will help to differentiate it from the competition.

☐ *Attractions and interesting things for guests to do while they are in the area.*

☐ *Transportation information.* This would include limo service, rental car companies, airlines, and other forms of transportation that could be used to travel to the facility.

PUBLIC RELATIONS

The term *public relations* is widely misunderstood and is often misused within business, and the hospitality business is no exception. Every business interacts with a variety of "publics" representing consumers, the general public, the financial community, the organization's employees, government, the media, suppliers, and many others. Public relations is the process by which the relationships with each of these publics is managed. All businesses have to realize that the public will be affected by what the company says and does. Public relations is most obvious in the event of a disaster, such as a hotel fire, but public relations encompasses many other facets and can and should take a positive tone as well. The following section will discuss aspects of public relations, offering guidelines for effective public relations, techniques that can be used effectively to manage public relations, and finally, a specific application of public relations—the opening of a hotel.

It requires great skill to effectively manage public relations, which is why many firms use external consultants and agencies to assist them with this effort. Public relations should be tied in as an integrated part of the overall marketing plan. Just as objectives, strategies, tactics, action plans, target audiences, implementation schedules, and methods for evaluation are a part of the development of a marketing plan, so too the same approach should be applied to public relations. Positive and beneficial public relations do not just happen by chance; they must be the result of individuals making it happen according to a plan.

One of the basic needs of public relations is for the organization to be able to provide accurate information. The development of a press kit can help to accomplish this goal. The essential components of a press kit follow:[3]

☐ *Fact Sheet.* This should contain basic information about the facility and the companies that own and operate it. Examples of the type of information necessary would be property name, address, telephone number; general manager's name as well as those of all of the department heads; number of rooms and suites; number of restaurants; number of lounges; special features of the product-service mix; and the size and capacities of the meeting facilities.

☐ *Description of the local trading area.* Where is the facility located, and what are the surrounding areas like?

☐ *Special features of the product-service mix.* Are there special aspects of the facility that should be mentioned, such as architecture, type of suites offered, type of food and beverages offered, or special services?

☐ *Specific details about the product-service mix of the facility.* This should provide information about each of the retail outlets.

☐ *Photographs.* Stock photographs should be maintained of both the exterior and interior of the facility, showing the facilities being used by guests.

☐ *Biographical sketch of the General Manager.*

The press kit is useful when interacting with members of the media, as well as the other publics. Figure 11.4 provides a list of those members of the media with whom the public relations personnel should be familiar.

Public Relations Techniques

Public relations can be applied in several ways. Some of the more common techniques include the following:

☐ *News releases.* These should be routinely sent to the media, providing information about people and events of potential interest. Certainly, not all of the releases will result in positive coverage, but some will.

☐ *Photographs.* These will be particularly attractive if they feature a famous personality or create a human interest angle.

☐ *Letters, inserts, and enclosures.* Letters might be sent to governmental officials urging them to take some type of action. Inserts can be used as envelope stuffers in employee paychecks, or they can be sent with follow-up correspondence with guests or clients.

☐ *House organs and newsletters.* These can be both internal and external, but should be focused on a specific target audience. The purpose is to communicate positive images, increase sales, and influence public opinion.

The Print Media
City editor
Food editor
Travel editor
Finance editor
Style section editor
Travel and tourism/business section editor
Feature columnists

Broadcast Media
Station manager
New director
New announcers
Station personalities

FIGURE 11.4
Public Relations Media Contacts

☐ *Speeches and public appearances.* Members of the management staff should be encouraged to speak before groups with either professional or civic applications. Special care should be taken to ensure that the speech is well prepared and delivered.

☐ *Posters, bulletin boards, and exhibits.*

☐ *Audiovisual materials.*

☐ *Open houses and tours.*

No discussion of techniques can be complete. However, the guidelines presented in Figure 11.5 provide several good ideas for increasing the effectiveness of public relations activities.

Public relations requires careful planning and attention to detail. Unlike advertising, in which the sponsor controls the content and the timing of the message, public relations requires coordination with many other parties. These parties do not have the interests of the hotel or restaurant as their primary objective. Figure 11.6 provides an example of a timetable developed to plan the public relations for the opening of a new hotel. It should be noted that the plans provide a framework around which more specific action plans and specific responsibilities can be developed.

SUMMARY

This chapter focuses on the important aspect of promotions and public relations. The elements of the promotional mix are presented and a communications model is illustrated. The role of sales promotion is discussed and includes increasing consumer awareness, introducing new products and services, increasing guest occupancy and customer counts, combatting competition, encouraging present guests to purchase more, and stimulating demand in nonpeak periods.

The two basic type of sales promotions strategies are push and pull. Push strategies attempt to push the product-service mix through the service delivery system, while the pull strategy encourages increased purchases and consumption by consumers. Several common techniques are discussed, including coupons, sampling, premiums, and contests and sweepstakes. Recommendations for managing and budgeting for successful promotions are also discussed.

Internal promotions are reviewed. A discussion of the lost revenue potential from missed selling opportunities is presented, as well as suggestions and recommendations for how these missed opportunities could be avoided. Specific material presented includes suggestions for training guest-contact employees to suggestive-sell more effectively. Aspects of training guest-

1. Always identify individual photographs when submitted so that recipient does not play "Editor's Bingo" in guessing who's who. Only send photos of people involved, not the person making announcement. In group shots, indicate individual identifications as "left to right, standing," etc.

2. Do not fold, staple, crease or otherwise mutilate photos, or write on front or back with a heavy hand, thereby damaging the photo.

3. Know the publications that you send material to so that you do not waste your company's money or the editor's time. Don't develop a reputation for sending out worthless material or your important releases may one day be overlooked and consigned to file 13.

4. Always provide needed information such as company's name and address (not just the public relations or ad agency's name and address), retail price or cost of the product so that the reader can evaluate its appeal and marketability, etc. Just the facts, no puffery.

5. Do not send too many releases at one time and then complain that the publication did not select "the most important." If one is most important from a product, marketing, design or production standpoint, send that separately or identify it properly. It is really best to space out releases. Few publications maintain files to "space out" releases since they receive hundreds each week.

6. Be brief and provide a summary of the release so that it can be judged quickly (and properly) and written efficiently by someone not an expert in your field. Complete information can be briefly stated without reams of company history!

7. Do not confuse trade magazines with Playboy, Playgirl, etc., and use scantily dressed models. Editors frequently choose not to use a picture if models are too obviously selected to trap the viewer with blatant sex appeal.

8. Be careful when placing logotype, model number, etc., on photos, so that it can be cropped off without destroying the product image. Providing this information in a corner of the photo may solve your product or brand identification problem. Otherwise your photo may not be used at all.

9. Remember the timing of magazine publishing and do not send out releases a week or so before promotion takes place, expecting them to be used "in time." You should not ask a publication to run a new product or display item before you are in production and/or your sales organization has told the trade about it in regular personal calls.

10. Do not threaten editors with loss of advertising if they do not run your items, or bait them with promises of advertising if they do.

These dos and don'ts were provided, "based on our frustrations and irritations," by the editors of "Hardware Retailing" magazine.

FIGURE 11.5
Guidelines for Public Relations

This schedule begins six months before the hotel opening, at which time the announcement of construction plans and the groundbreaking ceremony will have been completed.

150–180 days before opening

1. Hold meeting to define objectives and to coordinate public relations effort with advertising; establish timetable in accordance with scheduled completion date.
2. Prepare media kit.
3. Order photographs and renderings.
4. Begin preparation of mailings and develop media lists.
5. Contact all prospective beneficiaries of opening events.
6. Reserve dates for press conferences at off-site facilities.

120–150 days before opening

1. Send announcement with photograph or rendering to all media.
2. Send first progress bulletin to agents and media (as well as corporate clients, if desired).
3. Begin production of permanent brochure.
4. Make final plans for opening events, including commitment to beneficiaries.

90–120 days before opening

1. Launch publicity campaign to national media.
2. Send mailings to media.
3. Send second progress bulletin.
4. Arrange exclusive trade interviews and features in conjunction with ongoing trade campaign.
5. Begin trade announcement.

60–90 days before opening

1. Launch campaign to local media and other media with a short lead time—emphasizing hotel's contribution to the community, announcement of donations and beneficiaries, etc.
2. Send third and final progress bulletin with finished brochure.
3. Commence "behind-the-scenes" public tours.
4. Hold "hard-hat" luncheons for travel writers.
5. Set up model units for tours.

30–60 days before opening

1. Send preopening newsletter (to be continued on a quarterly basis).
2. Hold soft opening and ribbon-cutting ceremony.
3. Hold press opening.
4. Establish final plans for opening gala.

The month of opening

1. Begin broadside mailing to agents.
2. Hold opening festivities.
3. Conduct orientation press trips.

FIGURE 11.6
An Example of a Public Relations Timetable for a Hotel Opening

Source: Jessica Dee Zive, "Public Relations for the Hotel Opening," *The Cornell Hotel and Restaurant Administration Quarterly,* Vol. 22, No. 1, p. 21.

contact employees include product-service knowledge (cognitive aspect), physical skills (psychomotor aspect), attitude (affective aspect), and reassurance (affective aspect). Methods by which guest-contact employees could be trained are presented.

The broad field of public relations is introduced. Public relations involves the management of relationships with the "publics" with whom the firm comes in contact. Specific material presented includes the development of a public relations press kit, as well the most commonly utilized public relations techniques.

KEY WORDS AND CONCEPTS

☐ Spirit of hospitality

☐ Elements of the promotional mix

☐ Communications model

☐ Sales promotion

☐ Frequent guest programs

☐ Push and pull strategies

☐ Coupons and couponing

☐ Sampling

☐ Premiums

☐ Contests and sweepstakes

☐ Internal selling opportunities

☐ Guest-contact employee training

☐ Product-service knowledge, physical skills, attitude and reassurance aspects of training

☐ Entertainment

☐ The "publics" of public relations

Questions for Review and Discussion

1. What are the elements of the promotional mix?
2. Illustrate the components of the communications model. How can this model be used to improve communications?
3. What is the role of sales promotion?
4. What are several of the objectives of sales promotion? Which one(s) do you believe is (are) the most important? Why?
5. What is the difference between push and pull strategies? Use an example to illustrate the difference.
6. Cite and discuss the pros and cons of each of the major sales promotional techniques discussed in the chapter.
7. If you were given the job of designing and managing a sales promotion,

how might you use the guidelines presented in the chapter? What would you do differently?

8. What are the skill areas in which guest-contact employees must be trained? Which of these, in your opinion, is the most important? Why?
9. What is public relations? What do public relations personnel do?
10. What is a press kit? What should a press kit contain?

PART V

HOSPITALITY GROUP SALES

CHAPTER 12

Marketing Organizational Structure and Management

The chapter will introduce the organizational structure and management approach that is used in group sales and marketing. The emphasis will be placed on hotels because this is where the majority of the group sales occur. For this reason, the examples used in this chapter will be based on hotels. However, many foodservice operations derive a considerable proportion of their sales from group food and beverage functions. The concepts and principles discussed in this chapter will be applicable for these types of foodservice operations as well.

Of increasing importance to the success of any hospitality operation, sales and marketing encompasses a broad range of activities and responsibilities. The chapter will highlight the sales and marketing departmental structure and operation, the development and management of marketing plans and forecasts, and the management of the sales and marketing efforts of the entire sales team. Chapter 12 is divided into the following sections:

INTRODUCTION

DEPARTMENTAL STRUCTURE AND OPERATION
☐ Organizational Structure of the Sales and Marketing Department
☐ Interaction and Coordination with Other Departments and Agencies
☐ Coordination with External Publics

HOTEL MARKETING PLANS AND BUDGETS
☐ A Model for Developing, Implementing, and Evaluating a Marketing Plan
☐ Developing Accurate Forecasts

MANAGEMENT OF THE SALES AND MARKETING DEPARTMENT
☐ Manual Systems
☐ Automated Systems

SUMMARY

KEY WORDS AND CONCEPTS

QUESTIONS FOR REVIEW AND DISCUSSION

INTRODUCTION

Until very recently, the upper management ranks of businesses in general were dominated by individuals who had advanced through the organization's operations or financial departments. Few presidents or chief executive officers had spent the majority of their careers in sales and marketing. Today, this situation has changed. Within both large and small companies, the top executives often have strong marketing experience.

Marketing's role within the corporate structure has increased in its importance for two major reasons. First, the competitive situation has changed dramatically. Within the hospitality industry, there has been a great deal of new construction, resulting in a substantial increase in the number of available guest rooms. This growth in the inventory of available rooms has in some instances outpaced the demand for rooms. The result is increased pressure to maintain occupancy levels, with slightly increased average room rates and in turn increasing profitability. This increased pressure for profitability has resulted in greater importance being given to the sales and marketing function.

Second, all businesses, but especially the hospitality business, experience peaks and valleys of demand. Hotels such as resorts and business-oriented properties, which are targeted toward different market segments, experience peaks and valleys on different days of the week and seasons of the year. It is a major role of the sales and marketing department to try to maximize the high-demand periods (peaks) and to minimize the low-demand periods (valleys).

As the competitive situation has changed, marketing has increased in importance within the corporate structure. This increased stature has created the need for more professionalism and increased effectiveness. There are several characteristics of a well-managed hospitality organization that has a solid marketing orientation. The following are yardsticks by which organizations should be judged.

☐ *Customer orientation.* Is the guest the number one priority? Do the organization's employees try to stay in close touch and communicate with the customer, in order always to be ready to satisfy needs?

☐ *Strategic orientation.* The competitive environment is changing more rapidly than ever before. Those organizations that keep a close watch on the environment while they plan for the future will gain competitive advantages. Success calls for anticipating change, not merely reacting to it.

☐ *Adequate marketing information systems.* In this age of computerized data bases and computerized applications to management, it is critical that the organization have available accurate information in a timely fashion.

☐ *Integrated systems between marketing and operations.* If the business is to reach its full potential, the sales and marketing department must work effectively with all operating departments. Within hotels, for example, this is especially true for food and beverage and the front office departments. The sales and marketing staff must be able to make promises to the client that the operating departments will be able to satisfy. This calls for excellent communications and exceptional coordination between the departments so that client needs can be clearly articulated to the entire staff.

☐ *Operating efficiency.* The operating departments must be well coordinated and well managed to deliver the level of service desired by guests in a consistent manner. In addition, the marketing department must be organized in such a manner to deliver high-quality service to clients. This can be done through maintaining all files in an organized and up-to-date manner, keeping sales call reports up to date and complete, and distributing to the other operating departments in a timely fashion accurate and complete information concerning the groups that are scheduled to come into the hotel.

DEPARTMENTAL STRUCTURE AND OPERATION

Organizational Structure of the Sales and Marketing Department

The structure and organization of the sales and marketing department are critical to the success of the hotel. The exact organizational structure will depend on several factors, including the size of the hotel, the responsibilities of the sales and marketing staff, the standard operating policies that have been developed for the hotel, and the nature of the target markets of the hotel.

The organizational structure is dynamic—that is, it continues to change as the situation changes. Nothing is ever constant in a dynamic environment. The role of the sales and marketing department has changed in the last several years. For example, during the 1970s, the corporate-level sales and marketing department was responsible for sales, marketing strategy, marketing research, development of marketing plans, public relations, advertising and promotion, and all the other facets of the marketing mix. Those who worked at the hotel property level were charged with generating sales. Their job was to sell. Often, those at the property level were merely given sales quotas in dollars and number of guest room nights that they were expected to sell. All of the decisions related to marketing were made at the corporate level; at the property level the job was to sell.

This is no longer the situation. Those working at both the corporate level and the property level have responsibilities that cover the entire spectrum of sales *and* marketing. This change calls for a more sophisticated staff at the property level. Sales and marketing demands talents and skills that extend beyond simply selling the product-service mix.

A typical organizational chart for the sales and marketing function is illustrated in Figure 12.1. The major roles for which each individual is responsible are highlighted in the following paragraphs.

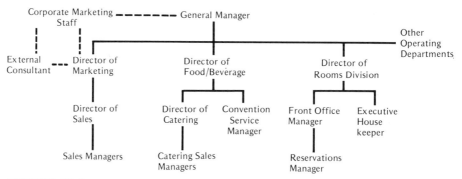

FIGURE 12.1
Organizational Chart for the Sales and Marketing Function within a Medium-sized (400-room) Hotel

General Manager (GM). This individual holds the ultimate responsibility for the success of the hotel property. The GM must work to establish the overall atmosphere, style, and tone for the property, and must help to differentiate it from the competition. This individual must work very closely with the director of marketing to develop the proper market segmentation and positioning strategies to assure success. It is imperative that the general manager be able to work with the other department heads and the representatives of the owners to develop both long- and short-range goals and objectives. It is the general manager's role to instill a "marketing-oriented philosophy" of putting the guest's needs first among all members of the staff. The general manager must also allocate resources among the operating departments in such a way that each has the necessary resources to accomplish the goals and objectives that have been established.

Director of Marketing (DOM). This individual is responsible for the professional operation of the sales and marketing department and the coordination with the other operating departments within the property. In addition, the director of marketing must coordinate plans and actions with the corporate marketing staff if the hotel is affiliated with a chain organization. All of the major chains maintain national sales offices in various geographic locations across the country. These offices provide support and leads for potential business to the director of marketing at the individual property level. In addition, the corporate marketing staff will provide support and training for those individuals employed in sales and marketing at the property level. The director of marketing must maintain excellent lines of communication with the corporate marketing staff to ensure that the plans being developed and implemented at the corporate level will be supported by and integrated with the plans being developed at the property level. The director of marketing also must coordinate the tasks of external consultants. The most commonly used external consultants are advertising agencies and public relations firms.

At the property level, the director of marketing has a wide variety of responsibilities. The director must develop, implement, monitor, and evaluate an annual marketing plan, the goal of which is to maximize the revenue generated by the various profit centers. The two largest profit centers are the rooms division and food and beverage department. In an average hotel, the rooms division will produce approximately 50–60 percent of the total revenue and food and beverage will contribute 30–40 percent. Contributions by other profit centers will be less and will depend on the nature of the hotel property and the number and size of the other profit centers. For example, a resort property will generate a considerable contribution from the recreational profit centers, so the percentage of the total revenue from rooms and food and beverage would be less.

The director of marketing is responsible for managing product-service mix development, marketing research activities, and strategic marketing planning. The development of the marketing plan and the financial goals and forecasts are under the control of the director of marketing. Another major aspect of the director of marketing's position is managing the sales team. This involves recruiting, interviewing, staffing, training, leading, and motivating this critical departmental work force.

In sum, the director of marketing is responsible for all aspects of marketing management at the property level. In the other chapters of this book, you have read about this wide variety of marketing topics. The director of marketing has responsibility for all of the aspects of marketing about which you have read. However, the director is not alone: He or she has a staff to help get all the tasks accomplished. Being a director of marketing is a large responsibility, but other members of the staff play a vital role.

Director of Sales (DOS).   As the second-in-command of the department, the director of sales is responsible for motivating, coordinating, and supervising the activities of the sales managers. The director of sales assists with the creation of specific programs and plans designed to increase revenue of profit centers. The director of sales engages in some personal selling, usually focusing on the major groups that the hotel is attempting to book.

Sales Manager (SM).   Individuals working as sales managers are primarily responsible for maintaining contact with existing clients and initiating contact with prospective clients for the purpose of booking group or convention business for the hotel. Sales managers make use of a variety of techniques, including personal selling, telephone sales, and direct mail. The number of sales managers employed by a hotel depends on the number of guest rooms and the percentage of the hotel's total room night demand that is generated by group rooms. In extremely large hotels, such as those with more than 1500 guest rooms, as many as thirty-five sales managers might be employed.

Sales managers are typically assigned to concentrate on a specific target market, so that they can establish a relationship with their clients. These market assignments can be made in a variety of ways, including geographic dispersion and by type of group. The latter is the most common. Sales managers are typically assigned to the association, corporate, medical, incentive travel, insurance, education, government, sports, unions, or group pleasure travel market segments.

The primary focus of a sales manager is on booking group room nights. Once a group has signed a contract, the details concerning the group's meetings, such as food and beverage needs or meeting rooms setup, are turned over to a catering sales manager, who then works with the clients in refining their ideas and servicing their needs.

Interaction and Coordination with Other Departments and Agencies

Each of the individuals working in the sales and marketing department plays an important role in coordinating efforts with the other departments of the hotel. In most hotels, once a group has signed a contract and committed to meet at the hotel, the meeting planner is then shifted to the catering department, where a catering sales manager works with the meeting planner to finalize all of the details of the group's meetings. Examples of details that normally must be discussed and worked out include food and beverage selections, layout or configuration of the meeting rooms, registration of those attending the meeting, audiovisual needs, entertainment, accounting and billing procedures, and a host of other details that must be decided if the group's meeting is to be a success.

The catering sales manager in turn coordinates planning with the convention service manager. The convention service manager is the main contact person once the group checks into the hotel; this individual works with others in the hotel to ensure that the client receives the services that were promised by the sales manager and the catering sales manager.

Coordination must also be achieved with the rooms division. The sales and marketing department must work closely with the front office manager and the reservations manager to ensure that the client's wishes for accounting and billing, room assignments, and other matters related to guest rooms and suites are carried out as promised and stipulated in the contract.

Coordination of all the small details is very critical to the success of the hotel's sales and marketing efforts. Murphy's Law suggests that if something can go wrong, it will. If you believe Murphy's Law, consider O'Brian's Postulate: "Murphy was an optimist." Attention to the smallest of details is necessary. Coordinating, checking up, and following up with all other departments within the hotel are critical activities for those working in the sales and marketing department.

Coordination with External Publics

Just as the hotel sales and marketing staff must coordinate with the members of other departments within the hotel, they must also work with individuals and groups that are external to the hotel. As mentioned earlier, the activities of advertising agencies must be coordinated, as well as communications with the chain's national sales offices and corporate headquarters.

One type of group with whom the sales and marketing staff works cooperatively is convention and visitors' bureaus (CVB). These are nonprofit umbrella organizations that represent a city or geographic area in the solicitation and servicing of travelers to that area. The convention and visitors' bureau brings together the efforts of government, civic associations, and the sales and marketing efforts of the hospitality industry.[1] Convention and visitors' bureaus are funded by two primary methods: by levying occupancy taxes on guest rooms and by selling memberships in the convention and visitors' bureau. They are typically operated by either the Chamber of Commerce or by the city government.

The primary purpose of the convention and visitors' bureau is to sell the entire city or destination rather than an individual hotel. Convention and visitors' bureaus focus on several different markets. First, they try to solicit potential business for the city or area from all types of groups, from large conventions and trade shows to smaller meetings that involve incentive travel. Second, they also focus on the transient market made up of individual travelers.

A second purpose that a convention and visitors' bureau performs is service. They may help to coordinate city- or areawide conventions by providing a housing clearinghouse, registration assistance, and other forms of support to both the traveler and the hotels in the area.

It is vitally important that the convention and visitors' bureau staff remain neutral when a prospective visitor or meeting planner representing a group selects a hotel property. Special efforts are made to make sure that all hotels in the city or area are notified when a meeting planner or site selection committee will be making a decision about potential hotels for a group. In this way, the individual hotels are able to submit proposals and the convention and visitors' bureau can remain neutral in the hotel selection process.

Convention and visitors' bureaus provide an extremely effective way to coordinate the sales efforts that several hotels would otherwise have to expend to solicit business from a diverse group of prospects. By taking a more macro-oriented or destination focus, the convention and visitors' bureau is able to bring group and transient business to the city or geographic area so that everyone will benefit.

HOTEL MARKETING PLANS AND BUDGETS

Earlier, in Chapter 4, marketing plans were discussed in considerable detail and a ten-step model was presented. The model presented earlier has application to the development of a marketing plan for hotels. The purpose of the model that follows is to provide a detailed outline for developing the very specific marketing plan required by a hotel that derives a considerable portion of its business from group sales.

A Model for Developing, Implementing, and Evaluating a Sales and Marketing Plan

    I. Situation analysis
        A. Product-service mix analysis
            1. Property strengths and weaknesses
                a. Location
                b. Parking
                c. Exterior and interior structure and design
                d. Food and beverage
                e. Guest rooms and suites
                f. Ballroom
                g. Other meeting rooms and public space
                h. Price
                i. Overall quality of products and services
            2. Current methods of marketing
                a. Advertising
                b. Public relations
                c. Internal sales promotion
                d. External sales promotion
                e. Personal selling
        B. Market analysis
            1. Identification of past and current situation
                a. Geographic profile of guests
                b. Demographic profile of guests
                c. Psychographic profile of guests
                d. Behavioral profile of guests
            2. Identification of new potential market segments
        C. Competition analysis
            1. Inventory of competition to include
                a. Number of guest rooms
                b. Occupancy level by month and year
                c. Guest market segmentation
                d. Rate structure
                e. Food and beverage facilities
                f. Meeting rooms and public space
            2. Assessment of the strengths and weaknesses of the competition
                a. Location
                b. Parking
                c. Exterior and interior structure
                d. Food and beverage
                e. Guest rooms and suites

        f. Ballroom

        g. Other meeting rooms and public space

        h. Price

        i. Overall quality of products and services

    3. Current methods of marketing

        a. Advertising

        b. Public relations

        c. Internal sales promotion

        d. External sales promotion

        e. Personal selling

II. Goals, strategies, and positioning

    A. Marketing goals and strategies

    B. Positioning strategy and positioning statement for the property

        This section involves as much art as science. The formulation of strategies and the subsequent market segmentation and positioning involve a great deal of creativity. The strategic marketing planning model presented in Chapter 4 should be examined before the strategies are finalized. Everything that follows in the remainder of the marketing plan flows from the critical decision concerning the nature of the positioning strategy and the positioning statement.

III. Annual and monthly objectives/forecasts for the following areas

    A. Occupancy

    B. Average room rate

    C. Total room sales

    D. Food and beverage sales

        1. Restaurant sales by outlet

        2. Lounge sales by outlet

        3. Group food sales

        4. Group beverage sales

    E. Other revenue centers

        1. Meeting room rentals

        2. Recreational facilities

        3. Retail stores and rentals

        4. Other revenue centers

        The development of objectives or forecasts does not need to be like pulling figures "out of the air." There are sound and rational approaches to the development of forecasts. A rational approach to forecasting will be explored in the next section of the chapter.

IV. Market segmentation and strategy—establish strategies for each appropriate segment

    A. Guest rooms and suites

        1. Transient

      2. Group rooms
        a. Association
        b. Corporate
        c. Medical
        d. Incentive
        e. Insurance
        f. Education
        g. Government
        h. Sports
        i. Unions
        j. Group pleasure travel (travel and tour group)
        k. Other group markets

Each property should develop market segments based on the business mix, the size of the hotel, and the number of staff members in sales and marketing. The eleven market segments shown here are likely to be the maximum number ever used within a marketing plan.

    B. Food
      1. Banquet areas/catering sales
      2. Each of the public food and beverage retail outlets
    C. Beverage
      1. Banquet areas/catering sales
      2. Each of the public food and beverage retail outlets
    D. Other revenue centers
      1. Meeting room rentals
      2. Recreational facilities
      3. Retail stores and rentals
      4. Other revenue centers

V. Action plans and implementation
    A. Develop a series of monthly action plans to solicit business from each of the targeted segments. A specific sales and marketing staff member should be assigned responsibility for each action plan, and completion dates should be specified.
    B. Develop a list of key accounts and discuss how business will be solicited from each of these accounts. A large percentage of a hotel's business is often generated by a few clients. These clients should be identified and plans for solicitation and service developed. Key account management will be discussed in Chapter 13.
    C. Develop a series of monthly action plans with regard to advertising to include
      1. Media selection
      2. Objectives of specific media
      3. Recommended media vehicles

D. Develop a series of monthly action plans with regard to sales promotion to include
   1. Internal
   2. External
E. Develop a series of monthly action plans with regard to public relations.

VI. Budget—develop a complete annual and monthly budget to include all items related to the marketing department. It is recommended that the standards established in *The Uniform Systems of Accounts for Hotels* be used to develop the budget.

VII. Evaluation/research
A. Develop and implement plans for monitoring changes in the market place.
B. Develop and implement plans for monitoring guest satisfaction.
C. Develop and implement methods to evaluate the actual performance against the marketing plan.
D. Develop and implement plans for other marketing research projects.

Each hotel company uses its own approach to developing a sales and marketing plan. Some are very detailed and are over 100 pages in length, while others are quite brief, perhaps less than 15 pages. The model presented in this chapter can be used as a guide in developing a marketing plan for a hotel property of almost any size. Each of the sections outlined can be expanded or reduced to fit the needs of the individual property or company.

Developing Accurate Forecasts

The task of preparing a forecast need not be overwhelming. With the use of computerized spreadsheets such as Lotus 1-2-3™, Supercalc 4™, or any of the host of other computer software programs available on the market, the burden of preparing a budget has been lessened. The computer software allows the user to focus on the "what if" situations and implications by having the computer manage the simple calculation and mathematical manipulation. Those responsible for preparing the forecast can develop a number of assumptions and see how these will affect the forecast.

Forecasts should be developed in a systematic manner and should be based on realistic assumptions and a realistic view of the future. Accurate forecasts are based on reality, not on wishes and hopes. The forecasting method presented in this section was originally developed by Peter Yesawich, the President of Robinson, Yesawich and Pepperdine. It represents an excellent model that is more fully developed than other forecasting models. It combines the work typically done by both the front office manager and the director of marketing to develop a total rooms revenue budget. Based on past performance, multipliers for food and beverage revenue, and for other revenue centers if desired, are added to the rooms revenue, resulting in a total revenue forecast.

Just as there are simple formulas that can be used to determine an advertising budget, such as the percentage of sales method, there are simple formulas that can be used to develop a forecast. The simplest is to apply some type of multiplier to the revenue figures for the past year. The multiplier is based on assumptions and to some extent guesswork. The market-based forecast proposed by Yesawich is grounded in sound methodology and reasoning. No forecasting methodology is foolproof; all are subject to error. However, this method makes use of a systematic approach that would seem to be less subject to error.

The model is based on six steps illustrated in Figure 12.2. The first step involves determining the amount of business that exists within the market in which the hotel competes. The second step is to determine the market share of the total demand and the fair share of business mix within the competitive group of your property. The third step is to examine each of the major market segments and assess the future demand with each segment. The fourth step involves developing an inventory of the competitive practices of the competing hotels. This information should be readily available through the marketing information system, as discussed in Chapter 5. Once this information is available, the next step is to assess the extent to which your own marketing efforts can preempt the competition. The fifth step is to determine priorities by deciding the proportion of your marketing effort and marketing resources that will be assigned to each market segment. The sixth, and final, step is to prepare the forecast for property occupancy, business mix, and revenues.

Step One—Determining Market Demand.   Before one can prepare an accurate forecast, it is necessary to estimate the total demand within the competing group of hotels. Once total demand within the competitive group is known, market share can then be calculated. Figure 12.3 illustrates an example of the outcome of this step. Note that information is provided for your property and for each of the competitors based on property size, occupied rooms, and occupancy.

Once the total demand is determined, the next step is to break the total demand into individual market segments. For the purpose of this example, four market segments will be used: individual commercial, group commercial, individual social, and group social. These market segments are defined as follows:

☐ *Individual commercial.* Guests who are traveling on business but are not part of a group

Step Task	**Assignment**
(1) Determine how much business exists within the group of properties that compete with your own.	Determine which properties constitute your competitive group, and then prepare a summary of area-wide demand expressed in terms of occupied rooms by market segment.
(2) Determine the extent to which you now penetrate existing demand.	Compute your property's market share of total demand and your fair share of the business mix within the competitive group.
(3) Determine which market segments are expected to grow, decline, or remain stable through the forecast period.	Classify each market segment as either growing, stable, or declining, and then express the expected change in occupied rooms.
(4) Survey the market practices of competitive properties, and then determine the extent to which you can preempt their approach to each market segment.	Prepare an analysis of competitive practices by market segment, and then determine whether you are capable of preempting consumer interest in favor of your property.
(5) Determine the proportion of your marketing effort that will be applied to each market segment.	Rank the market segments by assigned priority.
(6) Prepare the forecast.	Project occupancy, business mix, and revenues for the forecast period.

FIGURE 12.2
The Market Forecast: Step by Step

Source: Peter C. Yesawich, "A Market-Based Approach to Forecasting," *The Cornell Hotel and Restaurant Administration Quarterly*, Vol. 25, No. 3, pp. 47–53.

☐ *Group commercial.* Guests who are traveling on business as a part of an organized group

☐ *Individual social.* Guest who are traveling for pleasure but are not part of a group

☐ *Group social.* Guest who are traveling for pleasure and are part of a group

When preparing a forecast, any number and/or combination of market segments can be used. The number and makeup of the market segments selected will be determined by the business mix that the hotel attracts. Figure 12.4 illustrates the results of breaking demand down into market segments for your own property and those with whom you compete. Note that demand is broken down by each major market segment in terms of number of room

	Your Property	Competitor A	Competitor B	Competitor C	Competitive Group Total
Property size	275	250	300	230	1,055
Occupied rooms	67,753	55,760	65,520	59,232	248,265
Occupancy	67.5%	61.1%	59.8%	70.5%	64.4%

FIGURE 12.3
Descriptive Data for Competitive Group
Source: Peter C. Yesawich, "A Market-Based Approach to Forecasting," *The Cornell Hotel and Restaurant Administration Quarterly*, Vol. 25, No. 3, pp. 47-53.

nights occupied and the percentage of total room night demand that each segment contributes to the total number of occupied rooms for each property.

The data needed to complete this chart can be derived from your own internal marketing information system. Data concerning the competitor's performance should be estimated, based on your knowledge of their business mix. The total number of room nights occupied within each segment can be estimated based on the property's total occupancy percentage and the percentage of business that each market segment provides.

Step Two—Determine Market Share.   In order to assess current position and the potential for the future, the next step is to determine your

Rooms Occupied During Previous 12 Months

Market segment	Your property # rms.	%	Competitor A # rms.	%	Competitor B # rms.	%	Competitor C # rms.	%	Total # rms.	%
Individual commercial	21,681	32%	25,092	45%	23,587	36%	20,139	34%	90,499	37%
Group commercial	16,938	25%	10,037	18%	19,656	30%	8,885	15%	55,516	22%
Individual social	21,004	31%	20,631	37%	10,483	16%	20,731	35%	72,849	29%
Group social	8,130	12%	—	—	11,794	18%	9,477	16%	29,401	12%
Total	67,753	100%	55,760	100%	65,520	100%	59,232	100%	248,265	100%

FIGURE 12.4
Demand Analysis by Market Segment
Source: Peter C. Yesawich, "A Market-Based Approach to Forecasting," *The Cornell Hotel and Restaurant Administration Quarterly*, Vol. 25, No. 3, pp. 47–53.

property's market share for each of the identified market segments. By comparing your market share in each segment with the competitor's market share, you can see relative strengths and weaknesses. Figure 12.5 illustrates how this is done. The total number of rooms occupied for the competitive group listed by market segment is compared with your property's performance in the same segments. The market share is calculated by dividing your property's number of occupied rooms by the total number of occupied rooms within the competing group. The result in the example shown is a market share of 27.2 percent. The market share for each market segment can also be calculated in the same way, by dividing your property's total number of occupied rooms in the segment by the total number of occupied rooms in the segment within the total competitive group. The variance from fair market share is also useful to examine. The fair market share is the percentage of the market that your property would hold if you achieved the average performance within the competitive group. The variance from fair market share is the difference between the average for the total group and your property's performance.

Once the market penetration is determined, it is necessary to examine your property's performance against the competitors in terms of market share of the total demand and market share within each market segment. The two analyses are shown in Figures 12.6 and 12.7. Figure 12.6, Market Share Analysis, illustrates your property's expected market share if you achieve occupancy performance that matches the average for the competitive group, as well as the actual performance. These two figures allow you to calculate a

Rooms Occupied During Previous 12 Months

Market Segment:	Total for Competitive Group # rms.	%	Total for Your Property # rms.	%	Market Share	Variance from Fair Share
Individual commercial	90,499	37%	21,681	32%	23.9%	−5%
Group commercial	55,516	22%	16,938	25%	30.5%	+3%
Individual social	72,849	29%	21,004	31%	28.8%	+2%
Group social	29,401	12%	8,130	12%	27.6%	—
Total	248,265	100%	67,753	100%	27.2% (avg.)	

FIGURE 12.5
Market Penetration

Source: Peter C. Yesawich, "A Market-Based Approach to Forecasting," *The Cornell Hotel and Restaurant Administration Quarterly*, Vol. 25, No. 3, pp. 47–53.

$$\text{Expected market share} = \frac{\text{Your available rooms}}{\text{Total available rooms for competitive group}} = \frac{275}{1,055} = 26.0\%$$

$$\text{Actual market share} = \frac{\text{Your occupied rooms}}{\text{Total occupied rooms for competitive group}} = \frac{67,753}{248,265} = 27.2\%$$

$$\text{Variance from expected market share} = \text{Actual} - \text{Expected} = 27.2 - 26.0 = +1.2\%$$

FIGURE 12.6
Market Share Analysis

Source: Peter C. Yesawich, "A Market-Based Approach to Forecasting," *The Cornell Hotel and Restaurant Administration Quarterly*, Vol. 25, No. 3, pp. 47–53.

variance from the expected market share. Variances that are positive (as is the case in the example) indicate that your property is outperforming the competition, while negative variances indicate that you are not matching the performance of the competition.

Figure 12.7 illustrates how the variances from Figure 12.5 should be ranked from negative to positive based on the absolute size of the variance. As

Variance from Fair Share	Market Segment	Remarks
−5%	Individual commercial	Competitor's approach to this segment has been more aggressive and aided by more attractive "corporate" programs.
—	Group social	—
+2%	Individual social	The location of our property relative to the city's shopping district is preferable to that of our competitors; in addition, our weekend packages have been marketed well.
+3%	Group commercial	We have developed a close working relationship with meeting planners, maintain an aggressive field sales staff, and offer highly competitive group rates.

FIGURE 12.7
Fair-Share Analysis

Source: Peter C. Yesawich, "A Market-Based Approach to Forecasting," *The Cornell Hotel and Restaurant Administration Quarterly*, Vol. 25, No. 3, pp. 47–53.

with any type of variance analysis, any negative variance should be examined first and the largest variances should be examined second. Each of the variances should be examined carefully to determine the underlying reasons.

Step Three—Estimate Market Segment Growth.   The segments that you should look toward for the greatest growth potential are those for which total areawide demand is increasing, or those from which your property is not receiving the fair market share. Certainly a wide number of factors could influence the demand within any segment, including economic forces and changes in the number of available rooms within the area.

Total market demand should be projected for each market segment, as shown in Figure 12.8. This figure illustrates the anticipated change in the number of room nights produced by each segment. Along with the projection, it is wise to include the rationale or reasons behind the estimate.

Step Four—Survey of Competitive Market Practices and Your Own Marketing Plans.   This step calls for a careful assessment of the competitive

Demand Forecast (Next 12 Months)

Market Segment	Expected Change	Remarks
Growing segments:		
Individual commercial	+3% (2,715 room-nights)	Sustained economic recovery should increase commercial traffic to the city.
Group commercial	+2% (1,110 room-nights)	Local high-tech firms will schedule additional sales training meetings because of planned new-product introductions.
Stable segments:		
Group social	N/C	Current booking patterns suggest that demand from this segment will remain relatively flat.
Declining segments:		
Individual social	−2% (−1,457 room-nights)	Consumers remain cautious about discretionary expenditures for vacation travel; we also anticipate very strong price competition within this segment.
Net change	+2,368 room-nights	

FIGURE 12.8
Demand Forecast

Source: Peter C. Yesawich, "A Market-Based Approach to Forecasting," *The Cornell Hotel and Restaurant Administration Quarterly*, Vol. 25, No. 3, pp. 47–53.

situation. Your potential for increasing market share in the segments you targeted for growth in the previous step will be influenced by the actions of your competitors. The entire spectrum of competitive activities will influence your ability to reach your targets. Based on your knowledge of the situation, you must assess the extent to which you can preempt the competition. This analysis is shown in Figure 12.9.

Step Five—Determine the Proportion of the Total Marketing Effort which Will be Applied to Each Market Segment. All hotels have limited resources. It is not possible to do all things at once, even though we sometimes would like to. Priorities must be established. Figure 12.10 illustrates the determination of marketing priorities based on the assessment of the growth of various market segments, the competitive activities, and your own ability to preempt the competition. In the example shown, the individual commercial segment will receive the highest priority and a justification is provided to support this. Other segments and their relative priorities are also shown. High-priority segments are those in which you can preempt the competition and in which an increased investment of resources will likely produce an appropriate increase in occupied rooms. Maintenance priority segments are those in which you plan to maintain the status quo. An increase in marketing resources is not likely to result in enough of an increase in occupied rooms to warrant an additional expenditure, but if fewer resources are allocated a reduction in market share is likely. Low-priority segments are those that are

Market Segment	Can Competition be Preempted?	Required Strategies
Growing segments:		
Individual commercial	Yes	Introduce executive-traveler floors and offer more attractive corporate programs.
Group commercial	Yes	Promote special meeting incentive packages, including some new guest amenities.
Stable segments:		
Group social	No	—
Declining segments:		
Individual social	No	—

FIGURE 12.9
Summary of Competitive Practices
Source: Peter C. Yesawich, "A Market-Based Approach to Forecasting," *The Cornell Hotel and Restaurant Administration Quarterly*, Vol. 25, No. 3, pp. 47–53.

Market Segment	Remarks
High priority:	
Individual commercial	Represents largest percentage of our existing business; not currently receiving our "fair share"; demand expected to grow by 3%; can preempt competition.
Group commercial	Represents 25% of our existing business; should be able to preserve our positive variance on "fair share"; demand expected to grow by 2%; can preempt competition.
"Maintenance":	
Group social	Curently receiving "fair share"; demand not expected to grow in next 12 months; cannot preempt competition.
Individual social	Represents 31% of our existing business but demand is expected to decline by 2% during next 12 months; would have to compromise rate too much to preempt competition.

FIGURE 12.10
Determination of Marketing Priorities
Source: Peter C. Yesawich, "A Market-Based Approach to Forecasting," *The Cornell Hotel and Restaurant Administration Quarterly*, Vol. 25, No. 3, pp. 47–53.

likely to decline as a percentage of total market share regardless of the allocation of marketing resources.

The decision to allocate resources and determine priorities is vitally linked with the development of the marketing plan. Every effort should be made to exploit the market segments in which your property currently has strength and to build on this established business base.

The marketing priorities are then converted into more specific objectives, as shown in Figure 12.11.

Step Six—Prepare the Forecast.   The final step of the forecasting process is to develop the actual forecast and the subsequent revenue projections, which are shown in Figures 12.12 and 12.13. The specific objectives for increases in occupied room nights that you determined in a previous step (illustrated in Figure 12.11) are added to the present mix of business within each segment. The result is the projected mix for the forecast period, usually one year.

The projected number of occupied rooms in each segment is then used as the basis for projecting revenue. A targeted average rate must be determined for each segment, as well as a multiplier for food, beverages, and other expenditures by individuals in each segment. As shown in Figure 12.13, these three figures are multiplied together to produce the total revenue estimate for each segment. In turn, estimates should be included for local guests in the

Market Segment	Objectives	Expected Change in Rooms Occupied
High priority:		
Individual commercial	· Recapture 3 points of fair share. · Capture 20% of increased demand.	+2,715 +543
Group commercial	· Maintain positive variance from fair share. · Capture 30% of increased demand.	— +333
"Maintenance":		
Group social	· Maintain fair share.	—
Individual social	· Limit expected loss to 25% of area decline.	−364
Net Change		+3,227

FIGURE 12.11
Performance Objectives by Segment

Source: Peter C. Yesawich, "A Market-Based Approach to Forecasting," *The Cornell Hotel and Restaurant Administration Quarterly*, Vol. 25, No. 3, pp. 47–53.

	Occupied Rooms				
Market Segment	Present Mix # rms.	%	Expected Change	Projected Mix # rms.	%
Individual commercial	21,681	32%	+3,258	24,939	35%
Group commercial	16,938	25%	+333	17,271	24%
Individual social	21,004	31%	−364	20,640	29%
Group social	8,130	12%	N/C	8,130	12%
Total	67,753	100%	+3,227	70,980	100%

Note: This forecast represents a 5% increase over the previous year—an annual occupancy rate of 66.8%.

FIGURE 12.12
Forecast

Source: Peter C. Yesawich, "A Market-Based Approach to Forecasting," *The Cornell Hotel and Restaurant Administration Quarterly*, Vol. 25, No. 3, pp. 47–53.

Transient Guests	Occupied Rooms	×	Average Rate	×	Food, Beverage, Miscellaneous Multiplier	=	Total
Individual commercial	24,939		$68.50		1.35		$2,306,234.00
Group commercial	17,271		$55.75		1.40		$1,348,001.50
Individual social	20,640		$74.00		1.22		$1,863,379.20
Group social	8,130		$52.00		1.15		$ 486,174.00
Subtotal							$6,003,788.70
					Local guests		
					Food		$1,650,000.00
					Beverage		$1,200,000.00
					Miscellaneous		$ 65,000.00
Subtotal							$2,915,000.00
Total							$8,918,788.70

FIGURE 12.13
Revenue Projections
Source: Peter C. Yesawich, "A Market-Based Approach to Forecasting," *The Cornell Hotel and Restaurant Administration Quarterly*, Vol. 25, No. 3, pp. 47–53.

food and beverage area and other revenue centers, with the end result being a total revenue projection for the property.

There are many ways to develop a forecast. The value of the method developed by Yesawich is that it is based on a very rational thought process, while at the same time it is relatively simple to complete.

MANAGEMENT OF THE SALES AND MARKETING DEPARTMENT

As was discussed earlier in the chapter, the overall responsibilities of the director of marketing are very broad. This section of the chapter will focus on the management of a most important resource in the sales and marketing office—information. Information lies at the heart of everything that is done in the sales and marketing office. The filing system is the basis for managing this information and putting it into the hands of sales and marketing personnel when they need it. In most cases, the effectiveness of the sales and marketing office is only as good as the filing system and monitoring system that has been established.

Manual Systems

Many hotels use a manual filing system within the sales and marketing office. This approach is very effective if it is properly managed. The filing system is centered around the "master file." A master file is maintained for every group with which the hotel has done business or would like to do business. The master file contains a vast array of information:

☐ All written correspondence with the client.

☐ A running log of all telephone contacts with the client with notes concerning the dates, what was discussed, and who the sales and marketing person making the contact was. An example of a call report sheet is shown in Figure 12.14.

☐ A record of all personal calls that have been made on the client. An example of a personal call report sheet is shown in Figure 12.15.

DATE _____

ORGANIZATION _____

REASON FOR CALL _____

CONTACT'S NAME _____ TITLE _____

       ADDRESS   _____

                   _____

       TELEPHONE _____

CALL REPORT _____

_____

_____

_____

_____

_____

NEXT ACTION _____

_____

TRACE _____

COPIES OF REPORT TO _____

FIGURE 12.14

An Example of a Call Report Sheet Which is Maintained in the Master Account File

Source: Julia Crystler, *Situation Analysis Workbook* (Washington, DC: Hotel Sales and Marketing Association International and The Educational Institute of the American Hotel and Motel Association, 1983), p. 15.

FILE NO. _____

COMPANY: _____   SALESPERSON: _____

CONTACT: _____   TITLE: _____

ADDRESS: _____

_____

PHONE: _____

Meeting Potential

THIS HOTEL: Yes:____   NO:____

OTHER HOTELS: _____

_____

_____

MEETING DATES: _____   # OF ROOMS: _____

OF DAYS: _____   # OF OVERNIGHTS: _____   # OF PEOPLE: _____

CATERING: _____

BUSINESS TRAVELLERS: YES: ____   NO: ____   FREQUENCY: _____

COMMENTS

_____

_____

_____

_____

_____

_____

_____

_____

_____

TRACE DATE: _____

ACTION: _____

cc: General Manager
     Director of Sales
     File

FIGURE 12.15
An Example of a Personal Sales Call Report

Source: Julia Crystler, *Situation Analysis Workbook* (Washington, DC: Hotel Sales and Marketing Association International and The Educational Institute of the American Hotel and Motel Association, 1983), p. 23.

☐ All proposals that have been sent to the client as well as all contracts that have been signed. All internal and external records related to the group's planned functions within the hotel are maintained. Examples of a group room block and a group cover sheet are shown in Figures 12.16 and 12.17.

In short, the master file is a record of *everything*. If files are properly maintained and a sales manager leaves a property, a new sales manager should be able to pick up the master file and understand everything that has occurred in the past with the particular client.

Definite Cancellation		GROUP ROOM BLOCK	Meeting _____		
				MO Day YR	
Tentative Decision Date _____			Property _____		
Change From			File #		

Name of Group			
Division Name		Name of Meeting	
Name of Contact	Title	Salesperson	Today's Date
Address of Contact			
Area Code – Telephone Number		No. Of People	Total Room Nights

DAY	SUN	MON	TUE	WED	THRU	FRI	SAT	SUN	MON	TUE	WED	THUR	FRI	SAT
DATE														
RMS BLOCKED														
RMS PICKED UP														

NUMBER	Singles	Doubles	Twins	Triples	Quads	Suites
RATE	$	$	$	$	$	Suites
BILLING PROCEDURES	Room & Tax ___Individual ___Master		Incidental Charges ___Individual ___Master		Credit Code	
RESERVATION	___Individual __Card __ List __GTD __6pm			Cut Off Date	Rooms Commissionable At %	
Comps			Remarks			

Frequency Of Meeting	Meeting Type	Decision Process Date _____	No. of Exhibits
PAST & FUTURE HISTORY	MO/DAYS/YR	HOTEL	CITY/STATE
LEAD SENT ___			
Comments/Cancellation Comments			

FIGURE 12.16
An Example of a Group Room Block

Source: Julia Crystler, *Situation Analysis Workbook* (Washington, DC: Hotel Sales and Marketing Association International and The Educational Institute of the American Hotel and Motel Association, 1983), p. 31.

GROUP COVER SHEET

Date:_____

File #:_____

Group Credit Code:_____

VIP Credit Code:_____

1. Organization:_____

2. Dates:_____

      Major Arrival Date_____   Major Departure Date_____

      Group Arrival Time_____   Group Departure Time_____

3. Group Contact:_____

4. Hotel Contact:_____

5. Attendance:_____   Number of Rooms:_____

6. Rooming List:_____   Individual:_____

      Guaranteed:_____   Time Arrival:_____

7. Preregistration:_____   Quick Checkout:_____

8. Gratuities (Automatic):_____

9. Rates: Singles_____ Doubles_____ Twins_____ Triples_____ Quads_____ Suites_____

      E.P._____ M.A.P._____ F.A.P._____ Other_____

10. Comps, VIP's & Suites: State number of rooms, type of suite/accommodation, connectors required, rates, names of occupants, arrival and departure information.

NAME	TYPE	RATE	#PP	ARRIVAL DATE/TIME	DEPARTURE DATE/TIME	COMMENTS

11. Billing Instructions

      Non-commissionable   Commissionable to_____

      Each pays   Guest sign for all charges   Sign for room & tax only

      own bill   (Transfer to M/A)   (Guest pays all incidentals)

      Exceptions:_____

12. Check Cashing: Hotel policy (except as noted)_____

_____

13. Master Account: 14. Person(s) Authorized to Sign

      Account Name _____   Master Account

      Address   _____   _____

                     _____   _____

      Attn: _____   _____

      Phone #: ( )_____   _____

FIGURE 12.17

An Example of a Group Cover Sheet

Source: Julia Crystler, *Situation Analysis Workbook* (Washington, DC: Hotel Sales and Marketing Association International and The Educational Institute of the American Hotel and Motel Association, 1983), p. 33.

Master files are usually assigned a number for filing purposes. This number is cross-referenced with other filing systems that will be discussed later. Master files are often color-coded by market segment as well. For example, this can be done in such a way that all files in the state association market segment would be color-coded with blue. Other segments would be color-coded in similar ways.

When a master file is removed for use by a sales manager, a guide card is left behind in the master file. This card tells who has the file, who signed it out, and the date that the file was removed. In this way, if someone else in the office needs to examine a file that has been removed, it can be easily found.

In order to keep track of the numerically filed master files, several other files are maintained, all of which are cross-referenced with the numerical master file. Examples of other supporting files include the following:

☐ *Alphabetical files.* A complete listing of all clients and prospects for whom a master file is maintained. This file is consulted and is referenced to the numerical master file so that the master file can be pulled for further study.

☐ *Geographic file.* All clients and prospects within specific geographic areas are often maintained. In this way, if a sales manager is planning a sales trip to a specific geographic area, master files can be pulled for clients and prospects within the selected geographic area.

☐ *Market segments.* Files are often maintained for each market segment. These files are also cross-listed with the numerical master files.

Another vital file maintained by the sales and marketing office is the trace file. All master files should contain a trace date—that is, the date on which a sales manager is scheduled to follow up with the client. Trace dates are normally tied to dates when the client will be planning a meeting or making a decision about where to hold a meeting.

Two other records are of great importance to the sales and marketing staff. The *function book* is a record of reservations for the use of all public space—that is, ballrooms and meeting rooms. All vital data are recorded in the function book, and further detail is supplied by the client master file or the files maintained by the catering department. The function book should contain the following information for every group booked by the hotel:

☐ organization or group

☐ authorized client contact and the individual's job title

☐ type of function planned

☐ time required for the function

☐ total time the ballroom or meeting room is reserved, to include time for setup and breakdown of the room

☐ number of people who will attend the function

☐ type of meeting room setup

☐ who booked the function

☐ status of the contract as either tentative or definite

☐ any other comments that are appropriate

The control placed on the function book is critical. Most hotels will bolt the function book to a desk so that it cannot be removed. Second, one person is given the responsibility for entering all information into the function book. This eliminates the opportunity for less-than-ethical sales managers to erase a group function that has already been booked and to enter a group function that they have just booked.

The second set of records maintained in the sales office that are of daily interest to the sales and marketing staff is the *forecast book*. Every hotel maintains a mixture of guest rooms occupied by transient guests and those occupied by individuals who are part of a group. The forecast book shows daily limits, or ceilings, that have been set for the number of group guest rooms to be sold. As groups are booked into the hotel for future dates, the rooms they will occupy are subtracted from the allotment of group rooms for a particular day.

Hence, when a sales manager is discussing a possible meeting with a client, two sources of information must be checked and verified before a group can be booked into the hotel. The function book must be checked to ensure that public meeting space is available in which the group can meet, and second, the forecast book must be checked to determine the availability of guest rooms for those who will be staying with the group.

Automated Systems

Computer applications have had an impact on just about every phase of business, and the hotel sales and marketing office is no different. Automated systems allow the director of marketing to perform the following functions:

☐ *Automate all prospecting, selling, and booking activities, thereby reducing paperwork.* For example, automated systems assist the sales manager in checking for the best dates that satisfy the meeting planner's criteria, recommend the best rates based on the goals established by management, generate personalized letters and proposals, electronically file call reports, and manage the control of public space previously done manually in the function book.

☐ *Develop a rational approach to making decisions about which groups will be the most profitable to the hotel and which groups should be booked into the hotel.*

For example, systems provide information about how sales for all meetings and meal functions will affect sales and profits, why business is lost, and how to recapture lost business.

☐ *Monitor the performance of each individual member of the sales and marketing team, as well as the performance of the total department.* For example, automated systems give the director of marketing information about how productive sales managers are, compared with last year's performance or future goals; the average rate, room nights, and revenue each individual of the sales team is getting from each market segment; whether important actions are being traced and followed up; and how much business has been booked, compared with the goals for the period.

☐ *Assist with forecasting group business, usually done on a monthly basis.*

Automated systems, also known as *decision support systems,* allow the sales manager to have a wealth of information available instantly, for example, the following:

☐ The booking and account information for the client can be entered once and will be available later for many applications. Examples of these applications include management reports, contract generation, proposals and the detailed banquet event orders that are sent to the food and beverage department.

☐ A data base can be accessed to determine the prospects who should be contacted. Clients meeting the criteria established by the sales manager will then be generated by the system.

☐ All group bookings, both tentative and definite, can be monitored effectively. Hotels sell dates, rates, and space, all of which the automated system can help manage effectively.

☐ The group room block, or the total number of available rooms allocated for group business, can be monitored effectively. The function book of available meeting room space can be checked in the same manner. See Figure 12.18 for an example of how an automated system checks for available dates.

☐ Computer analysis can be applied to the critical decision, "Should we book this business?" "What rate should we offer in our proposal?" Figure 12.19 illustrates an example of this use.

☐ Routine trace files can be called up instantly by the sales manager.

Automated systems are clearly the direction of the future for the hotel sales and marketing office. These systems offer many advantages in comparison with manual systems. Examples of these differences are shown in Figure 12.20.

Delphi Identifies Best Available Dates

Eligible Dates: 5/11/90 – 5/26/90				Arvi- S M Dprt- T W	
Space Available All Days					
Rooms Needed	50	50	50	SSG/Contrib	
5/11-5/13 Grp Rooms	S	M	T	C	$72
Avail	400	350	320		
5/19-5/21 Grp Rooms	M	T	W	B	$94
Avail	330	285	275		

FIGURE 12.18
An Example of How An Automated System Checks for the Best Available Dates
Source: Newmarket Software Systems, Inc., 44 Newmarket Road, Durham, N.H. 03824.

Delphi Calculation of Contribution Profile

	Minimum Acceptable Profit —SSG—	Profit from — This Group —
Rooms	$9000	$8000
Catered F&B Events	$1000	$1800
"On Own" Dining	$1800	$1000
Other Income	$ 0	$ 200
Total Contribution	$11,800	$11,000
Above (Below) Minimum	($800)	
Contribution per Room-Night	$78.66	$73.33
Above (Below) Minimum	($5.33)	

FIGURE 12.19
An Example of How An Automated System Checks for the Best Contribution Profile From Potential Group Business
Source: Newmarket Software Systems, Inc., 44 Newmarket Road, Durham, N.H. 03824.

Manual	Automated
1. Account and booking information is entered on a scratch sheet.	All information is entered directly into the computer. If the account is an established one, entering the first few letters brings the name, address, contact person, and all other relevant information onto the screen. If the new booking is similar to a previous booking, the old entry can be duplicated and modified if necessary.
2. The same information is entered into the group room control log—the log is summarized manually.	The log is updated automatically; summary and forecast are calculated automatically.
3. The secretary types up group room block and function information.	The recap is automatically printed and includes all details on the group room block and the function events.
4. The same account and booking information is retyped in a confirmation letter.	Confirmation is produced automatically.
5. The same information is retyped in a contract.	Contract is produced automatically.
6. The banquet event order is typed and retyped with corrections using the same information as well as detailed menus, resource items, and comments.	Banquet event order is automatically generated by selecting menus and resources from the screen. Costs, consumption, and use at the time of the event are displayed.
7. Related follow-up correspondence is typed, referring to same account and booking information.	Follow-up correspondence is traced and generated automatically.
8. In order to execute market research and/or telemarketing activity, a data base is built by reentering the same booking and account information.	Integrated account booking information is available for database search for marketing, telemarketing, service history, and lost business tracking.
9. Reports are created by a review of the forecast books, diaries, and booking recaps. Summary of data is entered manually.	Diary is automatically updated each time a booking is entered; summary and forecast are automatically calculated.
10. Salesperson booking pace and productivity reports are created through manual tabulation.	Reports are generated automatically using data in the system.
11. Tracing is done by manual entry on 3 × 5 cards. Traced files are delivered by secretaries to sales manager, where they pile up on desks.	All activities are traced to the salesperson in accordance with a predeveloped plan. Daily trace reports remind the sales staff of such critical account and booking details as contracts due, credit checks to be done, block pickups, menus, and follow-up sales calls. Tentative and definite bookings are displayed and traced for follow-up. Numerous user-defined account traces and booking traces are generated for action steps.

FIGURE 12.20

An Example of a Manual Versus an Automated System

Source: *HSMAI Marketing Review*, Vol. 5, No. 2, p. 27.

SUMMARY

This chapter provided a detailed introduction to the field of hotel sales and marketing. Criteria to judge the effectively managed sales and marketing office are customer orientation, strategic orientation, adequate marketing information systems, integrated systems between marketing and operations, and operating efficiency.

The departmental structure is reviewed in detail and areas of job responsibility are discussed for the key positions of general manager, director of marketing, director of sales, sales manager, catering sales manager, and others. The vital link between the sales and marketing department and the other departments is discussed in detail.

Coordination with publics external to the hotel is vital to the success of the hotel as well. An example of a type of this external public is the convention and visitors' bureau. The purposes of a convention and visitors' bureau is to sell the entire destination rather than an individual hotel site, and to provide service.

A detailed model and outline is presented for developing a hotel marketing plan. Major sections of this model are situation analysis, goals, strategies, and positioning, annual and monthly objectives, market segmentation and strategy, action plans and implementation, budget, and evaluation and research.

The chapter provides a budget and forecasting model developed by Yesawich. The model is based on six steps: (1) determining the amount of business that exists within the market in which the hotel competes, (2) determining the market share of the total demand and the fair share of business mix within the competitive group held by your property, (3) examining each of the major market segments and assessing the future direction for each segment, (4) developing an inventory of competitive practices of the competing hotels and assessing the extent to which your own marketing efforts can preempt the competition, (5) determining the proportion of your marketing effort and marketing resources to be assigned to each market segment, and (6) preparing the forecast for property occupancy, business mix, and revenues.

The final section of the chapter focuses on the management of the sales and marketing department from two perspectives. First, a manual system is presented, as well as the major files and records needed. Second, an automated approach is discussed and examples of the systems applications are presented.

KEY WORDS AND CONCEPTS

☐ High- and low-demand periods

☐ Integrated systems between marketing and operations

☐ Key individuals: general manager, director of marketing, director of sales, sales manager, and catering sales manager

☐ Convention and visitors' bureau (CVB)

☐ Key elements of the sales and marketing plan: situation analysis, market analysis, competition analysis, goals, strategies, and positioning, objectives and forecasts, market segmentation and strategy, action plans, budget, evaluation and research

☐ Forecasting

☐ Market share

☐ Market segment

☐ Market demand by segment

☐ Manual versus automated systems

☐ Call report

☐ Group room block

☐ Group cover sheet

☐ Filing systems

Questions for Review and Discussion

1. How has the role played by the sales and marketing department changed in recent years?
2. What criteria were recommended for judging the effectiveness of the sales and marketing office? What additional criteria would you suggest?
3. Illustrate the organizational structure of the sales and marketing function. What are the job titles and major responsibilities of the key individuals?
4. How must the sales and marketing department interface with the operating departments if the hotel is to be successful?
5. What is a convention and visitors' bureau? What role does a CVB play?
6. Describe the process followed when a hotel is preparing a marketing plan. What are the major components of the marketing plan?
7. By what process or model is a hotel forecast or budget developed?
8. Cite and describe the major types of files maintained in a manually operated sales and marketing office.
9. What are the three major purposes of an automated sales and marketing system?

CHAPTER 13

Group Sales

This chapter is centered around the important subject of selling to the group market. Hotels and restaurants that are oriented toward the group market must engage in personal selling and solicitation if they are to be successful. The chapter is divided into two major sections. The first will concentrate on the different market segments that make up the group market, and the second will deal with personal selling.

INTRODUCTION

In the competitive world of hospitality sales and marketing, the ability to effectively identify potential business, qualify the prospects, engage in personal selling activities, and eventually book the business are critical to the success of the property. The range of activities that fall under the umbrella of personal selling is quite broad. Sales managers communicate with clients and prospects by means of the telephone, personal sales calls resulting from appointments, cold sales calls without appointments, calls made as a part of a sales blitz, and contacts with clients at professional meetings and conventions.

The role of sales has increased as the competitiveness of the group meetings business has intensified. Today, through the efforts of the major hotel corporations and professional associations such as the Hotel Sales and Marketing Association International (HSMAI), sales and marketing professionals employed within the hotel industry are better trained than ever before. They have to be, to be successful.

What makes a sales manager successful? A profile of a successful sales manager would reveal several factors that all contribute to the individual's success. Courtesy pays a big part in making the individual successful. It is imperative that the sales manager always strive to make certain that the client is satisfied. This means having to go the extra mile, or perhaps occasionally doing something that is not routine. It might even mean bending the rules or standard operating procedures (SOP's) in order to ensure client satisfaction. Courtesy also means being able to smile and handle a difficult situation even when those around you are angry or in a panic.

A second aspect in the profile of a successful sales manager is complete knowledge of the product-service mix that is being sold. The sales manager should know every square inch of the hotel property and should be able to answer questions that the prospect might raise. This knowledge would include items such as seating capacities of all meeting rooms in all seating configurations, policies with regard to groups meeting in the hotel, weight capacity of freight elevators and ceiling heights in all meeting rooms, audiovisual capabilities of the hotel, and food and beverage skills and talents of the hotel's staff, as well as many other aspects of the hotel's product-service mix.

A third part of the profile is professional appearance and behavior. This does not mean that the individual needs to be a "pretty face." Rather, the sales manager should present a professional appearance. This requires professional clothing, such as business suits, and personal grooming. First impressions are critical in selling, and professional appearance can be a real asset in establishing rapport with a prospective client.

A strong desire and a willingness to work is a fourth characteristic in the profile of a successful sales manager. Only a small percentage of sales calls and contacts will result in sales or signed contracts. A successful sales person must have the perseverance to keep going and to keep asking for the business, even when many others have said no. Keep in mind that if one call out of ten results in a signed contract, a sales manager has been told no nine times before making a sale. For this reason, when a prospect says no, the sales manager should say "thank you" knowing that the next prospect might say yes. A conversation with one of the leading salespeople for a major manufacturing company revealed an interesting philosophy when he stated, "I'm not in sales, I'm in rejections. I get rejected a lot more than I make sales."

Another quality that is a real asset in sales is organizational ability. Keeping in constant communication with dozens of clients and keeping all of the many separate details straight calls for superior organization. The ability to recall names and faces is also important; when the sales manager meets clients it is imperative to remember their names, who they work for, and other pertinent details. Following up with trace dates and the details of each client's contract calls for superior organizational skills.

A final quality that is an asset to the successful sales manager is a strong personality. This does not mean that to be successful in sales, one must be extroverted and the life of the party. Rather, it means that the individual needs to have some warmth, some empathy, and the ability to make others believe in and trust you. If prospects do not feel comfortable with the sales manager as a person, it is very unlikely that they will make a purchase.

Several studies have been conducted with the purpose of identifying the characteristics or traits of successful sales managers. The results of one such study are shown in Figure 13.1.[1]

Impression Criteria
    Appearance—neat and clean cut
    Dress—conservative and in good taste
    Demeanor—confident and with a sense of humor
    Attitude—friendly and sincere, possessing a "consumer is number one" orientation
    Voice and speech—talks to express and not to impress; has well developed listening skills

"Can do" Criteria
    Grades—upper 25 percent of graduating class
    Curriculum—tendency to take advanced and more difficult courses
    Extracurricular activities—has contributed to organizations, has held offices within the organizations, has experience working with volunteers
    Related work experience—part-time and summer jobs
    Career goals—interest in marketing and well-developed reasons for this interest

"Will do" Criteria
    Character—integrity, self-reliance, loyalty, idealism, principles
    Motivation—drive, perseverance, sense of responsibility
    Ability to get along with others—likes people, cooperative, has constructive attitude and maturity

FIGURE 13.1
Characteristics of Successful Sales Personnel

Hotel sales and marketing provides a dynamic environment in which to work. It is demanding and full of challenges, but the rewards are commensurate with the efforts required. The remainder of the chapter will explore aspects of hotel sales and personal selling.

SELLING TO GROUP MARKETS

Selling to Meeting Planners

Before a single telephone call or personal sales call is made, the sales manager must begin to develop a clear understanding of the nature of the buyer—the meeting planner. *Meeting planner* is a term used to describe someone who plans meetings that will be attended by all sorts of individuals. Meeting planners represent a vast array of different groups, from large national associations to small local civic groups. With this diversity comes a huge gap in talents and skills. Many meeting planners, especially those representing large associations and companies, are very knowledgeable professionals. They usually know as much or more about the operation of a hotel as the entry-level sales manager. On the other extreme are those individuals who only occasionally plan meetings and whom the sales manager must educate as well as sell. Such is the challenge faced by the sales and marketing team—selling to many different individuals, each wearing the title of meeting planner.

If sales managers are to effectively sell to the meeting planner, several things are necessary. First, sales managers must thoroughly understand the product-service mix that they are representing. They must know everything, or be able to find the answers quickly to questions raised by the meeting planner. Second, they must know how to sell. Selling is a skill that is learned and is then refined. Few individuals are born to be in sales; for nearly everyone, selling is a learned skill. Selling in the hospitality industry is just like selling in other industries, especially service industries: One must learn to sell effectively.

The nature of personal selling will be dealt with in greater depth in a later section of the chapter, but the paragraphs that follow will discuss selling to meeting planners. In order to sell effectively, the sales manager must possess a thorough understanding of the needs of the prospective client. The sales manager should be a professional in identifying client needs and then showing how the hotel's product-service mix will help to meet those needs. It is much easier to sell when you are demonstrating how your product-service mix will solve the client's problems than when you are merely trying to push your product-service mix.

Knowledge of the meeting planner's needs begins with background information about the group for which the meeting planner is working, as well as the more specific needs directly related to the meeting. For example, the needs of most meeting planners will fall into the following categories:

costs, location, image and status, professional service, adaptability and flexibility, and professional operations and management.

Costs. A meeting planner's desire to keep costs reasonable is a major need or objective. All meeting planners must operate within a restricted budget, yet they want to obtain the best "deal" for their dollars spent. In short, they want to book meetings with the hotel that will be able to provide the best price-value relationship. This does not necessarily mean the cheapest price, simply the best value for the dollars which are spent.

Location. Nearly all meeting planners begin with at least a general idea of the type of location that they are looking for. This will depend on the type of meeting being planned. Not every hotel need be located next to an airport, a lake, or a golf course, or boast of a great location. It is simply a matter of showing meeting planners how the location of a specific hotel will meet their immediate needs. *Location* includes both geographic location and the general environment surrounding the property. For example, a resort property may not be as easy to reach as a downtown hotel, yet it may have the type of environment that offers the opportunity for both meetings and recreation.

Image and Status. Meeting planners typically want to hold meetings at hotels that reflect the image and status of the client organization. This does not mean that the image must be upscale and exclusive, though this is certainly desirable. A image of budget and "no frills" is important to some groups. If these groups can be booked on a consistent and continuing basis, the profits will follow. The role of the sales manager is to link the image and status needs of the meeting planner to the perceived image, status, and positioning of the hotel, thereby creating a reason to buy.

Professional Service. Likely to be at the top of a list of complaints of nearly all meeting planners is the absence of professional service. The quality of service has been widely criticized within the United States. It is imperative that the sales manager be able to show the skeptical meeting planner that the hotel will be able to provide the level of service desired and expected by the client.

Adaptability and Flexibility. Every hotel has standard operating procedures (SOP's), yet at the same time to effectively sell to meeting planners, the sales manager must be able to demonstrate that the hotel will be flexible enough to meet the special requirements of the group. No meeting planner likes to be told, "We can't do that because it is not within the policies of the hotel." Meeting planners are not asking the hotel to do anything illegal or immoral; they simply want to work with sales managers and hotels that will adapt and work hard to meet their needs and special requests. The truly professional hotels that are indeed guest- and service-oriented will go out of their way to adapt to meet the needs of the meeting planner.

Professional Operations and Management.   A hotel is only as good as the staff and management that run the operating departments of the hotel. If the operations side of the business is poor, no amount of effort by the sales and marketing team will result in repeat bookings. Simply stated, the operations managers and the entire staff must function as a team, working *with* the sales and marketing staff to deliver to the meeting planner's groups the explicit level of products and service that were promised. Satisfying meeting planners means not only meeting their expectations, but surpassing the expectations as well.

If a sales manager is to be successful, he or she must help the meeting planner solve the problems faced in planning the meeting. This includes finding answers to all of the critical decisions that confront the meeting planner. The role of the salesperson begins with preplanning, which can be very important if the meeting planner is not experienced. The sales manager can assist the meeting planner with the following:

- ☐ Defining the purpose of the meeting as well as identifying who will attend and the total number of attendees

- ☐ Identifying the expectations of those who will attend the meeting

- ☐ Developing a central theme for the meeting

- ☐ Developing a schedule for the events that are planned

- ☐ Developing a budget for all meeting expenses such as rooms, food and beverage, and other expenses

- ☐ Developing criteria by which to select a geographic location and hotel site

- ☐ Deciding on first, second, and third most preferred meeting dates

In most cases, the meeting planner will have already done much of this preplanning before visiting with the hotel sales manager, but even so, the discussion related to some of these issues will serve to qualify the prospective client.

Once the preplanning is completed, the role of the sales manager becomes more critical. The meeting planner needs to make decisions about the type of guest room accommodations needed. This will include several particulars:

- ☐ Determining the total number of rooms that should be blocked, as well as the arrival and departure patterns of the attendees

☐ Assessing the need for hospitality suites and suites for VIP's and speakers

☐ Making decisions about the billing procedures, such as each guest being responsible for individual charges, all of the charges being billed to a master account, or some combination of the two methods

☐ Finalizing a meeting schedule to include the necessary meeting room configurations, meeting lengths, food and beverage functions, coffee breaks, and the proper audiovisual requirements

Once these issues have been discussed and determined, further discussion with the meeting planner is necessary to work out the details of the meeting room setups and meeting logistics. Some examples of the details that should be discussed follow:

☐ *Meeting room rental fees and setup charges.* If the group is meeting during a high demand period and is not generating sufficient room revenue and/or food and beverage revenue, a meeting room rental may be charged. This rental fee is often negotiable. Additional setup fees may be charged if special setup is required, for example, the 8 × 10 foot booths set up for exhibits. These often require additional utility connections for the exhibitor's displays.

☐ *Meeting room setups and configuration.* This includes theater style, in which chairs are placed in rows: this is appropriate for large groups. Schoolroom set up is used for groups in which a good deal of note taking is expected; this set up provides rows of tables and chairs all facing in one direction. For smaller groups the tables and chairs can be arranged in a variety of configurations such as T-shape, U-shape, hollow-square, and oval.

Once the meeting has been booked into the hotel, the catering sales staff begins to work more closely with the client in planning the food and beverage functions, such as breakfasts, lunches, dinners, receptions, coffee breaks, and entertainment for any of these functions. Creativity is of the utmost importance in this area. Every hotel needs to try to outdo the competition.

In the weeks and final days before the meeting is held, the hotel staff needs to work closely with the client to work out the final details concerning the meeting. The final details will include several areas:

☐ Registering attendees and providing them with the necessary information packets

☐ Distributing welcome gifts and/or baskets for dignitaries and VIP's

☐ Determining guarantees for food and beverage functions. Most hotels require final guarantee counts for food and beverage functions 48 to 72 hours before the actual event. A guarantee count is the number of guests for which the hotel will prepare and for which the client will be billed. Most hotels will prepare for 5 percent over the guarantee count. The client will be billed for the actual number of attendees or the guarantee, whichever is greater.

If the sales manager is to build a long-term relationship with the client, it is necessary to build a solid working relationship. This relationship is built on trust and the ability of the hotel's staff to deliver consistent products and services that meet or exceed the expectations of the meeting planners. While this may seem a very simple concept that every hotel should be able to deliver, it is much more difficult in the real world. However, the truly great hotels are able to do it each and every day. In the opinion of many meeting planners, one of the best hotels in the country is the Opryland Hotel in Nashville, Tennessee. While many hotels publish a meeting planner's guide that provides information about the hotel and the surrounding area, the Opryland Hotel has gone the extra step. The meeting planner's guide used by Opryland is in excess of 100 pages and provides information about location; transportation; reservation policies; credit and check-cashing policies; diagrams of all public meeting rooms; convention service department; conference equipment; exhibits and displays; security; preshipping procedures; placement of signs; catering department; audiovisual department; restaurants and lounges; room service; music and entertainment; retail shops and boutiques; recreation; special events; facts about Opryland USA Theme Park, the Grand Ole Opry, and the Nashville Network; publicity and promotion; weather facts and information; all of the services offered by the hotel; and information about the Convention and Visitors' Bureau of Nashville. Each of these sections is tabbed so that the information is very easy for the meeting planner to locate and review.

Selling Effectively to Different Group Markets

Selling to any group begins with understanding the needs of the prospective client and then showing the client how your hotel's product-service mix can satisfy those needs. In order to do this well, the sales manager must know a great deal of background information about the client's group, the group's needs, past meeting behavior and patterns, and objectives and plans for future meetings. The second step is to link the features offered by the hotel's product-service mix with benefits that the client will find attractive and that will satisfy the stated client needs and objectives.

Each group is different and it may be incorrect to stereotype specific types of groups. However, some broad generalizations about each group market segment can be made. The section that follows will provide a brief overview of some of the larger group market segments. For a more complete discussion of the group market segments, it is suggested that you read *The Group Market: What It Is and How To Sell It*, by Margaret Shaw. This book, published by the Hotel Sales and Marketing Association International, provides a thorough discussion of the major group market segments, including national associations, state and regional associations, corporations, medical meetings, incentive travel, insurance, education, government, sports, unions, and group pleasure market segments.

The next several paragraphs will focus on the two largest market segments, associations and corporations, as well as a third market segment, SMERF's. SMERF is an acronym that stands for a combination of several market segments—social, military, educational, religious, and fraternal. SMERF meetings are frequently held in conjunction with nonprofit groups that are often working with a very limited budget. They usually do not have a professional meeting planner. While some of the SMERF meetings are small, the total number of meetings that the SMERF market segment generates makes the overall contribution significant.

Association Market Segment

The association market is very broad, ranging from large national and international conventions attended by thousands of individuals to very small but expensive board of directors' meetings. When we think of the association market, we tend to think of the large conventions, but this is only a small segment of the total associations meeting market. According to research conducted by the American Society of Association Executives (ASAE) and the Hotel Sales and Marketing Association International (HSMAI), 56 percent of the association meetings are attended by fewer than 300 individuals, making even small and medium-sized hotels suitable for some association business. On the other hand, only about 10 percent of association meetings have more than 1000 attendees.[2]

Associations hold several different types of meetings each year, including the following:

☐ *Large annual convention for the entire membership.* This meeting is usually the largest that the association will hold. It will often include exhibits, especially within the trade association market.

☐ *Board of directors' meetings.* These are typically held three or four times a year and are often quite elaborate.

☐ *Seminars and workshops.* Associations provide continuing education for the members, and these meetings are held throughout the year.

☐ *Committee meetings.* Associations operate via a committee approach and each of the committees may need to meet several times a year.

The decision-making process and lead time for the association market can be quite frustrating for the hotel sales manager. This market segment is often assigned to the most experienced sales manager or the director of sales because that individual's additional experience will prove beneficial in working with this market segment. The meeting planners working with associations, especially the large associations, are normally quite experienced and professional, so the hotel's representative must be equally knowledgeable and experienced. The decision making is scattered among several people within the association. For example, the meeting planner may make the decision concerning where to hold small meetings and workshops, but decisions about the larger meetings such as the annual convention are normally made by the executive committee and/or the board of directors. For this reason, the sales manager must be prepared for a lengthy decision-making process. The initial contact may be with the association meeting planner, but it may take several weeks or months before the board of directors makes a final decision concerning the location for a large meeting. Decision factors are shown in Figure 13.2.[3] The lead time for planning meetings can also be quite long. For the largest of the national associations, it is common for the site of the annual

Factors Considered Very Important	Major Conventions	Other Meetings
Number, size, and caliber of meeting rooms	87%	39%
Quality of foodservice	80%	63%
Number, size, and caliber of sleeping rooms	70%	35%
Efficiency of check-in/check-out procedures	63%	44%
Assignment of one staff person to handle all aspects of meeting	59%	39%
Previous experience in dealing with facility and its staff	49%	36%
Availability of exhibit space	46%	9%
Provision of special meeting services, such as pre-registration, special equipment, etc.	28%	11%
Convenience to other modes of transportation	26%	21%
Number, size, and caliber of suites	26%	81%
On-site recreation facilities	23%	10%
Proximity to shopping, off-site entertainment, restaurants	22%	10%
Proximity to airport	15%	22%
Newness of facility	5%	4%

FIGURE 13.2
Decision Factors Cited by Association Meeting Planners

convention to be selected five to ten years in advance. Even smaller associations typically plan their annual conventions one to three years in advance. This lead time creates some real challenges for the sales and marketing staff. Even if a large annual meeting is booked now, the revenue will not be realized for quite some time in the future.

Associations often use the annual convention as a revenue-producing event, the revenue then being used to fund some of the association's annual operating expenses. For this reason, associations may be sensitive about such negotiable items as meeting room rental, complimentary room policies, guest room and suite rates. Keep in mind that association attendees will be paying their own expenses to attend meetings and may be very sensitive about prices for guest rooms, suites, and food and beverages.

Corporate Market Segment

This market segment is very broad and is widely solicited by hotels. The corporate market is quite different from the association market segment. The differences include needs and objectives, the type and number of individuals in attendance, and the lead time required.

Corporations hold many more meetings than associations. The meetings tend to be smaller, have a much shorter lead time, are less price sensitive, are subject to quicker site decisions, and involve fewer individuals in the decision-making process.

Corporate meetings are attractive to hotels for several reasons: They are held throughout the year rather than being concentrated in certain periods or months, and they do not require extensive meeting rooms. The typical corporate meeting involves fewer than 50 attendees, and the types of corporate meetings vary widely, including the following:

□ *Training meetings.* With the advent of new technology, corporations are always holding meetings to train new staff and provide update training for current staff. This type of meeting is perhaps the most common. Many hotels located near the offices of major corporations will solicit this type of meeting business on a continual basis.

□ *Sales meetings.* Most corporations maintain a sales staff that meets on a frequent basis. These meetings serve both to provide information to the sales staff and to motivate them. This is an excellent type of meeting to solicit because it often is less price sensitive.

□ *New product introduction meetings.* When a corporation introduces a new product, it is often done with great fanfare. The meeting is likely to be attended by dealers, corporate sales staff, and the media. This type of meeting can be very extensive and very price insensitive.

□ *Management meetings.* Management staff often needs to "get away" from the place of business to meet and discuss issues in a quiet environment, where they will not be interrupted by telephones and distractions of the office.

☐ *Technical meetings.* Technical specialists need to meet to discuss items of mutual concern. This type of meeting is less elaborate than the other types of corporate meetings.

☐ *Annual stockholders' meeting.* All publicly held corporations hold an annual stockholders' meeting that may be attended by a large number of individuals. Some food and beverage events associated with this type of meeting can be very extensive.

☐ *Board of directors' meetings.* These are perhaps the most elaborate and expensive, often featuring extensive food and beverage presentations. They also require more expensive and specialized meeting rooms within the hotel.

Meeting planning within corporations is typically spread among several departments. The very largest of corporations have established a meeting planning department, but this responsibility is often handled by someone within another functional area such as marketing or personnel. The decision making is usually rapid and does not involve too many individuals, far fewer than the association market. If the meeting planner is not the final decision maker, he or she is usually highly influential. Those factors of importance to the corporate meeting planner are shown in Figure 13.3.[4]

The association and corporate market segments represent the two largest market segments for group business. There are other market segments from which group business could and should be solicited. To discover more about these segments, further study is recommended. One excellent source is *The Group Market: What It Is and How to Sell to It* by Margaret Shaw.

PERSONAL SELLING

What is personal selling? Selling is an interpersonal process whereby the seller ascertains, activates, and satisfies the needs and wants of the buyer so that both the seller and the buyer benefit. Selling need not be one-sided; it can satisfy both parties. Prospective clients can derive benefits in that the burden of planning, organizing, and directing the various aspects of a group meeting function is taken away from the client. For most clients, this is a tremendous relief, as they no longer are directly responsible for the event. Of course, the hotel also benefits, through increased sales and profits.

Why should a hotel operation engage in personal selling? First, it allows the operation to be presented in an interpersonal manner to a prospective client. The sales presentation need not be supported by expensive visual aids. Sales calls and presentations can be as simple as having a sales manager engage in telephone and personal solicitation. These sales calls give the hotel

Site Selection Factor	Average Rating	Rank
Recommendations by other meeting planners	4.44	1
Hotel sales representatives	4.44	1
Recommendations by others in organization	4.38	3
National and regional sales representatives	4.25	4
Hotel-supplier correspondence files	4.11	5
Postconvention reports	3.95	6
Advertising by hotels in trade journals	3.61	7
Recommendations by hotel associates	3.54	8
Articles in business publications	3.47	9
Advertising by convention bureaus	3.29	10
Convention bureau sales representatives	3.08	11
Hotel associations	3.00	12
Airline publications	2.58	13
Airline sales representatives	2.56	14

Scale: 1 (unimportant) to 7 (important)
Average rating indicates average score

FIGURE 13.3
Decision Factors Cited by Corporate Meeting Planners
Reprinted from the 1985 Meetings Market Report, MEETINGS AND CONVENTIONS, Copyright © Murdoch Magazines, A Division of News America Publishing, Inc. All Rights Reserved.

operation exposure and provide the prospective clients with another choice when arranging group meetings and banquet functions. Second, sales calls allow for two-way communication between the hotel sales manager and prospective clients. Prospects are able to ask questions, and the representative has the opportunity to present the hotel operation more adequately than is possible through advertising. The representative can personally demonstrate how the operation will be able to satisfy the specific needs of the prospect.

Sales calls should be made on prospective clients as well as previous clients. Previous clients should receive follow-up calls to cultivate a continuing business relationship. If the previous experiences left the client feeling unhappy, this is all the more reason to follow-up with a sales call. Perhaps the situation can be corrected and negative word-of-mouth publicity prevented. Often the mere attention to the client's needs and a sincere effort to improve will be enough to convince the client the hotel should be given some additional business. There is nothing better than a satisfied client and nothing worse than an unhappy one.

Three basic types of sales calls are follow-up calls, initiating calls, and blitz calls. Follow-up calls are those arranged with representatives of groups and organizations that have previously been clients of the hotel. Their main purpose is to remind the client of the hotel's willingness to be of service and to solicit repeat business. Initiating calls are those made on people who have not been clients in the past but represent solid prospects. The purpose of these calls is to create awareness of the products and services and to encourage a site visit so that the prospective client may see firsthand what the facility has to offer. Few bookings are made at the time of initiating calls, but it is the first step in cultivating a better relationship. A sales blitz saturates an area by making many times the normal number of sales calls and distributing literature describing the product-service mix. A successful blitz reaches as many potential clients as possible. Sales blitzes often use a varied approach involving not only personal sales calls but also telephone selling as well as other forms of advertising using the mass media.

The Selling Process

Successful salespeople generally focus on four components of successful selling: (1) prospecting and qualifying, (2) planning and delivering sales presentations, (3) overcoming objections, and (4) closing the sale.

Prospecting and Qualifying. Identifying prospective clients is a critical activity if the sales manager's efforts are to be successful. Generally, 20 to 30 percent of all telephone sales calls are scheduled with prospective clients—those who have not previously booked a banquet or a meeting function with the hotel operation. No hotel can rely totally on repeat business; rather, the organization must commit itself to seeking and cultivating new business, allowing the organization to expand its market.

In the process of identifying and qualifying prospects, hotel sales managers should determine whether prospective clients represent good prospects before they invest a large amount of time. The following questions are helpful in determining whether a prospect is a good one:

☐ *Does the prospect have needs and wants that can be satisfied by the products and services of the hotel?* If the needs and wants of the prospect differ substantially from the product-service mix of the hotel and personal selling is undertaken anyway, sales managers are likely to be wasting both their own time and that of the meeting planner. In addition, it can create a poor image for the hotel, because the sales manager has not done enough background checking and homework to determine if the hotel "fits" the prospect's needs.

☐ *Does the prospect have the ability to pay?* It is important to determine whether the prospect has income or credit reserves to pay for a meeting or banquet function. This is a particularly important question to consider when dealing with small associations, corporations, and SMERF groups.

☐ *Does the prospect have the authority to sign a contract and commit the organization for the meeting function?* While not a total waste of time, it is terribly frustrating for a sales manager to cultivate prospective sales only to find that the individuals with whom they have been dealing do not have the authority to sign a contract and commit the organization for a function. It is important to know what the decision-making process is, who it involves, and when a decision will be made. If this information is not available from the hotel's records, the best way to find out is to ask the meeting planner.

☐ *Is the prospect readily accessible?* It is important that the sales manager be able to contact the meeting planner by telephone and schedule an appointment with the prospect. Part of the prospecting is determining the best time and method to contact the prospect. It may be difficult to schedule a sales presentation with such individuals as presidents of companies, and hence they may prove to be poor prospects.

Locating suitable prospects is a task confronting all sales representatives. What methods can be used to obtain leads that will result in good prospects? The following list represents a few potential sources:

☐ *Inquiries.* Often individuals visit or call the hotel operation and request information concerning banquets and/or meeting facilities. These individuals and the groups they represent are ready-made prospects.

☐ *Names given by existing clients.* This approach is sometimes called the "endless chain" or "networking." Simply ask each of the existing clients to supply the names of one or more individuals, groups, or companies that might be prospective clients. The resulting list is then qualified to determine the most attractive prospects, and personal selling begins. It is important to follow-up with a thank-you letter to the individual who supplied the name of the prospect, especially when the lead results in booked business. The mutual contact also serves as a means of introduction with the new prospect.

☐ *Centers of influence.* Every community has its own leaders and influential people. These individuals make excellent prospects because they tend to be active in the community; they are "joiners." Additionally, it is an excellent idea for the sales manager and other members of the management staff to belong to community and civic organizations. In this way, they can establish personal relationships with these community leaders.

☐ *Developed lists.* Often lists of prospects are simply developed from such sources as the telephone directory, chamber of commerce, and local clubs and organizations. These lists should then be qualified to identify the most likely prospects.

☐ *Direct mail prospecting.* Lists can also be used to initiate direct mail prospecting. Promotional material is mailed to a list of prospects, and the sales manager can either follow-up with a telephone call seeking an appointment or wait for an inquiry.

☐ *Corporate sales offices.* All of the major hotel chains maintain national and regional sales offices. One of the responsibilities of these offices is to direct prospective leads to the chain's hotels that are in the best position to service the prospective clients. In addition, hotels within a chain may refer potential business to other hotels within the chain. For example, if a sales manager has made a contact with a meeting planner and learns that the group is planning to meet in another city, the sales manager should contact the sales and marketing department of the chain's hotel in that city so that the potential business will not be lost to the competition.

☐ *Cold calls.* Finally, personal sales calls can be made without prior arrangements or appointments. These are called "cold calls." The sales manager simply contacts the prospect by telephone or may make a personal call to the prospect's office and ask to see the prospect. Rarely does this type of call result in a signed contract, but it does open some doors for future contact with the prospect. When made as personal sales calls, however, cold calls are quite time-consuming and, as a result, very expensive.

Planning and Delivering Sales Presentations.   Soon after qualifying a prospect as a good candidate for the product-service mix of the hotel, a sales manager should make contact with the prospect. This initial contact is usually done by telephone. Subsequent contact may also be by telephone, the sales manager may make a personal visit to the prospect's place of business, or the prospect may visit the hotel for a site inspection of the facilities. Sales managers should be assertive and honest. They should tell the prospect who is calling, the hotel they represent, and the reason for the call. It may also help to "break the ice" to mention a common associate or a common interest, but sales managers should be honest and up-front. They should not attempt to schedule the appointment under false pretenses, as this will only hurt in the long run.

The overall goal of any personal selling activity is, of course, to promote purchase on the part of the prospect. Rarely, however, does this occur without a well-planned sales presentation. The AIDA (awareness, interest, desire, and action) approach is one that has long been used in training sales personnel. To sell the prospect successfully, the sales manager must help move the prospect through each of the four steps of the AIDA model.

Before making the sales call, a sales manager should develop an outline of the presentation. What are the prospect's needs and objectives for the meeting or function? How can these needs and objectives be met by the hotel's products and services? It is important to make the products and services offered by the hotel as tangible as possible and to link them directly with the stated needs and objectives of the prospect. What points should be stressed? How should they be presented so that the hotel operation is perceived positively? What should the sales call accomplish?

It is not advisable to prepare a canned sales pitch that is merely replayed for each new prospect. Instead, a sales manager should be natural and straightforward, not waste words, and get right to the point. A sales presentation should begin with telling the prospect who is calling and what hotel is represented, and asking the prospect about his or her needs and objectives. These needs and objectives can then be used as the basis for the remainder of the sales presentation, as discussed in the preceding paragraph. It is important to let the prospect know that the hotel values, wants, and deserves the prospect's business. It may be best to use a checklist of points to be covered, for it is better to refer to a list than appear unorganized during the presentation.

It is also important to be aware of the nature of the prospect. Some individuals have time to sit and talk; others are too busy. A sales manager should be able to vary the presentation to suit the needs of the prospect. Every effort should be made to make the prospect comfortable by establishing rapport. Every effort should also be made to emphasize the strong selling points of the hotel operation's product-service mix, while linking these strengths to the stated needs and objectives of the prospect.

An acquired skill that sales managers can develop is the art of listening. Often sales managers feel that they must do all the talking if a sale is to be made. Nothing could be further from the truth. Selling also requires concentrating on what the prospect is saying and on nonverbal behavior. A good sales manager allows the prospect to ask uninterrupted questions and does not try to anticipate questions and jump in with a canned response before the prospect has finished asking the question. Listening is a learned skill, one that is critical to successful selling. Selling means focusing attention on prospects and learning to hear what they are really saying.

Overcoming Objections.　No matter how good a sales manager may be, sooner or later (and probably sooner) a prospect will object during the sales call. The prospect may object to a wide variety of things:

☐ *Price.* The perceived price value of the products and services being offered may not be high enough. This calls for the sales manager to reassure the prospect and to continue to negotiate.

☐ *Products and services offered.* The prospect may not feel comfortable with the assurances that the sales manager has made about the quality or consistency of the products and services provided by the hotel staff. It may be necessary to show the prospect firsthand how the hotel performs.

☐ *Hotel or hotel company.* The prospect may hold a negative image or impression about the individual hotel property or the entire chain. If this is the case, efforts must be taken to change the perceptions, and ask the prospect for a second chance, especially if the prospect represents a sizable piece of business.

☐ *Pressure to decide.* Sometimes the prospect simply does not like being put under pressure to make a decision immediately. This can occur when another group is thinking of booking the same space on the same days, or when sales managers are pressuring the prospect to decide in order to make their quota.

☐ *Individual sales manager.* Once in a while there can be a personality conflict between the sales manager and the prospect. Sales managers need to be flexible and able to work effectively with a wide variety of individuals.

For the sales call to be successful, of course, these objections must be overcome. A simple yet effective approach directs the sales manager to use these steps:

1. Listen; allow the prospect to explain the objections fully.

2. Reflect or rephrase the prospect's feelings to assure the prospect that you fully understand the objection.

3. Handle the objection. Several methods are used to effectively handle the objections that prospects will raise.
    a. *Agree and counter.* Acknowledge the prospect's objection, but then offer support for why the objection really is not important or is not an objection. It is important to offer support or a reasoned argument for your response. If the prospect has incorrect facts, that is easily remedied. If the prospect has an incorrect perception, this is much more difficult to change. Perception represents an individual's view of reality, and this is not easily changed.
    b. *Turn the objection into a reason for buying.* For example, if the prospect objects to the price it might be useful to talk about the hotel's employee-to-guest ratio and how this allows the hotel to provide a higher level of service than the competition and therefore is justification for the higher price.
    c. *Seek more information.* Often the stated objection is not the full reason why the prospect is not ready to make a commitment.
    d. *Postpone the objection.* If the prospect raises an objection early in the sales presentation and it would be best dealt with later, ask to defer it for a few minutes, indicating that it will be discussed at length. For example, if the prospect objects to the price, it is unwise to discuss price until the hotel's product-service quality is well established in the prospect's mind. It is imperative that objections be dealt with; do not just ignore them, hoping that prospects will forget about them—they will not.

4. Get a commitment from the prospect that the objection has been answered. If this is the case, it is advisable to ask for the business and attempt to close the sale. It is imperative to ask for the business.

Closing the Sale.   Despite otherwise successful sales efforts, many sales managers fail to get a firm commitment from the prospect. They simply fail to close the sale. Closure can be as simple as saying, "Can we confirm your meeting for October 15?" Closure involves summarizing the major selling points and striving for agreement on the part of the prospect. Simply stated, closure involves asking for business. A sales manager should not be shy, but should simply ask for business.

A number of methods can be used to try to close a sale. Among the most commonly used approaches are the following:

☐ *Continued affirmation.* If the sales manager can ask questions to which the prospect will answer yes, this can set up prospects for closing the sale. They have already responded positively to a series of questions, and the sales manager has led them to a point where he or she can then ask for the business.

☐ *Prestige or status close.* This is often used by upscale or exclusive properties. The sales manager discusses the other groups that have met in the hotel and by affiliating the prospect's group with the other more prestigious groups encourages the prospect to decide to hold the meeting or function at the hotel.

☐ *Assumptive close.* This is a bold approach in which the sales manager simply assumes that the sale is closed and asks the prospect questions that relate to details of the contract, or handing the prospect the pen and asking him or her to sign the contract.

☐ *Closing on a minor point.* This is useful in the case where the prospect has raised an objection that the sales manager has successfully dealt with. If there is agreement on the minor point, the sales manager can then ask for the business. This approach can be used by offering the prospect choices and asking "which" questions rather than "if" questions. In this way, the prospect will not respond with "no", but rather will agree and offer an explanation.

☐ *Standing room only.* If another group is looking at the same dates and space in the hotel, it may be useful to tell the prospect that he or she will need to make a decision quickly in order to reserve the meeting space and block of guest rooms.

Key Account Management

There is a rule that has been applied to sales for some time, called the 80/20 rule. This proposition holds that 80 percent of the profitable business will be generated by 20 percent of the customers. Not all prospects, guests, or meeting planners should be treated equally. Rather, special attention should be given to those that are producing the largest share of the revenue and profits, or have the potential to do so. The groups that make up this 20 percent are termed *key accounts*. They deserve special attention and extra personalized selling efforts.

Each sales and marketing department should keep a very close watch on the level of business provided by each account. Trends should be studied to determine which accounts are growing and which are declining. An analysis of each account should be conducted periodically to determine the total revenue and contribution margin for each account. Based on this analysis, accounts can be classified as shown in Figure 13.4.

Based on this analysis, key accounts can be identified and strategies and action plans developed to foster the development of exceptional accounts. Those accounts with the most current and likely business potential must be given extra attention, while those that are marginal should not consume too much of a sales manager's time and effort. Keep in mind that resources are limited and that they should be directed toward the accounts with the most profit potential.

SUMMARY

This chapter focuses on the vital link in hotel sales and marketing, the sales and solicitation of group business. The initial section of the chapter examines the selling function and the attributes that make a sales person successful. These attributes include courtesy, knowledge of the products and services

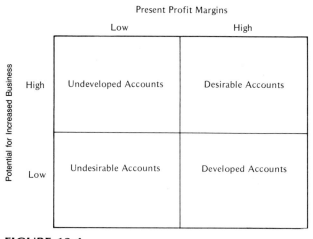

FIGURE 13.4
Account Profile

being sold, professional appearance, a strong desire and willingness for work, and finally a strong personality.

The role of the meeting planner is reviewed. Each meeting planner is different, and the needs and objectives of each group will be different, presenting a real challenge for the sales manager. However, common needs of meeting planners include costs, location, image and status, professional service, adaptability and flexibility, and professional operations and management. In working with a meeting planner, the sales manager should strive to build a solid working relationship, one based on trust and the hotel's ability to meet the meeting planner's needs and objectives. The sales manager should become a problem solver.

Selling effectively to group markets is discussed at length, especially as it relates to the needs and objectives of the association and corporate market segments. Characteristics of each of these markets are discussed and generalizations made.

The personal selling process is presented as including four important steps: prospecting and qualifying, planning and delivering the sales presentation, handling objections, and closing the sale. Suggestions are provided on how each of the steps can be handled by the effective sales manager.

Finally, account management is discussed. Not all clients should be handled in the same manner. Those with the potential to generate increased revenue and profits should be singled out for special attention.

KEY WORDS AND CONCEPTS

- [ ] Hotel Sales and Marketing Association International (HSMAI)
- [ ] Standard operating procedures (SOP's)
- [ ] Qualities and characteristics of successful sales personnel
- [ ] Meeting planner
- [ ] Meeting planner's needs: costs, location, image and status, professional service, adaptability and flexibility, and professional operations and management
- [ ] Methods by which a sales manager can assist a meeting planner
- [ ] Meeting room rental, setup charges, and meeting room configurations
- [ ] Guarantees for food and beverage functions
- [ ] Group market segments—association, corporate, and SMERF
- [ ] American Society of Association Executives (ASAE)

☐ Types of association and corporate meetings held

☐ Meeting planning, decision-making process, and those individuals involved in making the decision

☐ Complimentary room policy

☐ Types of sales calls—follow-up, initiating, and blitz

☐ The selling process—prospecting and qualifying, planning and delivering sales presentations, overcoming objections, and closing the sale

☐ AIDA

☐ Key accounts, 80/20 rule

Questions for Review and Discussion

1. Cite and discuss the attributes of a successful sales manager. Which one do you consider to be the most important? Why?
2. What do you see as the pros and cons to a career in sales?
3. What is the role of the meeting planner? How does this individual interact with the hotel sales and marketing staff?
4. Cite and discuss the nature of the association and corporate market segments, including decision making, lead time, types of meetings, and site selection criteria.
5. What are the steps in the personal selling process? Provide a brief description of the activities at each step.
6. By what criteria can a prospect be qualified?
7. When a sales manager encounters objections, how might these be handled?
8. What does it mean to close a sale? What methods can be used to accomplish this?
9. What is account management? How can it be done?

PART VI

MENU DESIGN AND PRICING STRATEGIES

CHAPTER 14

Planning and Designing the Menu

The printed menu is an extremely important marketing tool, for it facilitates communication between management and consumers. If the menu is poorly designed and produced, this communication process will deteriorate. A well-designed and well-produced menu, however, will increase management's chances for success. A good menu is designed to sell. There are, of course, many different types of menus for all segments of the hospitality industry. This chapter will focus most on commercial menus as used in hotels and restaurants. Similar principles can be applied to the design of other types of menus, such as those used within catering and banquet departments. In addition, cycle menus used in institutional operations will also be discussed.

The chapter focuses on the following major sections:

INTRODUCTION

MENU-PLANNING CONSIDERATIONS

337

SELECTING MENU OFFERINGS

PRODUCING THE PRINTED MENU
☐ Sources of Menu-Planning Expertise
☐ The Menu Cover
☐ Menu Copywriting
☐ Type Style and Paper Stock
☐ Menu-Planning Pitfalls to Avoid
☐ Wine Lists and Promotion
☐ Banquet Menus

ACCURACY IN MENUS

CYCLE MENUS
☐ Cycle Menu Patterns
☐ Marketing Cycle Menus

EVALUATING MENU EFFECTIVENESS
☐ The Importance of Menu Evaluation
☐ Methods of Menu Evaluation

SUMMARY

KEY WORDS AND CONCEPTS

QUESTIONS FOR REVIEW AND DISCUSSION

INTRODUCTION

The printed menu used by a foodservice operation affords management one of the best methods to communicate with the customer. The menu should provide more than a mere listing of the food and beverage offerings. The menu should influence the customer's selection of food and beverage items. Planning is crucial when creating menus; a successful menu does not result from chance. Careful planning and attention to design principles are needed at each step of the design process. No quick and easy formulas apply to all foodservice operations, but basic principles may be modified to fit the needs of each individual foodservice operation. The menu should complement the organization's other marketing activities. It should be designed to satisfy specific marketing objectives. A successful menu should, in fact, satisfy four major objectives.

First, the menu should further the goals of the marketing concept. Recall that the marketing concept holds that the needs and wants of the consumer should be given the highest priority. If the hospitality organization is successful in satisfying these needs and wants, then the marketing concept holds that financial success will naturally result. In short, if consumers are happy, the organization will experience increasing volume and should succeed. It follows too that if consumers are not satisfied, volume will decrease and the operation will not succeed. Therefore, every effort should be made to design the menu to include those food and beverage items that the target market segment(s) will find appealing. Establishing consumer needs and wants can be accomplished in some part through market research and analysis of internal marketing information systems and national menu census data.

Second, the menu should contribute to establishing the perceived image of the operation. For example, a menu used by an operation that appeals to young singles who desire a fun-filled atmosphere may use humorous names for menu items and cartoon drawings on the menu to establish the perceived image. A Mexican restaurant might use the drawings of a building with Mexican-style architecture on the front of its menu. The menu is one of the initial communication vehicles that the customer encounters after entering the hospitality operation. The menu's impact in the formation of a positive perceived image should not be discounted.

Third, the menu should act as a means to influence customer demand for menu items. Through menu clip-ons, menu item descriptions (copy), positioning of menu items on the menu, and special art work, the menu planner can influence customer demand. Extremely popular or profitable items are given extra attention or more prominent positioning, thereby making the customer more likely to select them. Attempting to influence customer behavior in this manner can result in a menu mix that not only increases the number of some menu items sold but can also substantially increase sales and gross profits. Experimenting with different menu mixes can result in substantially different levels of gross profitability, even without an increase in the total number of menu items sold.

Fourth, the menu is a vehicle to gain a competitive advantage. A successful operation often has selected menu items for which it is noted; these are called "signature items" and are promoted heavily on the menu, further adding to the competitive advantage. Hospitality operators should attempt to create certain signature items to enhance the perceived image of the operation and to create a distinct competitive advantage.

The menu should also be used to increase repeat patronage. This can be accomplished by providing not only items that have proven to be highly popular but also a wide enough selection to prevent menu monotony. The menu can also provide a competitive advantage in appealing to new target market segments. By closely studying menu census data, marketing information systems, and market research data, management can identify trends and alter the menu to take advantage of changing consumer tastes. The menu might also be used to expand the market, as a restaurant does when banquet services are promoted within the regular menu. The promotional piece draws customers' attention to additional product-service offerings that they may not otherwise have considered.

MENU-PLANNING CONSIDERATIONS

Several factors should be taken into consideration during initial stages of the menu-design process. Perhaps the most obvious factor is the consumer. What are the likes and dislikes of those who patronize the operation? What food items currently on the menu do they like most or least? A detailed sales history and other data provided by the marketing information system are invaluable in menu planning. Any menu must satisfy the consumer in order to be successful; therefore, a hospitality manager must fully understand consumer behavior and must always keep the consumer in the proper perspective. The entire business should be organized so that the consumer will derive satisfaction. Managers must always strive to provide consumers with exactly what they want to buy, not just what management wishes to sell. If the consuming public is demanding fast-food items, then a prudent hospitality manager should provide these, even though a manager may, in fact, prefer to produce something else. Management selects specific target market segments, and the needs and wants of these market segments must always be the first consideration when planning a menu.

Once the consumer's desires are determined, another consideration arises. What is the availability and cost of the needed food and beverage products? Many food items are seasonal, and some may be difficult to obtain in a fresh state or at a reasonable price on a year-round basis. Once a hospitality manager has determined that consumers desire a certain product, then a consistent source of supply must be located.

The skills of production and service employees must also be considered. If new menu items are introduced, do the current employees possess all the talents and skills necessary to prepare, present, and serve each new item correctly? If they do not, what training measures must be undertaken to teach them the necessary skills? Should additional employees be hired? These are important questions that a hospitality manager must ask during the initial stages of the menu-planning process.

The physical layout and design of the operation must also be considered. The layout and design of the kitchen is particularly important. Is the foodservice equipment capable of producing the new menu items? Decisions regarding space limitations, equipment capacities, and layout must be made. Modifications in the layout of the kitchen and service areas may be necessary to facilitate production and serving of new menu items. In other instances, additional equipment may have to be purchased to produce and serve the new items. For example, if a manager decided to switch from American table service to a combination of French and Russian table service, a considerable investment would have to be made in equipment.

Menus should provide consumers with the opportunity to select a nutritionally well-balanced meal. Certainly, institutional operations have a much stronger obligation to satisfy the nutritional needs of the clientele than do commercial operations. This is not to say, however, that commercial operations can ignore nutritional considerations. Every effort should be made to provide the consumer with the option of a meal that will satisfy one-third of the recommended dietary allowances. It is also important to remember, as numerous studies have shown, that consumers are more concerned and more knowledgeable about nutrition than ever before.

Finally, menus must be balanced, Menus will achieve increased success if they balance several aesthetic factors. Food and beverage items must be selected so that overall the menu is a balanced variety of the following:

- ☐ *Flavor.* Sweet, sour, spicy, hot, bland

- ☐ *Color.* Dark brown, golden brown, light green, dark green, white, red, orange

- ☐ *Texture.* Firm, soft, chewy, crisp

- ☐ *Shape.* Cubed, solid, ground, strips, balls, sliced

- ☐ *Preparation method.* Broiled, fried, baked, braised, boiled

- ☐ *Sauces.* A variety of both sauce and nonsauce items should be included.

SELECTING MENU OFFERINGS

Before the managers of a foodservice operation begin the layout and planning of a menu, they should give careful thought to the selection of menu items. Managers should list potential menu items in each menu item category. Table 14.1 breaks down categories representing many foodservice operations. Under each category, management should list several potential menu items. This process is called building the menu repertory. Potential items can be drawn from trade journals, recipe books, and a variety of other sources.

Once this listing is comprehensive enough to meet the operation's needs, management should rank-order each item in each category for its customer popularity and profitability. Based on these combined priorities, knowledge of the foodservice operation, and experience, management should begin to finalize the selection of menu items to be included on the new menu.

Management should also consider menu census data in selecting food and beverage items for the menu. Several of the industry trade journals

TABLE 14.1
Potential Menu Item Categories

Food	Beverages
Appetizers	Nonalcoholic
Soups	Cocktails
Salads	Beer
Entrees	Wine
Sandwiches	After-dinner drinks
Specialty items	
Desserts	

publish menu census reports. These reports represent the findings of national research studies undertaken by respected market research firms. Both *Restaurant & Institutions* and *Restaurant Business* magazines, for example, publish this type of data and report. Menu census reports usually contain useful information relating to (1) key menu trends, such as a concern for freshness; (2) trends that allow for regional differences and uniqueness; (3) best-selling items in American hospitality; and (4) menu census data broken down by type of operation.

While menu census data published by industry trade journals will not provide data specific to one operation, or one narrowly defined geographic location, these reports represent excellent sources for monitoring both geographic trends (national and regional) and trends by type of operation. When these data are combined with internally generated sales histories, marketing information systems, and managerial judgment, the result is a solid basis for decisions concerning menu item selection.

PRODUCING THE PRINTED MENU

Sources of Menu-Planning Expertise

All foodservice managers like to consider themselves professionals. Foodservice, like any other field, requires certain unique skills and expertise. Not all managers, however, possess all the necessary skills that the field demands. When a menu is planned and designed, layout, copywriting, and artistic skills are needed, yet many hospitality managers do not have a great deal of talent or skill in these areas. A wise manager recognizes these shortcomings and seeks professional assistance.

A wide variety of sources are available. Some sources can complete the entire menu from initial planning to final production and printing. Others may be able to offer expertise dealing with only certain aspects of the menu. The first source of assistance is a firm engaged solely in menu layout and design. Many menu-design firms offer stock menus as well as custom-designed menus tailored to each individual operation. In developing a custom-designed menu, they will completely design and produce the concept, design, typesetting, paste-up, photography, and printing. These services are not inexpensive, but the investment in professionally designed and produced menus is normally rewarded by increased sales and by the achievement of the manager's menu objectives.

Advertising agencies may also be able to assist in menu design. Agencies maintain individuals on staff who can produce photographs and artwork suitable for a hospitality menu. They also employ copywriters who may be able to add the extra flair that a menu needs to make it unique and to produce increased sales.

If a hospitality manager chooses to design a menu personally, the only outside help necessary is a top-quality printer. Most printers will be able to do the job adequately, but it is wise to work closely with a printer who has experience with menus. When selecting a printer, consider the following questions: Is the printer's equipment capable of producing the size, color, and style of the menu exactly as desired? Is the printer able to provide quick service on short runs when prices or menu items change?

The Menu Cover

First impressions are vitally important, so the design of the cover is critical. It sets the tone, creates the mood, and establishes the image of the foodservice establishment in the mind of the consumer.

The choice of cover designs is nearly limitless, but a number of factors may limit the selection process. Cost limitations may force a manager to select a more conservative and less expensive menu cover. If cost is of great concern, then only one color should be printed on a solid-color background. This can still have a dramatic effect, yet it remains relatively inexpensive. The length of service desired for the menu is another factor that should be considered when selecting a menu cover. If a long service life is desired, heavy-weight and grease-resistant paper stock should be used.

No concrete rules dictate exactly what should be included on a menu cover, so the following are only guidelines. The name of the foodservice operation and any artwork should appear on the front, while the address, phone number, hours of operation, and credit cards accepted should be included on either the back cover or else within the menu. The cover should reflect the theme and atmosphere of the hospitality operation and should be as creative as possible. Figures 14.1–14.6 all show high-quality menu covers. Each is unique and reflects the theme and image of its hospitality operation. All feature artwork that helps create an image in the consumer's mind and adds interest to the dining experience.

FIGURE 14.1
The Style and Sophistication of This Foodservice Operation Is Shown by the Drawing and Type Style

Courtesy: Restaurants No Limit, Inc., 4300 Baker Road, Minnetonka, MN 55343

FIGURE 14.2
This Restaurant Specializes in Fresh Fish, and the Cover Illustrates the Sources of Supply

Courtesy: Strang Corporation, Cleveland, OH

FIGURE 14.3
This Menu Cover Uses Creative Artwork for a Specific Image
Courtesy: Seaburg, *Menu Design, Merchandising and Planning,* 3rd Edition. VNR, Inc., 1983.

FIGURE 14.4
This Menu Cover Reflects the Formal Atmosphere of the Greenbrier Hotel. It Sets the Tone and Establishes an Expected Type of Dining Experience.
Courtesy: The Greenbrier Hotel, White Sulphur Springs, WV

We personally direct every activity

Any time is the right time for... Extra Billy's BBQ.

Don't even think about eating any place else!

Everything tastes better with our special BBQ Sauce!

Appetizers

Extra Billy's Cheese Pie
Cheesier than quiche; a different variation each day. Ask about today's selection. 2.25

Buffalo Style Chicken Wings
Hot, tangy, and crispy. Served with fresh vegetables and dip. 1.95

Onion Strings
Sweet, thin slices, crisply fried. EXTRA large portion! Plenty for one, enough to share. 1.95

Potato Skins
Original — served with sour cream. 1.95
BBQ — topped with our pit cooked, minced BBQ and melted Cheddar. 3.95

Smoked Sausage
Sliced rope links served with zesty mustard. 1.95

Smoked Shrimp
Served cold in the shell. 3.95

BBQ Ribs
Genuine hickory pit individual Billy Back Ribs. 3.95

Nachos
Regular — tortilla chips topped with melted cheese, jalapeño peppers, and salsa for dipping. 2.25
BBQ — tortilla chips with all of the above plus our pit cooked, minced BBQ, shredded lettuce, chopped tomatoes, and green onions. 3.95

Brunswick Stew
A cup of Virginia's favorite stew. 1.75

Salads

Salamagundi
Our large Chef's salad with Cheddar, Swiss, and smoked meats. 3.95

Extra Billy's Fruit and Vegetable Stand
B.Y.O. (Build Your Own) salad from a variety of fresh fruits and vegetables. Choice of Homemade dressings. 3.65

Burgers

Billy Burger
Our big 1/3 lb. handmade ground steak with lettuce and tomato garnish. 3.35

Cheese Choice
Your Billy Burger topped with American, Cheddar, Swiss, or Bleu cheese. 3.50

Billy's Bacon Burger
With American cheese. 3.95

Extra Billy Burger
Fresh mushrooms and melted Swiss cheese. 3.75

Side Orders

French Fries .85
Cole Slaw .85
Baked Beans .85
Potato Salad .85

Luncheon Platters

Served with your choice of two of the following: cole slaw, baked beans, french fries, and potato salad. (Or substitute the Salad Bar for an additional. $1.95)

BBQ Ribs
Genuine hickory pit Billy Back Ribs. 5.95

Liver Steak
Chargrilled Choice beef liver covered with sweet sautéed onions. 3.35

Delmonico Steak
U.S.D.A. Choice selected from the heart of the rib. 5.95

Sandwiches

All sandwiches include your choice of two of the following: cole slaw, baked beans, french fries, and potato salad. (Or substitute the Salad Bar for an additional. $1.95

BBQ Pork
Pulled pieces of hickory pit shoulder on a hickory bun. 3.50

Minced BBQ
A traditional BBQ lover's treat. 3.25

Beef Brisket
Tender, lean slices of our 14 hour hickory pit delicacy. 3.50

Smoked Turkey
Sliced turkey breast on a hickory bun. 3.50

Smoked Sausage
Spicy link sausage with zesty mustard. 2.95

Old Virginia Club
Ham, smoked turkey, and cheese with lettuce and tomato. 3.95

Fish
Selected daily. 3.50

Chicken Breast
Grilled and topped with baked ham and melted Swiss cheese. 4.45

Extra Billy's Favorites

Double Cheese Pie
Cheesier than quiche; a different variation each day. Ask about today's selection. 3.95

Billy's Skillet Omelettes
Prepared with 3 Grade A large eggs and Rebel know-how.
Billy's Best — tomatoes, onions, bacon, and Cheddar cheese. 3.25
Vegetarian Delight — Swiss cheese, mushrooms, and spinach. 3.25

Brunswick Stew
Virginia's favorite stew. A combination of chicken, pork, (forget the squirrel), tomatoes, limas, corn, and special seasonings. It's a meal in a bowl. Served with cole slaw. 3.50

Desserts

Freshly baked Apple Pie. 1.75
Ala mode. 1.95

Extra Chocolate Cake
Topped with ice cream and chocolate sauce. Plenty for three. 3.75

Lemon Cheese Pie. 1.50

Ice Cream. .85

Beverages

Pepsi	.75	Free Refills
Tea	.75	
Coffee	.75	
Milk	.75	

Extra Billy's Barbecue

Virginians have been enjoying barbecue long before Extra Billy's time.

There's only one authentic method of preparing barbecued meat, and it hasn't changed since the pits and smokehouses of Colonial times—the meat must be cooked slowly over the heat and smoke from a wood fire. That's the way we prepare our barbecue at Extra Billy's. But, like Extra Billy, we take the extra steps by using only real hickory logs and carefully trimming our meats before cooking them for up to 20 hours.

This requires extra time and effort, but the results are well worth it!

Take home BBQ to someone nice. Visit our Deli.

Party or Catering?

If you're thinking about cooking for a large group, ask us. We do it all the time.

FIGURE 14.5
This Menu Cover Sets the Tone for a Casual and Fun-filled Environment
Courtesy: Extra Billy's, Inc., Richmond, VA

FIGURE 14.6
Menu Covers Can Be Cut to Almost Any Shape Desired. This Cover Complements the Theme of the Restaurant, Which Is Mining.
Courtesy: Restaurants No Limit, Inc., 4300 Baker Road, Minnetonka, MN 55343

Menu Copywriting

The words appearing on the menu are referred to as copy. These words must be carefully chosen and must be designed to sell, rather than merely list, the available food items and prices. A well-written menu has a definite flair that can be translated into higher check averages and increased profits. As all managers are interested in increased sales, menu copy is an excellent starting point for reaching this goal. Menu copy can be divided into three main categories: (1) listings of menu items and prices, (2) descriptive selling of menu items, and (3) copy relating to extra services, special cuisine, or special features of the product-service mix offered.

Listing menu items and prices is the first and most basic step in developing menu copy, but it is important to consider the organization and sequencing of the items as well. In what order should the items appear on the menu? Should all the items receive equal attention? To answer the first question, one school of thought holds that the items should appear on the menu in the same order in which the customer would eat them. For example, appetizers should be followed by soups and salads, entrees, and then desserts. If a hospitality operation does not follow a rigid pattern of service, similar menu items should be grouped together. This might mean grouping sandwiches, side orders, pizzas, beverages, and complete dinners. All menu items should not receive equal attention on the menu. Not all items are equally popular with consumers, nor are they equally profitable to the operator. For example, why should a cup of coffee selling for $.95 be given the same amount of space and copy as a highly profitable entree selling for $17.95? Items that should be given special and bolder attention are those popular with consumers, profitable for the operation, or preferably, both.

Another school of thought is that menu items should be positioned so that the most popular and profitable items are seen first by the consumer. This will initiate the dining experience in a positive manner. Figure 14.7 illustrates the eye-movement pattern typical with threefold menus. Generally speaking, a consumer looking at a single-page menu will first focus slightly above the middle of the page. With a four-page menu, a consumer will focus slightly above the middle of the right-hand page when looking at the inner two pages.

Many hospitality managers merely list the menu items and the corresponding prices. The consumer's first reading of the menu copy is the "moment of truth" for any restaurant. The consumer is going to make a selection based on the presentation of the items on the menu. The menu should be designed with flair and should predominantly feature popular and profitable items. A menu lacking any descriptive selling of its items is dull, for if menu items and prices are merely listed, the menu looks like a telephone book, with names in one column and numbers in the other. Today's hospitality consumers are becoming more sophisticated and are demanding more. Consumers have been exposed to many innovative operations and are

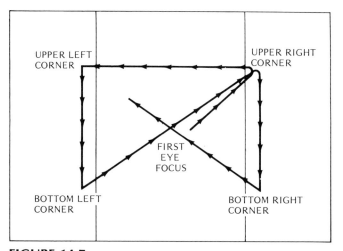

FIGURE 14.7
Eye Movement Across the Threefold Menu

increasingly less likely to patronize operations with dull and mundane menus and presentations. The menu should not merely list; it should sell!

All menu items cannot be given such extensive description, but most items can be given some extra copy. Copy can easily be developed to show an item's preparation, ingredients used, portion size, quality of steak or meat, or any other special features. It is not difficult to add flair to a menu. The copy need not be amusing, only accurately descriptive.

The third category of menu copy is related to extra services, special cuisine, or other interesting features. A hospitality menu should never contain any blank pages. Pages that do not contain menu items should be used to promote such extra services as banquets, takeouts, or other features. Menus should be treated as advertising space. Blank pages are a waste of money; they could be used to promote the operation. This copy may actively promote such profit-makers as banquets, or it may reinforce the operation's image by discussing the quality of products used or by describing any special furniture or paintings the hospitality operation might own. Use the space to the greatest promotional advantage. It is better to have a patron reading about the process by which the beef is aged than glaring across the dining room at a service person or reading where the silverware is manufactured. Figures 14.8 and 14.9 show menu copy used to promote extra services or cuisine or merely to enhance the operation's image.

Type Style and Paper Stock

Through careful selection of type style and paper stock, a manager can greatly improve a menu. Type style and paper stock can be used in combination to

FIGURE 14.8
Copy Explaining a Menu Item's History
Courtesy of: Strang Corporation, Cleveland, OH

create the desired impression. The menu is one of the few communication links with the consumer, so it must be both readable and attractive.

When selecting type style or paper stock, it is advisable to view the samples under the same environmental conditions as the consumer will see the menu. Do not, for example, select type style or paper stock under bright fluorescent lighting if the lighting in the dining room is low-level incandescent or candles.

Many different type styles are available in a wide range of sizes. Most printers have a wide enough selection to satisfy the needs of most foodservice operations. A few guidelines should be followed to make the final menu both readable and attractive. Type size is measured in points; type size ranges from 6 to 72 points. Most menus should not be printed in a type size of less than 12 points because smaller sizes are difficult to read. It is also advisable to use a larger type size for headings than that used for the remainder of the menu copy, so that the headings will be bolder and will stand out better. A combination of lowercase and capital letters should be used, for a menu made entirely of capital letters is more difficult to read.

The primary consideration when selecting paper stock is the length of service desired. If a menu is going to be changed weekly, it would not have to

The Greenbrier heritage.

Heritage. It's something passed on from generation to generation. For The Greenbrier, it began over a billion years ago when the mystical waters of White Sulphur Springs sprung forth from the earth.

But, it wasn't until 1778 that people flocked to the springs to drink and bathe in its "miraculous" waters. And, as word spread about the springs and the fertile land around it, settlers came in great numbers to the beautiful Greenbrier Valley nestled in the Allegheny Mountains.

Over the following two hundred years, White Sulphur Springs has entertained kings and presidents. In rustic cottages and in grandiose suites. The years have seen belles and beaux of high society. And the battle weary soldiers of the Civil War and World War II.

But, the greatest heritage The Greenbrier has to offer is its people. The ladies and gentlemen who serve you have a heritage of their own. From generation to generation, many of their families have passed on the prestige that goes with serving at The Greenbrier.

Possibly the truest reflection of The Greenbrier heritage is the Spa. With its mineral water baths and other relaxing treatments, the Spa is a rejuvenating experience. And when it comes to service, there's nothing quite like the individual pampering you receive at The Greenbrier Spa.

Another scene of individualized service is the sophisticated Tavern Room. A warm dining experience complete with brick archways, shining pewter and silver accented by the soft glow of candlelight. Dinner service is in the continental French style and, after dinner, the Tavern Room Lounge features your favorite popular and big band music for dancing and listening (seasonal).

Or enjoy dinner dancing in an informal, country club setting. A popular rendezvous for drinks, dinner and dancing is the Golf Club. An end-of-day relaxed atmosphere prevails as the sun sets over the golf courses and mountains. Dress as sporty or dressy as you like while you enjoy the view, cocktails, dinner and music for dancing. And every afternoon at the Golf Club there's the famous Greenbrier Buffet for fabulous luncheons (spring through fall).

Wherever you dine, and whatever you do, you're always a part of The Greenbrier heritage. That of "ladies and gentlemen serving ladies and gentlemen."

THE

Greenbrier

WHITE SULPHUR SPRINGS
WEST VIRGINIA 24986

FIGURE 14.9
Menu Copy That Sells the Consumer on the Heritage of The Greenbrier
Courtesy: The Greenbrier Hotel, White Sulphur Springs, WV

be printed on stock as heavy as one that will be changed monthly. For menus a manager is planning to use for an extended period of time, lamination may be applied, making the menu impervious to liquids and grease. High-quality paper stock may also be protected by a leatherette cover to increase the length of service of a menu.

Menus are not inexpensive to design and produce, and the cost of the paper will represent roughly one-third the cost of printing a menu. It is, however, false economy to use a menu after its useful life is over. A consumer is easily turned off by a menu that is dog-eared or stained. Prices that have been crossed out and written in by hand only draw unnecessary attention to price increases. A menu is an important communication tool. Its appearance should be the very best that a hospitality operation can offer.

Menu-Planning Pitfalls to Avoid

Despite the best efforts of hospitality managers, mistakes are made in menu design and production. The following are common menu pitfalls:

☐ *Being the wrong physical size.* Often a menu is too small to accommodate all the items. The result is overcrowding, which makes the menu difficult to read. On the other hand, some menus are so large that they become difficult for the guest to handle, particularly at a crowded table. Management should strive to achieve a happy medium.

☐ *Using too small a type size.* Often the type size is too small for many people. Not everyone has 20/20 vision, and many consumers are somewhat vain and do not want to put on glasses just to read the menu.

☐ *Failing to sell.* Many menus lack any sort of descriptive selling copy. These menus fail to communicate fully with the guest.

☐ *Treating all menu items equally.* Do not treat all menu items equally on a menu. A hospitality operation does not make an equal profit on all food and beverage items. To increase sales, special attention should be given to those items that are popular and/or profitable.

☐ *Using tacky clip-ons.* Make certain that any menu clip-ons do not cover any part of the regular menu. It is also advisable to have the clip-on printed on the same paper stock and in the same type style as the regular menu. In this way, the clip-on will appear as an integral part of the menu, not as an afterthought.

☐ *Forgetting the basics.* Be sure to include on the menu such basic information as hours of operation and credit cards accepted.

Wine Lists and Promotion

Wine has two major attributes. First, it offers a chance for romance and enjoyment. Second, it can be highly profitable, especially when a substantial volume is sold. These two attributes mark wine for special attention. Many aspects of menu design apply to the design of a wine list as well. The successful selling of wine depends not only on a well-planned wine list but also on personal selling by the service personnel. Several factors should be considered when designing a wine list.

First, an idea successfully used by many hospitality organizations is to link specific wines with individual entrees on the menu. Usually, two wines are suggested as being complementary to each entree. This copy is included directly on the menu, indicating either the names of the wines or the bin numbers of the recommended wines. Of the two wines suggested, one should be in the low-to-moderate price range and the other wine in the moderate-to-high price range. Being offered in different price ranges gives the guest a choice without having to feel as though the higher-priced wines are being promoted exclusively. Suggestive selling of wines to accompany each entree is highly recommended.

Second, a description of the wine on the actual wine list assists the guest, especially the novice wine drinker, in selection. Despite the increasing per-capita consumption of wine in the United States, many restaurant guests are unsure of themselves when they order wine. In many cases, where the name and vintage of the wine are the only listings, the guest does not have enough information to make an informed decision. If a description of each wine is included, the guest will feel more sure of the selected wine and will not feel nearly as anxious.

Finally, the most neglected aspect of selling wines is the service personnel. Often, they do not have the tools necessary to sell the wine properly. They need to be adequately trained not only in presenting, opening, and pouring the wine but also in selling it. Extra attention must be given to training the service personnel. In particular, they must be shown how to approach and assess the guests sitting at the table, get the wine list in the hands of the guest who is the decision maker, captivate the guest's interest by talking about the wines and how they will complement the selected entrees, and offer positive suggestions about which wines to recommend. In order to accomplish these tasks, the service personnel will need to receive training that focuses on product knowledge, the handling and serving of wine, and most importantly, techniques for selling wine successfully. It is very important that such personnel learn how to ask for the wine sale: If they don't ask for the sale, they will rarely receive it.

The marketing and promotion of wine is an aspect of menu planning and design that often does not receive adequate time and attention to detail. Wine is a profitable aspect of the operation, and professionally planned wine lists are a real asset.

Banquet Menus

Within hotels and restaurants that have targeted group business as a substantial part of their volume, the selling of group meal functions is critical. One of the aids to selling this type of group is the banquet menus. First and foremost, planning banquet menus is in many respects very similar to planning other types of menus. However, banquet menus do not have to be boring. The entree selections do not have to be limited to several varieties of roast beef, chicken, and ham. A great deal should be done with food and beverage presentation and the flair with which items are presented and served. This type of banquet presentation can make the occasion memorable.

The variety of menus and presentations offered by the leading hotels is nothing short of amazing. Theme parties of endless variety help to turn simple group meal functions into memorable events. A similar approach, albeit on a reduced scale, can be used by smaller hotels and restaurants that are active in the banquet business.

The actual presentation of banquet menus is often accomplished by way of a packet of information and menus for all meal periods. To assist the meeting planner in finding the type of information that he or she is seeking, the menus are often die-cut, as shown in Figure 14.10.

ACCURACY IN MENUS

With the growing sophistication of hospitality consumers has come an increased emphasis on accuracy in menus. Simply stated, this means serving exactly what the menu says will be served. For many years, restaurants have been subject to licensing, minimum wage, tax, and sanitation laws and codes, but the words placed on the menu were not legislated or controlled to any great extent. Consumer groups have, however, become more active in this area, and consumers are more aware of potential violations in accuracy in menu.

Los Angeles County was an early national leader in adopting legislation that focused specifically on accuracy in menus and imposed fines for violators. Accuracy in menus is centered around several areas where potential problems might arise, include the following:

☐ *Representation of quantity.* If food products are merchandised on the menu by a weight or volume, then that is the exact amount which must be served. Steaks are often merchandised this way. Also, sometimes an implication of size is made on the menu; for example, a cup of soup is less than a bowl.

☐ *Representation of quality.* Federal and state standards are sometimes used on a menu for products such as beef, poultry, eggs, fruits, and dairy products. If claims are made on the menu about a specific grade or standard,

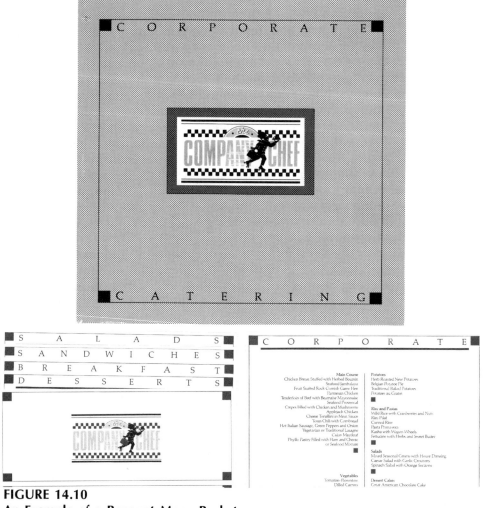

FIGURE 14.10
An Example of a Banquet Menu Packet
Courtesy: The Company Chef, Vienna, VA

this is exactly what must be served. For example, if a steak is merchandised as being prime, it must be USDA prime, not USDA choice or any lower grade. By USDA definition, ground beef is just that, ground beef. It can not contain any type of extra fat, water, or extenders.

☐ *Representation of price.* The menu should be very specific about what is included at the stated price. For example, if there is an extra charge for "all white meat" chicken entree the menu should clearly state this. If a 15 percent service charge is automatically added for parties of six or more, this should be stated on the menu.

☐ *Representation of brand names.* Brand names must be accurate as well. Blue cheese may not be substituted for Roquefort™ cheese. If Jello™ is used on the menu, then Jello brand must be served, not another gelatine product. Containers of products such as ketchup that are placed on the tables must contain the brand name stated on the label.

☐ *Representation of product identification.* The exact product stated on the menu must be served. A cheaper product should not be substituted. Examples of products that might cause an accuracy-in-menu problem include maple syrup and maple flavored syrup; whipped topping and whipped cream; butter and margarine; turkey and chicken; light meat tuna and white meat tuna; flounder and sole; ground beef and ground sirloin of beef.

☐ *Representation of point of origin.* The point of origin must be exactly as stated on the menu. If challenged, the restaurant manager should be prepared to substantiate the menu claim by showing packing labels or other documentation. Examples include Idaho potatoes, Maine lobster, Long Island duckling, Wisconsin cheese, Smithfield ham, Gulf shrimp, and Chesapeake Bay oysters.

☐ *Representation of merchandising terms.* Merchandising terms such as "our own special salad dressing," "chef's special sauce," or "finest quality" must not be used when the operation is unable to substantiate such statements. Commercially prepared salad dressing or sauces may not be called "house specialties." Other merchandising terms that may cause a problem include *fresh daily, ground daily, baked each day on our premises, low calorie,* and *kosher meat.*

☐ *Representation of means of preservation.* Food products may be preserved in a wide variety of forms, such as fresh, frozen, canned, or chilled. If these terms are used on the menu, they must be accurate.

☐ *Representation of food preparation method.* The method of preparation represented on the menu must be accurate. If a menu item is represented as charbroiled, it must be exactly that and nothing else. Other preparation methods include sauteed, baked, broiled, deep-fried, smoked, poached, and microwaved.

☐ *Representation of verbal and visual presentation.* Any representations by means of a picture or a server's comments must be accurate. For example, if a picture on the menu of a dessert shows whole strawberries, then it would be improper to used sliced strawberries in the actual item which is served. If a server states that the fish is fresh, then it must indeed be fresh, not frozen.

☐ *Representation of nutritional claims.* Menu merchandising terms such as *low calorie* must be able to be substantiated.

Figure 14.11 is the position paper of the National Restaurant Association concerning accuracy in menus. This is a standard that all foodservice operations would do well to uphold. Compromising standards is not only unethical; it is poor marketing as well.

Several sources of assistance are available for the hospitality manager who wishes to assure that the menu is accurate. Several state restaurant associations offer services that include review of menus. If the menu is approved, the hospitality operation is able to market this approval in numerous ways, including menu stickers and table tent cards.

Accuracy in menus should be a major concern when a manager is writing or reviewing a menu. The following are guidelines:

☐ *Read your menu!* Check the details on the menu with what your kitchen staff actually serves. If you have made changes in purchasing or preparation but have not listed them on the menu, take immediate action to bring the menu into accord.

☐ *Talk to your service personnel.* Are they aware of what you serve and where it comes from? Do they describe your menu items correctly? Remember that accuracy in menus includes the oral statements of employees as well as the printed menu. Perhaps a manager should conduct a menu review session with the entire staff.

☐ *Evaluate consumer comments and complaints related to accuracy in menus.*

☐ *Institute a training program in handling consumer complaints.* Standard operating practices should be developed for all possible situations.

Consumers expect and demand honest representation of food and beverages, and they have a right to get it. Accuracy in menu programs represent legitimate efforts by ethical business people and national and state restaurant associations.

CYCLE MENUS

Many managers of institutional operations such as hospitals feel that marketing does not play a part in the menu-planning and design process. Rather, their major focus is on the nutritional needs of the clients. Marketing should, however, be a major concern, in addition to nutritional concerns, because one of the biggest problems in institutional operations is menu monotony and lack of interest on the client's part. Management of institutional operations must give careful consideration to merchandising and marketing to increase client satisfaction.

POSITION STATEMENT

NATIONAL RESTAURANT ASSOCIATION

Accuracy In Menu Offerings

The food service industry has long recognized the importance of accuracy in describing its products, either on menus, and through visual or oral representation, both on ethical grounds and from the standpoint of customer satisfaction. The National Restaurant Association incorporated standards of accuracy in all representations to the public in its Standards of Business Practice, originally adopted by the Association in 1923. We reaffirm and strongly support the principles therein expressed.

"Truth in dining" or "truth in menu" laws and ordinances have been proposed in some government jurisdictions, and in a few cases adopted, in the belief that representations on restaurant menus present a unique problem in consumer protection. The National Restaurant Association believes that such legislation is unnecessary as Federal, state and many local governments have laws and regulations prohibiting false advertising and misrepresentations of products, and providing protection from fraud. In an industry such as ours, where economic survival depends upon customer satisfaction, misrepresentation is most effectively regulated by the severe sanction of customer dissatisfaction and loss of patronage.

To be equitable, the complexity of such legislation would be staggering. It is conceivable that standardized recipes for each menu listing would be required if regulatory refinement followed its logical course. The problems of enforcement, and proof if due process is observed, would be monumental, if not impossible.

The "truth in dining" movement is not confined to the proposition that restaurant menus be absolutely accurate in their representations. Legislation and ordinances have been proposed that would require the identification of a specific means of preservation, method of preparation or statement of food origin. Such requirements could unjustly imply that certain foods, processes or places of origin are unwholesome or inferior.

Government action must be confined to problems where its intervention can be effective and at a cost commensurate with the benefits to be gained.

Adopted February, 1977

One IBM Plaza/Suite 2600
Chicago, Illinois 60611
(312) 787-2525

FIGURE 14.11
National Restaurant Association Position Statement Concerning Accuracy in Menu Offerings

Courtesy: The National Restaurant Association

Cycle Menu Patterns

Central to the menu-design process in institutions is the cycle menu. Institutional operations have developed and used many different forms of cycle menus. For example, a very short cycle of perhaps five to seven days might be used in a hospital setting. A much longer cycle, perhaps four to six weeks, might be used for a university foodservice operation. This longer cycle is necessary to maintain customer interest.

Cycle menus can be designed using several patterns:

Typical.   This type of cycle begins each new cycle on the same day. For example the cycle might start on Monday and end on a Sunday, beginning the new cycle again on Monday.

Typical-Break Cycle Menu.   This type of cycle menu begins each new cycle on a different day so that the same foods are not repeated on the same day of the week. This helps to avoid the problem of serving meat loaf on Mondays. An example of this type of menu is shown in Figure 14.12.

Random Cycle Menu.   This type of cycle is used for extended "captive" customers, such as those found in schools or long-term hospital patients. In this type of cycle, each menu is assigned a letter and then the letters are picked at random and assigned to the individual day. An example is shown in Figure 14.12.[1]

For marketing, cycle menus are most important because they can be used to reduce consumer boredom. Cycle menus should be constantly updated with new menu items to maintain consumer interest. In institutional settings, this is of critical importance. Once consumers become bored with the menu selection, it is not long before negative feelings begin to develop in other areas, such as food quality, sanitation, and price. Several excellent books are devoted solely to planning and developing cycle menus. Managers with menu-planning responsibilities may wish to consult one of the following sources: *Menu Planning* 2nd Edition by Eleanor Eckstein, *Menu Planning, Merchandising and Marketing,* 3rd Edition by Albin Seaburg or *Management By Menu,* 2nd Edition by Lendal Kotschevar.

Marketing Cycle Menus

In addition to producing a printed cycle menu, management should give careful consideration to the merchandising and marketing of the menu. Many managers use innovative names for menu items, ones that spark consumer interest and accurately reflect the nature of the food items. In addition, management should plan special events to maintain consumer interest. These

TYPICAL-BREAK CYCLE

	MONDAY	TUESDAY	WEDNESDAY	THURSDAY
WEEK 1	MONDAY DAY 1	TUESDAY DAY 2	WEDNESDAY DAY 3	THURSDAY DAY 4
WEEK 2	MONDAY DAY 5	TUESDAY DAY 6	WEDNESDAY [DAY 1	THURSDAY DAY 2
WEEK 3	MONDAY DAY 3	TUESDAY DAY 4	WEDNESDAY DAY 5	THURSDAY DAY 6
WEEK 4	MONDAY DAY 1	TUESDAY DAY 2	WEDNESDAY DAY 3	THURSDAY DAY 4
WEEK 5	MONDAY DAY 5	TUESDAY DAY 6		

RANDOM-CYCLE MENU

DAY 1	DAY 2	DAY 3	DAY 4	DAY 5	DAY 6	DAY 7
A	J	L	Z	C	D	M
DAY 8	DAY 9	DAY 10	DAY 11	DAY 12	DAY 13	DAY 14
P	I	B	Q	N	E	W
DAY 15	DAY 16	DAY 17	DAY 18	DAY 19	DAY 20	DAY 21
F	O	H	R	V	K	S
DAY 22	DAY 23	DAY 24	DAY 25	DAY 26	DAY 27	DAY 28
U	G	X	T	Y	A	J

FIGURE 14.12
Samples of Cycle Menu Patterns

Courtesy: Nancy Loman Scanlon, *Marketing By Menu* (New York: Van Nostrand Reinhold, 1985)

special events should be periodically scheduled throughout the cycle (perhaps once a month). Special events might be used in a university hospitality operation to include the following:

☐ Ethnic dinners (Mexican, Asian, or English)

☐ Special decorations and decor changes in the dining room to reflect seasonal changes

☐ Special entertainment in the dining room

☐ Special presentation of food items, such as a meat entree (steamship round of beef) carved in the dining room

☐ Extended hours of service offering coffee, soft drinks, and light snacks during exam week, perhaps until midnight

☐ Birthday cakes presented to residents on request

☐ Dinners offered in separate dining rooms for identified groups, such as residents of a dormitory floor, thereby promoting unity

☐ "Sick baskets" delivered to students who have been hospitalized because of illness or accident

☐ "Build your own sundae" featuring several varieties of ice cream and toppings

☐ Hors d'oeuvres featured in the lounge before dinner begins

Cycle menus need not be dull. They should be designed with four objectives in mind: (1) to provide the consumer with the type of menu items desired, (2) to achieve the financial goals and objectives of the organization, (3) to provide adequately for the nutritional needs of the consumers, and (4) to maintain consumer interest and relieve monotony.

EVALUATING MENU EFFECTIVENESS

The Importance of Menu Evaluation

When managers design a menu, they seek to accomplish specific objectives. As with any effort, however, it is often difficult to ascertain the degree of success. Some measure of evaluation must therefore be used. Performance criteria must be established prior to implementing a new menu, and actual performance must be measured against these criteria. For example, management may give special treatment to a single menu item, such as prime rib, with the objective that this entree should constitute 30 percent of all entree sales. A simple method to evaluate this objective would be to calculate the percentage of total entree sales of prime rib. In the same manner, it would be possible to determine the degree to which each objective was achieved. After the menu has been in use for some time, perhaps a month or two, the degree of success for all objectives should be analyzed.

Methods of Menu Evaluation

Numerous methods can be used to evaluate menu effectiveness. The selection of one method over another is usually a function of time and money. Many hospitality firms have purchased computer software programs that allow a thorough analysis. Other operations use very simple, yet appropriate methods.

The simplest method used to evaluate menu effectiveness is simply to count the number of times that each item is sold. In most foodservice operations today, this information is readily available from the detailed tape printout and readings taken from electronic cash registers (ECR's). The ECR's use preset keys for each menu item, and so the number sold for each item is readily available. Based on this information, management can add or delete menu items or change the merchandising focus of the menu.

Another often-used approach is a comparison with menu census data. Menu census data allow management to compare sales figures and sales trends with regional and national data.

Finally, computer software is being used to a greater extent in evaluating menu effectiveness. Such an evaluation is based on financial performance rather than aesthetic evaluation. It is possible to use a variety of "off the shelf" software designed to perform this specific task, or to use more generic software such as Lotus 123™ or Supercalc 4™ to conduct your own analysis of a menu's performance.

Evaluation of menu effectiveness is an important aspect of the menu-planning and -design process. Management should invest time in evaluation because the results should be increased sales and improved profitability.

SUMMARY

This chapter is an overview of several important factors dealing with menu planning and design. The achievement of marketing objectives through the menu-design process must be considered. These objectives usually focus on the marketing concept, the enhancement of the operation's image, influencing the consumer's selection of menu items, and using the menu as a means to gain a competitive advantage.

Several factors that must be considered when planning a menu include consumer likes and dislikes, availability and cost of food and beverages, personnel skills and talents, physical layout of the hospitality facility, and the need for a nutritionally balanced menu. A simple technique can show how to select priorities for both profitable and popular menu items. Data from a national or regional menu census can also be used. Managers who lack the time and/or talent to produce high-quality menus should refer to sources of expertise for design assistance. The design and production aspects of the actual menu include menu cover, copywriting, type, paper stock, wine lists, and accuracy in menus. Managers should avoid common pitfalls of the menu-design process.

Selected aspects of cycle menus include both patterns and suggestions for improved marketing and promotion of cycle menus. Evaluating menu effectiveness is important, and widely used methods of evaluation are available.

The menu is of critical importance in the marketing efforts of a hospitality manager. It communicates, sells, creates the mood, and establishes the tone.

KEY WORDS AND CONCEPTS

- ☐ Marketing concept
- ☐ Menu mix and menu census data
- ☐ Menu-planning considerations
- ☐ Recommended dietary allowances
- ☐ Menu copywriting
- ☐ Type styles and paper stock
- ☐ Type sizes in points
- ☐ Menu-planning pitfalls
- ☐ Accuracy in menus—quantity, quality, price, brand names, product identification, point of origin, merchandising terms, means of preservation, preparation method, verbal and visual presentation, and nutritional claims
- ☐ Cycle menu patterns

Questions for Review and Discussion

1. What factors must be considered when planning a menu? How do they affect the menu-design process?
2. How should a manager select items to be included on the menu?
3. If you were a foodservice manager, what professional assistance would you seek when developing a new menu? Why?
4. Which of the menu covers shown in this chapter is the most effective and the least effective? How might each of these be improved?
5. How will length of service desired affect the menu cover selection?
6. What is menu copy?
7. What are the three categories of menu copy?
8. Of what value is descriptive copy?
9. Cite and discuss the guidelines for accuracy in menus.
10. What feelings do you have concerning accuracy-in-menu efforts? Why?
11. What role do business ethics play in menu development?

CHAPTER 15

Pricing Theory and Practice

Pricing is an important aspect of the marketing function for hospitality organizations. Management should strive to maintain a high level of perceived value, and indeed, many managers view this as the key element to increasing sales and profits. Successful pricing management involves a great deal more than merely plugging accounting or cost figures into a formula and generating a selling price. Successful pricing is a combination of many variables.

The chapter examines the following topics:

INTRODUCTION

PRICING THEORY AND STRATEGIES
☐ Pricing Objectives
☐ Broad Pricing Strategies
☐ Handling Price Changes

MARKETING FACTORS THAT AFFECT PRICES
☐ Environmental Factors
☐ Competitive Factors
☐ Consumer's Relative Perception of Value
☐ Cost Structure of the Organization

PRICING GUIDELINES AND POLICIES: INCREASING SALES AND PROFITS
☐ Cost Margin Analysis
☐ Determining a Breakeven Point
☐ A Model for Determining Prices

SUMMARY

KEY WORDS AND CONCEPTS

QUESTIONS FOR REVIEW AND DISCUSSION

INTRODUCTION

Pricing is a function of both marketing management and cost accounting. When managers establish prices they must take into consideration marketing factors such as the environment, competition, and the guest's perception of price-value, as well as the cost structure of the operation. Many managers view the establishment of prices solely as an outgrowth of cost accounting, but this simply is not true. Instead, the consumer and the entire marketing environment in which the foodservice establishment operates must be considered when developing prices for all types of hospitality products and services.

The establishment of prices is often done in a very haphazard manner. Many experienced hospitality consultants have found that managers often establish prices without a thorough knowledge of the cost structure of the operation and without in-depth knowledge of the marketing environment in which the business operates. This chapter explains the careful balance between the hospitality operation and the consumer.

PRICING THEORY AND STRATEGIES

Pricing Objectives

Before prices are established, management must carefully review the objectives to which they are aspiring. Pricing objectives typically can be classified into four categories:

☐ Financial
☐ Volume

☐ Competitive

☐ Image

Financial objectives focus on the level of profitability, rates of return on sales and equity, and cash flow. Well-managed firms will have specific objectives for financial performance and price changes will reflect these objectives.

Volume objectives focus on maximizing sales and building market share. In order for volume to be built successfully through price, the price must be as low as possible and very competitive.

Competitive objectives are centered on the relative position with competing firms and are set with several reasons in mind. These can include survival, eliminating competitors, or maintaining a parity position with competitors.

Image objectives are closely tied to the positioning strategy of the firm. This position might be that of the organization at the upper or lower end of the price spectrum. Hyatt Hotels has long been among the price leaders among the upscale hotel brands. They have used price to position their hotel properties as unique. At the same time, Econo-Lodge has long been a low-cost leader and has used image pricing to their advantage as well.[1]

The manner in which prices are established has tremendous impact on sales, profits, market share, and perceived value. When prices are established, management must consciously determine objectives. If producing the highest possible short-term profit is desired to improve cash flow, then higher prices must be established accordingly. If, on the other hand, sales levels are lower than desired, prices may be set somewhat lower to increase demand. This lower-price approach is based on the assumption that as prices are lowered, sales volume will increase and that as prices are raised, sales volume will decrease. If a larger share of the total market is desired, prices may be lowered still further to capture a larger percentage of the market in a given area.

Establishing prices by clearly defining pricing objectives is a useful process for any hospitality organization. Consider, for example, which of the following choices is most important: (1) having a larger percentage of the total market at a lower profit margin (large market share approach) or (2) having a smaller percentage of the total market at a higher profit margin (high short-term profits approach).

Broad Pricing Strategies

Along with the traditional cost-accounting approach to pricing, management must make decisions concerning basic pricing philosophies and strategies. Two commonly used approaches are market skimming and market penetration.

Market skimming uses a relatively high initial price to produce higher profits. The word *skimming* is an important one: The established price seeks to "skim" a small part of the total potential market. Market skimming can be used most effectively when the following conditions exist:

☐ A large potential market can be drawn from which a small percentage of individuals is willing and able to pay a higher price.

☐ Competition is not likely to undercut the established price for the same or a similar product-service mix.

☐ Management has established or can readily establish a high level of perceived value for the product-service mix, thereby helping to justify the higher cost in the consumer's decision-making process.

Market penetration operates from the opposite perspective. This approach means that the price should be set at the lowest possible level, based on fixed and variable costs. Initial profits may be small, and in fact, the initial months may not produce any profits, but by establishing the lowest possible price, the penetration approach seeks to acquire a larger and, management hopes, a loyal market share. This larger market share will generate increased sales volume and will, in time, produce larger long-term profits. Market penetration can be used most effectively when the following conditions exist:

☐ Target markets are extremely price sensitive, and any increases in prices will result in immediate and substantial reductions in volume.

☐ Lower prices are likely to discourage new competition from entering the market.

Neither approach is correct for all situations. Rather, management must carefully consider all the market conditions, opportunities, and threats. Management must remember that one of the most common reasons cited for failure in the hospitality industry is undercapitalization. Operations are opened without sufficient financial reserves; initial cash flows are not what was anticipated, and the venture fails. This type of situation occurs all too frequently in the industry.

The manipulation of price can have a tremendous impact on the sales volume of any hospitality organization. Figure 15.1 illustrates the traditional relationship between price and sales volume. In the figure, when the price, as measured by the average check, is established at $10 ($P_1$), the operation will serve 100 covers (D_1); at a price of $8 ($P_2$), the operation will serve 150 covers (D_2); and finally at a $6 price ($P_3$), it will serve 200 covers (D_3). Price and volume are inversely related, so that as price is decreased, volume will increase, and as price is increased, volume will decrease. If the managers of the foodservice operation illustrated in Figure 15.1 were not satisfied with the 100 covers served at a $10 check average, they might elect to lower the price to $8 and serve 150 covers, thereby generating additional revenue.

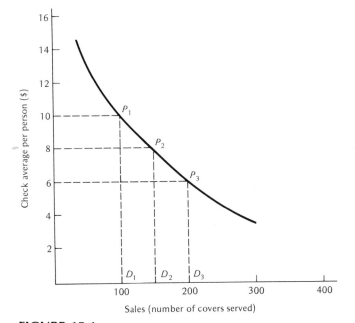

FIGURE 15.1
Relationship Between Price Levels and Demand (P_1, P_2, P_3 = price levels; D_1, D_2, D_3 = demand anticipated at price levels P_1, P_2, P_3)

Figure 15.2 illustrates another approach, nonprice competition. In this example, if the current price is $10 ($P_1$), the corresponding demand is 100 covers (D_1). Rather than lower the price to increase the sales volume, management instead chooses to shift the demand curve from the DC_1 position to the DC_2 position. How might this be accomplished? How can the demand be increased without an adjustment in price? Rather than relying solely on price as the variable that influences demand, management focuses attention on variables that can influence volume, such as marketing. By increasing the influence of such marketing activities as advertising, it is possible to shift the demand curve to a more favorable position without reducing prices.

When management establishes prices, several approaches can be used either individually or in combination: (1) cost-oriented pricing, (2) demand-oriented or perceived-value pricing, (3) competitively oriented pricing, and (4) maximum gross profitability pricing.

Cost-oriented pricing, as the name implies, is based on the costs associated with operating the hotel or restaurant. Numerous fixed and variable costs, such as food, labor, rent, insurance, and energy, may be examined as the basis for establishing menu prices. Cost-oriented pricing is the oldest pricing method and is the most widely used within the industry.

Demand-oriented or perceived-value pricing is pricing from the op-

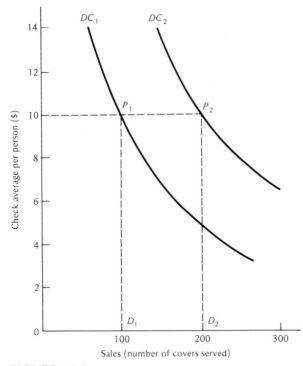

FIGURE 15.2
Nonprice Competition (DC_1 = demand curve 1, given existing market;
P_1 = current price level; D_1 = corresponding demand level on demand
curve DC_1; D_2 = corresponding demand level on demand curve DC_2;
DC_2 = demand curve 2, given expanded market)

posite perspective. For example, rather than thinking that a menu item costs x
dollars to prepare and should therefore be sold at x dollars plus some additional amount, perceived-value pricing examines price from the consumer's
viewpoint. What is the perceived value of the product or service to the
consumer? How much would consumers be willing to pay for this product or
service? This approach to pricing is frequently employed for unusual items or
highly personal service. For example, what is the perceived value of a flambé
dessert prepared at tableside? What is the perceived value of banquet services,
or the perceived value of the additional amenities that guests receive when
they stay on the concierge or executive-level floors that many upscale hotels
offer? These factors must be carefully considered when the perceived value of
a product or service is determined.

The goal of this pricing method is to increase prices to the highest
possible level without causing the number of guests to decline. This obviously
is not always easy to do, for the price of some products or services might be

raised slightly and the number of guests would fall dramatically. In other instances, larger price increases can be implemented with no reduction in demand. Economists refer to this as the elasticity of demand. A product or service is said to be inelastic if, when the price is raised or lowered, the demand for the product remains at roughly the same level as before the price was changed.

Within the hospitality industry, the price of food consumed away from home is thought to be fairly elastic. This means that the propensity of any individual to purchase a meal in a foodservice establishment is directly related to the price of that meal. If the menu price were increased dramatically, the number of units sold or sales volume is likely to fall just as dramatically. Because of this phenomenon, a sort of mental perceived-value game takes place between the management and the potential consumer. The growth in the use of cents-off coupons and other forms of promotion and bundling, or selling several products at a price lower than the total if they were purchased separately, illustrates the elasticity of the demand for some hospitality products and services.

This pricing approach boils down to the simple statement: The management simply charges "what the traffic will bear." What the traffic will bear varies tremendously depending on the situation. For example, if you were standing on a busy intersection at noon, and several foodservice establishments were within walking distance, then the price you would be willing to pay for lunch is likely to be influenced by the choices available. However, if you were at an amusement park and wanted to have lunch or if you were attending a sporting event and desired a meal, the only foodservice available to you may be operated by the owners or concessionaires of the facility. For this reason, the degree of competition has been reduced, and the result is that the consumer is likely to pay a higher price for the same meal. These facilities have the consumer as a "captive client," and as a result, they often raise prices far higher than would be possible if the degree of competition were higher.

Competitively oriented pricing, as the name implies, places the emphasis on price in relation to direct competition. Some firms allow others to establish prices and then position themselves accordingly, either higher or lower. This method assures that the price an operation charges for products and services will be within the same range as the competitive operations in the immediate geographic area. This method does, however, have several drawbacks. First, one operation may have a cost structure totally different from that of another operation. The first establishment might be brand-new and have a mortgage with a high interest rate that must be paid each month. On the other hand, the second operation might be well established and have a much lower payment each month. For this reason, the second operation would have lower fixed operating expenses and therefore could charge a much lower price, even if all other expenses were equal.

Second, other expenses might also vary among different operations.

Labor costs might be higher or lower depending on the skill level of the personnel, their length of service in the operation, or numerous other factors. In actuality, nearly every expense could vary considerably among different hotels and restaurants with the same basic product-service mix. For this reason, it is extremely risky for managers to rely on the prices of a direct competitor when setting their own prices. Each operation is unique and has its own unique cost and profit structure. This is not to say that management should not check to determine the prices a competitor is charging, just to keep an eye on the competition, but it does mean that prices should never be based solely on prices charged by a competitor.

Maximum gross profitability pricing takes into consideration the relationship between price, number of units sold (volume), cost of goods sold, and total profitabilty. Management attempts to find the pricing level at which the number of units sold at a specific price will produce the largest gross profit. This is not to say that the price will be established higher or lower than might otherwise be the case. Rather, it means that the ideal pricing level is at the point that results in the largest gross profit. This approach takes into careful consideration the relationships that exist among selling price, number of units sold, profit per unit sold, and total gross profit for the total number of units sold.

Handling Price Changes

Whenever managers make changes in price, there is the potential that it will have an impact on volume, sales, and profits. The overriding concern is the impact that price increases will have. There is not a quick and easy way to increase prices without some negative impact on consumers.

Many operators have increased prices successfully by simply repackaging the product-service mix. Within the foodservice segment, this can be done in two ways. First, menu items can be priced on an à la carte basis, with certain items priced at a lower margin than others to attract more customers. Fast-food organizations have used this approach for years. The mark-up as a percentage of selling prices is much lower on a hamburger than on the french fries and soft drinks that accompany the hamburger. The check average per person will be about $3.00, yet the main meal item is only $1.50 and is perceived as very reasonably priced. A second method is to offer the consumer something extra at the same time the price is increased. For example, rather than simply raising the price of a prime rib dinner from $11.95 to $12.95 and serving the same meal, many operators have found it desirable to include something extra, like expanding the selection of items available on the salad bar, and adjusting the price accordingly. In this example, the price of the prime rib dinner might be raised to $13.75 to include the cost of the extra salad bar items. Hotels have long used this approach successfully as well. As room rates have increased, the use of extra amenities placed in the guest rooms has increased, thereby raising the guest's perception of the price-value relationship. In recent years the number of hotels offering concierge or executive-level floors has increased, illustrating the consumer's willingness to pay a higher price when additional products and services are offered as a part of the price.

How should the managers of a hospitality organization respond when direct competitors adjust their prices? What impact will competitors' price changes have on sales? Management should consider several responses in response to competitors' price changes:

☐ *Maintain the current price and do nothing.* Make no overt response to the change in price. Maintain current prices and pay careful attention to daily and weekly sales figures. If a significant change in either sales (measured in dollars) or guest counts occurs, further action may be necessary. This strategy is best used when too much profit would be lost if prices were reduced, maintaining the current price would not adversely affect market share, and it would be relatively easy to regain market share.

☐ *Maintain the current price level and increase advertising promotion.* The principal idea behind this strategy is to counter the competition's price reduction with an increase in the visibility of advertising and promotion. When advertising is increased, it is believed, customer counts will either remain stable or will increase. The focus of the advertising should be the nonprice aspects of the product-service mix, negating the competition's price reduction.

☐ *Reduce prices.* In some instances, this may be the best strategy. When the price is reduced, the competitive advantage enjoyed by the competition is reduced or eliminated. Lower prices are a way to increase customer counts and improve profits. One caution is noteworthy here: Competition based solely on price is seldom effective as a long-term strategy and may have a negative impact on sales and profits. This strategy is used most effectively when economies of scale will allow costs to fall with increased volume, the market is very price sensitive and market share will be lost if prices are not reduced, and it would be difficult to rebuild market share if it were lost to the competition.

☐ *Increase prices and launch an increased advertising attack.* As the competition is promoting lower prices, one very effective method to counter these efforts is to increase prices and then initiate an advertising campaign emphasizing the higher-quality aspects of the product-service mix. This strategy can be used effectively to gain a competitive advantage in a situation that may initially appear to be competitively difficult.

MARKETING FACTORS THAT AFFECT PRICES

Four major factors have a significant impact on the establishment of prices for any hospitality organization: (1) environmental factors, (2) competitive factors, (3) consumer's relative perception of value, and (4) the cost structure of the organization. Figure 15.3 highlights several of the elements of each of these factors that have an influence on the determination of price. To establish an effective selling price, management must possess a thorough understanding of the interrelationships among these four factors.

Environmental Factors

As discussed in depth in Chapter 4, management must keep abreast with the developments in the broad business environment. The broad environmental issues that need to be examined on a regular basis include the economy, the social environment, the political environment, and the technological environment.

First, management must take into account the relative state of the economy within the geographic area in which the organization operates. What are the trends for future business growth, consumer spending, popu-

Environmental Factors
☐ Economic factors
☐ Social factors
☐ Political factors
☐ Technological factors

Competitive Factors
☐ Change in prices over time
☐ Competitors' reaction to price changes

Consumer's Relative Perception of Value
☐ Quality of products offered
☐ Quality of service
☐ Quality of atmosphere and environment
☐ Location
☐ Availability of competitive facilities

Cost Structure of the Organization
☐ Fixed costs
☐ Variable costs
☐ Semivariable costs
☐ Desired profits and return on investment

FIGURE 15.3
Factors that Affect Menu Prices

lation changes, and other economic indicators? On a broader scale, what are the national economic indicators projecting? What effect will changes in these indicators have on the hospitality organization?

Second, management must consider the effects of the social environment on prices. The shrinking pool of young workers has caused a shortage of labor for some hospitality operators. This in turn has driven up the average wage rate, which is directly related to price.

The third environment that management must take into account is the political environment. All levels of government have a tremendous impact on the operation of every hospitality operation in the country. For example, changes the federal government makes in the minimum wage laws have an immediate impact on hospitality operations. Government at the state and local level controls sales taxes, and additional taxes are often imposed on the hospitality industry. For example, suppose that the state sales tax is 5 percent and the local government is considering adding a 4 percent sales tax on restaurant meals or hotel rooms. The result in either case would be in effect a 9 percent sales tax. When the additional tax is imposed, what is the likely effect on the sales volume of an individual operation? As prices increase because of the additional sales tax, to what extent will this negatively affect sales volume? When consumers pay their bills, they are concerned with the total amount, and will not often think to consider that as much as 8 to 10 percent of the bill are taxes imposed at the state or local level.

The government also directly or indirectly influences prices through the control of the money supply, which in turn affects the interest rates an owner must pay as a part of the fixed costs of operating. As the supply of money is tightened by the Federal Reserve Board, the cost of credit increases, thereby increasing the cost of operation. Various levels of government also influence menu prices through taxes on profits, wages and salaries, property, sales along with license fees, and a host of other taxes and fees. It is a fact of business life that government at all levels has become and will continue to be a "silent partner" in every hospitality operation in the United States. When a manager is in the process of establishing or revising prices, the impact of the government must be identified and studied very closely. Governmental action is always an important concern in establishing prices.

The fourth change that managers must take into consideration is the changing technology. Even though the hospitality industry remains a service- and people-oriented business, the role that technology plays continues to grow. The impact of computer applications will continue to manifest itself.

Competitive Factors

Clearly, close attention must be paid to the actions that competitors take relative to price. Only in the event of a new product or service is pricing entirely proactive; in most cases it is reactive. As one competitor changes prices, so too will the others have to respond in some manner.

Most managers tend to be conservative when it comes to price changes. This is to be expected, for if incorrect decisions are made, the results can be disastrous. However, it is important that those involved in determining prices understand the competitive nature of the industry as well as the price-value perceptions of the consumers.

The following are four questions that every individual with price-setting responsibilities should consider:

1. Is the price an accurate reflection of the consumer's perceived price value?

2. Can the price make consumers who select the brand look good to their peers and to those whom they might influence?

3. How will prices change over time?

4. How will competitors react to price changes?[2]

Consumer's Relative Perception of Value

The consumer's relative perception of value must be considered when establishing prices. The perceptions of the consuming public are not easy to pinpoint, for they are ever-changing. Management must take this factor into consideration when establishing prices.

Perceptions of value held by the consuming public are divided into the following categories: quality of the products offered, quality of service, quality of atmosphere and environment, location, and availability of competing facilities.

Quality of Products Offered.   Every consumer who patronizes a hotel or restaurant forms an immediate opinion of the quality of the products offered. As the perceived quality of the products increases, the price the consumer is willing to pay for them also increases. This results because the consumer feels that as the quality of the product increases, so too does the value; hence the price the consumer is willing to pay also increases.

Consider, for example, the perceived value of two types of restaurant meals. The first meal consists of a baked potato, a small tossed salad, a piece of Texas toast and a 6-ounce USDA Choice top sirloin steak. Suppose that the selling price of this meal was $6.95. Given the food quality, this price represents value to the consumer, as is evidenced by the growing demand for "family or budget" steak houses. On the other hand, a consumer might easily pay two to three times this price for a similar meal in another restaurant, consisting of a baked potato, a tossed salad, rolls, and a 6-ounce USDA

Prime top sirloin steak. This meal can also represent value to a consumer who is willing to pay a higher price for the additional quality that a USDA Prime Grade top sirloin steak offers. In the eyes of the consumer, both meals represent a good value for the price. The first meal represents a good value because the consumer is able to obtain a steak dinner for less than $7.00. The second meal might also represent a good value to the consumer because the beef is of the highest quality available and therefore represents value. The quality of a meal and hence the perceived value is a subjective judgment on the part of the consumer. Generally, the consumer is willing to pay a higher price if the hospitality operation is offering increased quality.

In addition, the individual consumer's perception of value might easily change with the time of day and the individual's attitude at a particular moment. For example, a consumer might pay approximately $3.00 for lunch at a fast-food restaurant and would consider that lunch to be quality food at a fair price. The very same individual, however, might spend more than $25 for dinner on the same day and would perceive that as a good value as well. Perceived quality of hospitality products is therefore in a constant state of change; it depends on the individual and the moment for that individual.

Most corporations engage in some form of market research to determine the perceived quality and value of their products and services in the marketplace. These studies are critically important to these corporations, for even small shifts in perceived value can mean thousands of dollars of sales either gained or lost.

Quality of Service.   The consumer has historically shown an increased willingness to pay a higher price in those hospitality facilities offering increased personal attention and service. Consider the example of the widespread use of concierge or executive-level floors in hotels. Additional services are provided, but an appropriately higher and more profitable price is also charged for these services.

Considering the example from the preceding section. The budget or family steakhouse is usually designed so that the consumer passes through a cafeteria line and places an order for a main entree. The consumer then passes through the remainder of the service line and selects the accompanying items to complete the meal. At the end of the line, the consumer pays the cashier and proceeds to a table in the dining area. In contrast, the consumer expects and is willing to pay an increased menu price for the waiter or waitress service offered by the establishment serving the USDA Prime top sirloin steak dinner at a much higher price. As the quality of the service offered by the establishment increases, the consumer is willing to pay an increased price to cover the cost of this service.

Quality of Atmosphere and Environment.   The same example, taken one step further, points out that the higher-priced steak will usually be served in an environment offering more opulent atmosphere. Once again, the example holds true: As the level of atmosphere is raised, the consumer normally expects and is willing to pay a higher price.

Location.   The location of the facility and the resulting accessibility can have a direct impact on the price and perceived value. If, for example, a hotel is located in the downtown area within walking distance of the business and cultural centers, the price charged may be much higher than that charged by a hotel located in a less desirable location but offering the same level of products and services.

Availability of Competitive Facilities.   As the number of different options available to the consumer increases, the perceived value of any one of the available choices must be higher for it to achieve its desired share of the market. This point may be illustrated by the example of a locally owned family-oriented restaurant that had been doing business in the same location for a number of years. Over the course of five years of operation, the establishment had produced acceptable profits in each year except the first. With each succeeding year of operation, the establishment had increased sales and seemed to be moving in a most positive direction. Then one day, construction began on a new chain-owned and -operated family-oriented restaurant just a half block away. Once the corporate restaurant opened, business at the locally owned restaurant began to steadily decline, and within eight months, the establishment filed for bankruptcy.

What had happened? What had gone wrong? One of the reasons for the failure was that the perceived value by the local consumers was higher for the corporate establishment than for the locally owned establishment. The corporate establishment was able to offer a product-service mix perceived to be of a higher quality, which sold for the same price. The increased competition was more than the established operation was able to withstand. As a result, it was forced to close.

The consumer's perception of value is extremely difficult to understand precisely, but it is virtually certain that as the perceived value of a product-service mix is reduced, the volume of guests will also decrease. Consumers will most frequently patronize those establishments that offer "the most for the money," or the highest perceived value. If consumers perceive that they are not being given enough value for the money they are spending, they will no longer patronize establishments that offer low perceived value.

Cost Structure of the Organization

Professional managers must be aware of the cost structure of the operation. Establishing prices is a function of cost accounting, yet many operations have established prices without a complete working knowledge of the costs involved. Management must consider the fixed, variable and semivariable costs and the desired profits of the owner or stockholders. Each establishment will incur its own cost of operation. It is useful, as a point of comparison, to refer to average industry figures to determine how a particular facility compares, but one should not be tied to a strict comparison to "average" figures, for these figures may not reflect the unique and individual cost structure of a particular operation. When the time comes to establish prices, the unique cost figures for the individual operation must be considered on their own merits.

For example, a well-established foodservice operation may be able to charge a lower price than another foodservice operation charges for a particular item because the fixed costs for the mortgage might be lower than for a newer operation with higher fixed costs. The newer operation's adjusting prices to be closer to those of the older establishment might seem to be the recommended course of action when a manager is considering only the competition, but in the long run, it might be the fastest route to bankruptcy.

Many factors play a part in the decision to raise, lower, or adjust prices. First, the environmental factors of economic, social, political, and technological changes will have an impact. Second, the nature of competition and their actions will influence the manner in which prices are established. Third, the price-value perceptions of the consuming public concerning the quality of the product-service mix will have an impact on prices. Finally, the cost structure will determine, to a large extent, the prices the operation must charge to remain solvent and to produce the level of profitability that the owners demand.

PRICING GUIDELINES AND POLICIES: INCREASING SALES AND PROFITS

If the prices established by management must strike a very fine balance between the consumer's need for value and the owners' need for maximum return on investment, prices must be determined to induce new patronage. At the same time, prices should be developed so that the new prices will not drive away any of the current guests. Therefore, one of the major goals of any pricing method should be to maintain the current clientele while adding to the total volume by inducing first-time patronage.

Prices should be established with the maximum long-term profits of the firm in mind. It would be easy to set prices at a level that would produce very high rates of return for a brief period of time, but after a few weeks, the consumer would realize that the perceived price-value was very low. When this happens the total volume and profitability is likely to fall significantly. Therefore, the wise manager decides to focus attention on long-term rather than short-term profits. This pricing philosophy is most likely to enjoy the greatest long-term success. It is like the story of the hare and the tortoise, in which the slow but sure tortoise had eventually covered more ground than the speedier hare.

Many managers are tempted to reduce prices in the hope that more patrons will purchase the item and the result will be increased gross sales figures. This is a trap for the unwary manager. Simply stated, for the operation to enjoy increased gross revenue, many more patrons need to be served, and increased volume unto itself is no guarantee of increased gross sales. Figure 15.4 illustrates one example in which the gross revenue from a reduced price is lower, even though more guests (25 percent) were served.

The term *marginal revenue* refers to the difference between the gross sales at the old price and the gross sales at the revised, or "special," price. The goal of management should be to produce positive marginal revenue, or an increased total gross sales figure. In Figure 15.4, however, the opposite was the result. Even though the manager was able to serve 25 percent more patrons, the resulting gross sales figures were less than before the menu price had been changed. This reduction in gross sales is compounded by the two major expense items, for food and labor will have to increase for the operation to serve the additional 30 patrons. Therefore, the reduction in gross sales is even more dramatic when it is coupled with the resulting increase in expense. When both of these factors are combined, the obvious result is reduced profits, or increased losses, despite the fact that 25 percent more covers were served.

The caution for managers is this: Reduce prices as a means to increase volume only after all other marketing and merchandising avenues have been exhausted. A creative manager should be able to devise hundreds of marketing techniques that will result in increased gross sales. The truly professional manager can produce both increased volume and increased profits while holding costs below projected figures. Finally, the establishment of prices is not something to be left to chance. Prices should be established after careful analysis of the factors discussed earlier in the chapter.

Cost Margin Analysis

This is a technique that is particularly useful when analyzing menus. This section will provide a brief review of the technique. For a more complete

	Menu Price	Covers Served	Gross Sales
Luncheon Hamburger	$4.95	120	$594.00
Hamburger Special	$3.95	150	$592.50

FIGURE 15.4
Marginal Revenue

discussion of the technique, refer to "Menu Engineering" in *Computer Systems for Foodservice Operations,* by Michael Kasavana.[3] It combines the use of food cost percentages with the contribution margin relationship of the various menu items. The overall goal of cost margin analysis is to optimize the overall contribution margin to total sales, while trying to minimize the total food cost.

In order to use this analysis, each menu item is scrutinized based on three factors:

☐ Popularity

☐ Food cost percentage

☐ Weighted contribution margin or total contribution to profit

To complete the analysis, the following information is needed from the sales history and the accounting records: the number sold for each menu item, the food cost of each item, and the selling price of each item.

Each menu item is compared with the other available items. Menu items that sell above the average (mean) number of items sold are classified as popular, while those selling below the average number sold are considered unpopular. For example, suppose that the average number of each entree sold was 225 for a given period of time. Those entrees that sold in excess of 225 would be considered popular, while those selling fewer than 225 would be classified as unpopular.

The same type of calculation is completed based on potential food cost. Items with potential food costs below the average potential food cost for the group of menu items are considered low-cost items, while those above the average potential food cost for the group of menu items are considered high-cost items.

Finally, the weighted contribution margins for all of the menu items is divided by the total number of menu items to determine the average weighted contribution margin (AWCM), as shown in Figure 15.5.

The potential food cost and the average weighted contribution margin are used as the dividing lines when constructing a graph such as the one shown in Figure 15.6.

While a graph of this type will not by itself make the determination of prices any easier, it will provide a basis for identifying those menu items that are the best candidates for improving and building upon. For example, those items considered to be "problems" would be those with a very low contribution margin and a very high food-cost percentage or cost of goods sold.

$$\frac{\text{Weighted/Total Contribution Margin for the Group of Menu Items}}{\text{Total Number of Menu Items}} = \text{AWCM}$$

FIGURE 15.5
Average Weighted Contribution Margin

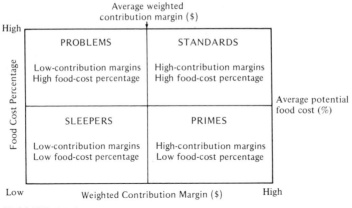

FIGURE 15.6
Cost Margin Analysis

Those considered "standards" have a high food-cost percentage, but at the same time have a very high contribution margin. Items with a low contribution margin and a low food-cost percentage are considered to be "sleepers", because they have potential. Finally, those items with high contribution margins and low food-cost percentage are considered to be "primes" because of their potential for contributing to profitability.[4] The example cited here has been related to a foodservice operation, but the same technique can be applied within hotels or other hospitality operations.

Determining a Breakeven Point

Another guideline that can be used when prices are being determined is the breakeven point. The breakeven point, as the name implies, is the point at which the operation's revenues match its costs. The breakeven point takes into consideration the revenues and fixed and variable costs. The breakeven

$$\text{Breakeven Point (BEP)} = \text{Fixed Costs} \div \left(1^a - \frac{\text{Variable Costs}}{\text{Total Sales}} \right)$$

For example, consider the following monthly figures:

$$\text{Breakeven Point (BEP)} = \$20,000 \div \left(1 - \frac{\$58,000}{\$90,000} \right)$$

$$= \$56,249.99$$

[a]1, or 100%.

FIGURE 15.7
The Breakeven Point

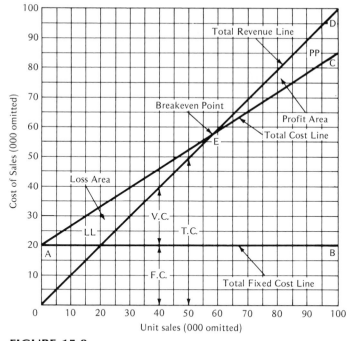

FIGURE 15.8
An Example of a Breakeven Chart

Courtesy: Jack Miller, *Menu Pricing and Strategy* (New York: Van Nostrand Reinhold, 1980), pp. 31–41.

point can either be displayed by means of a graph or it can be calculated by means of a formula. It is very simple to calculate and will provide a benchmark figure against which to compare the actual performance of the operation. The breakeven formula is shown in Figure 15.7, and the breakeven chart is shown in Figure 15.8.

A Model for Determining Prices

Barry[5] has suggested a model or framework that managers can use when they face actual pricing decisions:

Step One: *Recognize the pricing need and situation.* This can be the need to set a new price, change an existing price, or react to a price change made by a competitor.

Step Two: *Understand the life cycle differences.* Pricing must be approached differently in various stages of the life cycle, for the objectives will be different at various stages of the life cycle.

Step Three: *Prioritize pricing objectives.* The objectives discussed earlier in the chapter included financial, volume, competitive, and image objectives. Just as your product-service mix cannot be all things to all people and you must identify target market segments to be successful, so too you must determine which of the objectives is the most important.

Step Four: *Establish a basic pricing strategy.* The two broad pricing strategies discussed earlier in the chapter were price skimming and penetration pricing.

Step Five: *Set prices.* Using the information and methodology that is most appropriate for the situation, establish the prices.

Step Six: *Implement the prices.* This calls for the implementation, monitoring, and changes of prices as necessary.

SUMMARY

Pricing is by no means an easy task. Many variables must be considered as management attempts to strike an often delicate balance between consumer demand and the price level.

This chapter focuses on selected pricing theory and objectives, along with the broad pricing strategies of market skimming and market penetration. Pricing objectives can be classified as financial, volume, competitive, and image. Price and nonprice competition, in the form of cost-oriented pricing, demand-oriented or perceived-value pricing, and competitively oriented pricing must all be considered carefully. The delicate relationship between price and the level of sales that result are the most important consideration.

Four major factors have a significant impact on the establishment of prices for any hospitality organization: (1) environmental factors, (2) competitive factors, (3) consumer's relative perception of value, and (4) the cost structure of the organization. Management must carefully weigh the influence of each of these variables when establishing prices for the entire product-service mix. Management should not rely too heavily on a single variable.

Finally, several pricing guidelines and policies are discussed. These included the use of cost margin analysis and breakeven point calculation. The last section of the chapter provides a six-step model for approaching the establishment of prices.

KEY WORDS AND CONCEPTS

- ☐ Pricing objectives—financial, volume, competitive, and image
- ☐ Market skimming and market penetration
- ☐ Price and nonprice competition
- ☐ Cost-oriented, demand-oriented, competitively oriented, and maximum gross profitability pricing
- ☐ Marketing factors that affect prices—environmental factors, competitive factors, consumer's relative perception of value, and the cost structure of the operation
- ☐ Marginal revenue
- ☐ Cost margin analysis
- ☐ Breakeven point

Questions for Review and Discussion

1. What are the major pricing objectives discussed in the chapter? Which of these would you consider to have the highest priority? Why?
2. What are the major marketing factors that affect menu prices? What is the potential impact that each of these might have on the establishing of prices?
3. What marketing strategy and tactics might a manager in the hospitality industry employ to induce more patronage without lowering prices?
4. Discuss the term *consumer's relative perception of value*. How might this affect a manager when prices are established?

Notes

CHAPTER 2

1. Christopher H. Lovelock, *Services Marketing* (Englewood Cliffs, NJ: Prentice-Hall, 1984), pp. 1–9.
2. Lovelock, *Services Marketing*, pp. 49–64.
3. Leonard I. Berry, "Relationship Marketing," in *Emerging Perspectives on Services Marketing*, edited by Leonard I. Berry, G. Lynn Shostack, and Gregory D. Upah (Chicago: American Marketing Association, 1983), pp. 25–29.
4. Lovelock, *Services Marketing*, pp. 417–421.
5. Lovelock, *Services Marketing*, pp. 203–204.
6. William B. Martin, *Quality Service: The Restaurant Manager's Bible* (Ithaca, NY: Cornell University, 1986).

CHAPTER 8

1. James U. McNeal, *Consumer Behavior* (Boston: Little, Brown, 1982) pp. 5–15.
2. David C. McClelland, "Toward a Theory of Motive Acquisition," *American Psychologist*, Vol. 20, pp. 321–333.
3. George W. Wynn, "Consumer Behavior Models; An Introduction," in *Consumer Behavior: Classical and Contemporary Dimensions*, edited by James U. McNeal and Stephen W. McDaniel (Boston: Little, Brown, 1982), pp. 29–37.

4. Wynn, "Consumer Behavior Models," pp. 29–37.
5. Robert C. Lewis and Susan V. Morris, "The Positive Side of Guest Complaints," *The Cornell Hotel and Restaurant Administration Quarterly*, Vol. 25, No. 3, pp. 13–15.
6. National Restaurant Association, *Consumer Attitude Surveys* (Washington, DC: National Restaurant Association, 1975).
7. Stephen Hall, *Quest for Quality: Consumer Perception Study of the American Hotel Industry* (New York: Citicorp, 1985), pp. 1–14.

CHAPTER 9

1. Kenneth Roman and Jane Maas, *How to Advertise* (New York; St. Martin's Press, 1976), pp. 1–3.
2. H. Victor Grohmann, "Ten Keys to Successful Advertising," *Cornell Hotel and Restaurant Administration Quarterly*, Vol. 17, No. 2, pp. 3–7.
3. Roman and Maas, pp. 1–3.
4. C. H. Sandage, V. Fryburger, and K. Rotzoll, *Advertising Theory and Practice* (Homewood, IL: Richard D. Irwin, 1979), pp. 533–536.

CHAPTER 10

1. Howard A. Heinsius, "How to Select Advertising Media More Effectively," in *Strategic Marketing Planning in the Hospitality Industry*, edited by Robert L. Blomstrom (East Lansing, MI: Educational Institute of the American Hotel and Motel Association, 1983), pp. 256–258.
2. Harry A. Egbert, "Advertising for Hotels," in Blomstrom, pp. 280–284.
3. Robert T. Reilly, "Rediscovering Direct Mail: A Primer for Hospitality Firms," in Blomstrom, pp. 267–273.

CHAPTER 11

1. American Express, *Handbook of Restaurant Promotions*, pp. 3.1–3.4.
2. Ronald A. Nykiel, *Marketing in the Hospitality Industry* (New York: Van Nostrand Reinhold, 1983), p. 130.
3. Jacques C. Cosse, "Ink and Air Time: A Public Relations Primer," *The Cornell Hotel and Restaurant Administration Quarterly*, Vol. 21, No. 1, pp. 37–40.

CHAPTER 12

1.   Karen Colliton, "Effective Use of a Convention Bureau," *HSMAI Marketing Review,* Winter 1983/84, pp. 21–24.

2.   This section is based on the article "A Market-Based Approach to Forecasting" by Peter C. Yesawich, in *The Cornell Hotel and Restaurant Administration Quarterly,* Vol. 25, No. 3, pp. 47–53.

3.   Robert W. Horgan, "It's Time to Automate Your Hotel Sales and Catering Offices," *HSMAI Marketing Review,* Vol. 5, No. 2, pp. 24–27.

CHAPTER 13

1.   Carlton A. Pederson, Milburn D. Wright, and Barton A. Weitz, *Selling: Principles and Methods* (Homewood, IL: Richard D. Irwin, 1981), p. 42.

2.   Margaret Shaw, *The Group Market: What It Is and How to Sell to It* (Washington, DC: The Foundation of the Hotel Sales and Marketing Association International, 1986), p. 88.

3.   Shaw, p. 87.

4.   Shaw, p. 91.

CHAPTER 14

1.   Nancy L. Scanlon, *Marketing By Menu* (New York: Van Nostrand Reinhold, 1985), pp. 72–75.

CHAPTER 15

1.   Thomas E. Barry, *Marketing: An Integrated Approach* (Chicago: Dryden Press, 1986), pp. 375–381.

2.   Barry, p. 369.

3.   Michael L. Kasavana, *Computer Systems for Foodservice Operations* (New York: Van Nostrand Reinhold, 1984), pp. 149–188.

4.   David Pavesic, "Cost/Margin Analysis: A Program for Menu Pricing and Design," in *Dimensions of Hospitality Management,* edited by Robert C. Lewis, Thomas J. Beggs, Margaret Shaw, and Steven A. Craffoot (Westport, CT: AVI Publishing Co., 1986), pp. 291–305.

5.   Barry, pp. 370–371.

Index